LEGER AND THE AVANT-GARDE

CHRISTOPHER GREEN

Yale University Press
New Haven and London
1976

For my Mother and Father

Library of Congress catalog card number: 75-11499

International standard book number: 0-300-01800-2

Designed by John Nicoll and set in Monophoto Apollo

Filmset and printed in Great Britain by
BAS Printers Limited, Wallop, Hampshire

Published in Great Britain, Europe, and Africa by
Yale University Press, Ltd., London.
Distributed in Latin America by Kaiman & Polon, Inc., New York City;
in Australasia by Book & Film Services, Artarmon, N.S.W., Australia;
in Japan by John Weatherhill, Inc., Tokyo.

Acknowledgements

This book was written with the help of many people. I warmly thank them all. Madame Nadia Léger, Monsieur Georges Beauquier and the staff of the Musée National de Fernand Léger at Biot I thank for patiently answering my questions and for allowing me access to the whole of the museum's superb collection; Mrs June Larkin, Miss Inez Garson and the 1970 staff of the International Study Centre at the Museum of Modern Art, New York, Dr William C. Agee then of that Museum, and Anne d'Harnoncourt of the Philadelphia Museum of Art for their time and interest during my American stay; Mr Harold Diamond, Mr Manuel Greer, Mr Stephen Hahn, Mr Sidney Janis, Mr and Mrs Klaus G. Perls, Mr John Richardson, Mrs Daniel Saidenberg and Mr Eugene Thaw for their vitally important help in tracing works by Léger now in the USA and Canada; Mr and Mrs Herbert and Nanette Rothschild and their daughter Judith for an un-forgettable day with them and their collection; Monsieur Maurice Jardot of the galerie Louise Leiris and Monsieur Claude Bernard for their generosity in allowing me access to their photographic archives and in giving me information; Monsieur François Mathey of the Musée des Arts Décoratifs, Paris, and Monsieur Jean Leymarie, Madame Germaine Richet and Madame Françoise Cachin Nora of the Musée National d'Art Moderne, Paris, for their help and advice, and for allowing me to see much that was not on public exhibition; Dr Virginia Spate of the University of Cambridge for her patience in listening to my endless monologues and for retaining the energy to criticize and make suggestions; Mrs Angelica Rudenstine of the Solomon R. Guggenheim Museum for her serious consideration of my ideas and her unhesitating supply of often crucial information; Dr David Stewart for his support of my project while in Paris; Mr Peter de Francia for his always provocative discussion of Léger's work; Mr Douglas Cooper for bringing Léger to life in description; and I thank those who often unknow-ingly have provided support: Mr and Mrs Michael and Susan Compton, Mr John House, Mr L. F. Orton, Mr Richard Lanier and Professor and Mrs Robert Welsh.

I also owe a profound debt to all those who made it possible for me to see important works: to the staffs of the Solomon R. Guggenheim Museum, New York, the Chicago Art Institute, the Indianapolis Museum of Art, the Minneapolis Art Institute, the Art Gallery of Ontario, the Kunstmuseum, Basel and the Kunsthaus, Berne; and to the following collectors for allowing me to invade their privacy: Mr Lee A. Ault, Mr Edward Bragaline, Mr and Mrs Peter Bronfman, Mr Gordon Bunshaft, Mr G. de Menil, Madame E. Frigerio, Mrs Bernard Gimbel, Mr Wallace Harrison, Mr Joseph Hirschhorn, Mrs Edward Hokins, Herr Josef Müller, Mr Morton Neumann, Mr Stephen Paine, Mr Joseph Pulitzer Jr, Mr Nelson Rockefeller, Dr and Mrs Israel Rosen, the late Mrs Charles Russell, Mr James J. Shapiro, Mr David Solinger, Mr Sheldon H. Solow, Mr and Mrs Jerome H. Stone, Mrs Ayala Zacks, Mr Samuel Maslon and Mrs Wolfgang Schoenborn. Several collectors have also sent me photographs of their pictures, for which I thank them: Mr and Mrs Armand P. Bartos, Mr William A. Burden, Mr Nathan Cummings, Mr Harold Diamond, Mrs Lydia Malbin, Mr Samuel Maslon, Mr Joseph Pulitzer Jr, Dr and Mrs Israel Rosen, and Mr Richard K. Weil.

I owe a special debt to my teachers Mr Alan Bowness and Dr John Golding who are now my colleagues at the Courtauld Institute. I would not have been able to sustain my research without the constantly thoughtful and knowledgeable support of Alan Bowness. John Golding as well has always bolstered my morale, and during the final writing of this book I have become increasingly aware of how much my approach to painting in general and Cubist painting in particular owes to him. The emphasis I place on works of art themselves is the obvious result of his influence, which has been a presence behind my thinking since I first met him as an undergraduate at Cambridge.

Finally, I would like to thank Mrs Mary Cochrane, Miss Zillah Pettit and Miss Edwina Sassoon at the Courtauld Institute for their patiently efficient secretarial help, and the staffs of the Photographic Department, the book library, the Witt and Conway photograph libraries at the Courtauld Institute for their specialist expertise.

All illustrations are reproduced by kind permission of the owners. Specific acknowledgement is made as follows: plate 165, Archives Photographiques —Paris, Ancienne Collection Léonce Rosenberg; plates 78, 143, courtesy of The Art Institute of Chicago; plate 66, Galerie Claude Bernard, Paris; colour plate 8, Bulloz, 21 rue Bonaparte, Paris VI; colour plates 4 and 7, and plates 25, 68, 108, 123, 142, 145, 155, 169, 212, cliché des Musées Nationaux, France; plate 46, Walter Drayer, Zürich; plates 77, 157, and 189, Galerie Louise Leiris, Paris; plate 15, courtesy of Milwaukee Art Center; colour plate 2, The Minneapolis Institute of Arts; plates 17, 99, 110, 117, Philadelphia Museum of Art, A. J. Wyatt, staff photographer.

Contents

List of Plates

All paintings are oil on canvas unless otherwise stated.

COLOUR PLATES

1. Fernand Léger: *Le Balustre*, 1925. $51 \times 38\frac{1}{4}$ ins, Museum of Modern Art, New York.
2. Fernand Léger: *Les Fumées sur les toits,* 1911. $23\frac{3}{4} \times 37\frac{3}{4}$ ins, Minneapolis Institute of Arts.
3. Fernand Léger: *Contrastes de formes*, 1913. $39\frac{1}{2} \times 32$ ins, Museum of Modern Art, New York.
4. Robert Delaunay: *Formes circulaires*, 1913. $39\frac{1}{2} \times 26\frac{3}{4}$ ins, Musée National d'Art Moderne, Paris.
5. Fernand Léger: *La Partie de cartes*, 1917. $50\frac{3}{4} \times 76$ ins, Rijksmuseum, Kröller-Müller, Otterlo.
6. Fernand Léger: *Composition (Le Typographe)*, 1919. $97 \times 71\frac{1}{2}$ ins, Harold Diamond collection, New York.
7. Fernand Léger: *La Lecture*, 1924. $45 \times 57\frac{1}{2}$ ins, Musée National d'Art Moderne, Paris.
8. Fernand Léger: *Nature morte au chandelier*, 1922. $45\frac{1}{2} \times 31\frac{1}{2}$ ins, Musée d'Art Moderne de la Ville de Paris.

BLACK AND WHITE PLATES

1. Le Corbusier and Pierre Jeanneret: *Pavillon de L'Esprit Nouveau*, terrace garden and apartment unit, 1925.
2. Le Corbusier and Pierre Jeanneret: *Pavillon de L'Esprit Nouveau,* plans, 1925.
3. Le Corbusier: *Maison Citrohan* project, 1920.
4. Charles Plumet: *Maison de campagne*, from *Art et Décoration*, Paris, 1903.
5. Charles Plumet: *Maison de campagne,* plans, *Art et Décoration*, Paris, 1903.
6. Fernand Léger: *Nus dans un paysage*, 1909–11. 48×68 ins, Rijkmuseum, Kröller-Müller, Otterlo.
7. Paul Cézanne: *Cinq baigneuses*, 1885–7. $25\frac{3}{4} \times 25\frac{3}{4}$ ins, Oeffentliche Kunstsammlung, Basel.

8. Henri-Edmond Cross: *Nymphes*, 1906. $32 \times 39\frac{1}{2}$ ins. Present whereabouts unknown.

9. Fernand Léger: *La Couseuse*, 1909. $28\frac{3}{4} \times 21\frac{1}{2}$ ins, private collection, Paris.

10. Henri Rousseau (Le Douanier): *Portrait de Mme S.*, 1898. $18 \times 14\frac{3}{4}$ ins, sold Sotheby's, London, 3 July 1973.

11. Paul Cézanne: *Portrait de Mme Cézanne*, $35\frac{1}{2} \times 19\frac{3}{4}$ ins, National Museum, Stockholm (Grace and Philip Sandblom bequest).

12. Albert Gleizes: *La Femme au phlox*, 1910. $32 \times 39\frac{1}{2}$ ins, Museum of Fine Arts, Houston.

13. Pablo Picasso: *Femme assise*, 1909. $31\frac{1}{2} \times 25\frac{1}{2}$ ins, sold Sotheby's, London, 5 December 1973.

14. Pablo Picasso: *Trois nus*, 1908. $78\frac{3}{4} \times 70$ ins, Hermitage Museum, Leningrad.

15. Fernand Léger: *Essai pour trois portraits*, 1911. $77 \times 45\frac{3}{4}$ ins, Milwaukee Art Center.

16. Robert Delaunay: *Le Tour Eiffel*, 1910. $76\frac{1}{2} \times 45\frac{1}{2}$ ins, Oeffentliche Kunstsammlung, Basel.

17. Marcel Duchamp: *Portrait (Dulcinea)*, 1911. $57\frac{1}{2} \times 45$ ins, Louise and Walter Arensberg collection, Philadelphia Museum of Art.

18. Fernand Léger: *Les Fumées sur les toits,* 1911. $26\frac{1}{4} \times 22$ ins, Richard Weil collection, St. Louis.

19. View from the top floor of 13, rue de l'Ancienne Comédie, summer 1972.

20. Fernand Léger: *Femme nu,* 1911–12. Pen and ink on paper, 12×7 ins, sold by Parke-Bernet, New York, 12 May 1965.

21. Fernand Léger: *Etude pour Un Abondance,* 1911–12. Pen and ink on paper, $12 \times 7\frac{1}{2}$ ins, private collection, France.

22. Henri Le Fauconnier: *L'Abondance,* 1910–11. $125\frac{1}{2} \times 77$ ins, Haags Gemeentemuseum, the Hague.

23. Fernand Léger: *Les Fumeurs,* 1911. 51×38 ins, Solomon R. Guggenheim Museum, New York.

24. Fernand Léger: *Etude pour La Noce,* 1911. $32 \times 26\frac{3}{4}$ ins, private collection, France.

25. Fernand Léger: *La Noce,* 1911–12. $160\frac{1}{2} \times 128\frac{3}{4}$ ins, Musée National d'Art Moderne, Paris.

26. Umberto Boccioni: *Gl Adii,* 1911. $27\frac{3}{4} \times 38$ ins, Nelson A. Rockefeller collection, New York.

27. Fernand Léger: *La Femme en bleu,* 1912. 76×52 ins, Oeffentliche Kunstsammlung, Basel.

28. Paul Cézanne: *La Femme à la cafetière,* 1890–4. $51\frac{1}{4} \times 38\frac{1}{4}$ ins, Musée du Louvre, Lecomte Pellerin collection, Paris.

29. Fernand Léger: *La Femme en bleu (étude),* 1912. $51 \times 39\frac{1}{2}$ ins, Musée National Fernand Léger, Biot.

30. Fernand Léger: *Le Modèle nu dans l'atelier,* 1913. $50\frac{1}{4} \times 38\frac{1}{2}$ ins, Solomon R. Guggenheim Museum, New York.

31. Marcel Duchamp: *Nu descendant un escalier No. 2,* 1912. 58×35 ins, Louise and Walter Arensberg collection, Philadelphia Museum of Art.

32. Fernand Léger: *Etude de dinamisme linéaire, Montjoie!* Paris, no 8, 28 May 1913.

33. Fernand Léger: *Etude pour La Femme en bleu,* 1912–13. Wash and gouache, Mr and Mrs Leigh B. Block collection, Chicago.

34. Fernand Léger: *La Femme dans un fauteuil,* 1913. $51\frac{1}{4} \times 38\frac{1}{4}$ ins, Lydia and Harry L. Winston collection, Michigan.

35. Fernand Léger: *Dinamisme obtenu par contrastes de blancs et noir et complémentaires de lignes, Montjoie!* Paris, no. 9–10, 14–29 June 1913.

36. Fernand Léger: *Les Maisons sous les arbres,* 1913. $31\frac{3}{4} \times 23\frac{1}{4}$ ins, Folkwang Museum, Essen.

37. Fernand Léger: *Contrastes de formes,* 1913. $39\frac{1}{4} \times 32$ ins, private collection, Paris.

38. Fernand Léger: *Contrastes de formes,* 1913. $51\frac{1}{2} \times 38\frac{1}{2}$ ins, Louise and Walter Arensberg collection, Philadelphia Museum of Art.

39. Fernand Léger: *Dessin pour La Femme en rouge et vert,* 1913. Ink and gouache on paper, $24\frac{1}{2} \times 19$ ins, A. E. Gallatin collection, Philadelphia Museum of Art.

40. Fernand Léger: *Dessin pour Contrastes de formes no. 2*, 1913. Gouache and wash on paper, $19 \times 25\frac{1}{4}$ ins, private collection, New York.

41. Fernand Léger: *Paysage*, 1913. 35×29 ins, private collection, France.

42. Fernand Léger: *Contrastes de formes no. 2*, 1913. $25\frac{1}{4} \times 19$ ins, present whereabouts unknown.

43. Robert Delaunay: *Hommage à Blériot*, 1914. Tempera on canvas, $98\frac{1}{2} \times 98\frac{1}{2}$ ins, Oeffentliche Kunstssammlung, Basel.

44. Robert Delaunay: *L'Equipe de Cardiff*, 1912–13. $77\frac{1}{8} \times 51\frac{1}{8}$ ins, Stedelijk Van Abbemuseum, Eindhoven.

45. Gino Severini: *La Danseuse à Pigalle*, 1913. Measurements and whereabouts unknown.

46. Fernand Léger: *L'Escalier*, 1913. $57\frac{1}{2} \times 46\frac{1}{2}$ ins, Kunsthaus, Zurich.

47. Fernand Léger: *Dessin pour Nature morte sur une table*, 1913. Wash and gouache on paper, $25\frac{1}{2} \times 19\frac{3}{4}$ ins, galerie Beyeler, Basel.

48. Fernand Léger: *Nature morte à la lampe*, 1913. $24\frac{3}{4} \times 17\frac{3}{4}$ ins, Private collection, Dallas, Texas.

49. Fernand Léger: *Nature morte aux cylindres colorés*, 1913. $50\frac{3}{4} \times 76$ ins, Louis Carré collection, France.

50. Fernand Léger: *L'Escalier*, 1914. $57 \times 36\frac{3}{4}$ ins, Moderna Museet, Stockholm.

51. Fernand Léger: *Nature morte*, 1913–14. $39 \times 31\frac{1}{4}$ ins, Dr Emil Friedrich collection, Zurich.

52. Fernand Léger: *Le village dans la forêt*, 1914. $51\frac{1}{4} \times 38\frac{1}{4}$ ins, Oeffentliche Kunstssammlung, Basel.

53. 'Le fort de Vaux reconquis le 2 novembre', *Le Miroir*, Paris, 19 November 1916.

54. Fernand Léger: *Cuisine roulante*, 1915. Pen and ink on paper, $8 \times 6\frac{1}{4}$ ins, Musée National Fernand Léger, Biot.

55. 'Une Route nouvelle sur un champ de bataille ravagé de la Somme', *Le Miroir*. Paris, 8 October 1916.

56. Fernand Léger: *Sur la route de Fleury*, 24 October 1916. Pencil on paper, $6\frac{3}{4} \times 5\frac{1}{4}$ ins, Henriette Gomès collection, Paris.

57. 'Quelques phases de l'assaut qui, le 24 Octobre fit retomber le Fort de Douaumont entre nos mains', *Le Miroir*, Paris, 19 November 1916.

58. The cover of *Le Miroir*, Paris, 8 October 1916.

59. Fernand Léger: *Sur la route de Fleury, les deux tués*, 24 October 1916. Pen and ink on post-card, $4\frac{3}{4} \times 3\frac{3}{4}$ ins, private collection, France.

60. Fernand Léger: *Soldats dans un abri*, 1915. Pencil on paper, $8 \times 6\frac{1}{4}$ ins, Henriette Gomès collection, Paris.

61. Dunoyer de Segonzac: *Au repos*, *L'Elan*, Paris, no 6.

62. Fernand Léger: *Soldats dans un abri*, 1915. Pen and ink on paper, $7\frac{1}{2} \times 5\frac{1}{4}$ ins, private collection, France.

63. Fernand Léger: *Les Joueurs aux cartes*, September 1915. Oil and 'papier collé' on wooden fragment of crate, 39×26 ins, Dr and Mrs Israel Rosen collection, Baltimore.

64. Fernand Léger: *Paysage en Argonne*, 1915. Pen and ink on post-card, $3\frac{1}{2} \times 4\frac{1}{2}$ ins, Yvonne Dangel collection, Paris.

65. *Verdun, la rue Mazel*, after the bombardment of 1916. Post-card.

66. Fernand Léger: *Verdun, la rue Mazel*, 1916. Pen and ink on paper, $11\frac{3}{4} \times 7\frac{1}{2}$ ins, galerie Claude Bernard, Paris.

67. Fernand Léger: *Hissage de forme mobile*, 1916. Pencil on paper, $7\frac{3}{4} \times 5\frac{1}{2}$ ins, Henriette Gomès collection, Paris.

68. Fernand Léger: *L'Avion brisé*, 1916. Wash and gouache on paper, $9\frac{3}{4} \times 12$ ins, Musée National Fernand Léger, Biot.

69. Fernand Léger: *Paysage du front*, 1916. Wash and gouache on paper, Musée National Fernand Léger, Biot.

70. 'Couloir de l'infirmerie, Verdun, 1916.' From an album of photographs taken by General Mangin in 1916. Bibliothèque National, Paris.

71. Fernand Léger: *Soldats jouant aux cartes*, 1916. Pencil on paper, $5\frac{3}{4} \times 4\frac{1}{4}$ ins, Musée National Fernand Léger, Biot.

72. Fernand Léger: *Fragment, Etude pour La Partie de cartes,* 1916. Pen and ink on paper, $7 \times 8\frac{3}{4}$ ins, Museum of Modern Art, New York (gift of Mr and Mrs Daniel Saidenberg).

73. Fernand Léger: *Le Soldat à la pipe,* 1916. $51\frac{1}{4} \times 38\frac{1}{4}$ ins, Kunstssammlung Nordrhein Westfalen, Düsseldorf.

74. Fernand Léger: *Le Fumeur,* 1914. $39\frac{1}{2} \times 32$ ins, Bragaline collection, New York.

75. Gino Severini: *La Guerre,* 1915. Medium, measurements and present whereabouts unknown.

76. Gino Severini: *Dans le Nord-Sud, Sic,* Paris, no 4, April 1916.

77. Juan Gris: *Madame Cézanne (après Cézanne),* 1916. Pencil, $8\frac{3}{4} \times 6\frac{3}{4}$ ins, galerie Louise Leiris, Paris.

78. Paul Cézanne: *Madame Cézanne dans un fauteuil jaune,* 1890–4. $31\frac{1}{2} \times 25\frac{1}{2}$ ins, Chicago Art Institute.

79. Gino Severini: *Nature morte, Quaker Oats,* 1917. $23\frac{1}{2} \times 19\frac{3}{4}$ ins, Grosvenor Gallery, London.

80. Juan Gris: *Nature morte à la guitare,* 1918. $31\frac{1}{2} \times 23\frac{1}{2}$ ins, private collection, New York.

81. Pablo Picasso: *Guitare,* 1918. $31\frac{3}{4} \times 17\frac{1}{4}$ ins, Rijksmuseum Kröller-Müller, Otterlo.

82. Georges Braque: *Nature morte avec guitare et verre,* 1917. $23\frac{1}{2} \times 36\frac{1}{4}$ ins, Rijksmuseum Kröller-Müller, Otterlo.

83. Fernand Léger: *Soldat assis,* 1917. Pencil, wash and ink on paper, $20\frac{1}{4} \times 14\frac{3}{4}$ ins, private collection, France.

84. Fernand Léger: *Etude pour La Partie de cartes,* 1918. $36\frac{1}{2} \times 29$ ins, Staatsgalerie, Stuttgart.

85. Fernand Léger: *Composition (Etude pour La Partie de cartes),* 1918. $57\frac{1}{2} \times 45$ ins, Pushkin Museum, Moscow.

86. Fernand Léger: *Eléments mécaniques,* 1918–23. 83×66 ins, Oeffentliche Kunstssammlung, Basel.

87. Fernand Léger: *Dessin pour Eléments mécaniques,* 1918. Pen and ink on paper, $12\frac{1}{4} \times 9\frac{1}{4}$ ins, Oeffentliche Kunstssammlung, Basel.

88. Fernand Léger: *Dessin pour Le Poêle,* 1917. Pen and blue ink on paper, $6\frac{1}{2} \times 5$ ins, galerie Berggruen, Paris.

89. Fernand Léger: *Le Poêle,* 1918. Solomon R. Guggenheim Museum, New York.

90. Fernand Léger: *Les Hélices,* 1918. $32 \times 25\frac{3}{4}$ ins, Museum of Modern Art, New York.

91. Fernand Léger: *Le Moteur,* 1918. $63\frac{3}{4} \times 51\frac{1}{4}$ ins, Mme René Gaffé collection, France.

92. Fernand Léger: *Dans l'usine,* 1918. $39\frac{1}{2} \times 31\frac{1}{2}$ ins, private collection, France.

93. Fernand Léger: *Dessin pour Le Moteur,* 1918. Pencil on paper, $10\frac{1}{2} \times 13\frac{3}{4}$ ins, sold by Sotheby's, London, 8 July 1971.

94. Fernand Léger: *Nature morte,* 1918. $25\frac{1}{2} \times 32$ ins, private collection, Los Angeles.

95. Fernand Léger: *Le Typographe, 2e état,* 1919. $32 \times 25\frac{1}{2}$ ins, Staatsgalerie Moderner Kunst, Munich.

96. Fernand Léger: *Portrait de Philippon,* January 1917. Pencil, brush and watercolour on paper, $14 \times 10\frac{1}{2}$ ins, sold by Sotheby's, London, 2 July 1970.

97. Fernand Léger: *Le Fumeur,* January 1917. Pencil, brush and ink on paper, $20\frac{1}{2} \times 14\frac{1}{2}$ ins, sold by Sotheby's, London, 22 April 1971.

98. Fernand Léger: *L'Homme à la roue,* 1919. $36\frac{1}{4} \times 25\frac{1}{2}$ ins, present whereabouts unknown.

99. Fernand Léger: *Le Typographe,* 1919. $51\frac{1}{8} \times 38\frac{1}{4}$ ins, Louise and Walter Arensberg collection, Philadelphia Museum of Art.

100. Fernand Léger: *Le Mécanicien,* 1919. $19\frac{1}{2} \times 26$ ins, Munson Williams Proctor Institute, Utica.

101. Guillaume Apollinaire: *Calligramme* from the catalogue of the exhibition of works by Léopold Survage at the galerie Bongard, 1917.

102. Pierre Albert-Birot: *Poème imagé, Sic,* Paris, no. 24, December 1917.

103. Fernand Léger: Illustration for *J'ai tué* by Blaise Cendrars, Paris, 1918.

104. Fernand Léger: *Le Marinier,* 1918. $18 \times 21\frac{3}{4}$ ins, Museum of Modern Art, New York (gift of Mr and Mrs Sidney Janis).

105. Fernand Léger: *Le Remorqueur,* 1918. $25\frac{3}{4} \times 36\frac{1}{2}$ ins, Mme René Gaffé collection, France.

106. Fernand Léger: *Le Chauffeur nègre,* 1919. $25\frac{3}{4} \times 36\frac{1}{2}$ ins, private collection, France.

107. Fernand Léger: *Le Mécanicien dans l'usine,* 1918. $21\frac{1}{4} \times 25\frac{1}{2}$ ins, private collection, Chicago.

108. Fernand Léger: *Le Cirque Médrano,* 1918. $22\frac{3}{4} \times 37\frac{1}{4}$ ins, Musée National d'Art Moderne, Paris.

109. Fernand Léger: *Les acrobates dans le cirque,* 1918. $38\frac{1}{4} \times 46$ ins, Oeffentliche Kunstssammlung, Basel.

110. Fernand Léger: *La Ville (fragment)* 3e état, 1919. $51\frac{1}{4} \times 38\frac{1}{2}$ ins, Louise and Walter Arensberg collection, Philadelphia Museum of Art.

111. Fernand Léger: *Dessin pour La Ville,* 1919. Watercolour over pencil on paper, 15×11 ins, Société Anonyme collection, Yale University Art Gallery.

112. Fernand Léger: *Dessin pour La Ville,* 1919. Watercolour on paper, Perls Gallery, New York.

113. Fernand Léger: *Esquisse pour La Ville,* 1919. $32 \times 25\frac{1}{2}$ ins, Mr and Mrs Armand Bartos collection, New York.

114. Fernand Léger: *Dessin pour La Ville,* 1919. $19\frac{1}{4} \times 22$ ins, watercolour on paper, Musée National Fernand Léger, Biot.

115. Fernand Léger: *Esquisse pour La Ville,* 1919. 38×51 ins, private collection, New York.

116. Fernand Léger: Illustration for *La Fin du monde filmée par l'Ange Notre-Dame,* by Blaise Cendrars, Paris, 1919.

117. Fernand Léger: *La Ville,* 1919. $91 \times 117\frac{1}{2}$ ins, A. E. Gallatin collection, Philadelphia Museum of Art.

118. Léopold Survage: *Nice,* 1915. $39\frac{1}{2} \times 32$ ins, Greer Gallery, New York.

119. Fernand Léger: *Etude pour Les Disques,* 1918. $51 \times 38\frac{1}{4}$ ins, Los Angeles County Museum of Art.

120. Fernand Léger: *Les Disques,* 1918. $94\frac{1}{2} \times 71$ ins, Musée d'Art Moderne de la ville de Paris.

121. Fernand Léger: *Les Deux Disques dans La Ville,* 1919. $25\frac{1}{2} \times 21\frac{3}{4}$ ins, Harold Diamond collection, New York.

122. Fernand Léger: *Cylindres,* 1918. Pencil and wash on paper, $13\frac{1}{2} \times 10\frac{1}{4}$ ins, present whereabouts unknown.

123. Fernand Léger: *Les disques dans La Ville,* 1919–20. 51×64 ins, Musée National Fernand Léger, Biot.

124. Juan Gris: *Guitare et compotier,* 1919. $28\frac{3}{4} \times 21\frac{3}{4}$ ins, Niels Onstad collection, Norway.

125. Juan Gris: *Nature morte et carafe,* 1919. $28\frac{3}{4} \times 21\frac{1}{4}$ ins, private collection, Basel.

126. Gino Severini: *Nature morte avec raisins et mandole,* 1919. $17\frac{1}{2} \times 26$ ins, private collection, Florence.

127. Fernand Léger: *La Femme au miroir,* 1920. $36\frac{1}{4} \times 25\frac{1}{2}$ ins, Moderna Museet, Stockholm.

128. Pablo Picasso: *L'Arlequin,* 1918. $57\frac{3}{4} \times 26\frac{1}{4}$ ins, Joseph Pulitzer Jr collection, St Louis.

129 Fernand Léger: *L'Homme à la pipe* 2e état, 1920. $35\frac{3}{4} \times 25\frac{1}{2}$ ins, Musée National d'Art Moderne, Paris.

130. Fernand Léger: *Le Mécanicien,* 1920. $45\frac{1}{2} \times 34\frac{1}{2}$ ins, National Gallery of Canada, Ottawa.

131. *Winged Spirit,* Assyrian stone relief from the palace of Sargon at Karlsabad, 8th Century BC, Musée du Louvre, Paris.

132. Stele. Egyptian, stone, 12th Dynasty, Musée du Louvre, Paris.

133. Amédée Ozenfant: *Flacon, guitare, verre et bouteille à la table grise,* 1920. $32 \times 39\frac{1}{2}$ ins, Oeffentliche Kunstssammlung, Basel.

134. Charles-Edouard Jeanneret: *Nature morte à la pile d'assiettes,* 1920. $32 \times 39\frac{1}{2}$ ins, Oeffentliche Kunstssammlung, Basel.

135. Amédée Ozenfant: No. 133 as illustrated in *L'Esprit Nouveau*, no. 17 with 'tracés régulateurs'.

136. Grain elevators, illustrated in *L'Esprit Nouveau* no. 1.

137. Factory, illustrated in *L'Esprit Nouveau* no. 2.

138. Vilmos Huszar: *Stilleven Komposition*, 1918. *De Stijl* vol. 1, no. 3, January 1918.

139. Piet Mondrian: *Composition*, 1921. Private collection, Switzerland.

140. Gino Severini: *Maternité*, 1916. $36\frac{1}{4} \times 25\frac{1}{2}$ ins, Jeanne Severini collection, Paris.

141. André Derain: *L'Eglise de Vers*, 1912. 26×37 ins, National Museum of Wales, Cardiff.

142. Pablo Picasso: *La Femme assise lisant (La Liseuse)*, 1920. $65\frac{1}{4} \times 40\frac{1}{4}$ ins, Musée National d'Art Moderne, Paris.

143. Pablo Picasso: *Mère et enfant*, 1921. $56\frac{1}{4} \times 63\frac{3}{4}$ ins, Chicago Art Institute.

144. *Juno*, Roman copy of a 5th Century Hera, Museo Nationale, Naples.

145. Nicolas Poussin: *Elizieh and Rebecca at the Well*, 1648. Musée du Louvre, Paris.

146. Fernand Léger: *Le Grand Déjeuner*, 1921. $72\frac{1}{4} \times 99$ ins, Museum of Modern Art, New York.

147. Fernand Léger: *La Femme couchée*, 1920. $24\frac{1}{2} \times 36\frac{1}{2}$ ins, galerie Beyeler, Basel.

148. Fernand Léger: *Les Deux Femmes et la nature morte*, 1920. $28\frac{3}{4} \times 36\frac{1}{4}$ ins, Von der Heydt Museum, Wuppertal.

149. Fernand Léger: *Les Odalisques*, 1920. Mr and Mrs William A. M. Burden collection, New York.

150. Fernand Léger: *Le Petit Déjeuner*, 1921. $25\frac{1}{2} \times 36\frac{1}{4}$ ins, private collection, Minneapolis.

151. Fernand Léger: *Le Petit Déjeuner*, 1921. 40×53 ins, Mr and Mrs Burton Tremaine collection, Connecticut.

152. Fernand Léger: *Trois figures*, 1920. $36\frac{1}{4} \times 28\frac{3}{4}$ ins, Joseph Müller collection, Soleure.

153. Pablo Picasso: *Pierrot et arlequin*, 1920. Gouache on paper, $10\frac{1}{2} \times 8\frac{1}{4}$ ins, private collection, New York.

154. Fernand Léger: *Mère et enfant*, 1920–1. $25\frac{1}{2} \times 36\frac{1}{4}$ ins, present whereabouts unknown.

155. *L'Arithmétique*, French 15th century tapestry, Musée de Cluny, Paris.

156. 'Fresque de Puvis de Chavannes animé', Lieutenant Georges Hébert's course as taught at Deauville, *L'Illustration,* August 1919.

157. Fernand Léger: *La Mère et l'enfant*, 1922. $67\frac{1}{2} \times 94$ ins, Oeffentliche Kunstsammlung, Basel.

158. Louis Le Nain: *La Famille de paysans dans un intérieur*, circa 1642. $44\frac{1}{2} \times 62\frac{5}{8}$ ins, Musée du Louvre, Paris.

159. Illustration from *Omnia*, Paris, 1922.

160. Fernand Léger: *La Femme*, 1922. $25\frac{1}{2} \times 18$ ins, Perls Gallery, New York.

161. Fernand Léger: *Nus sur fond rouge*, 1923. $57\frac{1}{2} \times 38\frac{1}{2}$ ins, Oeffentliche Kunstsammlung, Basel.

162. Romain mosaic, from the Baths of Caracalla, as reproduced in *L'Esprit Nouveau* no. 13.

163. 10 HP BSA chassis, Salon de l'Automobile, Paris, 1922. As illustrated in *Le Monde Illustré*, November 1922.

164. 10 HP Citröen advertisement, *Le Monde Illustré*, 15 November 1919.

165. Fernand Léger: *Trois figures*, 1924. Josef Müller collection, Soleure.

166. Fernand Léger: *Le Remorqueur*, 1920. 41×52 ins, Musée de peinture et de sculpture, Grenoble.

167. Fernand Léger: *Les Pêcheurs*, 1921. 24×36 ins, galerie Beyeler, Basel.

168. Fernand Léger: *L'Homme au chien*, 1921. $25\frac{1}{2} \times 36\frac{1}{2}$ ins, Nathan Cummings collection, Chicago.

169. Fernand Léger: *Le Grand Remorqueur*, 1923. $49\frac{3}{4} \times 74$ ins, Musée National Fernand Léger, Biot.

170. Fernand Léger: *Paysage animé*, 1924. $19\frac{1}{2} \times 25\frac{1}{2}$ ins, Philadelphia Museum of Art.

171. Fernand Léger: *Deux hommes dans la ville*, 1924. Pencil on paper, $8\frac{1}{4} \times 9\frac{3}{4}$ ins, Musée National Fernand Léger, Biot.

172. Fernand Léger: *Les Visiteurs*, 1925. $36\frac{1}{4} \times 25\frac{1}{2}$ ins, Mr and Mrs Leigh B. Block collection, Chicago.

173. Giorgio de Chirico: *Joy of return*, 1915. $33\frac{1}{2} \times 27$ ins, private collection, California.

174. Fernand Léger: *Le Viaduc*, 1925. $19\frac{3}{4} \times 24\frac{1}{4}$ ins, Perls Gallery, New York.

175. Fernand Léger: *L'Homme au chandail*, 1924. $25\frac{1}{2} \times 36\frac{1}{2}$ ins, Mme S. Frigerio collection, Paris.

176. Fernand Léger: *Nature morte*, 1923. $31\frac{1}{4} \times 39$ ins, Museu de Arte de São Paolo.

177. Charles-Edouard Jeanneret: *Nature morte aux nombreuses objets*, 1923. $45 \times 57\frac{1}{2}$ ins, Fondation Le Corbusier, Paris.

178. Fernand Léger: *Eléments mécaniques*, 1924. $57\frac{1}{2} \times 38\frac{1}{4}$ ins, Musée National d'Art Moderne, Paris.

179. Fernand Léger: *Elément mécanique*, 1924. $38\frac{1}{4} \times 57\frac{1}{2}$ ins, Kunsthaus, Zurich.

180. Victor Servranckx: *Opus 47*, 1923. $40\frac{1}{2} \times 82$ ins, Musées Royaux des Beaux Arts, Brussels.

181. Fernand Léger: *Nature morte*, 1924. $31\frac{3}{4} \times 45\frac{3}{4}$ ins, galerie Beyeler, Basel.

182. Juan Gris: *Guitare et compotier*, 1921. $24 \times 37\frac{1}{2}$ ins, private collection, Basel.

183. Fernand Léger: *Nature morte*, 1924. $36\frac{1}{4} \times 24$ ins, galerie Beyeler, Basel.

184. Pablo Picasso: *Tapis rouge*, 1922. $31\frac{1}{2} \times 45\frac{1}{4}$ ins, private collection, London.

185. Fernand Léger: *Le Siphon*, 1924. $36 \times 23\frac{1}{2}$ ins, Mrs Arthur C. Rosenberg collection, Chicago.

186. Campari advertisement, *Le Matin*, Paris, November 1924.

187. Cigarette cases. *L'Esprit Nouveau* no. 24.

188. Still from the film *L'Inhumaine* directed by Marcel L'Herbier, 1923 (laboratory set here by Fernand Léger).

189. Fernand Léger: *Les Trois Pioes*, 1925. $25\frac{1}{2} \times 18$ ins, galerie Louise Leiris, Paris.

190. Still from the film *Ballet mécanique* directed by Fernand Léger, 1923–4.

191. Still from *Ballet mécanique*.

192. Still from *Ballet mécanique*.

193. Still from the film *La Roue* directed by Abel Gance, 1920–1.

194. Still from *Ballet mécanique*.

195. Le Corbusier and Pierre Jeanneret: *Pavillon de L'Esprit Nouveau*, the living room (sculpture on balcony by Jacques Lipchitz; painting Colour Plate 1), 1925.

196. Robert Mallet-Stevens: Entrance hall of the Ideal Embassy at the Exposition Internationale des Arts Décoratifs, Paris, 1925, with *Peinture murale*, 1924–5 by Fernand Léger. From *L'Amour de l'Art*, August, 1925.

197. Auguste Herbin: *Peinture*, December 1920. Gouache on paper, 21×15 ins, sold by Sotheby's, London, 11 December 1969.

198. Fernand Léger: *Ie état graphique, projet fresque,* 1922–3. Ink on paper, Musées Royaux de Belgique, Brussels.

199. Fernand Léger: *Fresque (extérieur) pour un Hall d'Hôtel*, 1922–3. *L'Architecture Vivante*, Paris, autumn/winter 1924.

200. Fernand Léger: *L'Architecture*, 1923. $25\frac{1}{4} \times 36\frac{1}{4}$ ins, private collection, France.

201. Robert Mallet-Stevens: *Aéro-club de France*, model exhibited at the Salon d'Automne, Paris, 1922.

202. Fernand Léger: *Peinture murale*, 1924. $70\frac{3}{4} \times 31\frac{1}{2}$ ins, Musée National Fernand Léger, Biot.

203. Fernand Léger: *Composition*, 1924. 51×39 ins, sold by Parke-Bernet, New York, 1974.

204. Fernand Léger: *Peinture murale*, 1925. $82\frac{3}{4} \times 31\frac{3}{4}$ ins, Josef Müller collection, Soleure.

205. Gerrit Reitveld and Vilmos Huszar: Room designed for an exhibition, Berlin, 1923. *L'Architecture Vivante*, Paris, autumn/winter 1924.

1.   Le Corbusier and Pierre Jeanneret: *Pavillon de L'Esprit Nouveau,* terrace garden and apartment unit, 1925.

INTRODUCTION
The Modern Artist and Modern Life: Idealist or Realist?

In 1925 the architect Le Corbusier supervised the construction of the Purist contribution to the Exposition Internationale des Arts Décoratifs, the Pavillon de L'Esprit Nouveau. Its site was peripheral, its size small, but encapsulating as it did the hopes of a visionary with a gift for cultural propaganda, it was able to make its point. The Pavillon was a house fitted out for living, and on its walls were paintings: still-lives by Amédée Ozenfant and Le Corbusier, with among them, certainly for some of the time, a canvas called *Le Balustre*, the contribution of Fernand Léger (Colour Plate 1, and Plates 1 and 2).

Le Corbusier's little building was an adaptation of a project first set out on paper in 1920, the 'maison Citrohan'. As a Citrohan house variant, it was, in a sense, an attempt to promote the development of a modern, realistic architecture for housing; an architecture as progressively realistic and practical as a 10 HP Citroën. Certainly Le Corbusier was convinced of the structural progressiveness of the Pavillon, but for him it was also as progressive and realistic in the lessons it taught about planning.

The building was a succinct response to new needs, and the economy of 'the machine-for-living-in' image was underlined by the distinctly modern need to get the most out of the least space, a need which the Pavillon plan answered with immense ingenuity (Plate 2). Within a relatively small cubic volume, the basic requirements for sleeping, washing, cooking, eating and relaxing are all satisfied, and by pulling together the various functions of entrance hall, dining room and living room in a single area, while minimizing the area taken for sleeping and washing, an illusion is created of expansiveness, of generosity in the space set aside for the waking moments of daily life.

Yet, if the Pavillon *can* be called progressive in its structure and mechanistic in the spare precision both of its forms and of its planning, it cannot either in its forms or in its planning be called realistic. Its forms do not follow with complete logic from its plan, and its plan is not based

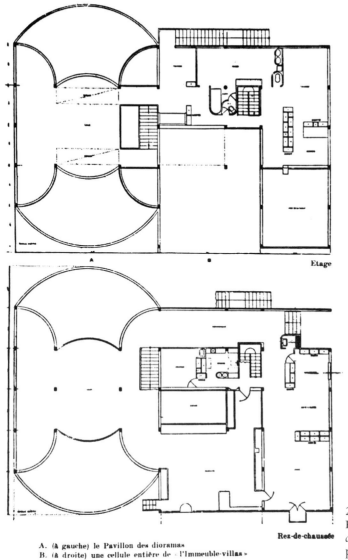

Etage

Rez-de-chaussée

A. (à gauche) le Pavillon des dioramas
B. (à droite) une cellule entière de «l'Immeuble-villas»

2. Le Corbusier and
Pierre Jeanneret: *Pavillon
de L'Esprit Nouveau,*
plans, 1925.

on the actuality of domestic life in the Paris of the early 1920s, but on an
ideal. The ideal was an ideal that embraced the city as a whole, since the
Pavillon was conceived of as but one perfectly working component in an
enormous apartment building made up of 660 such units. This building was
itself but one of dozens forming a single residential quarter in an ideal city
for three million, or in a plan for the reconstruction of central Paris—the
Voisin Plan. Le Corbusier's urban ideal, and therefore his idea of the part
to be played in it by the Pavillon, was realistic to the extent that it was
based on a geographical study of Paris itself as a route-centre, coupled
with a statistical study of changing demographic patterns and transport
needs;[1] but an *a priori* desire for absolutely clear distinctions between part
and part and for geometrically harmonious relationships directed his handling of fact. The tendency for business and administrative functions to

2

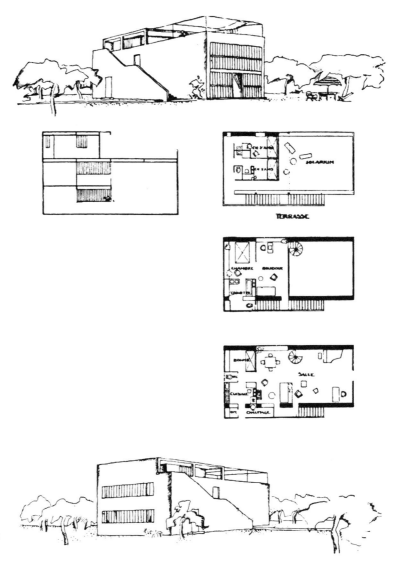

3. Le Corbusier:
Maison Citrohan
project, 1920.

displace housing at the centre of Paris, and the enormous growth in motor transport between 1908 and 1922, led Le Corbusier to plan a city which would completely separate a working centre dominated by tower blocks from residential zones dominated by lower slabs of apartments. Some of these slabs were to be made up of Pavillon-type dwellings and the whole complex was to be knitted together by road patterns and ordered with a clear geometric sense of composition. It was a plan controlled by a mind and an eye drawn to a classical ideal of order, a plan too finite and perfect to allow for the realities of organic change and individual variation, a plan providing for standardized residents living in standardized ways, as was the plan of its ideal residential cell, the Pavillon. The Pavillon implied the existence of a perfectly balanced man (proof against whim and the barbarism of children) while it awaited the construction of a city fit for him.

4. Charles Plumet: *Maison de campagne*, from *Art et Décoration*, Paris, 1903.

However, perhaps most symptomatic of Le Corbusier's idealism was not the perfect balance of the Pavillon's ideal city-dwelling inhabitant, but the perfect balance of the form taken by the building; and perhaps most striking of all as a demonstration of the dominant part played by a purely *formal* ideal in the designing of the Pavillon itself is the fact that its spare geometric precision did not necessarily follow from the economy of its plan, and was not the result of a logical design process. Indeed, there was one precedent for its plan whose context was emphatically rural, and whose forms, far from creating an ideal machine image, looked back to the rustic dream of the Arts and Crafts movement. Nothing could be further from the Pavillon or the 10 HP Citroën than the country cottage project by Charles Plumet published in *Art et Décoration* as early as 1903. Yet its plan, so space-savingly arranged about a galleried hall, is uncannily close to the Citrohan idea, and significantly, Plumet was one of the architects Le Corbusier wanted to work with in 1908 on his arrival in Paris (Plates 4 and 5).[2] Moreover, as Reyner-Banham has pointed out, the design of machines themselves, especially aeroplanes, did not in reality always conform to an ideal of geometric simplicity during the early and mid twenties.[3] The Pavillon was the product of a formal ideal in harmony with a machine ideal, however progressively realistic it was made to seem.

Yet it did contain, besides the equally idealist paintings of Ozenfant and Le Corbusier, at least some ordinary everyday products purchasable in the Paris of 1925—there *were* things that actually did conform to the ideal—the 'off-the-peg' metal staircase, the bent-wood chairs, the Roneo flush-fitting metal doors, the tables ordered from a supplier of hospital furniture.[4] And there was also in the double-height living room, for a period at least,

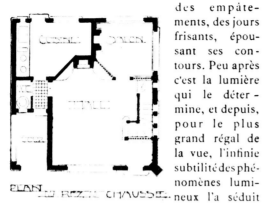

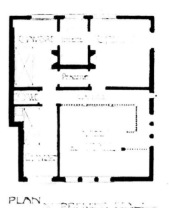

des empâte-ments, des jours frisants, épousant ses contours. Peu après c'est la lumière qui le détermine, et depuis, pour le plus grand régal de la vue, l'infinie subtilité des phénomènes lumineux l'a séduit discrètement de nuances légères, qu'enveloppe l'art si varié de sa pénombre. Ainsi du matin : les voiles de la nuit élargissent leurs mailles sous la caresse de l'aurore aux doigts de rose ; alors les choses commencent à appa-

5. Charles Plumet: *Maison de campagne,* plans, *Art et Décoration,* Paris, 1903.

one painting by an artist who was emphatically a realist, who tried to respond directly to the imperfect vigour of Paris as it was: *Le Balustre* by Léger.

Léger accepted the sheer profusion and conflict of Paris, and his paintings celebrated the vitality of what he saw. But, for all the outspoken realism of his approach to modern life, his painting fits perfectly in the ideal, harmonious setting of Le Corbusier's Pavillon, and it fits there for a significant reason which must qualify any analysis of his realism. The fact is that Léger looked at Parisian life not as an ordinary Parisian but as a member of a small, very special circle, the avant-garde, a loose-knit and shifting group of groups whose members constantly affected each other's way of seeing art and the city. What Léger chose to see in the world around him and the qualities he found in it were affected by the ideas, attitudes and products of those close to him in the avant-garde. In 1924 and 1925 he was close to Le Corbusier, so that he was persuaded to see at least some of the qualities essential to the Corbusian ideal in the reality of urban life, and to find a geometric clarity and a balance in the world as well as conflict. It was thus that he could paint a canvas for the Pavillon de L'Esprit Nouveau and remain a realist.

Since the avant-garde setting of art-works, ideas and attitudes was itself as much in flux as the city, Léger's view of reality, and therefore his painting, could not ever have stood still. He could not have produced a canvas, simple, precise and balanced enough to hang in the Pavillon either in 1910 or 1913 or even 1919, so different was the setting within which he worked at those times, so different his way of seeing reality. It is the intention of this book to explore the way Léger's painting changed in the twenty years that came before his contribution to the Pavillon de L'Esprit Nouveau, and to see it, especially after 1909, in the context of his changing view of modern life, and therefore in the context of his changing avant-garde surroundings, surroundings made up not only of the pictorial images he admired but of the ideas generated by the architects, the musicians, the poets, the thinkers, the engineers, the mechanics and the artisans, some of whom he knew, and all of whose work he responded to with ebullient conviction.

5

CHAPTER 1
Fernand Léger and the Development of a Dynamic Cubism

Cubism began as a private movement. It was the esoteric obsession of two painters, Picasso and Braque, their poet friends, Guillaume Apollinaire, Max Jacob and André Salmon, a German dealer, Daniel-Henri Kahnweiler, and a few serious amateurs.[1] The public *début* of Cubism was left to a small group of painters, who were encouraged by a common feeling of disillusionment with Impressionism to visit Kahnweiler's gallery on the rue Vignon. They worked, not like Picasso and Braque in Montmartre, but in Montparnasse and the industrial suburbs of Paris; they were not confined by a *fin de siècle* sense of withdrawal from society; and their public version of Cubism was very different from the Cubism of their acknowledged masters. This second phase of Cubism made its *début* in the spring of 1911 at the Salon des Indépendants. Here in a single room, 'Salle 41', were hung together, like a group manifesto, paintings by six artists; Henri Le Fauconnier, Albert Gleizes, Jean Metzinger, Marie Laurencin, Robert Delaunay and Fernand Léger.[2] The public *début* of Fernand Léger as a contributing member of the Parisian avant-garde coincided with that of Cubism, for his painting *Nus dans un paysage* (Plate 6) was his first large-scale attempt to make a really progressive pictorial declaration in the setting of a Salon.

The kernel of this group was formed during the years 1909 and 1910, when Albert Gleizes, Henri le Fauconnier and Jean Metzinger met. An important factor common to these meetings was the part played by poets as intermediaries: the poets Pierre-Jean Jouve, Paul Castiaux and Alexandre Mercereau were all directly implicated, Mercereau in particular making important introductions at his *soirées*.[3] The key to these connections between painters and poets was held by Gleizes, for between 1906 and 1908 he had been involved with Mercereau in a Tolstoyan attempt to found a community of artists in a large decaying house on the river Marne, the Abbaye de Créteil.[4] Among the poets involved were Georges Duhamel, René Arcos, Charles Vildrac and an older man, active in syndicalist politics, Henri-Martin Barzun, while among those who sympathized with the venture was Jules Romains, a poet whose impact was to be profound. Jouve and Castiaux were the editors of a little Parisian review, *Les Bandeaux d'Or*, which, after the collapse of the experiment for want of rent, published the work of the Abbaye poets. Thus it is clear that when Gleizes pooled his pictorial ambitions with those of Le Fauconnier and Metzinger he did so to form an alliance which embraced not only a group of painters but also an already cemented group of poets. The aims of these poets and of the painters who exhibited in 'Salle 41' were in many senses in the deepest harmony.

With these connections firmly established and with Gleizes, Le Fauconnier and Metzinger set on a course towards a style whose emphasis was on solid, geometricized form rather than on the formless light of Impressionism, Léger himself made contact with the group. He already knew Delaunay, and one or two drawings of nudes exhibited at the Salon d'Automne of 1910 initiated his meeting with the others.[5] During the months that followed, before the scandal of the next spring, Gleizes recalls: 'We found out in depth about each other'; at the same time Léger completed the *Nus dans un paysage*. He had begun the painting over a year before, working on it fitfully, independent of all groups; he finished it in the fresh, heady atmosphere of group activity, since, as plans for the 'Salle 41' went ahead, the friends met often to discuss their new concerns, both literary and pictorial. They met at the *soirées* of Gleizes and Mercereau, at the studio of Le Fauconnier on the rue Visconti[6] and at the Montparnasse café, the Closérie des Lilas. However, before exploring further the context of ideas within which the *Nus* was finished and the approach to reality that lay behind it, a pause is necessary to consider the nature of the style which it declared and of the style or styles which it dismissed.

'A battle of volumes', Léger later called the *Nus*;[7] but exactly how and when this concern with volume, with mass, came upon him is impossible to establish, because he was quick to cover his tracks. The simple self-confidence which was to become typical of his statements on himself and his work deserted him when he looked back at what preceded the *Nus*, and he destroyed soon afterwards all that he could find of his work from before 1909. There exists, therefore, no more than the most tantalizingly incomplete picture of the attitudes and the styles which it displaced.

Not a single oil is known to have survived from the crucial year 1908, and it is only possible to guess, using the recollections of contemporaries as a guide, at what Léger painted as the immediate prelude to the *Nus*. Looking back to the time of their first meeting, Gleizes wrote later of *'une Baignade en Méditerranée*, ... which proves how much he was affected by Impressionism'.[8] So idyllic a subject mentioned in an Impressionist context suggests connections with the Neo-Impressionist idylls of Henri-Edmond Cross (Plate 8), and there is one firm indication that Léger was indeed absorbed briefly by the concerns of the Neo-Impressionists. In his autobiography, the Paris-based Futurist Gino Severini, who almost certainly knew him by the autumn of 1911, recalls seeing a landscape by Léger which was to his eye close to the landscapes painted by himself and Boccioni while under the influence indirectly of Signac and the Neo-Impressionists.[9] There is good reason to believe Severini, since already among Léger's friends in 1908 was Delaunay, who in that year was deeply involved with

6.   Fernand Léger: *Nus dans un paysage,* 1909–11. 48 × 68 ins, Rijkmuseum, Kröller-Müller, Otterlo.

Metzinger in exploring the Neo-Impressionist colour-system. It seems, thus, that Léger's decision to reject colour for the realization in painting of form, may very well have been preceded by an intensive exploration of colour and light—that Léger turned against himself.

Yet there is an important sense in which Impressionism taken to the extreme of Neo-Impressionism would have given Léger a suitable foundation on which to build the style of *Nus dans un paysage.* For it was, especially by 1908 in the hands of Signac, Cross, the young Delaunay and Metzinger, emphatically an artificial style: a style concerned with creating an equivalent of the vitality of light in nature in terms which were purely pictorial. The *tâches* of colour in Cross's *Nymphes* are so large as to underline the artificiality of the painting's mosaic colour structure, even though their vibrant clashes are calculated to create a sensation of sunlight on flesh and foliage as dazzling as that of real sunlight. Paintings like this demonstrated that realism in painting, i.e., the attempt to realize on canvas the physical presence of things, did not necessarily mean the imitation of appearances, that the painter could use purely pictorial elements (here broad colour *tâches*) to create equivalence of sensation rather than absolute likeness.

8

7. (above) Paul
Cézanne: *Cinq
baigneuses,* 1885–7.
$25\frac{3}{4} \times 25\frac{3}{4}$ ins,
Oeffentliche
Kunstssammlung,
Basel.

8. (right) Henri-
Edmond Cross:
Nymphes, 1906.
$32 \times 39\frac{1}{2}$ ins. Present
whereabouts
unknown.

9. Fernand Léger: *La Couseuse,* 1909. $28\frac{3}{4} \times 21\frac{1}{2}$ ins, private collection, Paris.

Léger's *Nus dans un paysage* was an attempt to create not an equivalent of natural light effects, but an equivalent of mass. He aimed to evoke the weight, the sheer physical presence of three-dimensional form. He may have rejected colour as the dominant component, but he followed the basic approach to the realization on canvas of observed effects established by the Neo-Impressionists. He simply shifted his emphasis from light to form. The very way in which he created the sensation of mass both in landscape and in figures can be seen as a translation into tonal terms of the Divisionist approach to colour. In his *Souvenirs* Gleizes writes of volumes 'treated according to the graded zones procedure used in architecture or in mechanical models',[10] and it is this clear separation into tonal zones of the planes out of which masses are formed that corresponds to the clear separation of colour *tâches* out of which Signac, Cross, Delaunay and Metzinger formed their images of light before 1909.

Léger was repeatedly to acknowledge the preliminary importance of the Impressionists, but he acknowledged as his masters two painters above all, the Douanier Rousseau, whom he knew with Delaunay before 1909,[11] and Cézanne. It was Cézanne, he told Dora Vallier later, who answered his

10. Henri Rousseau
(Le Douanier): *Portrait
de Mme S.*, 1898.
$18 \times 14\frac{3}{4}$ ins, sold
Sotheby's, London,
3 July 1973.

need 'to fatten volumes',[12] but so, one might add, did the Douanier. The
Nus and its smaller relative painted in 1909, *La Couseuse*, tell much of
both debts, and so too do Léger's 1913 views on Cézanne, which often
apply as readily to the Douanier. These latter lay the emphasis particularly
on Cézanne's desire to idealize, to order and simplify the forms of nature,
and he quotes one of Cézanne's letters to Emile Bernard in support: 'His
(the artist's) way of seeing was much more intellectual than visual.'[13]
For Léger, Cézanne did not go far enough since he never realized that his
ability to idealize what he saw freed him from his dependence on the
model or *motif*; Rousseau must at times have gone far enough even by
Léger's standards.

La Couseuse (Plate 9) and *Nus dans un paysage* establish clearly the fact
that in 1909 as well as in 1913 it was indeed both Cézanne and the Douanier's
ability to idealize nature that most deeply affected Léger, and that even
at this early stage he could go far further than Cézanne, if not perhaps than
the Douanier. Cézanne's *Portrait de Mme Cézanne* (Plate 11) and the Douanier's
Portrait de Mme S (Plate 10) are very much the kind of figure paintings
that would have attracted Léger's attention on his visits in 1908 and 1909

to Vollard's gallery and to the ageing Rousseau's home in the 14e *arrondissement*. From a Cézanne like this he would have learned how the transitions between light and shadow could be simplified into distinct areas of warm and cool tones, thus intensifying the sense of three-dimensional mass. From a Rousseau like this he would have learned something only hinted at in the Cézanne: that the contrasts between light and dark could be so simplified as to make of the head especially an artificial geometric structure lacking the smooth transitions between light and shade that result from Cézanne's continued dependence on the first-hand observation of light effects—a structure which has the artificiality of a mask. In *La Couseuse* Léger applies the warm and cool tones of the Cézanne portrait, but applies them to a figurative structure even more sharply faceted, even more geometrically solid than the Rousseau portrait. So far has the process of idealization gone that one need no longer infer a model as a necessary starting-point. In order to create the sensation of figurative mass Léger needs no longer to paint the fall of light across surfaces as seen in life—he can construct his figure out of simple faceted solids closer to the pure world of Euclid than to life. However, like both Cézanne and Rousseau, Léger remains in *La Couseuse* and the *Nus* caught in the paradox central to Neo-Impressionism, because, as has been seen, he idealizes in order to strengthen the sensation created of mass and weight: he idealizes for a fundamentally realistic purpose. Indeed, both Cézanne and the Douanier justified a realistic purpose as much as they justified an idealizing method, and in 1913 Léger also quotes Cézanne on this point: 'To paint after nature, for an impressionist, is not to paint the object, but to realize sensations.'[14] From the beginning of his avant-garde career Léger aimed to balance a desire to render things palpably real on canvas with a belief in painting as an essentially non-imitative and pure art. In the *Nus* he idealized in order to arrive at a simpler, more solid sense of physical reality.

By returning to the pictorial and literary context within which the *Nus* emerged between the autumn of 1910 and the spring of 1911 a little more light can be thrown on the nature of Léger's idealizing realism, and on its significance to the alliance cemented in 'Salle 41'. The special force and simplicity that Léger gave his volumes ensured for the *Nus* an obvious independence,[15] but it was unmistakably at one with the works among which it hung, sharing in general terms the essential features of the group style they established. The balance struck by Léger between the pursuit of a massively solid realism and the simplifications of solid geometry was not isolated; it was fundamental as well to Gleizes's *Femme au phlox* (Plate 12), Metzinger's *Deux Nus* and Le Fauconnier's *L'Abondance* (Plate 22), and it was the result of an approach to reality which is equally evident behind the work of their literary allies.

By 1911 the writers involved with the 'Salle 41' Cubists had made their position regarding realism abundantly clear. Jouve and Castiaux's *Les Bandeaux d'Or*, Jacques Nayral's *Revue Indépendante*, and 'Unanimism', the movement initiated by Jules Romains, had come to stand for a lyrical reaction against the fantastic and obscurantist excesses of the Symbolists.[16] There were points of difference between individuals, but the one-time Abbaye de Créteil circle shared a common sense of involvement in the most ordinary aspects of everyday life. Their work was rooted always in experience, and they lionized above all Emile Zola, Emile Verhaeren, and Walt Whitman, the last of whom entered the Parisian literary world almost as if he was a contemporary with the 1908 publication in French of Léon Bazalgette's biography and the 1909 translation into French of *Leaves of Grass*.[17] Yet, this lyrical celebration of reality—what Georges Duhamel called a new optimism[18]—was balanced against a deep respect for the abstract, conceptual capacities of the poet. The aim was for a poetry of ideas, beautiful in its abstract forms, but always rooted in experience. Jean Metzinger contributed an essay on Alexandre Mercereau to the Montparnasse review *Vers et Prose* in the summer of 1911 and dwelt throughout on the problem of bringing into harmony idea and reality.[19] He saw Mercereau's *Paroles devant la vie*, of which parts were published in *Vers et Prose* in 1911,[20] as the climax of his career because, although its beauty lay in the beauty of Mercereau's ideas—an abstract beauty—it never lost touch with the reality of experience. The parallel between the approach of the poets and of the painters who met in Le Fauconnier's studio or the Closérie des Lilas was remarkably exact. Just as Metzinger wrote of Mercereau approaching the world of everyday experience through the medium of his intelligence, so in the *Revue Indépendante* Gleizes wrote of Metzinger subjecting appearances to the shaping power of the mind.[21] Again, just as the painters sought to reconstruct the components of reality in simple geometric terms, certain of the poets gave order to their lyricism by means of a clear and simple use of poetic artifice. Thus, Georges Duhamel, writing on Vildrac and Romains in 1910 and 1911, singles out their use of metric and verse forms as especially important,[22] and in 1910 he and Vildrac underlined the importance of poetic form by publishing a treatise on the subject, 'Notes sur la technique poètique'.

Léger's *Nus dans un paysage* was at one with the works among which it hung in a further fundamental respect, the conventional pictorial distinction between solid and space was broken down. His forest setting is built up in the same way as his nudes, out of facets hinged together and angled differently in relation to the picture-plane. He allows an illusion of plunging recession by superimposing hummock after hummock of lumpy ground, but gives the whole a common density and pushes the sky out of the picture area. The *sous bois* is as weighty as the nudes embedded in it, so that the entire picture surface becomes a simulated relief creating the sensation of mass. Le Fauconnier, Metzinger and Gleizes attempted an analogous unification of pictorial substance. It was perhaps the group's most revolutionary innovation, since it went further than the simplification of things to actually invent a new kind of reality, and, like the process of geometric faceting, it was an innovation for which they owed much to the first Cubists, to the private experiments of Picasso and Braque.

'And if Apollinaire and Max Jacob,' Léger told Dora Vallier, 'had not come to see us, it would not even have been possible to know what was happening in Montmartre. They told us to go to Kahnweiler's, and there we saw, fat Delaunay too, what the Cubists were doing.'[23] Kahnweiler himself has confirmed that it was after Léger had exhibited the *Nus dans un paysage* that Léger first came into the rue Vignon gallery, but it has repeatedly been pointed out that the dealer bought *La Couseuse* as early as 1910,[24] and both the circumstantial and the visual evidence suggests

13

persuasively that Léger, like the others of the 'Salle 41' group, owed a debt to the Montmartre Cubists at least equal to the debt he owed Cézanne and the Douanier.

It may well be that Apollinaire and Max Jacob were for Léger the intermediaries between Montparnasse and Kahnweiler, but it is unlikely that before he went to Kahnweiler's he had heard nothing of what was to be seen there. His years of apprenticeship, when *La Couseuse* was painted and the *Nus* begun, were spent in 'La Ruche', a strange decaying remnant of the Exposition Universelle on the rue Dantzig. As has been seen, he was at this time (1908–11) in contact with Delaunay, and so his life in 'La Ruche' could not have been altogether out of touch with advanced developments in the Parisian avant-garde. Delaunay was well informed: in November he had seen Kahnweiler's exhibition of Georges Braque's L'Estaque landscapes, and he was a regular visitor at the home of one of Kahnweiler's first clients, the German connoisseur and dealer Wilhelm Uhde, who in the autumn of 1909 was painted by Picasso and who by this date owned thirteen Braques.[25] Certainly Delaunay was excited by what he saw at that time,[26] and it seems at the least unlikely that he communicated none of his excitement and none of his knowledge to his friend.[27] Moreover, by the time Léger was at work on finishing the *Nus* for the spring 1911 Indépendants, he was close to Le Fauconnier, Metzinger and Gleizes, and they certainly must have showed off what they had learned from the Montmartre Cubists.

What then did the simplifying and unifying treatment of solid and space in *Nus dans un paysage* have in common with that of its closest relatives in the 'Salle 41' and of the Montmartre Cubists; and what was special to it? Closest of all the *Nus* relatives in the 'Salle 41', stylistically if not in subject, was Gleizes's *Femme au phlox* (Plate 12). Gleizes gives a solid unity to all pictorial substance, but he is not tempted by Picasso's newest mode, the mode of the 1910 *Portrait of Kahnweiler*, to break down the distinctions between figure, objects and setting. He firmly closes his facets by contour so that their surfaces cannot flow into one another, and he uses both colour and shape to state plainly the commonplace components of his subject. He is attracted by the massive simplicity of Picasso's heads of Fernand Olivier painted in 1909 at Horta de San Juan, by the unification of figure and setting achieved without ambiguity in canvases like *Femme assise* (Plate 13).

Such plainness of pictorial statement in the interests of a commonplace subject recalls the plain speaking of Léger's *La Couseuse*, and it is also found, though in the interests of a more than everyday subject, in the *Nus*. Like Gleizes, Léger firmly encloses facets, both those of figures and of forest scene, emphasizing the fact that his sharply divided surfaces cover tight, separated solids; like Gleizes, he does not allow the solid unification of figures and setting to undermine the importance of his subject, preferring to leave the muscular energy contained within his forest scene unblurred; but much more than Gleizes he uses the weighty components of his painting to generate force, and it is the sheer power of *Nus dans un paysage* that most indisputably asserts its originality within the context both of Montmartre Cubism and of 'Salle 41'. The very structure of the three nudes, even where their postures are static, conveys a dynamic power, but this

11. (right)   Paul Cézanne: *Portrait de Mme Cézanne*, $35\frac{1}{2} \times 19\frac{3}{4}$ ins, National Museum, Stockholm (Grace and Philip Sandblom bequest).

12. (below)   Albert Gleizes: *La Femme au phlox*, 1910. $32 \times 39\frac{1}{2}$ ins, Museum of Fine Arts, Houston.

13.   Pablo Picasso: *Femme assise,* 1909. $31\frac{1}{2} \times 25\frac{1}{2}$ ins, sold Sotheby's, London, 5 December 1973.

depicted dynamism is complemented by a dissonance which is purely pictorial, more directly capable of generating force. The solids of the painting are divided into groups united by similar size and shape: large, swelling forms—the back of the nude crouched in the centre, and the broad areas of grey-green above—small, nuggety forms—the bushes, heads, limbs, etc.—and finally the jointed tubular units of the trees. So clear is the separation between these contrasting types of solid that great force is generated by their collision: it is this, of course, that lies behind Léger's phrase: 'a battle of volumes'. So uncompromising and all-embracing an emphasis on the dynamic, and on cacophonous formal collision, looks back beyond the Picasso of 1909 to the Picasso of the great figure-paintings of 1908, to the rhetoric of *Trois Nus* (Plate 14); but the sheer range of

16

14.   Pablo Picasso: *Trois nus,* 1908. 78¾ × 70 ins, Hermitage Museum, Leningrad.

Léger's contrasting armoury of forms is unprecedented, and their force was unchallenged in the 'Salle 41'.

The violence of the *Nus* is further accentuated and its novelty underlined by looking at it from the point of view of its subject-matter. A woodland scene with nudes obediently postured for effect rather than comfort was one of the staple crops of French academic art, and it had by 1909 been given the reviving palliative of fresh avant-garde use. Cézanne's *Baigneuses* gave the subject a new revolutionary status, Matisse returned to it in *Luxe, calme et volupté* and *Joie de vivre,* as did André Derain, Orthon Friesz[28] and, of course, Henri-Edmond Cross (Plate 8). It is unimaginable that Léger could have conceived *Nus dans un paysage* unaware that its subject fitted into this tradition, but his painting does not merely fit into its past context, it confronts the old with an abrasively new interpretation. The nude is no longer an image of simplistic harmony, as in Cross's *Nymphes* or Matisse's *Joie de vivre.* It is an image of power, and it is formed, as has been seen, not to work *with* the elements of landscape but against them.

17

Cézanne's *Baigneuses*—for instance the nudes in *Cinq Baigneuses* (Plate 7) which was exhibited at the galerie Bernheim-Jeune in 1910—might often anticipate the massive strength of Léger's nudes, but Cézanne's nudes do not anticipate their muscular dynamism, nor their antagonism to each other and to their natural setting. An old theme is given an aggressively new, anti-harmonious interpretation.

In the aggressive novelty with which Léger treated an old theme and in the dissonant power of his pictorial collisions he declared a view of life whose violence was to be a constant throughout his career, and it is a view of life which is partially if fitfully illuminated by its literary context. An analogous concern with effects of conflict is found not so much in the then current work of the Abbaye de Créteil poets and their sympathizers, as in the work of their acknowledged masters—in Bazalgette's French translation of Whitman's *Leaves of Grass* and in Verhaeren's collections, *Les villes tentaculaires* (1895) and *Les forces tumultueuses* (1902). Of the Abbaye poets themselves, only Henri-Martin Barzun in the first two books of his *Terrestre Tragédie*, seems to anticipate the force of the *Nus*.[29] Barzun's long poem is a celebration of man: its scale of reference in time and space is vast, its tone dramatic. The titles given to its sections reveal the emphasis given to themes of dynamism and struggle: thus, the first book is entitled *Le Souffle*, and subtitled *Energie-Volonté*, and is divided into four sections: *L'Effort humain, L'Idée, Vouloir* and *Puissance*. Like Verhaeren and Whitman, Barzun senses a rhythmic force interpenetrating and unifying all things; it is the key to an essentially violent view of life profoundly in tune with that declared by Léger's painting.[30]

Barzun's *Terrestre Tragédie* also contains passages which seem to echo the view of the relationship between man and nature expressed by Léger in the *Nus*—that view which accentuates conflict between man and nature; but perhaps the most apt and illuminating parallel of all is found elsewhere. In one of the first passages of criticism devoted to the *Nus*, Apollinaire made a mistake which is especially revealing: he described Léger's figures as 'woodcutters'.[31] Léger himself leaves no sign that might thus identify them, but so well does the image of woodcutters seem to fit the nudes that commentators have repeatedly been tempted to return to it, attracted by the violence implicit in the woodcutter's relationship with the forest.[32] Yet, it is not in the poetry of Apollinaire that the woodcutter as an image takes on a power truly in tune with the power of Léger's nudes, it is rather in the poetry of Whitman, and it was possibly to a particular passage in the *Leaves of Grass* that Apollinaire's mind was drawn when he first saw the painting, for, in a passage devoted specifically to the woodcutter, the American provides a text in praise of human power that might have been written for Léger. It begins:

> The axe leaps!
> The solid forest gives fluid utterances,
> They tumble forth, they rise and form,
> Hut, tent, landing, survey,
> Flail, plough, pick, crowbar, spade. . . .[33]

After which follows a passionately compiled catalogue of all things formed in wood, given the refrain, 'The shapes arise!', ending with a universal

18

celebration of 'the main shapes'—'Shapes of turbulent manly cities, . . . shapes bracing the earth and braced with the whole earth.' Whitman's vigour, the force of his language, effectively conveyed in Bazalgette's French translation, and the fusion of the destructive and the constructive in the image of man as woodcutter is so closely in tune with the violence of Léger's *Nus* in their forest setting that one is tempted to read a definite allegorical intention into the painting. But Léger's refusal to make specific allusions invalidates such a reading: his nudes are no more than nudes, set without attributes in a forest which could be any forest. In the most general of terms his big painting conveys the confrontation between nature and man.[34]

Léger's pictorial vocabulary of simplified forms tonally graded and his abrupt division of pictorial forces collaborates with the power of his nudes to destroy the peace of the Arcadian 'idyll', and thus with the *Nus dans un paysage* he declares the potential not only of a new style in painting, but also of a new approach to reality—an approach which celebrates above all the power of man both to destroy and to create. It was the first major painting to declare Léger's personal Cubist alternative. His Cubism was to move in directions which could never have been prophesied from the closest of studies of the *Nus*, but with this painting he declared plainly and irrevocably the violence that was to be crucial to his alternative at every stage. It was in a real sense a beginning.

* * * * *

At the Salon d'Automne of 1911 the group which had given Cubism a public face at the Indépendants made a second public statement, but with some subtractions and some additions. Robert Delaunay was the most important defector, although he was not yet in positive opposition to the group; the most important recruits were Roger de La Fresnaye and the Villon brothers, Jacques and Marcel (Duchamp). Léger, Gleizes, Metzinger, Le Fauconnier, de La Fresnaye, Villon and Duchamp showed together in 'Salle 8'. Léger, who had spent the summer at home in Normandy,[35] brought to the Salon a second manifesto work, *Essai pour trois portraits* (Plate 15); it was even larger than *Nus dans un paysage*.

With *Essai pour trois portraits*, Léger so accentuates the unification of figures and setting that the separate integrity of things is often lost in the movement of the whole. He breaks the three stiffly posed figures into fragments and dislocates their limbs. Yet by thus fragmenting them he does not deny their solidity; neither does he open the contours of every form to allow a shifting, over-all sense of surface flow. Certain figurative components—the arms, hands, parts of the torsos—are isolated as tightly closed cylinders or blocks, each polished to a dull metallic sheen, and it is in between these solid members that the figures are penetrated by the movements set up around them. Whirling and spilling bundles of luminous form break into them, each with its origin in the observed effects of light—as it spills through the window to merge with the uppermost head, as it catches the shirtfront of the young man and wraps around the back and arm of the chair. There is established a clear contrast between the passage of light and the weight of figurative form, both elements of the contrast moving in interpenetrating, contradictory rhythms. Broken down into

19

15.   Fernand Léger: *Essai pour trois portraits*, 1911. 77 × 45¾ ins, Milwaukee Art Center.

16. Robert Delaunay: *Le Tour Eiffel*, 1910. $76\frac{1}{2} \times 45\frac{1}{2}$ ins, Oeffentliche Kunstssammlung, Basel.

mobile sequences of facets, the fall of light becomes the instrument of penetration set in dynamic counterpoint against the rotation of solid forms. The result is a painting which is both less simple than the *Nus*, and, for all the static rigidity of its subject, more pictorially dynamic—a painting whose essential qualities are contrasting rhythm and interpenetration.

Essai is far closer than the *Nus* to the work of the Montmartre Cubists, now certainly known by Léger at Kahnweiler's gallery, but, lacking the elusiveness of Picasso and Braque's current style, it remains at a distance. Its rhythmic dynamism is, of course, alien, and so too is the literal descriptiveness of the devices by which Léger announces his subject and breaks down its integrity. The figures may be fragmented, but their identity remains clearly declared, the three most recognizable and complete images being the three heads. Their features are faceted and simplified, but by contrast with the cylindrical artificiality of the limbs they are near naturalistic, and the strong sense of individual presence that they carry makes them indeed 'trois portraits'.[36] The solidity of three figures recognizable as people is thus penetrated by a moving force recognizable as light; where the interpenetration of figure and setting in Picasso's Kahnweiler portrait is presented as a purely pictorial event, here it is presented as an observed event—an event taken from life. Léger is still clearly a painter concerned with the realization of his sensations, but he has become absorbed more in the sensation of rhythmic interpenetration than in the sensation of 'a battle of volumes'.

The closest contemporary relations of *Essai* were not hung in the 'Salle 8': they were Robert Delaunay's latest versions of *Le Tour Eiffel*, one of

21

which had been shown at the Indépendants in the spring. Their subject separates them from Léger's painting, but their dynamic force and the literal descriptiveness with which they express the themes of interpenetration and fragmentation is very much in tune.

Although Delaunay did not show in the 'Salle 8', there is good reason to suppose that when Léger came back from Normandy in the autumn of 1911 the two friends were still frequently in contact. Their approaches were deeply in sympathy, and in Paris they were easily accessible to each other, for either late in 1910 or early in 1911, just before or just after the completion of the *Nus*, Léger had moved to 13, rue de l'Ancienne Comédie,[37] which was within short walking distance of the Delaunay's apartment at 3, rue des Grands Augustins.

The version of *Le Tour Eiffel* in the Kunstmuseum, Basel (Plate 16) is close to that which hung in the 'Salle 41'.[38] Like Léger, Delaunay identifies here the processes of dynamic interpenetration and fragmentation with a particular subject, the tower, whose likeness he leaves unmistakable, the axis of the painting. Again, like Léger, he breaks its structure apart by means of penetrating forces whose origins lie in observed fact—the floating softness of white clouds and the angularity of sudden light-shafts. So closely related is the operation of Delaunay's dynamic devices to the operation of Léger's that a direct, causal relationship must be suggested: Léger, it seems, did not forget the lesson of the *Tours* while in Normandy. Yet, although *Essai* was not, therefore, an unprecedented variant on Cubism when it was hung in the 'Salle 8', Léger's choice of a subject so far from Delaunay's, the deeply personal nature of his figurative simplifications and of his faceted passages of light all combine to assert its independence.

The more emphatic breakdown of the boundary between solid and setting was a quality declared not only by Léger's contribution to the 'Salle 8', but also in their more or less literal ways by Gleizes's *Portrait de Jacques Nayral*, Metzinger's *Le Goûter* and Marcel Duchamp's *Portrait, Dulcinea* (Plate 17). The dynamic energy of *Essai* was unchallenged, but especially in the case of Gleizes and Duchamp the sensation of rhythmic interpenetration was crucial, and in the case of Léger it declared a significant modification of his dissonant view of reality, a modification whose character is to some extent revealed by the treatment of the interpenetration theme in the work of the poets.

In 1908 the Abbaye de Créteil published Jules Romains's collection of poems *La Vie Unanime*. The ideas central to these poems were to obsess all the Abbaye writers and their sympathizers especially during the formative period of what might be called second-phase Cubism, 1908–12.[39] Romains believed that by feeling people can so identify with each other and with their surroundings that they can lose their isolation, become one. It was this idea that lay behind the theory called 'Unanimism'. For Romains, the emanation of Unanimist forces could become so strong as to achieve a visible, physical form breaking through the barriers between things,[40] and this is a central theme both in *La Vie unanime* and his next collection of poems *Un Etre en marche* (1910). Poets like Pierre-Jean Jouve in *Les Ordres qui changent* (1911) and René Arcos in *Ce qui naît* (1910) might not have seen this dissolution of barriers exactly as Romains did, but they shared his belief in the interpenetration of people and things, and in general terms it is a belief which parallels the move towards effects of interpenetration so clear in the painting of Gleizes, Metzinger, Duchamp and Léger at the Salon d'Automne of 1911. The physical rather than psychological nature of penetration in Léger's *Essai* may discourage specific reference to the poetry of Romains, but the fact remains that boundaries are broken down and a new fluxing, open relationship between things is made possible—a relationship which would have held much meaning for poets who no longer considered the separateness of things but the continuity of movement between them.

The penetrative movement of light was not the only device by which Delaunay and then Léger could break open the integrity of things and make them part of a continuous fluxing dynamic theme. Delaunay's tower is not a single view image but an amalgam of many views, so that his sudden shafts of light shatter a structure already tilted, twisted and broken apart by movement, by dramatic changes of aspect.[41] The example of Picasso and Braque—above all the Picasso of the Horta de San Juan figure-paintings (Plate 13)—lies behind this attack on static perspective,[42] but Delaunay achieves an effect of fragmentation more radical even than the Picasso of 1909, because he conveys the changing of viewpoints by completely severing one tower aspect from another, creating an effect not unlike cinematic cutting which is destructive in a new and emphatic way.

With *Essai pour trois portraits* Léger too moved into the attack on single viewpoint perspective, but his attempt is neither as radical nor as dynamic as Delaunay's in the *Tours*. Figures are fragmented by the action of light alone, not by the action of cutting from one viewpoint to another, and mobile perspective is only tentatively given a place in the painting. The heads are, in fact, the only unmistakable displays of the new shifting perspective in action, and they are little more than simple adaptations from the Picasso of 1909. All three are seen three-quarter face, turned to the left, like so many of Picasso's Horta heads, and all three are subjected to an identical sequence of changes, following rather timidly the guidelines set by Picasso. Thus, on the vertical axis provided by the nose the cheeks are pulled forward so that the forehead is folded and the chin twisted. Even the mode of modelling and dividing from each other the facets of the three heads is close to Picasso's. Léger builds with clearly separated and modelled lumps of matter, whose forms are often crystalline in their simplicity, yet which are securely locked or hinged onto one another. For this reason, as in the Horta heads, the act of changing viewpoint does not fragment. Each aspect is attached as part of a single mass to the next, and so the sensation is created, not of cutting abruptly from one aspect to the next, but of a continuous sliding movement around unbroken and unbreakable structures.

Once again, however divergent their Cubist variants, all the painters who exhibited in the 'Salle 8' agreed on the need for a concerted attack on single viewpoint perspective. For all of them the stimulus of Picasso and Braque was crucial—the indebtedness of Léger and Delaunay was by no means the exception—but the reason for their common acceptance of the new mobile perspective is less obvious. It lies in the deeper question of meaning, in the special significance they attached to this new, more radical reaction against orthodox pictorial representation; and in this is revealed a further factor crucial to Léger's modified view of reality.

'Today', announced Gleizes and Metzinger in their personal statement of Cubist principles, *Du cubisme*, 'oil painting allows the expression of notions of depth, density and duration *(la durée)*, thought inexpressible, and encourages us to present within a limited space, governed by a complex rhythm, a true fusion of objects.'[43] *Du Cubisme* was published by Eugène Figuière, publisher of Romains, Arcos, Mercereau, Jouve and others of the circle, in December 1912. It was Gleizes's and Metzinger's considered comment on what had been established in the 'Salle 8'. The 'fusion of objects' has already been described as it occurs in Léger's *Essai*; for Gleizes and Metzinger, the principal way by which 'duration' could be expressed was by the shifting of viewpoints.[44] *Du Cubisme* was certainly not a statement on Cubism whose every contention was agreed with by the other painters of 'Salle 8', but on the special capacity of mobile perspective to convey *la durée* they probably did agree, and the term *la durée* introduces a figure whose importance both to them and to their poet friends was fundamental, the philosopher Henri Bergson.

'The influence on my generation of the philosophy of M. Bergson,' wrote the critic Tancrède de Visan in 1910 'is only comparable with that exercised by Descartes on Malebranche or by Hume on Kant.'[45] De Visan was discussing poetry, but he pointed at the same time to a major influence on second-phase Cubism.

Bergson's intention was to replace the methods and assumptions of nineteenth-century positivism with an approach to reality which was not based on the logical and ordering qualities of the intellect. His attempt reached a point of some completeness with the 1907 publication of *L'Evolution créatrice*. Here he rejects the mechanical approach of science, according to which reality is split up into the separate parts of a logical system, and he rejects the finalist approach, according to which the order of reality represents the result of a master plan. The certainty provided by scientific analysis is, he maintains, irrelevant to any profound understanding of reality, since on the one hand it ignores the fact that reality is experienced as a continuity of relationships rather than as a collection of separate items, and on the other ignores the factor of time. The concept of *la durée* is central to his concept of time. 'Duration is the continual progress of the past which eats away at the future, swelling as it advances.'[46] For Bergson, *la durée* is the constantly growing force of what has occurred in the past behind both the evolution of new forms—plants, animals, etc.— and of new experiences—of each individual's consciousness. Man, he believes, is always aware of this force, and because the past is thus given a constant place in the present, all mechanical notions of time as subdivisible into hours, minutes and seconds are invalidated. Life, for him, is an irreversible movement forward, driven by past accumulations, and to break its passage down into units is to interrupt the continuity of its movement. 'Duration, for us,' he writes in *L'Evolution créatrice*, 'is like an endless flow. It is the core of our being, we feel it keenly, that essence which we communicate with. It is in vain that a dazzling prospect of a universal mathematics is presented to us, we cannot sacrifice experience to the demands made by a system.'[47]

24

There is no concrete evidence that the second-phase Cubists themselves actually attended Bergson's lectures, but the ideas expounded in his books, particularly those from *L'Evolution créatrice* mentioned above, had been absorbed so much into the work and, no doubt, the talk of their literary allies, that by 1911 the Bergsonian view—no doubt often blurred or simplified—was the common property of the avant-garde. With the introduction to the group of the Villon brothers a new centre for discussion was established at the Puteaux studio of Jacques Villon, and it is well known that *L'Evolution créatrice* was the subject of much talk there.[48] Moreover, the publications of the Abbaye circle between 1908 and 1912 demonstrate beyond doubt the importance to their entire approach of the Bergsonian view. The notion of interpenetration itself, with its attendant destruction of physical barriers in favour of a rhythmic continuity, is obviously at least in part Bergsonian, and, when extended to involve the factor of time, as in Jules Romains's 1911 novel *Mort de quelqu'un*, the connection is even more obvious.[49] Indeed, René Arcos's poem *Ce qui naît,* also published in 1911, revolves entirely around the theme of *la durée*. 'From the dedication on,' wrote Georges Duhamel in 1911 'the idea of duration impresses itself on the reader . . . . The poem seems like an episode and, of itself, allows the time it invokes to take control.'[50]

Thus, when Gleizes and Metzinger link the process of moving about a subject as manifested in Cubist painting to the expression of *la durée*, they link the new common factor found in the work of themselves, Marcel Duchamp, Roger de La Fresnaye and Léger to an idea, indeed a philosophy, which was of great significance both to the poets and to the painters. Arcos's *Ce qui naît*, being poetry and therefore by nature sequential, carries, in the Bergsonian sense, its own duration within itself; it evolves, driven by the rhythm of its words and the accumulated sum of its images and ideas. Painting cannot so straightforwardly involve the factor of time, because it makes its impact more or less in a single instant. The attraction of Picasso's and Braque's invention lay at least partially in the way it could involve the factor of time in a single painted image, for it allowed the results of a continuous and mobile process of study to be merged into a single composition. In their different ways the figure-paintings shown by Gleizes and Metzinger in 'Salle 8', and the three heads of Léger's *Essai* convey the duration of their conception—the mobile, evolving process which has culminated in their pictorial realization—as literally and straightforwardly as they do their identity.

If it was possible to introduce the factor of time into a painting by conveying the changing aspects of the artist's relation to the model, it was also possible to do so by conveying the changing aspects of the model's relation to the artist: by setting the model itself in motion. There was one painting in 'Salle 8' which attempted to do this: Marcel Duchamp's *Portrait, Dulcinea* (Plate 17). Duchamp's painting was much more a purely intellectual work than those exhibited around it, for its subject had no physical presence. It was an imaginary event: the process of Dulcinea (itself an imaginary name) stripped bare in his mind. To this end he repeats the figure five times, the five images being allowed to flow into each other through opened contours.

The insubstantial fluidity of Duchamp's painting echoes the insubstantial

17.   Marcel Duchamp: *Portrait (Dulcinea)*, 1911. $57\frac{1}{2} \times 45$ ins, Louise and Walter Arensberg collection, Philadelphia Museum of Art.

fluidity of his subject; it is utterly alien to the substantial vigour of Léger's *Essai*. Yet, Duchamp's focus on the movement of his subject rather than of himself makes a link with Léger's painting, because it is the only other work exhibited in 'Salle 8' which shows signs, though in a far less all-embracing way, of a comparable approach to motion. Virginia Spate has recently noted that in *Essai* Léger makes a small experiment in the representation of movement by the repetition of images.[51] It involves only the woman seated on the right, but, however peripheral an incident, it is of

26

great interest. The woman is circled as if by a sash of hands loosely knit together; the hand of the figure standing behind falls on her shoulder to hold her left hand which rises to meet it. Then, below, her left hand appears once more, repeated twice, implying a movement either down and away from, or up and towards the hand on her shoulder. The continuity of the sequence of images ties together the effect of movement. Time enters the painting in a new way. Yet, in the final analysis, this particular temporal incident, left unmentioned by commentators for so long, demonstrates the fact that, though indirectly based on Bergsonian thinking, the new approach to reality that lay behind *Essai* was not strictly Bergsonian; for, the practice of conceiving time as a succession of points, or movement as a succession of 'stills', was considered by Bergson fundamentally alien to the unbroken continuity of flow crucial to his concept of *la durée*.[52] Léger almost certainly absorbed the elements of his new approach, not from the careful contemplation of Bergsonian ideas, but in an unstructured way from what he heard and saw in the avant-garde around him, the result being, in philosophical terms, far from consistent.

The breakdown of physical barriers to create an interpenetrating continuity of rhythm, the introduction of mobile perspective, the sequential depiction of movement—all these features of *Essai pour trois portraits* were the product of a new approach to reality. They were features which took Léger further from the orthodox representation of things, but they did not take him further from realism. A new idea of experience—involving rhythmic interpenetration, movement and a sense of the past in the present—meant new pictorial methods aimed at the capture on canvas of experience. In *Essai*, even more clearly than in the *Nus dans un paysage*, Léger takes every interpenetrating, every mobile and every durational effect from observed reality. The painting is an attempt to present in paint the quality of sensations experienced in life; the sensation of moving around the three heads, the sensation of light flowing through the window, the sensation of a hand briefly, peripherally in movement.

*   *   *   *   *

The question of how fundamental Léger's realistic intention remained as he developed a more dynamic and more durational variant on Cubism is answered in a less complex way by a look at a series of smaller oils. They are private paintings and the urban view which was their subject still exists almost unchanged (Plate 19). The series is called *Les Fumées sur les toits*.

The probability is that the series, including the small, coarsely painted version in the St Louis collection of Richard K. Weil (Plate 18) described by John Golding as 'almost certainly' the first, was painted during the latter half of 1911,[53] and the importance given in these canvases to rhythmic interpenetration and mobile perspective suggests an approach to reality at least as dynamic and durational as the approach expressed in *Essai*. They are portraits of a particular place (the Quartier Latin) seen from a particular window (in Léger's rooftop studio at 13, rue de l'Ancienne Comédie), but seen with an eye for the dissonance and the dynamism of certain types of effect. All these effects are realistic, and Léger's determination to declare their realism is conveyed by the fact that, as they are developed and intensified in the most finished of all the versions, the painting in the Minneapolis Art Institute (Colour Plate 2), so their representational identity is clarified too. The process of accentuating the pictorial effects of contrast and interpenetration does not obscure their representational meaning. Thus, line separates forms more crisply in the Minneapolis than in the St Louis version, and colour is more wide-ranging, a pale pink being introduced among the greys and browns for the broadest, most central area of roof-surface. The result is that with clearer separation comes clearer representational definition: the roofs are more clearly roofs, the smoke, smoke, and the shafts of light shafts of light. The contrast between the hard, angular weight of buildings and the floating cursiveness of smoke, between the nimbus forms of a rain sky and the sudden penetration of sunlight, the observed origin of every pictorial incident is, in fact, more clear-cut in the Minneapolis *Fumées*. Paradoxically, an increase of pictorial power parallels an increase of descriptive lucidity.

The linear force given by Léger to the penetrations of clouds and light-shafts draws the *Fumées* closer to Delaunay's *Tours* than the *Essai*, but perhaps as important as a link with the series are Delaunay's four paintings on the theme of *La Ville*, they too taking as their subject a rooftop view across Paris.[54] Delaunay's emphasis here on the merger of light effects, especially in the last two versions (painted in 1911), took him away from the linear dynamism of the *Tours* towards an art of weightless, transparent colour; and these canvases are therefore stylistically alien to Léger's *Fumées sur les toits*. Yet these parallel series demonstrate in their common subject and the manner of its treatment a common intention to extract from a broad, embracing view of Paris, an image of rhythmic interpenetration, the one focusing on the movement of colour, the other on the expressive force of form and line. For both, the city theme is crucial.

'The city', writes Georges Duhamel in 1910, *à propos* of Jules Romains, 'is the greatest God. Imposing organism, superior expression of life, it possesses more than anything else: form, that is to say fixity in the midst of mutability. The uninterrupted renewal of its substance does not alter its identity.'[55] For the poets as much as the painters, the city was perhaps the most powerful symbol of the rhythmic interpenetration of living things, and of *la durée*. It looked towards the future and was in constant flux, yet it possessed the fixity—the form—of an identity built up over centuries. It conveyed both the movement of change and the prolongation of the past into the present, and it was therefore central both to Jules Romains's *La Vie Unanime* (1908), and between 1908 and 1910 to his poems *Un Etre en marche*.

Once more, however, it is one of the acknowledged masters of the Abbaye poets and of Romains who most strikingly anticipates Léger's dynamic view of the city: Emile Verhaeren, whose *Villes tentaculaires* (1895) comes especially close. At the apex of Delaunay's view was the Eiffel tower, his own special obsession; at the apex of Léger's was Notre Dame. Neither emphasizes the presence of these landmarks as symbols, but they remain fleetingly visible among the rhythms of the paintings and therefore fleetingly effective as such. Where the iron tower is obviously a symbol of modern life, of present movement into the future, so the Cathedral stands for the

18. (above) Fernand Léger: *Les Fumées sur les toits,* 1911. $26\frac{1}{4} \times 22$ ins, Richard Weil collection, St. Louis.

19. (right) View from the top floor of 13, rue de l'Ancienne Comédie, summer 1972.

past, as indeed do the forms of the old roofs of the 'quartier' across which Léger looks. The presence of the past in the city is essential to Verhaeren's view of 'les villes tentaculaires'.

> Oh! the Centuries upon Centuries that lie upon this city,
> Great with its past
> Unceasingly ardent—and inhabited,
> As at this time, by ghosts![56]

The modern dynamism of his city interacts with the presence, above all in buildings, of the past. Similarly, Léger's modern, dynamic view of the old 'quartier' and the Cathedral confronts a selfconsciously *new* energy with the fixed forms of the past, so that the collision between the immutability of aged buildings and the mobile destructiveness of the new vision becomes in itself a dynamic contrast. Notre Dame is partly obliterated by the movement of smoke—it is *not* immutable to Léger's eye. Verhaeren provides a briefly evocative image as summing up:

> The red factory bursts forth where once only the fields glittered;
> Smoke in black clouds erases the church roofs . . .[57]

The action of smoke and light as the agents of dynamic penetration and dissonant force are not the sole means by which the structural stability and wholeness of the old 'quartier' buildings and Notre Dame are destroyed. Mobile perspective deforms the very structure of the space within which the buildings stand, and it is in this way that the immutability of the old city is most radically confronted with the destructive power of Léger's new approach to reality. Once again, and conclusively, the origin of this deformation lies in observed experience, it is, for Léger, realistic. Delaunay's views of the Eiffel tower in the *Tours* were from the ground, and he could move freely around it; Léger's view of the 'quartier' was from a window (Plate 19), and so his relationship with the *motif* could not so easily be mobile. As a result there are no abrupt and dramatic dislocations and twistings of the structure of buildings; line does not cut one extreme change of aspect from another. But, as far as his restricted position allows him, Léger does with the *Fumées* succeed in conveying the sensation of a shifting relationship between eye and *motif* (Col. Plate 2). Thus, the section of roof to the right of the pink one has slid downwards and taken on an exaggerated tilt as if the result of an opposing view looking rightwards out of the window, and elisions of this kind occur repeatedly, given strong emphasis by the tilting of the entire view to accentuate the counterthrusts of diagonals: the effect is created altogether of a rotating rhythm, as if the solid forms of the buildings below have begun to turn on a hub at the centre of the painting. They and Notre Dame are made mutable, but even this most all-embracing dynamic effect is manifestly the product of experience.[58]

*   *   *   *   *

The *Fumées,* being unexhibited products of studio experiment, are a private demonstration of the realistic intention and the dependence on first-hand observation that lay behind the development after the *Nus* of Léger's new dynamic Cubism, but there is an even more private layer of evidence provided by his surviving exploratory figure-drawings, a group

30

20. Fernand Léger: *Femme nu,*
1911–12. Pen and ink on paper,
12 × 7 ins, sold by Parke-Bernet,
New York, 12 May 1965.

of which, despite the preposterous early dates on many of them, seems to
have been done at the time of the *Fumées*. The group in question is decisively
carried through with a thick-nibbed pen or quill on paper, and *Femme nu*
(Plate 20) is typical of them, introducing as it does all the basic qualities
of the *Fumées*.[59] Line here rarely acts to separate one component from
another, but generates movement, guiding the eye through the gaps
strategically left in contours so that a fluid, open relationship is created
between one part and another, and between figure and space; and the figure
itself is made mobile, turning about its central axis with the action of
mobile perspective to produce a swivelling structure as dramatic as
Delaunay's *Tours*. Léger concentrates once again on effects of interpenetration and dynamic change, and once again every effect is manifestly the
result of first-hand exploration: for this drawing, like many others in the
group, was probably done at the Académie de la Chaumière where nude
models were available, and although it is impossible to establish conclusively
that it was made directly from a model, the traces of a penetrating first-
hand study remain in the unsimplified shaping of forearms, thighs, knees
and hips.

Yet, however much it may seem simply another demonstration of the
realism at the core of Léger's dynamic Cubism, *Femme nu* itself is related
to an isolated attempt by Léger to go beyond realism into allegory, and the
nature of the allegory involved allows a final literary gloss on the view of
reality that was essential to his new style, that guided his eye to the least

31

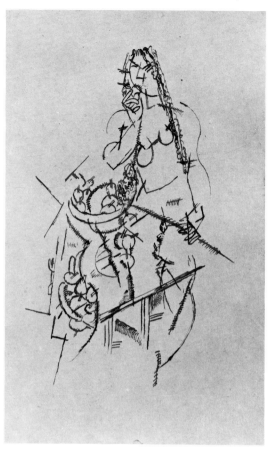

21. Fernand Léger: *Etude pour Un Abondance,* 1911–12. Pen and ink on paper, $12 \times 7\frac{1}{2}$ ins, private collection, France.

fixed and least stable of visual effects. The allegorical connection is made because the figure from *Femme nu* is used again, accompanied by a plentiful supply of fruit, in another drawing which was illustrated, with the caption 'Etude pour un Abondance' (Plate 21), in the first edition of *Du Cubisme* by Gleizes and Metzinger. When the book was published in 1912 Gleizes and Metzinger were in regular contact with Léger, so the title they give must be taken seriously;[60] it announces Léger's probable intention late in 1911 to paint a sequel to Le Fauconnier's star turn at the 1911 Indépendants, his elaborate allegory of fruitfulness and regeneration, *L'Abondance* (Plate 22).

The theme of *l'abondance* was profoundly important not only to Le Fauconnier, but also to the poets of the circle, especially in 1911. René Arcos's *Ce qui naît* is evidence of this fact, but perhaps most obviously in tune with Le Fauconnier's canvas is the section *Paroles devant la femme enceinte* from Alexandre Mercereau's *Paroles devant la vie*, which section was published in full in the summer 1911 *Vers et Prose*.[61] Mercereau, unlike Le Fauconnier, chooses to contemplate a pregnant woman, but it is above all her significance as symbol of fruitfulness that concerns him, and at one point his imagination seems almost to fuse with that of Le Fauconnier, because he builds around the idea of *la femme enceinte* a symbolic setting, like the setting for Le Fauconnier's symbolic mother, though more elaborate,

22.   Henri Le Fauconnier: *L'Abondance,*
1910–11. 125½ × 77 ins, Haags Gemeentemuseum, the Hague.

combining the image of man the cultivator with the image of man the
labourer—on the land, in the mines and on the sea.[62]

The Bergsonian justification for such a concern with themes of regeneration and fruitfulness is not difficult to establish, since for Bergson organic
regeneration and evolution were especially powerful expressions of *la
durée*. And, moreover, anticipating both Mercereau and Le Fauconnier's
use of symbolic images, Bergson believed that the image, for instance, of a
mother and child could trigger an intensified awareness of *la durée*—of
'the living being' as 'above all a stage of transition' and of the fact that 'the
essence of life is contained within the movement which transmits it'.[63]

Yet, in the final analysis, though Léger's flirtation with the idea of an
allegory devoted to abundance underlines once again his commitment to
the dynamism of the Bergsonian view, and though it shows him briefly
sharing Mercereau and Le Fauconnier's commitment to images symbolic
of evolutionary change, it shows him only halfheartedly and not at all
convincingly tempted by the use of such symbols. It shows, in fact, how
profoundly alien allegory was to his new dynamic and realistic style. For
Léger's nude is neither manifestly a mother, nor pregnant, and she is
certainly not, like Le Fauconnier's, at work; she is merely a nude eating
fruit. Indeed, so understated is the allegory, that the theme of *l'abondance*
would seem almost irrelevant but for the title supplied in *Du Cubisme.*

33

1. (left) Fernand Léger: *Le Balustre*, 1925. 51 × 38¼ ins, Museum of Modern Art, New York.
2. (above) Fernand Léger: *Les Fumées sur les toits,* 1911. 23¾ × 37¾ ins, Minneapolis Institute of Arts.

23. (left) Fernand Léger: *Les Fumeurs,*
1911. 51 × 38 ins, Solomon R.
Guggenheim Museum, New York.

24. (right) Fernand Léger: *Etude
pour La Noce,* 1911. 32 × 26¾ ins,
private collection, France.

The meaning of the drawing is carried by the linear and formal movement
extracted from figure and still-life: Léger expresses an abundant vigour
sensed in all things through the interpenetrating vigour of graphic effects
alone.

It is tempting to see this failure ever actually to make a full-scale painting
on the theme of *l'abondance* as a conclusive pointer to the anti-symbolic
nature of Léger's dynamic Cubism. Perhaps he realized that to elaborate
the allegory to the point of easy legibility would rob his idea of direct
visual impact. Even when thus tempted, perhaps he realized that allegory
was a pointless luxury for a painter who made observed fact the basis of
his work, and whose purely graphic or pictorial means—line and form—
could convey so much. Certainly, it was not the vague symbolism of the
Etude pour un Abondance that led him forward as a painter during the next
year, but rather the dynamic realism of *Essai pour trois portraits* and the
Fumées. He may have shared some of the Bergsonian attitudes of poets like
Mercereau and Romains, but for the moment he was not further tempted to
paint as if a poet.

* * * * *

Both the *Nus dans un paysage* and the *Essai pour trois portraits* declared a
violent, a dissonant view of reality, but the latter fused this with a view
which embraced the Bergsonian themes of interpenetration and of duration.
Moreover, with the move into a more fluid, durational style, above all in
the figure studies of 1911 and in *Fumées sur les toits,* the essential dependence
of Léger's art on his experience of life at first hand was underlined, for the
tendency to idealize observed effects, to simplify forms, so dominant in
the *Nus,* was reversed in the interests of immediacy, of generating a convincing sense of contact with the *motif.*

The most developed and most ambitious painting to explore the fluid,
linear style of the *Fumées* in terms that thus stressed contact with the

37

motif was *Les Fumeurs* (Plate 23). Here Léger brings to a conclusion the realistic experiments in cityscape and figure-drawing of 1911.[64] The painting is dynamic and interpenetrating in precisely the same way as the *Fumées*, but, introducing as it does, strong figurative foreground incident, and framing the distant view of landscape between curtains, it makes of the interpenetration theme something more complex, a theme involving the interpenetration not only of figure and setting, but of near and far, foreground and background. Moreover, it seems to be a durational painting in a way even more insistently dynamic than *Essai pour trois portraits*, for it has been pointed out by Virginia Spate that the two heads, so clearly repeated and so directly connected by the suggested continuity of a diagonal movement, are in fact almost certainly but one, doubled by motion. *Les Fumeurs* is, it seems, a single *fumeur* multiplied, so that the spatial and durational flux caused by effects of mobile perspective and interpenetration is joined by the effect of observed physical movement. And every one of these effects could not be more emphatically grounded in the observation of physical fact—everything is instantly recognizable as an incident taken from experience. The hard grey heads, the pears, the poplars modelled in deep green, the houses, the ball-like clouds in the distance—all declare their identity with an almost naïve directness, and so too do the large, swirling motions of softer form—the purple *repoussoir* curtains and the puffs of tobacco smoke; and, besides motion, as in *Les Fumées*, once again the agents of fragmentation and interpenetration are smoke and light, cutting through the solidity of things as Léger saw them in life.[65]

This emphasis on the subject observed at first hand was not to remain unchallenged for long, for over the next year Léger's pursuit of conflict was to lead him to confront the strong descriptive element in his painting with an equally strong anti-descriptive element which was to renew with increased conviction the impetus away from representation towards abstraction. The *Essai pour trois portraits, Les Fumées* and *Les Fumeurs* for a while blurred the paradox central to his art, as to all Cubist art, the paradox of a deeply realistic purpose carried through in uncompromisingly anti-representational terms; over the next year that paradox was to emerge again with a force unequalled even by the *Nus*.

CHAPTER 2
From Dynamic Cubism to the Pure painting of *Contrastes*, Autumn 1911–Spring 1913

At the Indépendants of 1912 Léger showed a painting catalogued as *Composition avec personnages*. Recently this has been shown to have been the enormous canvas *La Noce* (Plate 25).[1] Where *Les Fumeurs* (Plate 23) brought Léger's 1911 experiments to a conclusion, *La Noce* at once looked back to the pictorial results of those experiments and looked forward to new pictorial possibilities, no longer directly dependent on the observation of nature.

As a composition, *La Noce* is still close to *Les Fumeurs*, and so too are its major rhythmic, interpenetrating effects. On the left the canvas is closed off by a *repoussoir* succession of shifting surfaces modulated as if by atmosphere—the equivalent of the curtain, while in the middle the massed figures of the wedding procession are unfolded as a succession of cylindrical and nuggety solids felt, like the solid poplars and houses of *Les Fumeurs*, in constantly tangible relief. Across these cut the outlines of a rising and mobile mist into which at certain points the figures merge lending a tinge of their colour—yellow and pink at the centre—to its shifting substance. This shifting substance has the interpenetrating effect of the smoke of *Les Fumeurs* and is painted with precisely the same feeling for the transitions of light and the force of linear accent,[2] but, like the succession of *repoussoir* forms, it has absolutely no declared origin in the subject as seen in life. Its softness and the mobility of its outlines act therefore in a new way. It becomes, by contrast with the tangible descriptiveness of figurative and landscape form, an anti-descriptive, abstract element—an element whose *raison d'être* appears to lie not in the subject but in the need for pure pictorial effects of dynamic interpenetration.[3]

This is not the only evidence of an incipient move away from first-hand contact with the subject; the spatial setting of the scene provides evidence of a different, less purely pictorial kind. The teeming figures of the wedding procession are not set within an unfragmented space deformed by the movement of the painter's eye; instead they are piled up as part of a loose,

25.   Fernand Léger: *La Noce*, 1911–12. $160\frac{1}{2} \times 128\frac{3}{4}$ ins, Musée National d'Art Moderne, Paris.

relief structure, through whose right flank are pierced pockets of landscape depth, seen in emphatic high viewpoint perspective. A sudden vista of poplar ornamented countryside and a jumbled village scene are blended into the surface movements of the painting and set in violent perspectival contrast against them. The near and the far interpenetrate, but not as factors in a continuous spatial experience, so that the feeling of first-hand contact with the subject is undermined, and the impression is given of a free combination of separate views brought together at second hand by memory.

Between 1911 and 1913 Léger's approach to the reality of modern life did change, as will become clear, but, more obviously important, his approach to the relationship between painting and subject changed; and the move suggested by *La Noce* away from first-hand observation was prophetic of a move increasingly in the direction of abstraction, a development which was more and more profoundly to underline the paradox of a realist art committed to purely pictorial effect. The move towards abstraction is the dominant theme of this chapter, but before it can fully assert itself a pause is necessary to consider what lay behind Léger's decision to introduce purely pictorial interpenetrating effects and to fragment the space of *La Noce*, and essential to an understanding of this is a broadening of the context within which Léger's art can be seen, to include Milan and Italian Futurism.

*   *   *   *   *

The story of Léger's relationship with Futurism can only fully be told by turning back two years to the first Parisian manifestations of the movement as a movement of painters. On 11 April 1910 the 'Manifesto tecnico' of Futurist painting was published, signed by the artists Boccioni, Carrà, Russolo, Balla and Severini.

The manifesto appeared on 18 May in *Comœdia* translated into French, and, although there was much in it that would have struck the second-phase Cubists as alien, the decision to paint 'dynamic sensation', and the idea expressed that 'everything moves, is in flux',[4] would have struck Léger and Delaunay in particular as profoundly in tune with their aims.[5] The development of F. T. Marinetti as leader, oracle and manifestation of the Futurist movement was rooted as much in the Parisian as in the Italian avant-garde. Indeed, he had himself visited the Abbaye,[6] was actively involved in Closérie des Lilas circles[7] and was, like the Abbaye poets, an admirer of both Verhaeren and Whitman. His dynamic view of life, though more obsessive in its focus on the world of industry and machines, was therefore deeply in tune with that of Mercereau and Romains, and it finds significant echoes in the Manifesto produced by the painters, making of it a document whose strongly lyrical and Bergsonian caste would have added much-needed support to the convictions of the second-phase Cubists—above all, of course, to those of Léger and Delaunay. It is, in fact, difficult to believe that the dynamic Cubism of these two developed without knowledge of the Manifesto, for Léger's use of multiplied images to convey physical movement in *Essai pour trois portraits* and *Les Fumeurs* seems specifically to refer to it, since the multiplication of images in movement

41

was one of the most radical proposals made by the Futurist painters in 1910.[8] Yet at this early stage the Futurists could only have stimulated peripheral stylistic change, because their verbal propaganda was not supported by the visual propaganda of paintings, and their ideas did not offer anything that the Cubists could not get from their own philosophical and literary environment. All they could offer in 1910 and 1911 were a few hints at possible pictorial innovations and what must have appeared an unbalanced emphasis on modern life in its mechanical and industrial aspects, the whole underlined by the ecstatic fervour of their evangelism.

Boccioni and his friends arrived themselves in force to see the 'Salle 8' at the 1911 Salon d'Automne, and to visit the studios of the Cubists, including Léger,[9] but not even the Paris-based Gino Severini could at this time offer far-reaching pictorial innovations to supplement the still diffused impact of the 1910 Manifesto. Léger may have been tempted by the idea of depicting movement successively, but there can be no doubt that the features most essential to the *Fumées sur les toits*, the *Essai pour trois portraits* and *Les Fumeurs* evolved without Futurist assistance. The dynamic Cubism of these paintings *anticipated* the emergence of a truly radical Futurist style.

On 5 February 1912 the first Parisian exhibition of Futurist painting opened at the galerie Bernheim-Jeune. It turned Futurism from a distant source of support into a powerful, new avant-garde force, and the innovations of *La Noce*, at least in part, seem to be manifestations of Léger's reaction to it.

The Futurist painters' most dramatic change of position between the 1910 Manifesto and the February 1912 exhibition was their rejection of a Neo-Impressionist focus on colour in favour of an anti-Impressionist focus on form and line. New ideas on the expression of dynamic interpenetration in painting were developed, ideas generated by the Futurists' own experience of Cubism during their October 1911 visit,[10] and therefore ideas which were naturally far more adaptable to the methods of Léger and his friends. The most recent of the paintings shown—for instance, Boccioni's *Stati d'Animo* (Plate 26)—made these new ideas pictorially available, while the long statement, which served as catalogue, gave them persuasive verbal form.

Dominant among the new means by which the Italians sought to express the sensation of dynamism without Neo-Impressionist colour *tâches* was what they called 'force-lines'. 'Each object, by means of its lines, reveals how it will be decomposed according to the direction of its forces . . . . Moreover, each object influences its neighbours, not by reflections of light . . . , but by a real coming together of lines and by real conflicts of plane against plane, which follow the emotional law dominant in the painting . . .'[11] The way in which the Futurists intended to translate an observed conflict of lines and planes into purely pictorial incident, as an expression of the dynamic rhythm within things, closely parallels the approach to line and plane developed by Léger and Delaunay during 1910 and 1911. But the Futurists gave to line and plane a degree of pictorial independence from the *motif* which is more in tune with the anti-descriptive smoke-like forms of *La Noce* than with the always *motif*-bound forms of the *Fumées* and *Les Fumeurs*. 'It may be noted, furthermore, that in our paintings there are *tâches*, lines and colour-zones which do not relate to anything in reality, but which, following a law determined by our internal mathematics, musically guide and augment the emotion of the spectator.'[12] Futurist 'force-lines' could be sensed intuitively, without actually being observed.

The other crucial innovation found in Léger's *La Noce*, the fragmentation of space into disconnected pockets of depth, is also profoundly in tune with an idea central to the Futurists' catalogue preface, the idea of 'simultaneity'. The Futurists declared their desire to fuse into a single image all that they or their subject could be affected by during any one phase of experience—their surroundings both physical and psychological. They wished to convey the 'simultaneity of the ambiance', and this, they believed, led inevitably to the 'dislocation' of objects, to the scattering of details, once all was freed from the limitations of logic.[13] They wanted a kind of painting which would synthesize both 'what is remembered and what is seen'.[14] The inclusion of past impressions—of memories—as so crucial a part of 'ambiance' suggests that the idea of 'simultaneity' here expounded owed much either directly or indirectly to Bergson, for it demonstrates a profound awareness of *la durée*. However, the Italians derived from the idea of *la durée* a far more all-inclusive approach to reality than had the French with the invention of mobile perspective. They did not merely allow themselves to include more of a *motif* than could be seen from one particular position, they allowed the free combination of many *motifs* in a single image—of the many images crowded together in a single phase of consciousness. Where reality for the second-phase Cubists in 1911 had been the isolated still-life, landscape or figure explored from many angles at once, reality for Boccioni and his friends was the multiplicity of experience on every level, both sensory and psychological. The Cubists had concentrated on the changing shape of the *motif* itself, revealed as a complete whole; the Futurists now proposed to concentrate on the changing shape, not of the *motif*, but of the painter's multi-layered experience of the *motif* at first or second hand. 'The dynamic sensation', for them, had become more than merely optical.

Just as the anti-descriptive elements in *La Noce* can be called 'force-lines', so its fragmented space can be called simultaneous in the Futurist sense, for Léger condenses into the setting of his wedding group an idea of its rural ambience; his village and field vistas are quite independent of each other, and in their dislocation effectively freed from the limitations of logic, in particular from the spatial logic of the *Fumées*. He does not merely present the subject as seen at first hand, he also presents an idea of its ambience, using apposite memory-images.

That the innovations crucial to *La Noce*—its anti-descriptive elements and its fragmented space—were a direct response to the ideas announced at the Bernheim-Jeune exhibition seems at least possible, and this is underlined by an analysis of the painting's relationship with the only surviving oil study for it (Plate 24) and, through the study, with *Les Fumeurs*. The fact is that the study is actually closer to *Les Fumeurs* than to *La Noce* itself, since, lacking the scything invasion of smoke-like elements so crucial to *La Noce*, and including but one poplar ornamented vista, it remains a simple conflict between central figurative masses and broader areas on the flanks: it has neither the specifically Futurist force-line dynamism nor the simultaneity of the final canvas. The implication is plain: that Léger began *La Noce* while still working within the terms of *Les Fumeurs*, and that only later were his crucial Futurist innovations introduced. Furthermore, it seems that these innovations could well have been introduced late in the process of painting the final canvas, for a close look at the overlapping of paint-layers, especially along the accented right edge of the central invading sequence of forms, indicates that this certainly, and possibly the village vista as well were additions to an otherwise complete composition. The temptation is strong to conclude that during the month or so between the opening of the Futurist exhibition and the opening of the Indépendants, Léger made a conscious and clear-cut attempt to turn *La Noce* into a more up-to-date, a more emphatically Futurist image and to apply the lessons taught by the catalogue preface and by the paintings he had seen at Bernheim-Jeune.

Boccioni was the Futurist whose work at the Bernheim-Jeune exhibition came closest to Léger's, echoing on occasion the combined descriptive and anti-descriptive dynamism of *La Noce*. Thus, in the *Stati d'Animo* triptych he gives to his interpenetrating forces a more than merely descriptive quality, so that, for instance, the undulating expansion of lines in *Gli Adii* (Plate 26) at once describes the movement of smoke around the locomotive, and expresses the chaotic emotions generated by the experience of parting,

26. Umberto Boccioni: *Gl Adii*, 1911. $27\frac{3}{4} \times 38$ ins, Nelson A. Rockefeller collection, New York.

making especially close contact with *La Noce* through Boccioni's force-lines and fragmentation of space.

La Noce may in part anticipate Léger's move away from the subject towards a more purely pictorial stance, but it remains an essentially realist painting, and its subject remains vital to its effect. The descriptive element is there not merely to contradict the anti-descriptive element but to fix the interpenetrating forces released by the painting in reality, and on this level of subject-matter too, the alliance between Léger and the Futurists is clear. The durational presentation of changing group emotions in the three panels of Boccioni's *Stati d'Animo* gave the paintings a strong Unanimist flavour.[15] At the 1912 Indépendants *La Noce* was one of a group of very large second-phase Cubist paintings with equally Unanimist themes— André Lhote's *Dimanche*, Albert Gleizes's *Baigneuses* and Robert Delaunay's *La Ville de Paris*—all of which represented in part a reaction to the Futurists, and within this group it would have represented emphatically the most positive, the most sympathetic reaction. Jules Romains had used the psychological force of a funeral as a central Unanimist image in his 1911 novel *Mort de quelqu'un* and, as a poet, he was continually drawn in *La Vie Unanime* and *Un Etre en marche* to public events with the capacity to unite people; it is in this context that Léger's subject should be seen.[16] *La Noce* is an attempt, by the creation of an ambience and by both pure and impure dynamic effects, to convey the unanimity of awareness and feeling generated by a public occasion. The exuberant, generalized energy of the subject was perfectly suited to the exuberant, generalized energy of Léger's dynamic Cubism, reinforced by the immediacy of anti-descriptive forms and of force-lines. In the swirl of a constantly animated occasion uniting many people, the past of a man and a woman is caught up and pushed forward into the future: the movement of a temporal, a psychological and a physical dynamism combines to create a concentrated image of interpenetration and *la durée*.

Even in its most abstract elements, in its central invasion of anti-descriptive forms, *La Noce* is at root still a realist painting, but Léger's adaptation of force-lines relates to reality in a way rather different from that of the force-lines in Boccioni's *Gli Adii*. While Boccioni derives his force-lines specifically from effects observed in his subject coupled with its fluxing emotional content, Léger derives his from effects observed in other, altogether separate subjects—the effects of smoke rising from city chimneys or from a smoker. He purifies these effects by lifting them out of their original context and placing them as pure pictorial incidents in a new context. In this way he can both be more free of his subject than Boccioni and at the same time retain for his anti-descriptive forms a strong sense of reality. The direct heirs of observed effects, these forms are worked with a feeling for atmospheric modulation of tone as tactile and as convincingly weightless as the smoke of the *Fumées* and *Les Fumeurs*. Léger shows himself in every detail of *La Noce*, however 'abstract', still to be concerned with creating on a flat canvas the sensation of reality, of the heavy or the light, the hard or the soft, of movement, of duration and of conflict. The signs of an incipient move away from the subject do not mark an incipient move away from realism.

*   *   *   *   *

Léger and the second-phase Cubists may have found much in the Bernheim-Jeune Futurist exhibition, but its catalogue preface began with a violent attack on their painting. The attack concentrated on the relationship between style and subject-matter. The French, the Futurists felt, were obsessed with the immobile, the frozen, with the 'traditionalism of Poussin, Ingres and Corot';[17] and, worst of all, they suppressed the subject, ignoring the fact that modern painting was impossible 'without, as point of departure, an absolutely modern sensation'.[18] Indeed, they even worked from the posed model, hardly a modern starting-point and were therefore utterly rejected by the Futurists. These vigorous criticisms were obviously aimed at such 'Salle 8' exhibits as Gleizes's *Portrait de Jacques Nayral*, Metzinger's *Le Goûter* and Léger's *Essai pour trois portraits* (Plate 15), and, as has been seen, *La Noce*, with its overtly dynamic subject, answered them.

Yet Léger's sympathy towards at least this part of the Futurist attack on Cubism—the demand for modern, dynamic subjects—did not last long, for *La Noce* was his last attempt before 1914 to paint an overtly mobile subject from contemporary life, and his only attempt before 1914 to create a simultaneous ambience. Immediately after the Indépendants of 1912 he turned to the problem of giving dissonant force to an absolutely static traditional subject—a woman seated at a table. The result was *La Femme en bleu* (Plate 27), exhibited in its final form at the Salon d'Automne in October. With it he moved against his previous position, and joined the counterattack on the Futurist dogmas of February 1912, a counterattack which had already gathered force at the Indépendants, initiated by Gleizes's and Delaunay's directly provocative use of the posed female nude.[19] With it too, he moved more decisively away from the descriptive realism of *Les Fumeurs,* finding for anti-descriptive forces an even more central place in his art.

During the period in which Léger conceived and executed *La Femme en bleu* there was, partly as a reaction against the shock of Futurism, a fresh intensification and expansion of Parisian avant-garde activity. After the public demonstration of solidarity in the October 1911 'Salle 8' there may have been no sequel at the 1912 Indépendants, but meetings continued at the Closérie des Lilas and in the Puteaux studio of Jacques Villon, and ambitious plans were put into action for that autumn, plans which in themselves initiated discussion, and which required by their nature a considerable amount of coordination. There was the plan for a *maison cubiste* at the Salon d'Automne,[20] and also the plan for a full-scale 'Salon' to represent the Parisian avant-garde in its entirety, the Salon de la Section d'Or.[21] The man behind the *maison cubiste* was Léger's old Norman friend André Mare, and the idea was to demonstrate by means of an architectural and decorative ensemble how the new painting could provide a new environmental style. The architecture itself was the work of Raymond Duchamp-Villon; and Marcel Duchamp, Jacques Villon, Metzinger, Gleizes, de La Fresnaye, Laurencin and Léger all contributed to its decoration—Léger a small painting whose identity has been forgotten. The project led to regular meetings at Puteaux, some of which Léger must certainly have attended. He was also positively involved as a potential exhibitor in the 'Section d'Or' project, which again was conceived and developed at Puteaux, this time by the Villon brothers, helped by the public-relations

27.   Fernand Léger: *La Femme en bleu*, 1912. 76 × 52 ins, Oeffentliche Kunstssammlung, Basel.

flair of Apollinaire and the money of a newcomer to the circle, Francis Picabia.

Not only during these months of revived group activity was Léger constantly involved, listening and no doubt contributing, but they were months during which he was established as a major figure in the avant-garde. This is a fact which, as Golding has pointed out, was made abundantly clear at the 'Section d'Or' itself, where, among the more prominent contributors, Gleizes, Picabia and de La Fresnaye could be seen to owe profound debts to his discoveries.[22] The new ideas released among his friends deeply affected his own attitudes, and he deeply affected theirs: it was a mutually interactive relationship.

Among the ideas much discussed at Puteaux and in Montparnasse between April and October 1912 was one of those specifically singled out for attack by the Futurists, the idea of tradition, and the fact that the Futurists associated it with Cubism in the Bernheim-Jeune catalogue preface indicates that it was a topic of serious avant-garde concern by February. The central question that arose from this concern was the question of how a modern art, emphatically of its time, could in fact belong to a tradition. Once again, behind this concern lay the fundamental Bergsonian concept of *la durée*, for, if life as a whole was believed to carry the impetus of the past into the present, then so too were the arts. As early as September 1911, Gleizes attempted to outline the ideal relationship between past and present in his *Revue Indépendante* essay on Metzinger. Here he states the absolute need for progress in art if art is effectively to reflect the progress of man. However, he sees this constant state of 'renaissance' as pushing forward an unbroken flow of evolution, so that the modern is always tied to the past. Cubism he therefore situates in a moving stream which has emerged from the past, a stream given a new direction by Cézanne, but centuries older than Cézanne. This he chauvenistically calls the 'French tradition'. Gleizes himself, Metzinger and the Villons were particularly affected by the idea of such a tradition in which to place their work; it was an idea developed further in *Du Cubisme*, and in another article by Gleizes, this time singling out the idea for separate treatment, 'Le Cubisme et la Tradition'. 'We consider . . .', he writes here, 'that the works of the most independent artists today have their origins in our national tradition.'[23] The great exponents of that tradition, besides Cézanne, were, he declared, the French primitives, Fouquet, Clouet, Poussin, Claude, Philippe de Champagne, the brothers Le Nain, Chardin, David and Ingres, and its fundamental characteristics were an over-riding concern with form in its own right and with the values of lucidity and order. Cézanne emerges once again as the great prophet because of the conviction with which he refocused the energy of French painting on these fundamentally 'French' concerns.

At Puteaux and in Montparnasse this sense of tradition—so decisively anti-Futurist by nature—led to a complementary interest in the order of proportion. The treatises of Leon Battista Alberti and of Leonardo were read, and the Villon brothers with the Montmartre-based newcomer to Puteaux, Juan Gris, actually attempted to apply systems of proportion based on the *section d'or* to their compositions.[24] Constant abstract principles were sought beneath the surface of stylistic change. Léger did not apply any such system in the composing of *La Femme en bleu*, but he did move

48

28. Paul Cézanne: *La Femme à la cafetière*, 1890–4. $51\frac{1}{4} \times 38\frac{1}{4}$ ins, Musée du Louvre, Lecomte Pellerin collection, Paris.

away from the dynamic compositional mode of *La Noce* to a kind of composition which is more stable. Its formal clashes create, of course, immensely powerful discharges of energy, but long, rhythmic sequences of forms are avoided and with them sensations of unbroken movement. Colour planes are used to prevent the extended diagonal thrusts and the tumbling profusion of *La Noce* from taking control. Léger's static subject is not transformed into a constellation of dynamic pictorial effects; it is activated by conflict, by the disruption of movement. Within a structure approaching stability a dissonant rather than dynamic force is released. The balance of a quasi-traditional compositional mode is confronted by a thoroughly modern, disruptive energy.

Yet, most of all, it is obviously the traditional quality of Léger's subject that declares the relationship between *La Femme en bleu* and the past. The seated woman of the painting is not merely in a general sense traditional, but also in a particular sense, referring directly to one of Cézanne's most tried subjects—that most aptly perhaps of *La Femme à la cafetière* (Plate 28).[25] However, with its openly Cézannist subject, *La Femme en bleu* does not merely spell out its relationship with the tradition revitalized by Cézanne, it also, even more than *Nus dans un paysage*, dramatizes the distance between Cézanne and Léger and throws into relief the disruptive modernity of Léger's painting. For the traditional subject of *La Femme en bleu* is not left unchallenged. It is the object of a new invasion of anti-descriptive form even more pictorially pure than the invasion of smoke-like forms so crucial to *La Noce*. The smoke-like forms are still there, slicing into the hard metallic components of the seated woman, but they are joined by flat, intensely blue planes, whose connections with observed reality are very tenuous. In *La Noce* Léger had used the deep blue of a costume at the summit of the composition and the green of another to the right of centre as strong contrasting incidents among the predominant greys. He takes this idea further in *La Femme en bleu*, intensifying the force of pure colour areas thus localized among neutral greys, and in so doing he moves further from the description of effects towards pure pictorial contrasts. In *La Noce* the costume colours had been modulated enough by tonal modelling to suggest their costume identity and to dilute their force; in *La Femme en bleu* Léger's blue planes are hardly modulated at all, and this, coupled with their sharp angular shaping, frees them from any overt reference to costume. Léger flattens colour to give it the fullest possible realization as *pictorial* fact. Just as he had extracted the flowing forms of rising smoke to use them anti-descriptively in *La Noce*, so here he extracts the intense blue of his model's dress to use in a pure, undiluted state for direct pictorial effect.

Léger's intentions, however, were still by no means entirely pure, for a look at the relationship between the Basel version of *La Femme en bleu* and the large, so-called *Etude* at Biot (Plate 29) shows clearly that he was concerned with strengthening the collision between anti-descriptive and descriptive elements as he moved from one stage to the next. Thus, not only are strategic points of pictorial contrast sharpened in the more elaborate Basel canvas, but so too is his treatment of descriptive effects clarified. The turned back of the chair, the woman's head and hands are all given increased definition in both formal and descriptive terms, sharpening the sense of a subject, and therefore the sense of a subject under attack. Among the angular blue planes and the shifting surfaces the parts of the figure and her setting stand out, like the hands and watch-chain of Picasso's Kahnweiler portrait, as clues to a subject which is still very much there but whose identity and importance has been decisively challenged.

Léger's static and traditional subject for the Salon d'Automne and his balanced compositional treatment of it may have been anti-Futurist, but as much as this it was his determination to undermine the subject's significance—to make it so obviously no more than an excuse for his painting—that gave *La Femme en bleu* anti-Futurist point, for in the February 1912 Bernheim-Jeune catalogue the Futurists specifically attacked the tendency to say 'that the subject in painting is without any significant value'.[26] Such a tendency must therefore have been current by the beginning of the year, and in April, at precisely the moment when Léger was beginning work on *La Femme en bleu*, Guillaume Apollinaire gave it verbal expression with an article published in the first number of *Soirées de Paris* called 'Du

29.   Fernand Léger: *La Femme en bleu (étude),* 1912. 51 × 39½ ins, Musée National Fernand Léger, Biot.

sujet dans la peinture moderne'. Here Apollinaire pointed to a general move among painters away from the subject, a move which, he felt, must lead to its eventual dissolution. He counselled the avoidance of 'careful representation', and added, 'The subject no longer counts, and if it does, it does so against the will of the painter',[27] exactly echoing the attitude which seems to have been behind Léger's attack on the model in *La Femme en bleu.* The Futurists' Bernheim-Jeune catalogue preface and Apollinaire's article make the point that Léger's move away from the subject, so clear in his Salon d'Automne canvas of 1912, was part of a broader avant-garde move, a move which through the year gathered speed.

51

The tendency to emphasize pure pictorial effect at the expense of the subject had been a tendency inherent to a certain extent in Apollinaire's position as a critic four years earlier,[28] but it was almost certainly given its decisive 1912 shape by Robert Delaunay, who was able to inform his correspondent Wassily Kandinsky of the current search for 'pure painting' months before such a search had actually affected the work of any other painter in Paris.[29] Delaunay himself was, it is reported, often at the Puteaux discussions, and so must have played a part in stimulating the idea of painting without subject-matter as a coming concern, but in April he ensconced himself with his wife Sonia in the valley of the Chevreuse, where he began a new series of paintings, the *Fenêtres*, which heralded an attempt at a complete break with the second-phase Cubist circle.[30] That spring and summer, therefore, it was left more to Apollinaire, helped by his rich friend Picabia, to act as promotor of the new tendency towards 'pure painting'; and when Delaunay returned to Paris in the autumn, so independent did he consider his own art, so outside the general movement of group activity, that he did not exhibit the *Fenêtres* in the 'Section d'Or'.

'The young painters of the extreme schools,' wrote Apollinaire in April 1912, 'want, therefore, to make pure painting. This is an entirely new plastic art. It is only at its beginning and is not yet as abstract as it would like to be.'[31] Purity had not yet been achieved, and it seems that not even Apollinaire himself at this stage considered that absolute purity should be achieved, since Gabrielle Buffet-Picabia reports that Picabia had to persuade him on the point when all three visited England in July.[32] But Picabia too was still far from 'pure painting' in the autumn, as his major contribution to the 'Section d'Or', *Danseuses à la source*, testifies, and the extreme view that he stood for seems to have been no more than a stance taken up for the purposes of debate. At Puteaux during the spring and summer of 1912 an uncompromising 'pure painting' seems thus to have been no more than an extreme theoretical possibility, allowed its head in discussion, but not in painting. Léger's *La Femme en bleu*, with its conflict between the pure and the descriptive, echoes the unresolved state of the debate. Yet, egged on by the arguments of Delaunay, Picabia and Apollinaire, the attack Léger mounted here on the traditional seated female subject of Cézanne declared even more clearly than *La Noce* the direction of his efforts—the imminence of a truly uncompromising move away from the subject. In 1954 Léger recalled his 1912–13 phase as 'the battle for liberation from Cézanne'. '(His) grip was so strong,' he said, 'that to get free of it I had to go as far as abstraction. Ultimately, in *La Femme en bleu* . . . , I felt that I had freed myself from Cézanne and that at the same time I had moved a long way from Impressionist melody.'[33] As he declared his independence from Cézanne, he declared too the direction of his emphatically modern art —towards 'pure painting'.

*   *   *   *   *

During the last weeks of 1912 and the early months of 1913 Léger executed a series of nude studies in pencil, ink and gouache, some large and elaborate, which culminated in *Le Modèle nu dans l'atelier* (Plate 30), a work almost the size of *La Femme en bleu*. Writing on the 1913 Salon des Indépendants,

Apollinaire notes that Léger had displayed great 'artistic conscience', 'because, not having yet achieved his aim, he did not want to send his large canvas,'[34] but, whatever doubts Léger might have expressed to Apollinaire, the probability is that he did send the painting to the Salon, for it is illustrated in André Warnod's *Comoedia* review, and inscribed on its back in Léger's hand is the inscription: 'Le Modèle nu dans l'atelier Salon des Indépen . . . F. Léger Dan . . . 1912–13 (Complémentaires).'[35]

Le Modèle nu is the most complete declaration of the distance and the direction in which he travelled towards 'pure painting' between the Salon d'Automne of 1912 and March 1913, and, stylistically, the distance he had moved by that month from *La Femme en bleu* is immediately obvious. He does not achieve his pictorial drama at the expense of dynamic continuity: the central, rising succession of swelling masses is not disrupted by alien, angular planes, but is pulled together as an unbroken sequence of linear movements. Flat, angular colour planes are shifted to the flanks of the canvas, as part of a powerful, contradictory setting, and the central flow of forms is given substance in a new and significant way, using a treatment of surfaces first tentatively explored in a couple of rural landscapes during the summer of 1912.[36] In the development which led from *La Noce* to *La Femme en bleu*, Léger had evolved three distinct types of surface treatment for the realization of his formal contrasts; the shifting, tactile surface, the flat colour plane, and the tonally modelled solid. The last of these, being the most overtly descriptive, was given special importance as one of the major contrasting forces in *Les Fumeurs*, *La Noce* and *La Femme en bleu*. It was, however, not only the most descriptive but also the least pictorially forceful of Léger's means, since simple tonal modelling deadens surface and keeps form away from touch in an illusory pictorial space. In *Le Modèle nu* such deadened surfaces are cut to a minimum, and certain of Léger's central surfaces, in a new way for him, use highlight to create a sense of curvature and at the same time of conflict, conflict *flat* on the surface, each darker patch of colour confronting each patch of highlight in clearly two-dimensional terms. Thus, *Le Modèle nu* is dissonant in a new way even as it returns to the fluid dynamic effects of *Les Fumeurs* and *La Noce*.

Moreover, although Léger does thus return to the dynamism of his 1911 and early 1912 experiments, he moves even more decisively away from the subject, for the long elliptical lines and swinging surfaces of his nude are in no sense specifically figurative, and only the five short strokes of black in the centre and again upper right, referring as they do to the hands, can with certainty be associated with a nude model. Indeed, the forms of Léger's nude are, of course, derived not from the figure at all, but from the smoke of *Les Fumeurs* and the *Fumées sur les toits*, with the more recent *Paysage* as intermediary (Plate 41).[37] The fact is that Léger did not 'abstract' this nude, extracting from the model simplified forms and qualities, rather he *translated* it into a range of forms 'abstracted' from other subjects —the movement of smoke and foliage in landscape and cityscape. He took further the process first used in the painting of *La Noce*, but the model as necessary starting-point was now totally redundant, for his vocabulary of contrasting forms had been purified to the extent of all-embracing versatility. So far, indeed, had Léger moved from the model that the un-

resolved conflict between the descriptive and the anti-descriptive central to *La Femme en bleu* was at last superceded—descriptive form had finally been removed from his repertoire.

There seems to have been one further stimulus behind the development of the dynamic central theme of *Le Modèle nu*, a stimulus other than the smoke and foliage forms developed in Léger's own landscapes and cityscapes, a stimulus which *was* figurative. The series of figure-drawings behind the painting was begun soon after both the Salon d'Automne and the 'Section d'Or', late in 1912, and one of the works hung at the 'Section d'Or' was Marcel Duchamp's *Nu descendant un escalier, no. 2* (Plate 31). The final composition of *Le Modèle nu dans l'atelier*, with its diagonal motion of curvilinear forms in an angular setting, is closely analogous with Duchamp's,

30. (left)   Fernand Léger:
Le Modèle nu dans l'atelier,
1913. $50\frac{1}{4} \times 38\frac{1}{2}$ ins,
Solomon R. Guggenheim
Museum, New York.

31. (right)   Marcel
Duchamp: *Nu descendant
un escalier No. 2.* 1912.
58×35 ins, Louise and
Walter Arensberg collec-
tion, Philadelphia Museum
of Art.

while Léger's title is phonetically almost the echo of the earlier title, so
that it seems possible that his painting was at least in part a direct response
to *Nu descendant*. Yet, if it was a response, *Le Modèle nu* was an antagonistic
response, and in the nature of the criticism it levels against Duchamp is
found a final demonstration of the anti-descriptive direction of Léger's
painting, of its direction towards 'pure painting'. Where Duchamp adapts
the Futurist use of repeated images to describe movement diagram-
matically,[38] Léger rejects his own earlier use of repeated images in *Essai*
and *Les Fumeurs*; and where Duchamp is concerned with the depiction of
a moving subject, Léger is concerned with making, out of a static subject,
a dynamic painting. Léger opposes illusory dynamism with his new purely
pictorial dynamism, and it seems to have been to underline this point

55

that he did so in terms in such a way comparable with the *Nu descendant*.

Just over a year after Léger had decided to send *Le Modèle nu* to the Indépendants, he recalled it in the second of his Académie Wassilief lectures. His recollection sums up the attitude to painting and to subject-matter which it declares: 'With the most commonplace, the most banal of subjects, a female nude in a studio . . . you replace advantageously locomotives and other modern machines, which are difficult to take home. Everything like that is a means to an end; there is nothing of real interest but the manner of presentation.'[39] His dissonant and dynamic view of reality no longer found pictorial expression through the force of subject-matter, either traditional or modern. It found expression in the release of pure pictorial forces: the manner of execution was what mattered. Within a few months of *Le Modèle nu*, Léger was to arrive at paintings with no subject at all—the pure painting of contrasts.

*   *   *   *   *

Although Léger does seem to have exhibited *Le Modèle nu,* at the 1913 Indépendants, Apollinaire's brief mention of the painter's unwillingness to send 'his large canvas' because he had not 'achieved his aim' suggests that Léger was not altogether happy with it. And a careful analysis of the first Académie Wassilief lecture reveals an approach to painting which is not strictly in tune with *Le Modèle nu* and which looks forward, in fact, to a style with significantly different qualities.

Delivered on 5 May 1913 at Marie Wassilief's predominantly Russian 'Académie' on the avenue du Maine,[40] the lecture was almost certainly composed just after Léger finished work on *Le Modèle nu*. It was published in two parts in *Montjoie!*. He opens this first extended defence of his beliefs with a declaration on the fundamental importance of pictorial effect over and above that of subject; he then goes on to define the terms essential to what he calls, significantly enough, 'pictorial realism', i.e., an art based on pictorial effect: 'pictorial realism is the simultaneous ordering of the three great plastic quantities: lines, forms and colours. No work can aspire to pure classicism, that is to say to endurance beyond the epoch of its creation, if it sacrifices completely one of these quantities to the detriment of the two others.'[41] In order to place his art in the continuing context of a tradition, Léger invents a comprehensive Trinitarian view of painting, a view which is not classical in the sense that it demands the balanced order of static compositions, nor in the sense that it defines in detail rules of proportion, but which is classical in the sense that it defines broad principles considered to have a constant validity. He demands a kind of painting which does not merely concentrate on the quality of pictorial effect, but which uses *all* the basic elements of painting. *Le Modèle nu* was certainly not stylistically complete in this way.

The drawing of a reclining nude illustrated in the first published part of Léger's lecture was significantly captioned: 'Etude de dynamisme linéaire' (Plate 32). It is a study which has the characteristic divided surfaces found in other pen drawings of the group, but Léger's caption makes it clear that line was his dominant interest. As has been seen, the freshness of *Le Modèle nu* came of the new way in which Léger harnessed dynamic linear

32. Fernand Léger: *Etude de dinamisme linéaire, Montjoie!* Paris, no 8,
     28 May 1913.

rhythms to dissonant highlit surfaces, but, for all its freshness in this
respect, the painting still remained so exclusively concerned with line and
surface that it lacked a firm, substantial sense of form, and at the same time
it still allowed positive, unmodulated colour no more than a limited role
in the composition. The highlit surface did, it is true, give the impression
of curvature and therefore of underlying substance, but here, as in the
renovated smoke-forms of the *Paysage* so closely related to *Le Modèle nu*
(Plate 41), these curving surfaces evoke a fluid underlying substance
without either the fully rounded volume or the weight of a figure. In order
to achieve the complete dynamic style whose basic principles are defined
in the 1913 lecture, Léger needed to find a way of evoking solid three-
dimensional volumes by means of his mobile line and divided surfaces,
and a way of involving colour in this pursuit of form.

It was by exploring yet further the dissonant possibilities opened up
by the static subject of *La Femme en bleu* that Léger took up the pursuit of
form as a result of his new ideas: an old idea acting as a new starting-
point. One of the earliest stages in this redevelopment was a gouache and
water-colour study obviously made in the presence either of the Biot or
the Basel *Femme en bleu* (Plate 33).[42] The positioning of the seated woman
in *La Femme en bleu* and much of her setting, are repeated in general terms,
but fundamental changes have been made which are prophetic. The angular
blue plane which invades the torso of *La Femme en bleu* is replaced by a
curving breastplate form, giving the figure substance at its core, and the two
arms have been transformed into simple jointed elements implying in their
sequence an unbroken rhythm around the torso. The continuity of this
movement is new, but more important is the new and coordinated sense
of mass conveyed by the upper half of the figure. This results not merely

57

33.   Fernand Léger: *Etude pour La Femme en bleu*, 1912–13. Wash and gouache, Mr and Mrs Leigh B. Block collection, Chicago.

from the highlit treatment of surfaces, but from the shaping of forms. Léger does not, as in the early 1913 nude studies and *Le Modèle nu*, rebuild the figure out of all-purpose abstracted elements, he reduces the forms of limbs and torso to simple geometric solids; the arms thus become cylinders and the torso a segmented drum.[43] Rather than merely animating gently swelling surfaces close to the picture plane, highlighting, where used on the cylinders of the arms, gives a metallic sheen to the firmly and fully rounded surfaces of three-dimensional solids. The effect is achieved both of surface conflict and of tangible, weighty form.

34. Fernand Léger: *La Femme dans un fauteuil*, 1913. $51\frac{3}{4} \times 38\frac{1}{4}$ ins, Lydia and Harry L. Winston collection, Michigan.

The new solidity of *La Femme en bleu* in this study, and the new continuity of rhythm set up by her arms would both of themselves suggest a date after the Biot and the Basel oil versions, but the suggestion is made conclusive by the fact that the two crucial new features, the jointed cylindrical arms and the breastplate torso, are found almost exactly repeated in the large and brash *Femme dans un fauteuil* (Plate 34). Here Léger's 'classical' dynamic style is complete; all the three 'great plastic quantities, lines, forms and colours' are actively and equally engaged in the movement and drama of the painting. Yet once again, though wholly transformed, the subject is a woman seated in three-quarter view with a glass on the table beside her—the subject of *La Femme en bleu*.

Here, not only are the components of the figure simplified to give a comprehensive feeling of its mass and weight, but every single surface is highlit, and the colour patches which bracket highlights, completing the effect of curvature and therefore of volume, are heightened to an unmodulated primary pitch. Thus, colour at its simplest and most powerful is integrated with form, also at its simplest and most powerful: it is made to play an active part in the effect of form. The advantages for Léger of engaging colour in this way are obvious. The less insistent colours of the central forms in *Le Modèle nu* had been enough, since the effect of three-dimensional form allowed by the shaping of elements was relatively shallow, but here, where the effect of three-dimensional form is so strong, an equally strong emphasis on the flatness of colour-components is needed, and it is achieved by the undiluted power of primary red, blue and yellow. Furthermore, for all the rough speed of his execution, Léger is careful to keep the edges of each colour patch away from the line which bounds it, so that each surface becomes a sequence of abrupt clashes between the separate *quantités plastiques* (black line, strident colour patch and white, form-building highlight). In this way colour and line can move in separate sequences across the canvas even as they combine to suggest volume. The jointed cylinders of the arms set up, both by line and by the successive repetition of elements, a strong rotating rhythm, as in the *Etude pour La Femme en bleu*, which is divided in two by the implied movement of reds on the left and of blues on the right. A flat dissonant and dynamic style is declared, which has form.[44]

This question remains: when did Léger finally make his step, by way of a re-evaluation of form, into the complete new style of *La Femme dans un fauteuil*? Delevoy dates the *Femme dans un fauteuil* itself 1912, and there is a related gouache study in a Chicago collection signed and dated 1912.[45] However, the fact that Léger was so fully involved in the *études linéaires* during the early months of 1913, and that *Le Modèle nu* was his public statement for the Indépendants in March, indicates that he did not make his final step until the spring of that year. Certainly one would expect him to have used his most advanced ideas to illustrate the *Montjoie!* publication of his lecture in May and June, and there are no illustrations here in the complete, 'classical', dissonant and dynamic style. The spring and early summer of 1913 seem to mark a period of crisis for Léger as a painter, a period during which he was driven to crystallize his beliefs in verbal form for the first time and to profoundly question not only *La Femme en bleu* but all that had come after it. Out of this period of thought and experiment,

60

backed by doubt, came both a new, apparently less pure figure style, straightforwardly legible in every respect, and, alongside it, an utterly illegible, pure alternative.

*   *   *   *   *

Yet, in the final analysis, Léger's new figure style, for all its apparent impure legibility, was but another declaration of the ultimate irrelevance of the figure subject—it too was in a crucial sense a declaration of pictorial purity, since, evolving as it did from transformation after transformation of a single figurative idea—*La Femme en bleu*—it repeatedly made the point: 'There is nothing of real interest but the manner of presentation.' It too asserted the primacy of direct pictorial effect.

The first of the Académie Wassilief lectures was given a significant title: 'Les Origines de la peinture et sa valeur représentative.' More than the classical need for a complete style involving all 'the three great plastic quantities', the lecture focused on the problem of representation and 'realistic value' in painting. Léger maintains that the representation or imitation of things is totally irrelevant to 'the realistic value of a work', that realism lies in the complete reality of the sensation generated by the painting—a thing in its own right, made out of 'the simultaneous ordering' of lines, forms and colours.[46] His conclusion is put thus: 'The "rapports" of volumes, lines and colours are becoming the generators of all artistic production and of all influence exercised on artistic *milieu*, as much in France as abroad . . . Pictorial contrasts used in their purest sense (complementaries) of colours and line, of form, are from now on the armature of modern paintings.'[47]

Within months of the appearance of the second part of Léger's lecture in *Montjoie!* he had produced paintings entitled simply *Contrastes de formes*. With these paintings he declared most uncompromisingly of all the purity of his approach, for it was with them that he dismissed the subject altogether.

*   *   *   *   *

The second part of Léger's lecture in *Montjoie!* was accompanied by a reproduction captioned: 'Dynamism obtained by black and white contrasts and linear complementaries (heightened drawing)' (Plate 35). The caption implies that the content of this lost gouache is simply and purely the dynamic sensation created by its contrasts, and there is not a single overt clue in the gouache to give it an identity. However, the study relates closely to a pair of oils whose identity as landscape paintings cannot be doubted; one of these is *Les Maisons sous les arbres* (Plate 36).[48] The relationship between the Essen landscape and this illustration, and its stylistic affinities with *Le Modèle nu*, point to an early 1913 date, probably during the spring, and with this painting Léger takes the implications of the small *Paysage* (Plate 41) an important step further, following the lead of *Le Modèle nu*. He no longer puts together a complete and coherent landscape image by means of the landscape elements at his disposal, but rather uses them freely as pure contrasting forms. Thus, on the left a rhythmic succession of deep green foliage forms rise as weightlessly as smoke clouds,

35.   Fernand Léger: *Dinamisme obtenu par contrastes de blancs et noir et complémentaires de lignes, Montjoie!* Paris, no. 9–10, 14–29 June 1913.

paired on the right by an expanding succession of green hemispheres,
while between them, held into the painting by them, are bunched a jostling,
angular array of deep red planes, relieved just above centre by a single
rectangular slat of blue. The red planes derive from buildings, the blue
rectangle from a roof, but they are as weightless and as pictorially liberated
as the foliage forms around them, and they move as close to the picture
plane. The leaf-green shades and a certain suggestion of landscape recession
to the right of the blue rectangle reinforce the landscape identity of *Les
Maisons sous les arbres* but are gone in the *Montjoie!* illustration. Here the

36. Fernand Léger: *Les Maisons sous les arbres*, 1913. $31\frac{3}{4} \times 23\frac{1}{4}$ ins, Folkwang Museum, Essen.

single blue rectangle is joined by two others, translated of course into black, so that a rocking, rising rhythm is created up the centre of the composition, and the swinging foliage forms on the left of *Les Maisons* are joined on the right by an echoing combination. One can see clearly how Léger arrives at a new and simpler idea by reshuffling his formal elements, how the *motif* as such no longer exists, and how the representational purpose of forms has atrophied to nothing.

Both *Les Maisons sous les arbres* and the *Montjoie!* illustration are stylistically incomplete by the standards of the first Académie Wassilief lecture, in

37. Fernand Léger: *Contrastes de formes*, 1913. 39¼ × 32 ins, private collection, Paris.

the same way as *Le Modèle nu*: they achieve dynamism and dissonance without a fully rounded sensation of form. This is tacitly accepted by the caption of the illustration, where only 'black and white contrasts and linear complementaries' are mentioned, but Léger seems to have made an attempt to approach full realization in the oil, for, where (in the illustration) the surfaces of foliage are highlit, here they are modelled. In so anti-illusionistic a pictorial setting the result is anomalous, and, more important, the fluid shaping of foliage forms keeps an effectively massive realization of three-dimensional form still out of reach. Only the cloud-puff succession of hemispheres on the right are so shaped as to be thus effective, and in them is contained the potential for a comprehensive future development.

Léger needed to solidify the linear and surface features of his dynamic idea into an underlying, complementary composition of simple, geometric volumes; and it is the conclusion of this process that is found in a particular *Contrastes de formes* (Plate 37). The suggestion carried by Léger's *Montjoie!* illustration of a connected sequence of rectangles, zig-zagging into and out of the shallow space of the composition, is taken here to its logical end. The rectangles, now a strong, unmodulated red, are pulled together by white rectangles to form a central feature of spilled flat planes. On either side the rhythm of foliage forms has been translated wholesale into tumbling cylinders, which are in their metallic simplicity utterly alien to the forms of landscape. Only the clear contours of their elliptical faces retain something of the linear *élan* so essential to the tree-forms in the 1913 *Paysage* and *Les Maisons sous les arbres*. It is impossible here to guess at the stages by which this transformation has occurred, but by means of it Léger both achieves the formal weight he lacked in the illustration for *Montjoie!* and in *Les Maisons sous les arbres*, and loses touch altogether with nature.

The *Contrastes de formes* with the zig-zag centrepiece is unique in the series, and so without a broader investigation it would be misleading to suggest that the process of manipulation and purification followed above— from landscape into pure pictorial contrast, lies behind the series as a whole. Yet a broad investigation from which such conclusions can be drawn

64

38. Fernand Léger: *Contrastes de formes*, 1913. $51\frac{1}{2} \times 38\frac{1}{2}$ ins, Louise and Walter Arensberg collection, Philadelphia Museum of Art.

39. Fernand Léger: *Dessin pour La Femme en rouge et vert*, 1913. Ink and gouache on paper, $24\frac{1}{2} \times 19$ ins, A. E. Gallatin collection, Philadelphia Museum of Art.

40. (left) Fernand Léger: *Dessin pour Contrastes de formes no. 2*, 1913. Gouache and wash on paper, $19 \times 25\frac{1}{4}$ ins, private collection, New York.

41. (right) Fernand Léger: *Paysage*, 1913. 35×29 ins, private collection, France.

42. (far right) Fernand Léger: *Contrastes de formes no. 2*, 1913. $25\frac{1}{4} \times 19$ ins, present whereabouts unknown.

is possible, and it reveals too just how the abstract cylinder was brought into landscape.

The largest and strongest of the series is the *Contrastes de formes* (Plate 38). It represents a crucial stage in a long and sharply focused investigation, which involved at least nine other oils and a large number of wash and gouache studies.[49] These studies and oils account for almost all the rest of the *Contrastes*. Their exclusive common feature is the elongated diamond shape, split in two down the middle, which seems to shove apart two converging cylinders at the top of the composition, and for this reason they can be called the 'kite device' *Contrastes*.

An early stage of the 'kite device' series is found in the wash and gouache *Dessin pour Contrastes de formes no. 2* (Plate 40). Here, between angular fragments rise a succession of broad elliptical planes; a single oblique line splits each one down the middle, and on the surface of the broadest and highest this has led to a curious secondary development. In order to emphasize the contrasting force of the oblique line Léger brushes dark wash up against it on the left and heightens the other side with white gouache; a procedure which threatens to separate the oblique altogether as the axis of an angular contrasting form, lit on one side and shadowed on the other—the 'kite device' in embryo. Here, at its summit, the configuration arrived at loosely, but convincingly, relates to the configuration of elliptical cloud form and diagonal light-shaft which surmounts the 1913 *Paysage* (Plate 41), other echoes of that composition being found at the base, while on the right a sharp triangle of white seems to have been

lifted unchanged from *Les Maisons sous les arbres*. The *Dessin* is clearly a free combination of cloud, building and foliage forms so far from their origins in nature as to be almost unrecognizable as such.

Out of the *Dessin* evolved *Contrastes de formes no. 2*, a small oil painted on cardboard, whose sketchy quality and size convey its experimental purpose (Plate 42). Here Léger moves from a horizontal to a vertical format and by doing so is able to focus entirely upon the central, rising succession of ellipses. These are regrouped between a bracketing framework of tall, angular planes. The 'kite device' is not so clearly in evidence as in the *Dessin*, but the new grouping of ellipses brings the composition closer to the final 'kite device' *Contrastes*.

Any of these *Contrastes* can show how the final form of the series emerged from the *Dessin* and the *Contrastes de formes no. 2*. The ellipses of *No. 2* are regrouped again in the lower half of the 'kite device' composition, and it is possible to see in the way they are remodelled how they are translated into the split faces of cylinders, for they are extended, sometimes on both sides, by paired lines, paired patches of dark wash and white highlights, which very simply complete the illusion. Above, the uppermost central ellipse finally splits into the separate and contrasting forms of cylinder-face and sharp, insistent kite form.

The Philadelphia *Contrastes* and all its relatives count for almost all of the *Contrastes* (besides the variant with zig-zag centrepiece);[50] thus, in the last analysis it becomes clear that the *Contrastes de formes* as a body were indeed the result of the progressive metamorphosis of landscape ideas, a process which led ultimately to pictorial results so far from their origins and so compositionally free of any representational limitation, that they achieved purity.

This fact throws new light on the *raison d'être* behind Léger's attempt at 'pure painting', for it shows how a particular line of exploration, backed by a complete lack of interest in subject-matter *per se*, led him, as if by its own momentum, to such an extreme pictorial conclusion, and it is of great interest that at the beginning of this line of exploration lay, not figure-painting, but landscape. The motivation behind the final process of metamorphosis was, as has been seen, the need for a fully rounded realization of form. In figure-painting this led naturally back to the geometric simplification of the human figure, and thus to a new style which declared its subject more, rather than less, straightforwardly than before, even though Léger's emphasis was so strongly pictorial. However, the forms of landscape did not lend themselves so naturally to geometric solidification, and so, in order to achieve the degree of formal realization needed for a complete pictorial statement, Léger did not simplify the elements of landscape, he remodelled them altogether and thus allowed them to lose contact finally with nature. The cylinder, so easily the product of figurative simplification, was the key to the process: it both effectively solidified the surface play of fluid foliage or smoke forms, and purified it. Where the figure of *Le Modèle nu* approached 'pure painting' because Léger constructed it from forms whose origins lay in landscape, the elements of landscape in the *Contrastes de formes* cross the border into 'pure painting' because they are remodelled in terms whose origins lie in the figure. The tubular language of *La Femme dans un fauteuil* is proved as versatile and as fundamentally pure as the soft surfaces with cutting edges developed out of *Les Fumées sur les toits*, *Les Fumeurs* and *La Noce*.

The intimacy of the relationship sustained by Léger between his pure *Contrastes de formes* and his still evolving figure style demonstrates finally just how far the distinction between the two kinds of painting was broken down. A single important figurative innovation is enough to make the point: the innovation made by Léger in the treatment of head and bun with the 1913 gouaches which led from *La Femme dans un fauteuil* to the 1914 *Femme en rouge et vert*. The gouache *Dessin pour La Femme en rouge et vert* is one of these studies (Plate 39). Here the face itself is treated as a thin ellipse, split in two halves, one light, one dark, and the features are reduced to a few hastily drawn lines on the lighter half. On either side and behind are grouped two sequences of highlit cylinders, each converging on the ellipse of the face: Léger has now expanded the simplified bun of hair and split the result into two separate features, each seen in three-quarter view. Conceptually this is a durational incident; pictorially it creates an effective focal element in the composition, and it is possible that its motivation *was* pictorial alone, for the 'kite device' focal element in the *Contrastes* as established in the Philadelphia variant is strikingly analogous. The pure and the figurative almost fuse here in a single formal development.

Moreover, for all their distant landscape origins, the very structure of the 'kite device' *Contrastes* has strong figurative overtones, a fact which applies to all the oil variants known to this writer, but which again is perhaps best illustrated by the most ambitious variant (Plate 38). Not only is the 'kite device' here formally analogous with the head in *Dessin pour La Femme en rouge et vert*, but it is compositionally analogous as well. It is at the apex of all pictorial movement. Léger gives it a clear metallic blue colour, intensifying the blue and the sensation created of metallic sheen by his use of highlighting for the paired cylinders. These polished blue volumes are throughout the painting his 'figurative' forms, since they are his solid forms. As small cylinders, they are spilled down the left flank of the painting to create a rotating rhythm close to that set up by the cylindrical arms of the woman in Léger's figure study, while, as the elliptical surfaces and paired cylinders of the central field, they suggest that broader, falling motion suggested by her breastplate torso. Even the idea of separating the rotating run of cylinders from the central body of forms by a succession of flat red and white planes is echoed by the succession of stepped planes that separate the left arm from the torso in the figure study; and, of course, both dynamic groupings of volumes are placed within analogous settings of sharp angular forms.

Yet neither the landscape origins of the *Contrastes* nor their strong figurative flavour should detract from the simple pictorial immediacy of their impact. Just as they are no longer landscapes, so they are not figure-paintings; only elaborate pictorial comparison can make them seem to be either, and then only in the pursuit of causes rather than effects. Léger does achieve in them the purest possible statement of his dynamic and dissonant view. They are in one sense flat, for line and colour are separated as flat elements; yet in another sense they are solidly three-dimensional because of the simple geometric solidity of their volumes. They have, in fact, what for Léger were the features of a complete style and no subject to compromise it: they are 'Pictorial contrasts used in their purest sense (complementaries) of colours and line, of form . . . .' and that is all.

* * * * *

Up to this point an essentially unbalanced idea of Léger's move away from the representation of subjects to an art of pure pictorial contrasts has been given, for the process has been followed in relative isolation as if the impetus behind it were Léger's own ideas supported to a limited extent by the speculative example of Delaunay, Picabia and Apollinaire combined with the internal, progressive logic of his painting. Such an idea is un-balanced, on the one hand because it can only give a partial impression of the range and power of the stimuli behind the development, and on the other because it implies that Léger's art changed no more than pictorially, reflecting no significant change in his view of reality as a whole. Only by looking at the entire avant-garde context within which he made his move towards a pure dynamic and dissonant style can a fuller idea of the stimuli behind it be formed, and at the same time of the view of reality that was its ultimate *raison d'être*. Only in this way, too, can the question be answered of how so pure a style could remain still for Léger a fundamentally realistic style in the simplest physical sense—a style concerned with the realization in painting of the richness and power of life experienced at first hand.

3. Fernand Léger: *Contrastes de formes*, 1913. 39½ × 32 ins, Museum of
Modern Art, New York.

4. Robert Delaunay: *Formes circulaires*, 1913. $39\frac{1}{2} \times 26\frac{3}{4}$ ins, Musée National d'Art Moderne, Paris.

CHAPTER 3
Léger's *Contrastes* and the Parisian avant-garde, 1913–14

For Léger, his pursuit of a new and pure art, which found such direct expression in the *Contrastes de formes,* was not isolated. He saw it as part of a collective avant-garde effort—an effort which embraced all the arts. This belief is forcefully presented in his May 1913 Académie Wassilief lecture. For him the sense of common purpose which had led to the Salon de la Section d'Or was not spent, but had been canalized now into a collective move towards the pure dynamism and dissonance of contrasts. There was a considerable amount of truth in this belief.[1]

The Puteaux and Courbevoie studios of Jacques Villon and Albert Gleizes were still important meeting-places, and so too was the Closérie des Lilas, but by spring 1913 entirely new meeting-places, and new outlets, for the poets and painters had been established. From April 1912 the review *Soirées de Paris* was active, with Guillaume Apollinaire as one of its editors, and it provided a social centre around its patron the Baroness d'Oettingen (Roche Grey) and her brother Serge Férat, at whose functions were recorded, among others, Picasso, Raynal, Severini and Léger.[2] It was a new centre for discussion and an organ for the dissemination of 'pure painting', along with other ideas.

The collective mood gathered power in February 1913 with the first number of another new review, *Montjoie!*, in which, as has been seen, Léger's first lecture appeared three months later. *Montjoie!* announced in its first issue the existence already of 'a group of writers, musicians, and artists', whose needs the review set out to answer.[3] Its war-cry was: GIVE A LEAD TO THE ELITE. *Montjoie!*'s editor was Ricciotto Canudo, and the offices of the review on the Chaussée d'Antin at the foot of Montmartre became another centre for that group mentioned in his editorial. Among them were, during the next eighteen months, Mercereau, Henri-Martin Barzun, Apollinaire, Gleizes, de La Fresnaye, Diaghilev and Léger.[4]

For all its declared intention to 'give a lead', *Montjoie!* was unable—or perhaps unwilling—to formulate a group aesthetic or programme. Yet such an attempt was made by another new review, founded in December 1912 by the one-time Abbaye de Créteil poet Barzun, and called *Poème et Drame*. Barzun's faith in the power of a growing collective mood, expressed in the second number of *Poème et Drame* (January 1913), is very closely related to that of Léger as expressed in May. There is, Barzun announces, 'a foundation of identical tendencies', and this common foundation is ultimately the result of 'the new beauty'—a beauty simultaneously available to all: 'The point is that the same wonderful facts strike our senses.'[5] Like Barzun, Léger saw the dynamic force of his new style as the reflection of 'present-day life, more fragmented, faster than that of previous epochs'— a 'new beauty'; and he saw its force as universally valid, encouraging the development of a new sensibility. Moreover, though Léger had rejected the Futurist dogmas of February 1912, he was aware that the Futurists themselves had moved beyond them, and, like Barzun, saw the Italians as an important part of the new collective effort.[6]

Barzun was, like Léger, a regular visitor at Puteaux, and he provided those who met there with yet another opportunity for contact and discussion, though in more formal circumstances than Canudo's Monday *soirées* at the offices of *Montjoie!*. Between late 1912 and July 1913 there were nine 'Dîners des Artistes de Passy'. At these dinners lectures were given on such topics as Berlioz, Mallarmé and Cézanne, and in the July number of *Poème et Drame* a list of all those who on one occasion or another had attended is given: among those mentioned are: Paul Fort, Alexandre Mercereau, Gleizes, Le Fauconnier, Marie Laurencin, Apollinaire, Duchamp-Villon, Picabia, Auguste Perret, de La Fresnaye, Metzinger, Nayral, Canudo, and Léger.[7] Until autumn 1913, when *Poème et Drame* isolated itself from the most positive figures in the avant-garde, the review and the dinners formed an important forum for ideas of the pure, 'the new beauty' and dynamism in poetry, painting, sculpture and music, almost as important for nine months as *Soirées de Paris* and *Montjoie!*. All three of the new reviews and the meeting-places they provided were actively involved in the development of the collective fabric of ideas—embracing the Futurists as well as the French—which Léger saw as the ambience out of which the pure *Contrastes de formes* and all their relatives emerged.

*   *   *   *   *

As has been seen, by the autumn of 1912, when Léger exhibited *La Femme en bleu*, the most decisive pictorial evidence of the move towards pure painting was Delaunay's series of *Fenêtre* paintings brought back from the valley of the Chevreuse, paintings of whose purity Delaunay himself was firmly convinced.[8]

Delaunay exhibited these canvases at the Der Sturm gallery in Berlin at the beginning of 1913 and he was accompanied there by Apollinaire, who became that year, more than anyone, the champion of his ideas, finding in the *Fenêtres* a conclusive verification of the views he had expounded on *Le Sujet dans la peinture*. A central part in Apollinaire's promotion of Delaunay was played by his book, *Les Peintres cubistes*, which declared the emergence of a new movement in painting called Orphism. The aim of this movement was said to be the creation of pictorial structures combining elements invented by the artist, who remained apart from nature[9]—Delaunay's professed aim—and the Orphists Apollinaire named were Delaunay, Picabia, Duchamp and Léger. Delaunay was undoubtedly the impetus behind the idea of such a group, and it existed more in the realm of ambition than in the realm of fact—the ambition behind it coming of the drive towards 'pure painting'.

Apollinaire's idea of Orphism was general to the point of vagueness, but Orphism for Delaunay was based on specific aims and methods, which he outlined in a statement published in *Der Sturm* (January 1913) to complement his Berlin exhibition of the *Fenêtres*—'La Lumière'. As Léger was to do in his May lecture, so here Delaunay concentrates on the action of contrasts; they are for him too the essential factor in pictorial construction; but his emphasis is on the simultaneous contrasts of colour alone. This Orphist doctrine represents a return to the theoretical basis of Neo-Impressionism, but the dot is rejected and so pure is Delaunay's emphasis on colour, that the subject is rejected also. Working on the basis of Eugène Chevreul's *De la loi des contrastes simultanées des couleurs,* Delaunay focused on the way that colours can change each other when juxtaposed;[10] he thought of these changing relationships, by which, say, a blue can make a yellow more orange, as changes of light frequency or rhythm, and aimed to use them to stimulate the eye to movement and the mind to an awareness through this experience of the dynamic, fluxing quality of light. He aimed to synthesize the elements essential to our optical experience of the world, i.e. of light, and for him the movement of colours was no less than the essence of all visible reality.[11]

The emphasis on purity in Delaunay's theory was not the only point at which he strayed from his Neo-Impressionist sources; he strayed also in his repeated emphasis on rhythmic movement, and in the special meaning he gave to the term 'simultaneity'. His emphasis on rhythmic movement was certainly in part a reaction to the early 1912 Futurist invasion, and the special meaning he gave to the term 'simultaneity' has a specifically anti-Futurist slant—a slant which throws into sharp relief the distance between the Futurist accent on the subject and his own accent on pure pictorial effect. Delaunay's knowledge of Neo-Impressionist colour theory led him to the belief that he could develop a dynamic art, which was simultaneous, on the basis of the mutability and mobility of colours in simultaneous contrast—an art based on the direct pictorial effect of colour-movement, apprehended all at once in a single instant, rather than on the successive description of movement so characteristic of Futurist dynamism.[12] Thus, whereas for the Futurists in February 1912 simultaneity had meant the simultaneousness of the ambience—an experience combining emotions and the memories of people, events and things—for Delaunay, by winter 1912, it meant the simultaneousness of a single experience of contrasting colours on a flat picture plane. Delaunay's 'simultaneity' was optical rather than psychological and it could therefore, anticipating Léger's *Contrastes de formes*, eschew representation altogether.

Yet the significance of Delaunay's 'pure painting' did not, for him, end in the excitement of pure optical sensation. Although his Orphism was a declaration of independence, he retained the fundamental desire of the 'Salle 41' and 'Salle 8' Cubists to convey through painting the essential quality of an idea of existence as a whole.[13] He was convinced that by confronting the spectator with the colour structure of light in such a way, he could make the spectator deeply aware of the dynamic, fluxing quality of all existence. In 'La Lumière' he writes of wishing to communicate 'the idea of the vital movement of the world'.[14] His foundation remained as that interpenetrating, dynamic idea of life as movement whose most respected champion was Bergson.

In April 1913, exactly a year after the first of the *Fenêtres* were painted, Delaunay and his wife Sonia rented a house near the Château Louveciennes and it was probably then that he began to paint a new series called the *Formes circulaires*.[15] These canvases were first shown at the Berlin Herbst-salon of September–November, and the earliest could be seen to anticipate Léger's *Contrastes de formes*; they represent Delaunay's current work during that important summer and were certainly known in Paris before the autumn. Starting from separate studies of sun and moonlight, they culminate in three large oils which fuse the full range of colour movements from sun to moonlight, a powerful metaphor for the continuity of *la durée*. These were Delaunay's most complete pure expressions of his dynamic idea of simultaneity, and so, in order to understand the relationship between his contrasts and those of Léger, it is best to look at Léger's series alongside the *Formes circulaires* rather than the *Fenêtres*.

Delaunay's *Formes circulaires* (Colour Plate 4) is typically expanding and dynamic. It is one of the sun studies, and, like all the series, its subject is the key both to its expanding motion and to its colour. Delaunay had insisted in 'La Lumière' on the fact that his starting-point was light *in nature*, and it is known that this series was based on a first-hand study of sunlight and moonlight at Louveciennes.[16] This does not mean that the movement of colour contrasts in the painting imitates the natural effect of sunlight: it means, of course, that Delaunay aims to create an equivalent sensation. However, for all the purity of his forms and of the colour theory behind his contrasts, the fact that the painting derives from and refers to the observed effect of natural light gives Delaunay's treatment of colour and pictorial space a strong naturalistic quality. He sets his expanding sun-disc in a misty, shifting envelope of browns, which provokes the illusion of infinite space, and his colours are subtly modulated, even where hot and positive, to give the illusion of atmospheric light. Only the red band of the peripheral sun ring sits flat on the picture plane. Every other colour area shifts hazily somewhere in the depth behind it. In 'La Lumière' Delaunay gave special emphasis to the creation of depth by colour, completely ignoring the qualities of mass and volume. *Formes circulaires* is deeply spatial in its luminosity, continuous in the flow of its movements, and as insubstantial as air.

Léger's *Contrastes de formes* (Colour Plate 3) is an oil as important in the 'kite device' series as Delaunay's Paris *Formes circulaires* is in his sun and moon series. Its contrasts are dramatically discontinuous and it masses together the weight of many cylinders. Léger ignores the fundamentally Neo-Impressionist aim to create in paint an equivalent of the sensation of light in nature. His emphasis is on attaining the greatest possible dynamism and dissonance and, because his means have been developed through pictorial experiment rather than the study of light, his contrasts engage line and form as well as colour. Colour itself is used in the New York *Contrastes* as a flat element—the planes of red, blue and yellow are scattered from edge to edge of the canvas, unmodulated in their intensity: they do not expand into a limitless brown depth. The whole picture area is treated as a textured surface to give material support to this emphasis on pictorial flatness; the broad-weave canvas is primed with studied coarseness and colour is thickly scrubbed over it in patches, always *on* the roughened picture plane.[17] Léger achieves not only linear and chromatic movement, but also, by means of his division of pictorial elements, dramatic discontinuity of effect. Where Delaunay juxtaposes his colours one against another, Léger divides his colour patches by means of the white highlights, black lines and the primed canvas.[18] The differences are profound, and led, as Léger later recalled, to the end of his alliance with Delaunay.[19]

The timing of the Orphist campaign makes it difficult to doubt its significance as a major stimulus behind Léger's move to pure contrasts, for the climax of Delaunay and Apollinaire's effort coincided with the crisis in Léger's art which came to a head with *Le Modèle nu*. He talked in his May 1913 lecture of 'an art of dynamic divisionism', and there can be no doubt that the sudden brightening of his colour range and the clear division of his contrasting forces one from another reflected a revived interest in Neo-Impressionist colour theory, even if partly antagonistic to it—an interest almost certainly stimulated by the early 1913 propaganda of Orphism. And yet the theory of contrasts and the style which Léger developed between the spring and autumn of 1913 were profoundly different from Delaunay's. He arrived at a style which was both more dissonant in its impact, and in a sense less Impressionist—a style which reflected an essentially different attitude both to painting and to reality.

*　　*　　*　　*　　*

Neither Léger's nor Delaunay's emphasis on the purity of painting led them to ignore the manifold developments in music, poetry and ideas that gave broad avant-garde support to their art of movement and contrast, and served to create the common tendency picked out by Léger himself in his first Académie Wassilief lecture.

Apollinaire was not merely important as critic-champion, but as poet, for late in 1912 and early in 1913 his poetry was transformed, in part by the example of the *Fenêtres* and the approach behind them.[20] In December 1912 *Soirées de Paris* published a long poem by Apollinaire, *Zone*; a month later, in the January 1913 number of *Poème et Drame* a shorter poem was published, *Les Fenêtres*. These two pieces represent two vital early stages in what has been called Apollinaire's *changement de front*, and *Zone* is almost certainly the turning-point. Pär Bergmann has noted that, according to Gabrielle Buffet-Picabia, she, Picabia and Duchamp were present at a reading of the longer poem in October 1912, and Michel Decaudin has suggested that it was finished either then or in September,[21] precisely at the moment when Delaunay's new pure paintings and ideas were fresh in Apollinaire's eyes and mind. It was in Delaunay's studio that *Les Fenêtres* was completed, and the poem appeared in the catalogue of Delaunay's *Der Sturm* exhibition in January 1913.

Zone announced for Apollinaire a new kind of poetry which was concerned with the raw dynamism of life as well as with a private inner world of emotion; *Les Fenêtres* achieved an immediacy which is both more condensed and more exclusively concerned with the senses. It knits together snatched fragments of conversation,[22] with passages (almost certainly added in Delaunay's studio) which have an immediate visual impact. The famous opening is a pure evocation of light:

> From the red to the green all the yellow dies . . .

Delaunay is undoubtedly behind this new immediacy of effect. But involved in Apollinaire's *changement de front*, as an influential ally was another personality who could teach a lesson as direct as Delaunay's. By the early months of 1913 a new force had entered the Parisian avant-garde: Blaise Cendrars, who was already a friend of Apollinaire, the Delaunays and Léger, was to be seen at the Closérie des Lilas, Puteaux and the *Montjoie! soirées*. *Zone* is intimately linked in subject, tone and imagery to Cendrars' first important poem, *Pâques a New York*,[23] which was published the very month of the first recital of Apollinaire's poem in October 1912.[24]

It is the clashing combination of exotic, often religious imagery with the dynamic and the modern that so closely links *Zone* to the Cendrars poem. By the beginning of 1913 the images of the present-day were in control of both poets' work: *Les Fenêtres* shows the beginning of the process for Apollinaire; for Cendrars, it begins with his second major poem *Prose du Transsibérien et de la petite Jehanne de France* and the first of his *Dix-neuf poèmes élastiques*. A common source of dynamic effect in *Les Fenêtres*, *Prose du Transsibérien* and the first of the *Dix-neuf poèmes* is contrast, not merely pure contrasts of rhythm, but contrasts of imagery. Cendrars achieves a more dynamic, disruptive brand of contrast than Apollinaire, moving very abruptly in *Prose du Transsibérien* from flowing sentences to long runs of images, for instance:

> Tric-trac
> Billard
> Caramboles
> Paraboles
> La voie ferée est une nouvelle géométrie . . .[25]

Yet, like Apollinaire, he retains in *Prose* a sense of flow from image into image by sound and analogy,[26] a sense of continuity in motion perhaps more in tune with the 'simultaneous contrasts' of Delaunay than with the violently disruptive contrasts of Léger. The link between *Prose du Transsibérien* and Delaunay was a real one.

As Robert and Sonia Delaunay well knew, in comparison with painting, poetry suffered from the basic defect of successiveness.[27] Yet, they did believe that the successive rhythms of verbal contrast could be endowed with extra force by alliance with visual simultaneity. Early in 1913 Cendrars and Sonia Delaunay collaborated to produce 'the first simultaneous book', a presentation of *Prose du Transsibérien* which gave the verbal movement of the poem a pure colour accompaniment.[28] It was published in the autumn, designed to unfold as a continuous script—a single visual experience fusing colour and words. In this way the successive movement of the eye

through the text was complemented at every stage by 'simultaneous contrasts'; words against colours, and colours against colours.

Thus far in the argument it appears that Cendrars's use of contrast in *Prose du Transsibérien* ran parallel with that of the Delaunays, but, in fact, it seems probable that Cendrars directly influenced the work especially of Robert, late in 1912 and early in 1913. The nature of this influence being literary, it follows that it directed Delaunay away from the uncompromising purity of the *Fenêtres* towards a less pure idea of painting—an idea which allowed the subject back and which was more obviously the expression of 'the new beauty'.

Prose du Transsibérien is not an anti-Futurist poem; indeed, in many ways it is very much in tune with Futurism as it had developed during 1912. Cendrars, like Léger, Apollinaire and Henri-Martin Barzun, was able by the end of 1912 to accept positively certain Futurist ideas, among which was the concept of simultaneous ambience given a literary application. In *Prose du Transsibérien* Cendrars combines a shifting composition, constructed from memories, with the modern experience of a train journey

78

43. (left) Robert Delaunay:
Hommage à Blériot, 1914. Tempera
on canvas, $98\frac{1}{2} \times 98\frac{1}{2}$ ins, Oeffentliche
Kunstssammlung, Basel.

44. (right) Robert Delaunay:
L'Equipe de Cardiff, 1912–13.
$77\frac{1}{8} \times 51\frac{1}{8}$ ins, Stedelijk Van
Abbemuseum, Eindhoven.

—a combination with a very specific Futurist precedent in Severini's
Souvenirs d'un voyage. His journey through memories of Russia, of his early
childhood, and of many other experiences in other places is given continuity by the train journey on the Trans Siberian Express: the remembered
speed of the train helps break down the old unities of space and time.
The train becomes a symbol of the drawing together into one simultaneous
ambience of disparate thoughts, places and times.[29] Again, where he
wanted speed and force of impact Cendrars's use of verbs and nouns
undecorated by adjectives and adverbs clearly relates to Marinetti's 1912
invention—*parole in libertà*;[30] so that, not only by its creation of a physically
mobile theme hooked onto the symbolic movement of a train, but often
also by its language, the Cendrars poem conveys a strongly Futurist
experience of life. Ironically, it was this that found a place in the anti-
Futurist art of Robert Delaunay.

Thus, the sequel to the *Fenêtres* was not only the pure *Formes circulaires*,
but also a return to what Spate has aptly called the 'literary simultanism'
of Delaunay's earlier *Ville de Paris*. At the end of 1912 and the beginning
of 1913 Delaunay turned back to the use of literary images in allegorical
formation with two paintings taken from a news photograph of rugby
players, the two versions of *L'Equipe de Cardiff*. The first was completed
for inclusion in the January 1913 *Der Sturm* exhibition (Plate 44), the second
larger version was completed by March for the 1913 Indépendants.[31]
Here, the pure 'simultaneous contrasts' of colours are combined with
legible modern images—the tower, the wheel, the rugby players—and,
in the larger version, with the words: 'Delaunay—New York—Paris'.
These paintings initiated a series of literary simultanist allegories of 'the
new beauty' alongside the *Formes circulaires* which culminated in the

1914 *Hommage à Blériot* (Plate 43). The clarity with which Delaunay presents his images in *L'Equipe de Cardiff*, undistorted by Cubist perspectival complications, and the immediacy with which he uses the words Paris and New York to convey the shrinkage of distance by wireless, telegraph and steamship, both so much in tune with the simultaneity of *Prose du Trans-sibérien*, underline the part played by the Swiss poet in his change of direction.

Delaunay was not alone in his move towards an art which both employs pure pictorial contrast and is simultaneous in the literary, Futurist sense. By the Indépendants of 1913 a definite return to modern poetic imagery was observable in Parisian avant-garde painting. Albert Gleizes's *Joueurs de football* was another pointer to this trend, and it led Apollinaire to declare in *Montjoie!* the return of the subject in painting.[32] Almost before 'pure painting' had begun, the reaction against it had set in, allied to the acceptance of a Futuristically simultaneous emphasis on 'the new beauty' — the modern world.

*   *   *   *   *

In the second Académie Wassilief lecture (June 1914) Léger expounded an idea of 'the new beauty' which was very close to that of Gleizes, Cendrars and Delaunay, and he focused on the way that the experience above all of speed in cars and, significantly, trains, had fragmented the very nature of consciousness. For him, modern life was both 'more condensed and more complicated': 'Modern man registers a hundred times more impressions than the artist of the eighteenth century; to such an extent that . . . our language is full of diminutives and abbreviations.'[33] It was this, he believed, that lay behind the condensed force and the fragmentation of modern painting.

However, Léger was not tempted to make the connection between his pure pictorial contrasts and modern life too obvious by developing his own team of modern poetic images to perform in forward-looking allegories. The purity of his *Contrastes* and of his approach to *La Femme dans un fauteuil* may have been in part a response to the plea made by Delaunay and Apollinaire for 'pure painting', but so independent was the pictorial process of evolution out of which it emerged that when he achieved purity early in the summer of 1913, he achieved it *against* the current trend, which was back to the subject.

More important, although Léger's idea of modern life was fragmented, like that of Delaunay, it was also fundamentally opposed, a fact indicated by the abrupt and powerful contrasts of his painting, so alien to Delaunay's 'simultaneous contrasts'. In the second Académie Wassilief lecture he sums up the basic qualities of modern painting as its 'condensation', 'variety', 'its rupture of forms';[34] and in his discussion of contrast in modern life he concentrates therefore on the vigour of 'rupture' rather than on the continuity of relationships. The landscape is 'broken apart' by the motor-car, the train, and by the 'red and yellow poster', and, since such violence is the essence of modern experience, it must also, Léger declares, be the essence of modern painting.[35] Thus, when he comes to discuss his 'plastic means' he dismisses the term 'harmony', so much used by Delaunay and Apollinaire, in favour of a term which has seemed in description of his new painting repeatedly apt—the term 'dissonance'. By grouping the forms, lines and colours of the painting in opposing phalanxes: 'You get ... combined sources of tones, lines and colours acting against other contrary and dissonant sources. Contrasts = dissonance, and as a result maximum expressive effect.'[36] In the final analysis, the impetus behind Léger's attack on the merging colour harmonies of Delaunay, and his dogmatic demand for the sudden stridency of local colour, came of the conviction, brought forward into a more contemporary context from his earliest avant-garde statement (the *Nus dans un paysage*), that the fundamental quality of modern life was conflict. Léger's violent image of life as a whole found support in modern experience, and his dissonant variant on the idea of 'the new beauty' was not isolated.

Paradoxically, as Delaunay moved into a literary brand of painting encouraged by the poetry of Cendrars, the latter considered in pure terms, turned towards more forceful, dissonant effects closer to Léger's painting. This is clear in the first two of the *Dix-neuf poèmes élastiques*, *Journal* and *Tour*, which were written in August 1913, no more than a month or two after Léger had turned to his 'dynamic divisionism', as he and Cendrars moved together into close friendship.[37] All at once the fluid sense of movement from image to image so typical of *Prose du Transsibérien* is destroyed by the sharpness of the breaks between one image and another, as here in *Tour*:

> Gong tam-tam zanzibar bête de la jungle rayons X
> express bistouri symphonie . . .[38]

A dissonance is achieved emphatically in tune with Léger's painting.

The first six months of 1913 saw two further powerful and effective demonstrations in support of an art of dissonant contrast; they could both have positively contributed to the final development of Léger's new style and they provide a further gloss on the violence of his view of reality. One was the May 1913 opening of the Ballet Russe production of Igor Stravinsky's *Le Sacre du Printemps*, the other was the development between December 1912 and August 1913 of Henri-Martin Barzun's 'Dramatisme'.

The impact of *Le Sacre du Printemps* on the Parisian avant-garde was profound, and, according to the poet Sebastien Voirol, Léger was among those most impressed. It was an experience, Voirol pointed out, of significance to all the arts.[39] Stravinsky's theme was not modern life, it was the cyclical energy of all life as a continual process of regeneration—the theme so deeply explored by the Abbaye poets and all followers of Bergsonian philosophy. But the way that Stravinsky approached the alliance of music and movement in the expression of this universal theme was very much in tune with Léger's approach to pictorial movement and contrast. On 29 May, in precisely the same number as the first part of Léger's first Académie Wassilief lecture, *Montjoie!* published a statement by the composer: 'Ce que j'ai voulu exprimer dans, *Le Sacre du Printemps*'. It begins with a declaration of faith in abstraction surprisingly close to Léger, but perhaps equally important is the recurrent emphasis he gives to a disruptive view of the force of life. Thus, for him, the dance of the adolescents at the river in the first scene is an attempt to express in the opposing rhythms of groups of dancers the clash of universal forces,[40] and this, coupled with the accent throughout the ballet on *rondes* and spirals creates a clear link with the rotating dynamism of Léger's 'dynamic divisionism'. One cannot talk of exact connections, but one can be certain of the importance of *Le Sacre du Printemps* as part of the common tendency out of which Léger believed that his 1913 style emerged.

That Barzun was part of the common tendency and that his bias was towards an idea of life as conflict follows from his earlier championship of dynamic force in the first two books of *La Terrestre Tragédie*—so much in tune with Léger's *Nus dans un paysage*—and his poetry during 1912 and 1913, unlike Stravinsky's ballet, was founded on the experience of modern life. His own particular brand of simultaneity, with its use of clashing voices in groups, led to a vituperative break with the advocates of visual simultanist poetry—Apollinaire and Cendrars—but this did not occur until after the autumn number of his review *Poème et Drame*,[41] and before the fuse was lit by his cultural megalomania his energy earned him serious respect. For Barzun, 'the new beauty' was a compound of that boisterous beauty celebrated by Whitman, and that metallic, dynamic beauty celebrated by Marinetti;[42] it led to an idea of vital force as contrast very close to Léger's idea of contrasts. The violent dissonance of the content, if not the form, of his 1912 *Hymne des forces* is perhaps the closest of all literary analogies to the *Contrastes de formes*:

> World! thou sacred work, alone of souls given grace!
> Oh! create Contradictions in me!
> Unite the Antagonisms! . . .
> Oh, I pray thee, search no more—destroy nothing:
> Give the wonderful drama of the world freedom
> To unleash its titanic forces . . . .[43]

In March 1913, when Léger turned from the unsuccessful *Le Modèle nu* towards his complete 'dynamic divisionism', this passage was published in *Poème et Drame*. In a sense, though perhaps too limiting a sense, the style that he developed that summer might have been called a pure pictorial ally of Barzun's so-called *Dramatisme*.

*   *   *   *   *

Barzun, Apollinaire, Cendrars, Delaunay, Gleizes, Léger and many others owed to the Futurists, as has been suggested, at least something of their approach to 'the new beauty'. A complete idea of the avant-garde ambience in which Léger's new style was developed and the idea of reality it sought to embody is not possible without considering the stimulus which the Italians increasingly provided during the latter half of 1912 and 1913.

The Futurists were themselves in no doubt as to Léger's debt: after the first part of his May 1913 lecture was published in *Montjoie!* Carlo Carrà wrote from Paris to Ardengo Soffici that the figure-drawing which appeared as illustration (Plate 32) was sheer plagiarism, expressing a merely superficial understanding of the Futurists' experiments. Like its close relative, *Le Modèle nu* (Plate 30), it was certainly not plagiarism, but it did seem to reflect—perhaps superficially—an awareness of Futurist experiments,[44] and Carrà's indignation is explained by the fact that his own painting *Simultaneità* of 1912 was particularly relevant.

However, from the point of view of the development of Léger's 1913 'dynamic divisionism' the painting of Carrà was of minimal importance, and it was another Futurist who most of all seemed to belong to the common tendency he discerned towards an art of contrasts, towards 'pure painting'; Gino Severini. Severini's 1912 *Danseuse* experiments had with elaborate decisiveness declared the illustrative, successive nature of the Futurist approach to mobile subjects, but early in 1913 he took the lessons learned from these experiments closer and closer to pictorial purity in oils like *Danseuse à Pigalle* (Plate 45). With a Futurist emphasis on dynamic, inter-penetrating effect, he joined the move away from the subject. Here, in *Danseuse à Pigalle*, the illustrative nature of his repeated forms—their identity as arms, legs and head—has finally been subordinated to the purely visual rhythms they create. His use of tonal modelling to suggest mass in relief and his rejection of line are opposed to Léger's purpose, but the successive, rotary movement of forms and the localization of strong colours on a predominantly grey ground are obviously very much in tune with Léger's emergent 'dynamic divisionism'. Léger may have rejected the illus-trative use of successive rhythms advocated by Marcel Duchamp as well as the Italians, but he accepted the purely pictorial possibilities of rhythmic repetition—a fact which is made clear as much by *Le Modèle nu* as by *La Femme dans un fauteuil* and the *Contrastes de formes*. It was the month before Léger's first Académie Wassilief lecture, in April 1913, that Severini held a one-man exhibition at the Marlborough Gallery in London, in-cluding some of the recent *Danseuse* paintings,[45] and he justified his work with a short catalogue preface which comes uncannily close to Léger's lecture. Not only does he share Léger's view that the intensity and rapidity of modern life demand synthesis and therefore breed abstraction, but also his view that the concision of modern language is a symptom of this.[46]

45. Gino Severini: *La Danseuse à Pigalle,* 1913. Measurements and whereabouts unknown.

A direct interchange of views seems at the least possible, and there can be no doubt that Severini's new experiments and ideas were easily available during the spring and early summer, for he returned to Paris in May and was a prominent figure at the Closérie des Lilas.[47]

It is clear, therefore, that between the summers of 1912 and 1913 Léger's painting openly declared an alliance with Futurism, and it was an alliance given definitive verbal expression with the second part of the 1913 Académie Wassilief lecture to be published by *Montjoie!*. Two months later, in the Futurist review *Lacerba*, Boccioni declared that even as early as the Bernheim-Jeune exhibition he had seen Léger as 'the most gifted and promising' of the Cubists, and that now, with the Académie Wassilief lecture, his promise had been fulfilled. For the Italian, Léger's lecture was 'a genuine act of faith in Futurism'.[48]

The purely pictorial alliance with Futurism declared by Léger's 1913 'dynamic divisionism' was inevitably the result of a more profound alliance between Léger and the Futurists, an alliance of approaches to reality, in particular, of course, to the reality of modern life. Like Barzun's and Léger's idea of 'the new beauty', that of the Futurists was not only simultanist and fragmented by the experience of speed, but dissonant, focused on conflict.[49] However, it was not only the dissonant Futurist view of 'the new beauty' that added impetus to the development of Léger's *Contrastes*, it was also the status they gave to the machine in the hierarchy of modern experiences.

Léger's 'dynamic divisionism' may have been developed in the direction of maximum pure pictorial effect, yet an integral factor in its development was the creation of an unmistakable mechanistic image. Both the pure *Contrastes* and their figurative relations share an emphatic machine character, a machine character underlined above all by the figure-paintings of 1913–14, by *La Femme dans un fauteuil* (Plate 34) or *La Femme en rouge et vert*. Constructed of cylinders, drums and ovoids, their surface polished to a high sheen, Léger's women have here become a new kind of machine whose action is rotary. The highlight is not, after all, merely an artificial pictorial device, but the maker of a mechanistic effect. 'That theory,' Léger said of his theory of contrasts in the second Académie Wassilief lecture, 'is not an abstraction but a formula taken from the observation of natural effects which can be seen every day.'[50] The geometric solids of the *Contrastes de formes* have just such a source in the 'natural effects' of machine forms and metal surfaces, and this is a fact which is given yet further and more specific support by Léger looking back at the pre-1914 period from the vantage-point of ten years later. In a text of 1923 he writes of a year when the Salon de l'Aviation was installed next to the Salon d'Automne in the Grand Palais, remembering the impact of the aeroplanes and their engines when he turned from the hanging of the paintings to the machine exhibits close by: he remembers 'beautiful hard metal objects, complete and functional, treated in pure local colours, the steel playing against vermilions and blues with infinite variety of effect'; he remembers a dominant 'geometric power'.[51] The evidence that the incident recalled occurred in 1912 is persuasive. It is also probable that it was the same Salon de l'Aviation which was recalled when Léger told Dora Vallier of a visit to the Salon de l'Aviation 'before the 1914 war' with Marcel Duchamp and Constantin Brancusi, where above all the motors were what he loved.[52] These were the real *motifs* or models whose impact lay behind the rotating formal combinations of the *Contrastes de formes* and their figurative relatives. Landscape and figure were unimportant to pictorial effect, but the aero-engines seen by Léger at the 1912 Salon de l'Aviation were absolutely essential to it.

Léger's move towards a controlling mechanistic quality may have been the result of the real drama of machines experienced at first hand, but it depended ultimately on the desire to seek out such experiences, and there can be no doubt that the Futurists gave impetus to that desire during the months leading first to the 1912 Salon de l'Aviation, then to *Le Modèle nu* and beyond. Yet, certainly as effectively as the link it demonstrates with the Futurist approach to modern, mechanized life, the relationship between Léger's 'dynamic divisionism' and his first-hand experience of the machine brings back into focus the fundamental realism of his new style. It demonstrates that his belief in the evidence of his own eyes as the essential raw material of his art did not weaken as the idea of 'pure painting' strengthened its grip; he still worked towards pictorial effect by extracting from his surroundings the elements which were for him most essential to his awareness of dynamism and interpenetrating conflict. However versatile, however unrealistic his forms could seem, they always remained at root realistic, presented on the canvas to create that intense sensation of weight, of metallic solidity and of power in motion that he experienced in the machinery of modern life. In the same way, however purely pictorial was the fragmented, rhythmic sensation generated by his sequences of forms and colours, for him they always remained at root the generators of experiences derived from the fragmented nature of the world seen at speed, from the window of the railway-carriage or the motor-car. Léger remained a realist, but the reality he chose to paint had been modernized.

*　　*　　*　　*　　*

Léger's 'dynamic divisionism' had one further profoundly important characteristic: it eschewed the final pictorial statement. Léger's pictorial ideas from the end of 1912 to 1914 were open-ended, always capable of revision, development, even metamorphosis: they were in a continual state of evolution. The metamorphosis of *La Femme en bleu* into *La Femme dans un fauteuil* is itself a demonstration of this fact, as are the many small but telling variations found in each of the 'kite device' *Contrastes*, but the intitiation and evolution of the other main themes of 1913 and 1914, which ran alongside the still evolving *Contrastes*[53] and their figurative relations, is just as revealing a demonstration.

Of the other evolving themes to be established between the summers of 1913 and 1914, one of the most mechanistically dynamic was the *Escalier* theme. This theme was evolved in two distinct ways, one very much in line with the mechanistic figure-paintings of 1913,[54] above all *La Femme en rouge et vert* (Plate 39), the other not. There are two major versions of this other theme, the *Escalier* dated '13', now in the Kunsthaus, Zurich (Plate 46), and the version dated '14', now in the Moderna Museet, Stockholm (Plate 50).[55] The Zurich painting is clearly independent as a pictorial

46.   Fernand Léger: *L'Escalier*, 1913. 57½ × 46½ ins, Kunsthaus, Zurich.

47. (above)   Fernand Léger: *Dessin pour Nature morte sur une table,* 1913. Wash and gouache on paper, $25\frac{1}{2} \times 19\frac{3}{4}$ ins, galerie Beyeler, Basel.

48. (above right)   Fernand Léger: *Nature morte à la lampe,* 1913. $24\frac{3}{4} \times 17\frac{3}{4}$ ins, Private collection, Dallas, Texas.

49. (right)   Fernand Léger: *Nature morte aux cylindres colorés,* 1913. $50\frac{3}{4} \times 76$ ins, Louis Carré collection, France.

idea from the figurative descendants of *La Femme dans un fauteuil* (Plate 34). Where those figure compositions were relatively free of gravitational effects, so that Léger could scatter relatively small volumes and colour patches over the whole picture surface, this composition is emphatically gravitational: its volumes combine to create a strong sense not only of their individual weights but of their weight in concert, as a pair of figures. One figure, its cylinders a deep, receding blue, is set in front of the other, whose billiant vermilion cylinders thrust out chromatically onto the picture plane, flattening what is perspectively an illusion of depth. The large, simple cylinders of the two torsos, set spinning in tiers one on top of another, are the key both to the new sense of weight and to the new stridency of colour effect.

A clue to the origin of this new pictorial idea is provided by a gouache study for a *Nature-morte sur une table* dated 1913 (Plate 47).[56] The central feature of the gouache is two large cylinders one on top of the other, their partly exposed faces ridged and creviced; they are intimately related to the tiered cylinders of *L'Escalier* in its Zurich form. Indeed, so close is the relationship that in the gouache they seem to take on the identity of a machine torso, for above them is a form very close to Léger's then current head forms—a split oval bracketed by a pair of metallic bands. Yet, Léger's pencil inscription leaves no doubt as to the actual *non*-figurative starting-point for the composition: it is quite simply a still-life on a table with fork and open book, and its connections with a more obviously still-life idea developed during 1913 underline this fact.

The more obvious still-life in question is the small, roughly painted oil (Plate 48). This and Léger's other still-lifes in the new style are of special interest because they involve a new *motif*. Léger did not arrive at this series by merely translating an old pictorial idea into the new terms, he worked, probably by memory, from new arrangements of objects scattered on a table.[57] The objects in this *Nature-morte* are still legible enough for the nature of their pictorial transmutation to be visible. The fruit-bowl becomes an inverted cone, set upon a short cylinder with distorted cubic base, the fruit rotating as a collection of spheres in its flattened bowl; objects are simplified, fragmented and distorted for pure pictorial effect.

This small still-life is related to the gouache still-life through a very large oil, *Nature-morte aux cylindres colorés* (Plate 49), a canvas more ambitious in scale even than the Zurich *Escalier* itself. With this still-life Léger so emphasizes pure pictorial effect, so simplifies and distorts his objects that they are almost illegible. There are two bowls, each with the characteristic inverted cone, cylinder and cube structure of the New York fruit bowl; the cup from the smaller painting loses its curved profiles so that it becomes a third conical form, and beneath it Léger suggests a fourth cone of which the saucer is the top surface. A combination of spinning metallic volumes emerges, far from its origin in still-life, but close to the spinning cylinders of the gouache *Nature-morte sur une table* (Plate 47) and also, therefore, close to the machine-figures of the Zurich *Escalier*.

Thus, it seems that the Zurich and Stockholm *Escalier* theme was the result of a remarkable sequence of metamorphoses, by which the forms of still-life objects were purified into simple geometric combinations, which

50.   Fernand Léger: *L'Escalier,* 1914. 57 × 36¾ ins, Moderna Museet, Stockholm.

were then distorted and regrouped until they were pictorially free enough to be translated into a figurative guise. This process of metamorphosis at once demonstrates the ultimate irrelevance of declared subject-matter in the *Escalier* paintings, as elsewhere, and the evolving, unconcluded nature of every stage of their evolution, from still-life to figure themes. This openness to change, this lack of conclusiveness, was a feature of Léger's 'dynamic divisionism' in all its manifestations.

* * * * *

Léger was not content to see a pictorial idea as evolving merely through the changes between one painting and another in a series; it was, for him, necessary that every act of painting should be constantly open to change. For this reason, as he moved from *La Femme en bleu* into his new style of 1913–14, he developed an increasingly simple, flexible technique, a technique open at all stages to spontaneous invention.

The *Nature-morte* of either late 1913 or early 1914 (Plate 51) is a re-latively small painting; it has neither the scale nor the certainty of a work at the end of a series, like the successor to the Zurich *Escalier* (Plate 50), and yet both are painted with equal speed and openness to invention. Léger first primes them in grey, the primer having that roughcast quality, accentuated by rough handling, which was commented on above in the *Contrastes*. Then the linear movement and the shaping of the volumes are established in black with long and decisive strokes of the loaded brush, their execution obviously accomplished at speed and almost all in a single session. Shape gives volume, but the grey surface remains dead without colour, and Léger himself describes the next stage: 'Only when I'd really got the volume, as I wanted it, did I begin to put in the colours. But that was hard. How many canvases were destroyed . . .'[58] The fre-quent superimposition at their edges of colour patches over outlines makes it clear that in both these paintings colour was indeed a response to the preliminary stimulus of outline, its application following as a separate stage in the process of execution. Red, yellow, blue and violet are literally scrubbed on with the brush, the colours taken straight from the tube, and then finally, when they are nearly dry, the highlights are added to give the paintings a completely solid, mechanical and dissonant presence.

In general terms the technique used in these two canvases is used in all the paintings in the new style.[59] There is slight over-simplification in the analysis given above—for instance, late linear and colour changes occur in both the works discussed—but such irregularities are merely further expressions of Léger's emphasis on flexibility throughout the creative process.

There are two basic ways in which the new technique differs from that of *La Noce*, *Les Fumeurs* and *La Femme en bleu*: on the one hand, in the clarity of the division during the working process between line and colour; on the other, in the sheer speed of execution, from which follows the invariable roughness of finish. Léger's earlier practice was to draw in his lines with the brush and then, with care, to work up his surfaces, strengthening lines where required. This led to a smooth, integrated result. The move towards a clear separation of outlining from surface colouring

51. Fernand Léger: *Nature morte*, 1913–14. 39 × 31¼ ins, Dr Emil Friedrich collection, Zurich.

is already visible in *Le Modèle nu dans l'atelier* (Plate 30) where there is also a prophetic roughness of effect, but, like the new style, the new technique did not reach maturity until the sudden breakthrough of summer 1913—until the *Contrastes*, their figurative and still-life relatives.

With his new simplicity and speed of method Léger produced paintings whose coarse confidence stood out in the circle of Puteaux, *Montjoie!* and *Soirées de Paris*. They conveyed by their very coarseness, the spontaneous, open-ended nature of his pictorial ambition; the fact that his work continued without conclusions, each phase creating stimulus for the next—a perpetual becoming.

*   *   *   *   *

Once again, Léger's constantly evolving approach to pictorial themes was not isolated: it was part of the common tendency which was so important to him.

As with the move towards 'pure painting', Robert Delaunay was a significant figure in the early drive towards such an approach. His major 1910–13 themes were only in a few special cases developed in the conventional way from studies to the final state; for instance, *La Ville de Paris* and *L'Equipe de Cardiff*; the 1910–11 *Tours*, the 1911 *Villes*, the 1912 *Fenêtres* and the 1913 *Formes circulaires* were all evolving series on a set theme. Spate has pointed out that the smaller oils on the *Fenêtres* and *Formes circulaires* themes were never used as studies to be followed carefully in the larger, more complete versions, and that Delaunay worked out each variation *on* the canvas.[60] Late in 1912 and early in 1913 this serial approach to thematic evolution was combined with an increasing need for spontaneity in the execution of ideas, not only in the work of Léger, but also of Francis Picabia and the Futurists.

On his arrival in New York from Paris (January 1913) Picabia gave these concerns especially effective verbal and visual expression. His watercolours on New York and Harlem themes formed series of a manifestly open-ended, evolving kind,[61] and he gave repeated emphasis to spontaneity in the many published statements made during his three-month stay. However, more directly important as a stimulus to Léger was the Futurist approach to spontaneity. Spontaneity was fundamental both in the presentation of their manifestoes, and in the irrational, intuitive manner by which they believed the artist could divine and then express the simultaneous movement of forces around him.[62] Severini suggests that behind this emphasis on spontaneity lay, as behind so much else, the thinking of Henri Bergson.[63] For Bergson, in *L'Evolution créatrice*, intuition was 'instinct which has become disinterested, self-conscious, capable of considering its aims'. It led us, he believed, to the 'very core of life'; and, for him indeed, the 'aesthetic faculty' was itself the intuitive ability to make contact with the movement of life.[64]

René Arcos's *Ce qui naît* of 1911 had tied a central durational theme to a free *vers libre* form,[65] and in the same way the Bergsonian notion of intuition was extended by the Italians implicitly to support a free, evolutionary approach to composition. Thus, in *Le Futurisme* (1911) Marinetti describes Futurist *vers libre* as the 'perpetual dynamism of thought', expressing 'the dynamism of our consciousness', a perpetual becoming.[66] And there is a freely evolving quality about the succession of studies that led up to Boccioni's *Stati d'Animo* at the Bernheim-Jeune exhibition, an accent on evolution found also, perhaps most influentially, in Severini's *Danzatrice* series, and in Boccioni's later series of drawings, oils and sculptures which culminate in the bronze, *Forme uniche della continuità nello spazio*. Boccioni, certainly, aimed in the latter at a clear, conclusive statement, but the evolution of his idea was always free, never planned, and at its beginning lay an intuitive perception of the nature of forms in movement. Again, it is Bergson who provides the fundamental justification: 'The more we dig into the nature of time,' he writes in *L'Evolution créatrice*, 'the more we will understand that duration means invention, the creation of forms, the continual elaboration of the absolutely new.'[67]

But Bergson's attitude was, in fact, closer to that of Léger during 1913–14 than to that of the Futurists, since he considered not only repetition but also the definition of conclusions as activities of the intellect, and saw both as alien to intuition. Indeed, it was possible in 1913 to see his philosophy itself as an evolving, never concluded thesis, for this is the view put forward by René Gillouin in *Montjoie!* no. 4, 29 March 1913: 'In that incomparable book *Evolution créatrice*,' Gillouin writes, 'which is the *De Natura rerum* of our time, M. Bergson was not able and did not wish to mark anything but the essential rhythm and the general direction of life; it is less a philosophy of life than the matrix of every future philosophy of life.'[68]

Allied to Delaunay, Picabia and the Futurists, it was thus as a particularly committed exponent of the Bergsonian approach to life and art that Léger rejected not only the rigid planning of a classical method with its careful succession of studies, but also the certainty of conclusive pictorial statements. He always retained his need for clearly defined compositional ideas during the 1913–14 period, always working by way of studies, usually in gouache or wash, towards set themes,[69] but he could not allow himself the satisfaction of a final statement: every pictorial statement was potentially a new beginning. There was never an *état définitif*.

*   *   *   *   *

Léger's 'dynamic divisionism' had fifteen or sixteen months in which to run its course; at the end of that period, in August 1914, came war, and an experience of reality so violent that his ideas and his painting irrevocably changed. Yet it was a long enough period for the developing progress of his work to declare a direction—hardly marked enough to be called definitely new, but discernible.

Between the first Académie Wassilief lecture of May 1913 and the second of June 1914 there is a detectable shift of emphasis. The first is concerned with the nature of pictorial as against descriptive realism, with the essential values of painting, and with the historical pedigree of the tendency Léger wished to encourage. It only briefly and vaguely touches on the connection between the new 'dynamic divisionism' and 'present-day life'. That such a connection is fundamental is made clear, but Léger emphasizes the purity of the style.[70] The second lecture begins thus: 'Nowadays pictorial realization is the result of the modern way of thinking and is closely linked to the visual aspect of appearances which are, for the painter, inspiring and necessary.'[71] Here Léger is concerned above all with the *connection* between his contrasts and 'present-day life'. His exhaustive exposition of the pure use of contrasting elements for dissonant effect is attached firmly to accounts of actual day-to-day experiences, and he insists that his art is *not* abstract. As has been seen, this declaration of realist intentions does not lead him to demand the depiction of modern, mechanistic subjects, but it does lead him to demand that the raw material of modern life should be related to every pictorial statement in a very tangible way. The change between the first and the second lectures cannot be called fundamental and it is accompanied by no fundamental change in Léger's painting, but it does reveal a shift of emphasis which echoes a

93

52. Fernand Léger: *Le village dans la forêt*, 1914. $51\frac{1}{4} \times 38\frac{1}{4}$ ins, Oeffentliche Kunstssammlung, Basel.

parallel pictorial shift—a shift away from the dynamic declaration of purity for the sake of purity back towards a more open admission of the artist's debt to the first-hand experience of life.

The *Contrastes de formes* were almost exclusively a 1913 series—only a few are dated 1914;[72] apart from these, *all* the other series which continued into the spring and summer of 1914 straightforwardly state a subject. However, the subject in these instances still remains, at least in part, a foil against which to set pictorial effect, as the dynamism of *Le Modèle nu* had been set against the static traditionalism of its subject. Thus, it is not surprising to find that the only theme which was an invention of the six months leading up to the war was developed from a landscape subject, banal almost to the point of naivety, *Le Village dans la forêt*.

In the 1914 Académie Wassilief lecture Léger returned to the remembered experience of smoke and roofs seen from his rue de l'Ancienne-Comédie studio to illustrate how a dynamic grouping of contrasted forms could be found in an observed effect.[73] It is to the old idea of angular houses set against cursive shapes, here the bulbous shapes of trees, that Léger returns with this new landscape theme. And he does so fully conscious that he is confronting the landscapes of Cézanne.

The key to his attitude to Cézanne is found in the 1914 lecture. Here Léger remarks that, although Cézanne seems to have sensed 'plastic contrast', the fact that he lived in a less dynamic and dissonant period prevented him from understanding it, and in particular prevented him from understanding the collision he sensed between houses and trees in the countryside.[74] Léger was himself, he believed, capable of showing just how such a theme—houses and trees—could be transformed by the 'multiple concept' which had fragmented his experience of reality.

There are at least five oil variations on the new landscape theme, each one a development from the last; the largest and most developed version is the *Village dans la forêt* (Plate 52). Never once in the versions that survive does pictorial development mean a move further from legibility. This fact leads inescapably to the conclusion that Léger was very careful not to allow the fact of houses and trees to be obscured by the processes of fragmentation and distortion, that the subject was of constant and fundamental importance to the paintings and that the declaration of purity for the sake of purity no longer mattered. Moreover, though the subject may in a sense remain a foil for the dynamism of pictorial effect, with this series Léger once again makes the point, already tellingly made with the 1911 *Fumées sur les toits*, that the properties of dynamic pictorial conflict can be found in the world of appearances itself. The seated figure of *La Femme dans un fauteuil* is manifestly not the source of pictorial effect. The landscape of the *Village dans la forêt* theme is. Léger demonstrates that modern life has transformed his way of looking at the world so dramatically that he is able to experience its violence in the least violent and least modern of scenes—in a calm, rural landscape. The exclusive purity of the approach which led to the *Contrastes de formes* is denied, and it is perhaps significant that Léger chooses for his new 1914 theme a landscape subject—precisely the subject which had been so completely subordinated to pictorial effect in the development of the *Contrastes*—for in this way, not only does he confront the landscapes of Cézanne with a new purity, but also the *Contrastes* themselves with a new impurity.

The direction tentatively suggested by Léger's 1914 Académie Wassilief lecture and by his 1914 *Village dans la forêt* series was *back* to the subject. Seemingly, 'pure painting' threatened to become for Léger too distant from the first-hand experience of reality. His still indecisive move was the prelude to a change which was to be dramatically decisive, for on 4 August 1914 war was declared, and Léger's attitude to painting entered a new phase of transformation. By the end of the year he was a sapper in the trenches. Suddenly he had left the purified world of the Parisian avant-garde for a world where poets and painters were insignificant oddities, and mechanized violence was the norm. In the face of so dramatic a declaration of the new reality 'pure painting' finally became meaningless; a lifeless irrelevance.

CHAPTER 4
Léger's War, the War-time avant-garde, and *La Partie de cartes*

In 1919, two years after Léger's war at the front had ended, Blaise Cendrars attempted to describe the quality and significance of his friend's art. It was an art, he wrote, 'which declares the transformation of Cubism, indeed its disappearance. Léger moves on into depth and the more he progresses, the more he approaches the subject.'[1] For Cendrars, his friend's work was a declaration of faith in the brutal power of modern subjects—a rejection of the conventional Cubist repertoire of portrait, still-life and landscape. Behind its committed optimism he diagnosed a cause: the war—the experience above all of machines at war: 'Enormous volumes which shift themselves with agility . . . squadrons of aeroplanes, convoys of lorries . . . the breech-block of a 75.'[2]

Léger agreed with Cendrars's diagnosis.[3] 'Three years without touching a paintbrush,' he wrote to Léonce Rosenberg in 1922, 'but contact with reality at its most violent, its most crude . . . the war made me mature, I'm not afraid to say so.'[4]

What was the nature of Léger's war experience? How did it turn him not merely back to the subject, but back to the overtly modern subject? How, if at all, did it change his idea of modern life and of the way painting should create the effect of its dynamic dissonance? Two writers help to give us an idea of what it was like: Cendrars and Henri Barbusse. Barbusse was unconnected with the circle in which Cendrars and Léger moved before the war, but he served like them as a common soldier in the ranks, seeing action in 1915 around Notre-Dame-de-Lorette near Vimy ridge, and his novel *Le Feu* published in November 1916 describes with great sympathy the life and character of the unit with which he fought. It provides a glimpse—sometimes journalistically realistic—of what day-to-day living was like for the ordinary infantryman. Cendrars served as a corporal in the Foreign Legion on the Somme and also around Notre-Dame-de-Lorette, until in the Champagne offensive of September 1915 he lost his arm. Léger was not in contact with him during this time,[5] but in November 1918, when both of them were back in Paris, he illustrated Cendrars's most explosive early attempt to express his experiences at the front, the prose piece *J'ai Tué*, and the feelings conveyed are often close to those of the painter. These feelings find fuller expression combined with a far more extensive description of people and places in his autobiographical *La Main Coupée* published nearly thirty years later. The facts provided by military historians and the day-to-day information provided by press reports allied to the picture composed by Barbusse and Cendrars make it possible to construct an idea of the context in which to see Léger's dozens of drawings made at the front. These *dessins de guerre* are the prime evidence of how 'reality at its most violent, its most crude', the reality into which he was thrown, deepened and broadened his idea of modern life and how ultimately it transformed his art.

* * * * *

Léger did not fight on the same sectors of the front as Barbusse and Cendrars. Where he was and what he did is known, though not in detail, through the information collected by Douglas Cooper,[6] through a few military documents which survive at Biot,[7] through Léger's later statements, and through the many inscriptions, obviously made at the time, on the *dessins de guerre*. He served in the 1e génie (1e Bataillon, 5e compagnie, 5e corps), at first as a sapper, and the earliest indication of his whereabouts is a drawing mentioned by Cooper inscribed 'Le Neufour, le 10-7-15'.[8] Le Neufour is a small village on one of the main routes through the Forêt d'Argonne and it is clear that Léger stayed in the Argonne at least until after September 1915 since other inscriptions give that date coupled with 'Argonne' or 'Le Neufour'.

During 1915 Le Neufour was three or four kilometres behind the first line—well in artillery range of the Germans—and probably served as a rest post for the units engaged.[9] The Forêt d'Argonne, especially late in June and through September, was the scene of the most violent fighting on the entire Western front.[10] It was here that the Germans developed their techniques of intensive bombardment as preliminary to infantry assault, and French losses were heavy—over 26,000 officers and men in the four weeks of the summer attacks, mainly the victims of shelling.[11] The French trenches were often open to the weather and were always in range of the highly sophisticated German trench artillery, the two first lines at times coming close enough to be in grenade range. Between rests of a week or two, units were brought to the point of physical and mental collapse, exposed daily to the weather, the vermin, and the danger of death by typhoid[12] if not by shelling or hand-to-hand combat. The sapper's job was particularly dangerous: they acted as miners digging tunnels beneath 'no-man's-land' for surprise attacks—a strategy used with comparative frequency in the Argonne. Léger's introduction to trench warfare could not have been more merciless.

On 13 October 1915 General Von Mura announced the end of the phase of German attacks in the Argonne, for resources were now required in Champagne, where a strong French offensive was under way, and as backing for a new plan—the attack on Verdun some forty kilometres

Photographie aérienne du fort criblé d'obus avant l'attaque qui nous l'a rendu —

En reprenant le fort de Vaux à l'ennemi qui, pour s'en emparer, avait fait tuer des dizaines de milliers d'hommes, les admirables soldats du général Mangin ont reconstitué dans son intégrité le camp retranché de "la plus puissante forteresse" du principal ennemi". En dix jours nous avons repris ce que les Allemands avaient mis cinq mois à nous arracher avec des pertes qui ne dépassent pas le nombre des prisonniers capturés. Cette photo très agrandie a été prise au-dessus du fort à 2.600ᵐ d'altitude.

53. 'Le fort de Vaux reconquis le 2 novembre', *Le Miroir,* Paris, 19 November 1916.

east of the forest. Until February the war for Léger was certainly a little quieter and a series of gouache and wash drawings marked 'A' for Aisne and dated '16' (Plates 61, 62 and 63) indicate that he was posted to a less dangerous area.[13] On 21 February 1916 the Battle of Verdun opened and with it a phase in Léger's war probably even more testing than the Argonne phase, for it was at Verdun that the intensive bombardment techniques rehearsed in the forest attacks of the previous summer reached their destructive apogee. From February until the summer, bombardment followed bombardment and counterattack followed counterattack with efficient ferocity as the Germans moved forward from Fort Douaumont, finally by July almost as far as Fort Souville.[14] Léger, now a stretcher bearer, was at the front for most of this time,[15] and he was there again in the autumn when the French turned the Germans back. On 15 September he sent a postcard to Jeanne, his future wife, who was now living in his new Parisian studio at 86, rue Notre-Dame-des-Champs, saying he was 'off to the front'.[16] Very shortly afterwards his unit was moved up ready for action, since a postcard drawing of a '100 de marine' gun sent from the Verdun area to another friend in Paris, Yvonne Dangel, is inscribed '13-10-16', a week before the French artillery bombardment which announced Nivelle's counterstroke. It shows one of the guns brought up in readiness. The French bombardment lasted four days and on 24 October came the advance, the French gaining some three to four kilometres from Fleury and Souville to Fort Douaumont. Léger was there, probably just behind the first line of advance,[17] and made many quick pencil sketches inscribed 'Route de Souville' or 'Route de Fleury' dated the 24th. The advance exhilarated him and he sent a drawing of two dead Frenchmen—*Les deux tués* (Plate 59)—to Yvonne Dangel with a short note, stating proudly: 'It bears a celebrated date, that of the retaking of Douaumont. The sketch was made that very day in the middle of a rather ordinary artillery concert.'[18] On that day, with Verdun a heap of rubble and the country north of it a cratered desert (Plate 53), the German effort was brought forcibly to a halt, and Léger was one of the survivors.

The Battle of Verdun lasted eight months; in those months more than 300,000 French soldiers died. General Pétain and then General Nivelle organized their forces so that no unit spent more than four days at a time on the first line, but even behind the line, at rest, men were in constant danger from the German heavy artillery. Verdun itself, which was always ten kilometres or more behind the first line, was systematically destroyed during the battle by artillery fire. A glimpse of what Léger saw during those months is provided in his 1954 interview with Dora Vallier when he describes a soldier 'reduced to pap' by a shell—not an uncommon event.[19] He would certainly have seen the worst both behind and in the first line because the stretcher bearers lived with the infantry units in the trenches and charged with them, actually carrying their stretchers.[20] Historical accounts can evoke little of the sheer horror of destruction that Léger must have experienced there—Henri Barbusse's fictional sergeant in *Le Feu*, a veteran of Verdun, comes closer to an effective evocation with his description of trees reaped like corn, of bodies tossed spiralling fifteen metres into the air by blasts which could wipe out thirty men at a time, of the shattered houses in Verdun itself, of the sense of defencelessness, the terror, 'which for months never ceased'.[21]

Léger stayed in and around Verdun through December, making dated sketches of the ruined town (Plate 66); as the battle reverted to the still dangerous monotony of normal trench warfare he continued to survive and he continued to draw. Then, at last, after more than two years exposed to violent death, in the spring of 1917 he escaped. He was gassed on the Aisne front, and his war ended.

*   *   *   *   *

99

We glorify war, the only purifier of the world.[22]

Marinetti had as early as 1909 aligned the Futurist commitment to dynamism and dissonance with a passionate glorification of war. The ideal of violence in art reflected an ideal of violence in life, and in October 1913 Marinetti, Boccioni, Carrà and Russolo signed the *Programma Politico Futurista*, which declared as a central demand the initiation of popular national violence in war.[23] German militarism satisfied the Futurist dream and Marinetti dubbed 1915 'this futurist year'.[24] In Rome and Milan he organized anti-neutrality demonstrations, and his plea for action, 'Guerra sola igiene del mondo', was published. War was, for him: 'The school of ambition and heroism all must attend.'[25] Marinetti's pitiless romanticism would have found dramatic fulfilment in Argonne and Verdun in 1915 and 1916.

Of the Futuristically inclined in the Parisian avant-garde, Ricciotto Canudo was at least one who celebrated the drama of front-line fighting, but both Léger and Cendrars looked for something other than the spectacle. Ironically enough, the war did not exaggerate the Futurist bent already so strong in Léger; it emphasized instead the essentially independent force of his realist convictions. He did not explosively represent scenes of explosive action in the Argonne and at Verdun, his subjects were most often calm everyday scenes. There are exceptions, but the *dessins de guerre* are most of all his records of daily life as a soldier, they are about the ordinary rather than the extraordinary aspects of his war experience. His unit would have spent only a few days at a time actually in the first line and then he would have known heavy physical work under fire, digging as a sapper or carrying the wounded as a stretcher bearer; he would not often have known the thrilling rush of an assault.[26] Even for Cendrars, who courted danger on the front, such moments of excitement were rare in the routine of an infantryman's life,[27] and Barbusse makes it clear that both in the first line and behind it the monotony of waiting far exceeded the thrill either of aggression or fear: 'It's all waiting in war. We have become machines for waiting.'[28] He describes a day-to-day existence in which, between isolated moments of destructive madness, the simplest pursuits—eating, smoking, letter-writing—assume enormous importance. Léger does not celebrate a Futurist dream, he records a less glorious reality—most of all, the subjects that presented themselves as he waited.

The need simply to report the nature of life in the trenches as authentically as possible is conveyed very strongly in the work both of Barbusse and of Cendrars. Barbusse's *Le Feu* is close to journalism, and Cendrars recalls in *La Main Coupée* that he took a camera to the front, photographing the men of his unit, explosions, bombardments, old corpses in the barbed-wire and the *poilus* he lived with, sending the results to the popular illustrated magazine *Le Miroir*.[29] Léger himself never used a camera on the front, but a look at his choice of subjects for the *dessins de guerre* alongside the hundreds of war photographs published in *Le Miroir* during 1915 and 1916 reveals that he too seems to have selected from his surroundings with very much a journalist's priorities, looking more for the authentic than for the violently dramatic.

There were, of course, photographs of action in *Le Miroir* as in the other illustrated magazines, *Le Monde Illustré* and *L'Illustration*—photographs

54. (left) Fernand Léger: *Cuisine roulante,* 1915. Pen and ink on paper, $8 \times 6\frac{1}{4}$ ins, Musée National Fernand Léger, Biot.

55. (below) 'Une Route nouvelle sur un champ de bataille ravagé de la Somme', *Le Miroir.* Paris, 8 October 1916.

of soldiers crawling prone under fire, of units scrambling forward in attack, and of shell-bursts—but there were also *types* of front-line photograph which recorded less dramatic events and certain of these closely parallel or anticipate groups of front-line drawings produced by Léger. Thus, the group of pen drawings made in the Argonne of horse-drawn supply wagons on their way to the line record a subject which would have been familiar to the point of boredom for any *poilu* on the march (Plate 54), but which also occurs on occasion, viewed from precisely the same angle in the illustrations of *Le Miroir* during 1915 and 1916 (Plate 55).[30] Thus too, a popular genre of front-line photograph was the town or village after the bombardment—a genre which enjoyed a special vogue in postcards, and Léger's drawings of Verdun after the bombardment find a close parallel in many such postcards (Plates 65 and 66) as well as in the illustrated page dedicated to the ruined city in *Le Miroir* (16 July 1916).[31] And again (this time in action), a popular genre was the infantry assault seen from behind, the photographer himself obviously moving forward among the troops, and Léger's drawings of the advance of 24 October 1916 are on occasion very much of this type (Plate 56), anticipated by analogous photographs and closely paralleling the extraordinary records of the same event which appeared a month later in *Le Miroir* (Plate 57). His backview figures, weighed down by their greatcoats, create the same authentic *un*dynamic effect, and the sketchy technique echoes the unfocused fuzziness so essential to the on-the-spot conviction of the *Miroir* photographs. Yet certainly the

56. (left) Fernand Léger: *Sur la route de Fleury,* 24 October 1916. Pencil on paper, $6\frac{3}{4} \times 5\frac{1}{4}$ ins, Henriette Gomès collection, Paris.

57. (below) 'Quelques phases de l'assaut qui, le 24 Octobre fit retomber le Fort de Douaumont entre nos mains', *Le Miroir,* Paris, 19 November 1916.

most extraordinary indication of the parallel between Léger's coverage of front-line themes and that of the photographers is the fact that the subject of one important drawing made during the advance of 24 October seems actually to have been in part suggested by a photograph. The cover of *Le Miroir* a fortnight before takes as its subject the tumbling, broken forms of two dead soldiers in a shell-hole (Plate 58),[32] exactly the subject of *Les deux tués,* the drawing so proudly sent as a memento of the retaking of Douaumont to Yvonne Dangel (Plate 59). Léger needed actually to experience the two corpses in a shell-hole at first hand before he could draw it, but his decision to select that particular subject and endow it with special significance in so finished a drawing must, at least subliminally, have been influenced by *Le Miroir.*[33]

The subjects of the *dessins de guerre* were, in the final analysis, the subjects not of a Futurist nor of a chronicler concerned with the scale and significance of events, but of a realist with an eye for the authentic. Moreover, they are popular subjects in a very definite sense, being the kind of subjects chosen for the popular illustrated magazines. The importance of this last point is demonstrated best of all by the subject of the largest group of *dessins de guerre*—the common soldier himself, the *poilu* at rest, on the move, or wounded. The *poilu* is the central hero not only of *La Main Coupée* but also of Barbusse's *Le Feu;* indeed, so strong was Cendrars's sense of identity with the men of his unit that in *La Main Coupée* he recalls how he refused to leave them to become a sergeant.[34] For him, as for Barbusse, as

APRÈS UN DUEL A MORT ENTRE UN FRANÇAIS ET UN ALLEMAND DEVANT COMBLES

L'offensive qui devait nous donner Combles les a mis face à face dans une tranchée bouleversée. Comme les guerriers de jadis, ils ont lutté corps à corps de toute leur vigueur, de toute leur haine, jusqu'à la mort.

58.   The cover of *Le Miroir*, Paris, 8 October 1916.

59.   Fernand Léger: *Sur la route de Fleury, les deux tués,* 24 October 1916. Pen and ink on post-card, $4\frac{3}{4} \times 3\frac{1}{4}$ ins, private collection, France.

for Léger, the war was not a chance merely to become absorbed in the energy of a technological melodrama, it was a chance to live with and become involved in the lives of ordinary men. Thus, Léger afterwards repeatedly insists on the importance of the *poilus* themselves in persuading him to move back to a more overt, a more straightforward realism, and, in a sense, the subjects he chooses are the subjects they might have chosen—a point supported by the fact that many of the *Miroir* photographers were *poilus* as well, like Cendrars.[35] In 1915 and 1916, in the Argonne and at Verdun, Léger not only saw modern reality in all its mechanized dynamism as never before, but identified with a group of men utterly alien to the avant-garde 'elite'—to use Canudo's mode of addressing them—from which he had come in Paris. His approach both to reality and to the way that reality should be given pictorial expression was profoundly changed as a consequence, and the range of the subjects which he chose to record is but one symptom of this change.

Barbusse sums up the distance between the new front-line circle in which Léger moved for two years and the avant-garde circle he had left. His feelings when he writes of the men in his unit indicate, even if imperfectly, something of the need Léger must have felt to change his priorities as an artist, to move back closer to the reality of popular themes:

We are combatants . . . and in this war almost no intellectuals, artists, almost none of the well-off have risked themselves at the loopholes or under the tin hats, even briefly . . . . In spite of age differences, differences of background, culture, position, everything, in spite of the great gaps that once separated us, we are in general terms the same. Within the same rough outline, there are hidden and revealed the same pattern of life, habits, the same simplified nature of men who have returned to the primitive state.[36]

If Cendrars and Barbusse are to be believed, the *poilus* were too immersed in the squalor, danger and boredom of front-line life to find it splendid. It is not, therefore, surprising that Léger's realism led him away from the Futurist obsession with war as the ultimate festival of violence and as the ultimate glory. 'War is filth,' said Cendrars to an enthusiast on the front.[37] War was never the cause of celebration in the *dessins de guerre*.

*   *   *   *   *

How then, if at all, did the style or styles of Léger's *dessins de guerre* reflect the change of priorities suggested by his popular subjects? Did he in any significant way adjust his pictorial values according to the special qualities of what he saw and recorded?

Léger was not alone as an artist sketching on the front. During 1915 certain of the more conservative painters on the fringe of the pre-war avant-garde—Dunoyer de Segonzac, Luc-Albert Moreau, Jean Marchand and André Favory—sent back drawings to Amédée Ozenfant's Parisian review *L'Elan,* and their most common theme was the *poilu*. In *Au repos,* reproduced in *L'Elan* no. 6, late in 1915 (Plate 61),[38] Segonzac applies a light, nervous pen technique to the job of noting at speed the essentials of grouping and posture, of particular *poilus* in a particular place and time. Léger needed to do much more than merely record. If the dynamic Futurist fantasy did not persuade him to glory in the violence of war, the qualities of dissonance, contrast and machine dynamism brought to the fore by his pre-war pictorial experiments remained central to the way he absorbed and set down the reality of the trenches. Thus, even though Léger's pencil sketch of soldiers in a shelter (Plate 60), one of many, shares with Segonzac's drawing a need to capture the essentials of grouping and posture, it shows a need right from the beginning to simplify forms in order to extract dissonant contrasting effects, and it was these effects that Léger focused on in more finished pen drawings like *Soldats dans un abri* (Plate 62). The solid, geometricized components of the *poilus* are pulled together as the rotating core of the drawing, their rotation set dramatically against the insistent verticals of the trees, and by means of varied hatchings and cross-hatchings Léger achieves with his areas of shading an effect both of volume and of flat surface contrast directly comparable with the flat colour-patch contrasts of his pre-war paintings. The result is a long way from Segonzac's acute graphic journalism, and Léger's lack of sympathy with the descriptiveness of a straightforwardly journalistic approach is underlined by the *collage* made on a piece of shell-crate which was worked

60. Fernand Léger: *Soldats dans un abri*, 1915. Pencil on paper, $8 \times 6\frac{1}{4}$ ins, Henriette Gomès collection, Paris.

61. Dunoyer de Segonzac: *Au repos, L'Elan,* Paris, no 6.

62. (left)   Fernand Léger: *Soldats dans un abri*, 1915. Pen and ink on paper, $7\frac{1}{2} \times 5\frac{1}{4}$ ins, private collection, France.

63. (right)   Fernand Léger: *Les Joueurs aux cartes*, September 1915. Oil and 'papier collé' on wooden fragment of crate, 39×26 ins, Dr and Mrs Israel Rosen collection, Baltimore.

up from the pen drawing, the *Joueurs aux cartes* (Plate 63). Here, as in 1913 and 1914, outlines drawn at speed precede white highlights coupled with colour patches (red, blue and yellow paper with white oil paint), and the roughness of the untreated wood accentuates the flatness of the effect, creating an image altogether as concentrated and dynamic as any developed in the purer circumstances of peacetime Montparnasse.[39] Only the fading of the red and yellow scraps of paper has subdued its force. Given the chance of a month in his studio at the end of 1915, Léger, it seems, would have translated his Argonne experiences into pictorial results often still at one with his earlier dissonant ideals. However journalistic his choice of subject may have been, and however plainly he set out to declare the identity of that subject, he remained determined to make a direct impact with contrasting pictorial elements on a flat surface.

Léger may not have celebrated the drama of violence on the front, but at the same time he could not ignore it—mechanical destruction was always present, even if only in the background or in the distance. His pre-war art of contrasts allowed him to find in the calmest of subjects—the inward-looking immobility of his friends playing cards—something of the machine force so mercilessly released around them. The new, brutal reality of the Argonne gave fresh purpose to old means.

*　　*　　*　　*　　*

106

64. Fernand Léger: *Paysage en Argonne,* 1915. Pen and ink on post-card, $3\frac{1}{2} \times 4\frac{1}{2}$ ins, Yvonne Dangel collection, Paris.

It is an index of the new and growing importance of Léger's subject-matter that, where in 1913 and 1914 every subject invited the same stylistic treatment, in 1916, on the Aisne front and at Verdun, different types of subject began to encourage different types of treatment, so that the nature of graphic effect increasingly, though never altogether, became the direct function of subject-matter. The drawings and gouaches made during 1916 can be grouped by subject into three distinct categories, all of which are anticipated by the Argonne drawings; drawings of the front-line setting—town and country; drawings of guns and aircraft; and drawings of *poilus*—on the move, resting, wounded and dead. Both the drawings of front-line settings and the drawings of machines declare, even if not always, new stylistic directions which on occasion follow from the subject, which have no precedent in Léger's 'dynamic divisionism', and which are therefore the exclusive progeny of his war experience.

Just as men at rest behind the front were for Léger charged with the potential for violence, so, both in the Argonne and afterwards, places where there was still calm enough to pause and sketch contained a dynamic force to be released in his drawings. Already in the Argonne he had applied what for him were new as well as old graphic means in order to release this force from the quietness of a country scene. *Paysage en Argonne* (Plate 64), sent as a postcard to Yvonne Dangel in September 1915, is Léger's record—'slightly cubist'[40]—of a particularly perfect moment of rural peace; only the presence of two soldiers hints at the near-by noise of war (it was the time of the last desperate German attacks). Yet he succeeds in creating, without either repeating the means used in the *Village dans la forêt* series or sacrificing the identity of his subject, an all-over graphic

108

force of some intensity. This is achieved by the collision of contradictory forms and linear directions, but most prophetically of all it is achieved on the left of the drawing by the collision of two contradictory spaces—a kind of contrast unprecedented in Léger's work. Slightly at an angle, the vertical of a treetrunk rises to literally cut the space of the scene in two, like a fault in rock strata. Here, a new kind of disruptive technique accompanies a return to the disruptive, discontinuous and dispersed kind of composition which had preceded Léger's 'dynamic divisionism'—the compositional mode of *La Femme en bleu*. It was a compositional mode particularly well suited to the dispersed open-air qualities of this kind of landscape *motif*— much more so than the centrifugal unity of the *Village dans la forêt* canvases —and *Paysage en Argonne* suggests that Léger's return to it may have been the natural result of his return to the first-hand observation of landscape subjects on the front.

The group of scribbled pen-and-ink sketches of the town of Verdun made in December 1916 after the bombardment of the summer and autumn are undoubtedly the most inherently violent of all Léger's attempts to draw front-line settings.[41] Here there is an obvious drama in the subject itself, but still Léger avoids action for the calm of the aftermath: the pyramids and columns of stone stand among the surviving trees like grotesque monuments. The shells have ceased to fall with the German retreat. Yet, a *motif* so brutally vandalized could not have offered more ideal raw material; Léger himself did not need to fragment, twist and break open what he saw, the high-explosive shells had done that already. *Verdun, la rue Mazel* (Plate 66) is typical of the shattered compositions—dispersed and disruptive rather than centrifugal and continuous—which were the predictable outcome of what he saw. The ruins of the town are flung across the paper as an uncoordinated chaos of formal collisions—advertising letters against buildings, buildings against telegraph poles, roofs against sky, the only unbroken succession of forms in the drawing to give the effect of rhythmic continuity being the flying succession of clouds. It would have taken a drive towards pure pictorial effect of extreme, even blind obstinacy, to extract a unified rotating movement of volumes from scenes like those recorded in the postcards of the time (Plate 65). Here it seems certain that the return to a dispersed and disruptive compositional mode *was* the direct consequence of Léger's subject.

'We are beneath a vault of shells,' writes Cendrars in *J'ai Tué* . . . 'There are locomotives in the air, invisible trains, collisions, concertina crashes. The double blow of the "rimailhos" is counted. The puffing of the 240 . . . The mad cat-call of the 75. An arch opens over our heads.'[42] Cendrars could not have known bombardments to compare with those Léger knew in the Argonne and especially at Verdun; to Léger, already so struck by the gleaming geometry of aero-engines, the power and precise efficiency of the guns used by the French and the Germans in 1915 and 1916 must have seemed stupendous. It was, it will be remembered, his heightened awareness of machines that Cendrars specifically mentioned when in 1919 he wrote of the impact of the war on Léger's work, and Léger himself was often equally specific on the point. If there was after all and without doubt a sense in which he echoed the Futurist desire to celebrate war, it was in his desire to celebrate 'the geometric and mechanical

65. (left) *Verdun, la rue Mazel,* after the bombardment of 1916. Post-card.

66. (left) Fernand Léger: *Verdun, la rue Mazel,* 1916. Pen and ink on paper, $11\frac{3}{4} \times 7\frac{1}{2}$ ins, galerie Claude Bernard, Paris.

67. (right) Fernand Léger: *Hissage de forme mobile,* 1916. Pencil on paper, $7\frac{3}{4} \times 5\frac{1}{2}$ ins, Henriette Gomès collection, Paris.

splendour'[43] of machinery in war, for that plainly was the desire that lay behind his drawings of guns and aircraft.

So adaptable were the machines of war to his 1913–14 'dynamic division-ism' that his 1916 drawings of them are almost all, like the Argonne drawings of *poilus* and supply-trains, reaffirmations of his earlier approach. What is new is that, instead of hiding their machine identity beneath the conventional subjects of figure-painting, still-life and landscape, they declare that identity straightforwardly, as fact. In the Verdun drawing *Hissage de forme mobile* (Plate 67) Léger explores once again the collision between tubular volumes and angular planes but he makes it absolutely clear that this is a formal collision found in the observed forms of a French gun emplacement. Where so often in the series of 1913 and 1914 there had been a contradiction between subject and style, which exposed the in-significance of the subject, in these studies there is an obvious close connection between subject and style, which reinstates the modern subject —the machine as machine.

111

68.   Fernand Léger: *L'Avion brisé*, 1916. Wash and gouache on paper, 9¾ × 12 ins, Musée National Fernand Léger, Biot.

In two of the 1916 war machine studies Léger went further than a mere reaffirmation of his pre-war pictorial approach: his new mechanical subjects suggested new pictorial directions which were to be of great importance after the war. *L'Avion brisé* (Plate 68) is one of a group of gouaches executed on the Aisne front. The subject is a crashed aircraft, and Léger takes a side view to create a novel dynamic effect. Beneath a sharp, angular rhythm of green-tinged fields, the gay orange wings and flanks of the aircraft flow together in a waving, rocking motion so that the effect is produced of two contrary lateral movements across the sheet, something different from the rotating movements which were the dynamic rule in Léger's 1913 and 1914 series. The contrast is still between cursive and angular, but a fresh view of a fresh machine subject (the Salon de l'Aviation exhibit *after* the event) has suggested a new way of rhythmically pulling forms together in a unity of contrasts.

The second of the forward-looking war machine studies is also from the

69. Fernand Léger:
Paysage du front, 1916.
Wash and gouache on
paper, Musée National
Fernand Léger, Biot.

Aisne front group of gouaches, *Paysage du front* (Plate 69), but it is altogether more radically novel. Here it is not the subject as such that stimulates
novelty, but Léger's decision to completely transform and reconstruct it,
using with some daring techniques of fragmentation and cutting that
recall his 1912 flirtation with the Futurist notion of simultaneity. The
bloated volume of an observation balloon rises to float in an architecture
of narrow vertical slats which tie it securely to the paper edge. From
behind these slats, as if contained in small compartments, emerge other
items—wheels and ladders being the most obviously recognizable. A
dispersed, disjointed machine composition is created where the fragmented elements of the machine subject are scattered among alien abstract
planes, which act with angular sharpness to cut them off from each other.
An uncompromising simultanist approach, careless of spatial unity, has
allowed Léger to arrive at a new kind of machine image, alien to the
rotating continuity of his pre-war 'dynamic divisionism'. This gouache
makes it clear that even before the Battle of Verdun Léger knew that his
intensified involvement with reality on the front need not necessarily
lead him back to an art of simplified if dynamic representation, that he
could still fragment and translate the forms of his new subjects to a very
high degree, creating an image which, for him, isolated their essential
qualities with great pictorial effectiveness. However, *Paysage du front* is a
rare experiment; Léger was too close to his subjects for so drastically destructive a pictorial treatment to be repeated often in 1916. It is very much
an isolated prelude to the pictorial themes of peace.

113

70. 'Couloir de l'infirmerie, Verdun, 1916.' From an album of photographs taken by General Mangin in 1916. Bibliothèque National, Paris.

At Verdun and on the Aisne front the *poilu* was far too important a figure for his identity to be destroyed in the interests of pictorial action, and the many drawings of *poilus* are especially clear statements of their subject. As in the Argonne, Léger's starting-point with *poilu* subjects was the quick first-hand sketch, usually in pencil, and many of these rough records survive at Biot. Most of those done before the French counter-offensive of 24 October are of the stretcher bearer's life off-duty behind the lines, under canvas or in dug-outs (Plate 70): the men sit and talk, turn to greet friends or play their interminable games of cards.[44] The accent remains on speed of line to grasp the essentials of grouping, pose and gesture; there is some formal simplification, but compositions are dispersed, their figurative components not yet pulled together into strong centrifugal movements (Plate 71). Yet, again as in the Argonne, it is clear that these on-the-spot sketches were considered as no more than a preliminary stage in the processing of reality, since there are other more considered *poilu* drawings where the precise description of gesture is of little importance and where the raw material collected from first-hand sketching is further simplified and rearranged to create a dynamic centrifugal image. In dealing with the human figure, as so often in dealing with the war machine subject, Léger continued to reaffirm his pre-war pictorial values.

Fragment, Etude pour La Partie de cartes (Plate 72) is one of the more considered *poilu* studies. One of a closely related pair drawn on the Aisne front early in 1916,[45] it restates the subject of the Argonne *Soldats dans un abri* (Plate 62), but Léger rediscovers the subject in the cramped and oppressive gloom of a subterranean dug-out. He therefore can concentrate even more closely than in the card-player *collage* (Plate 63) on the figures bent inwards around the table, and with this closer focus comes a more condensed centrifugal composition. The table is lit by two candles and its surface is broken by ridged lines which fan outwards as if to materialize the candlelight. Around this central area the heads, limbs and torsos of the card-players are rotated, their curved surfaces and shaping contrasted with the broken angular planes of the table and the timbered dug-out walls. Once more a dynamic violence is extracted from a scene of quiet concentration, and once more the process of geometric simplification has subordinated the individual characters of the *poilus* to a uniform sense of the mechanistically solid. Yet, much more than in the Argonne drawing,

114

71. (right) Fernand Léger: *Soldats jouant aux cartes*, 1916. Pencil on paper, 5¾ × 4¼ ins, Musée National Fernand Léger, Biot.

72. (below) Fernand Léger: *Fragment, Etude pour La Partie de cartes,* 1916. Pen and ink on paper, 7 × 8¾ ins, Museum of Modern Art, New York (gift of Mr and Mrs Daniel Saidenberg).

73. (left) Fernand Léger: *Le Soldat à la pipe*, 1916. $51\frac{1}{4} \times 38\frac{1}{4}$ ins, Kunstssammlung Nordrhein Westfalen, Düsseldorf.

74. (right) Fernand Léger: *Fe Fumeur*, 1914. $39\frac{1}{2} \times 32$ ins, Bragaline collection, New York.

Léger here modulates his areas of shading to stress illusionistically the solid reality of the *poilus*, and thus, more than before he begins to challenge the flat divided surface, to model. He may reassert the pre-war pictorial values of his 'dynamic divisionism' but in this partial way his revived sense of duty to the subject undermines those values.

Perhaps the most convincing evidence that the *poilu* was for Léger the most deeply significant of his 1916 subjects, is the fact that when at last a few weeks' leave in Paris gave him the chance to paint on a relatively large scale, he chose to paint neither front-line settings nor guns nor crashed aircraft, but his mechanistically forceful idea of the *poilu*. The result was the coarsely worked oil, *Le Soldat à la pipe* (Plate 73), whose origins lie in drawings made at the Verdun front of a single wounded *poilu* sitting with his tunic unbuttoned and head bandaged, waiting.

Le Soldat à la pipe, being his first war painting, is the first product of Léger's war experience which can directly be compared with his pre-war work. From it can therefore be gathered an especially clear idea of how his decision to declare the modern identity of his subjects influenced his attitude to pictorial effect even when his aim remained dynamically dissonant in a broadly pre-war sense. The obvious pre-war counterpart is a 1914 variation of *Femme en rouge et vert* in which the feminine identity of the figure has been challenged by the addition of a pipe; this is *Le Fumeur* (Plate 74). The pose and setting of Leger's pre-war figure are remarkably close—indeed, were it not for the rough pencil preliminaries that survive, one would be tempted to conclude that *Le Soldat à la pipe* was *Le Fumeur* slightly rearranged and dressed in uniform. Yet, however slight the change of posture, Léger's presentation of the figure is in an important sense new. The brilliantly coloured volumes of *Le Fumeur* have been replaced by volumes modelled in gun-metal grey, bringing the descriptive suggestions implicit in the tonal modelling of the Aisne front card-player *Fragment* to the most straightforward of pictorial conclusions. No longer a scintillating play of colour patches flat on the picture-surface, the head, limbs and torso of the figure unequivocally assert his weight and solidity, and at the same time his identity as machine-man.

The idea of man as machine had been strong in Henri-Martin Barzun's 1912 *Hymne des Forces*, and its origins predictably lay in the ideas and ideals of the Futurists. Marinetti in particular conceived of modern man as evolving towards a more and more emphatically mechanical physical form.[46] Though pure in their emphasis on pictorial effect, there can be no doubt that Léger's 1913–14 figure series, by wedding the machine-like and the human in so all-embracing a way, gave convincing expression to the machine-man idea. *Le Fumeur* is a particularly clear pre-war statement of the theme, but with *Le Soldat à la pipe* it is given an altogether new clarity of definition. This certainly is in part the *raison d'être* behind Léger's return to the gun-metal grey of simple tonal modelling. The war so deepened the significance of the machine-man metaphor that he could not but underline its significance in his work—the deadening of surfaces paid high dividends in terms of content. His experience showed him, it seems, that the *poilu* was not merely evidence of the energy and the strength of character possessed by ordinary men, but evidence of the ultimate anonymity of the individual in the context of great armies, subject to the sheer power of mechanized warfare. In *J'ai Tué* Cendrars describes himself face to face with: 'The torpedo, the gun, mines, fire, gas, machine guns, all the anonymous, demoniac, systematic, blind machinery [of war].'[47] Léger condenses into the figure of his wounded *poilu* something of his intensified awareness of that force and at the same time—with great simplicity—a strong sense of its blind, mechanistic anonymity and of its power to make everything absorbed into it equally anonymous.

Finally, the figure has acquired a new stability, without loss of impact, for, where the rotating succession of geometric volumes and colour patches in the pre-war *Le Fumeur* is uninterrupted, here in *Le Soldat à la pipe* Léger interrupts the continuity of movement in a way which looks back to *La Femme en bleu*. Vertical planes slice down into the right shoulder and the features of the face are abruptly cut into by a jagged area of red. The violence of collision generates dissonant force and there is enough successive rhythm to generate dynamic effect too, but, as in *La Femme en bleu*, the violence of movement is disciplined by the stabilizing influence of verticals. The lessons relearned above all in the 1916 gouache *Paysage du front* (Plate 69) are applied to add a more balanced sense of structure. The uncompromising verve and idealism of Barzun and the Futurists is challenged by a machine-man image which is both more sombre in its metallic greys and more dignified in its intimations of stability—the image more of a realist confronted with the actual effects of mechanized warfare, than of a dreamer immersed in visions of mechanical power.

*   *   *   *   *

Back at Verdun after his 1916 leave, Léger covered, as has been seen, the full range of his war subjects, drawing the French heavy guns positioned for the October bombardment and the ruins of Verdun itself in December (Plate 66). Yet, most significantly, he made a series of drawings culminating in a pair of water-colours, which were aimed at the composition of another major pictorial theme dedicated to the machine-man image of the *poilu*. The series is called *Les Foreurs* and came to its conclusion in December 1916.[48] That a final large-scale painting was envisaged is indicated by the fact that Léger went as far as colour studies, and that one of the more elaborate drawings is inscribed optimistically 'dessin pour les foreurs'.

From the isolated anonymity of *Le Soldat à la pipe*, Léger turns in the trench-digger theme to the uniformity of *poilus* working together—a group digging themselves in—a subject which, treated on his mechanistically simplified terms, could convey not only the machine-man metaphor in military uniform, but also that sense of group identity—'the same simplified nature'—characteristic of the infantry unit, especially as described by Henri Barbusse. The enforced intimacy and unison of action that Léger experienced in his unit on the front seems to have brought back to the surface of his consciousness the Unanimist feeling for the group which had so concerned him at the time of *La Noce*—his last pre-war excursion into the painting of popular, contemporary subjects. This feeling for the Unanimity of the group is already conveyed in the earlier studies of *poilus*, and so it is not surprising that the single figure of *Le Soldat à la pipe* should have given way to the group subject which could convey a broader and deeper idea of the *poilu* on the front.

However, Léger's sketches for *Les Foreurs* led to no great painting, for in the spring of 1917 he was gassed. Safe in hospital it was another *poilu* group subject that was to channel his energies towards a large-scale painting, *La Partie de cartes* (Colour Plate 5). Here, at last, the reinstatement of the modern popular subject was conclusively declared on canvas, and the bright, divided surfaces of 'dynamic divisionism' were conclusively rejected. It was with this work that Léger looked forward to a new period of peace with a new sense of priorities as a realist—a period in which the potential not only of his machine-man simplifications but of his straight-forward machine studies, his revival of dispersed and disruptive compositions, and his experiments in simultanist fragmentation could be fully realized on a large public scale, on canvas. The war did not disturb his fundamental idea of the modern world as mechanistic and violent—indeed, it deepened this conviction. What it did was finally to convince him that he should declare openly in his painting the existence of this mechanistic violence in modern places, modern things and modern men; and out of this return to the subject came new pictorial directions allied to a profound reappraisal of the old.

*   *   *   *   *

La Partie de cartes is a very elaborate and highly finished painting. It is larger than any pre-war Léger other than *La Noce*, and behind its high finish lies a period of gestation far longer and more exhaustive than ever before. On the back of the canvas is the inscription: 'fait à Paris en con-

119

valescence, décembre, 1917', but the origins of the work lie in the Argonne more than two years before. It was an expansive, carefully rehearsed pictorial gesture, which, though not exhibited in 1918, declared with the insistence of a manifesto Léger's new direction, away from 'pure painting'. For Léger, in 1954, it was his first attempt 'deliberately to extract [his] subject from the times'.[49]

Although *Le Soldat à la pipe* is the *poilu* as machine-man, the fact of the figure's military identity is not made clear—the *képi* is half-concealed and there are no tabs or buttons to make recognition immediate. Buttons, stripes, medals, *képis* and helmets all pointedly announce the military identity of Léger's card-playing *poilus*. Here, therefore, for the first time in a full-scale painting Léger emphatically and conspicuously found his subject in 'the times'. He finally rejected the conventional figure-painting, still-life and landscape subjects of his pre-war 'dynamic divisionism'.

La Partie de cartes, marking as it did Léger's return from relative isolation in the trenches, can with meaning be situated in a Parisian avant-garde context. In the perspective of war-time avant-garde activity, one can begin to understand the way in which Léger's new priorities were to relate to post-war Paris, and to those developed by the artists and poets who stayed away from the front.

With Léger and *La Partie de cartes* as the reference-point for the inquiry, the question is: did the common idea of a dynamic, dissonant art dedicated to the machine and modern life survive the war years, and, if not, what replaced it?

The war robbed Paris of many others besides Léger and Blaise Cendrars. Ricciotto Canudo, the leading spirit behind *Montjoie!*, volunteered for the Foreign Legion with Cendrars. Guillaume Apollinaire, the leading spirit behind *Soirées de Paris*, was by the end of 1914 an artillery officer. Of the artists, among those quickly in uniform were Duchamp-Villon, de La Fresnaye and Georges Braque, while the war kept away from Paris Gleizes and Picabia, who were at first in New York, and the Delaunays, who travelled to the security of the Iberian peninsula. Avant-garde activity was kept alive in Paris by the presence of the foreigners and of those not strong enough in health to fight. Especially prominent from the first were Picasso and Juan Gris, but the chief representative of the pre-war tendency towards a dynamic art dedicated to modern life was Gino Severini, who, initially driven by the war to Barcelona, had returned to Paris by July 1915.[50]

Severini's pre-war celebration of the dynamic and the mechanical had reached a very high pitch by the August 1914 declaration of war, combining poetic modern images—trains, the Metro, guns—with words, force-lines and colours in a complex style, more literary than the literary simultanism of Delaunay's *L'Equipe de Cardiff* (Plate 44) or *Hommage à Blériot* (Plate 43). His paintings on war themes made during the autumn and winter of 1915 retained this simultanist complexity, but on occasion, as in *La Guerre* (Plate 75), approached a more stable compartmented structure. These latter were the paintings which especially made an impact in January 1916 in a one-man exhibition of Severini's work held at the galerie Boutet de Monvel in Paris.[51] Here the Italian was presented as a painter whose approach still carried the Bergsonian emphasis on the many-layered dynamism of experience, and whose work was still aggressively anti-

75. Gino Severini: *La Guerre*, 1915. Medium, measurements and present whereabouts unknown.

rational and poetically impure. In February 1916 Pierre Albert-Birot, editor
of the newly founded review *Sic*, published an open letter to Severini, and
his comments on the war paintings underline their simultanist complexity:
'Plastic synthesis of the idea "War" . . . You try to represent for us the
complex, fugitive image which appears on the screen of your mind when
you push the button: idea of "War".'[52]

   The simultanist stance of Pierre Albert-Birot's review *Sic* is conveyed
by its sub-title: 'Sons Idées Couleurs Formes'; *Sic* brought back to life
many of the concerns which had given direction to the circles of *Poème
et Drame*, *Montjoie!* and *Soirées de Paris* during 1913 and 1914, and for a
while Severini was a responsive simultanist ally working for dynamic
effect in praise of the modern world. A spiralling composition of pure and
verbal forces contributed to the April 1916 number of *Sic* (Plate 76) is

76. Gino Severini: *Dans le Nord-Sud, Sic,* Paris, no 4, April 1916.

demonstration enough of this. Through the rest of the year and into 1917 Albert-Birot constantly presented his own experiments in graphic and verbal simultanism—his poetry focusing on modern life imagery[52]—while his review acted as a platform for the odd poem by Apollinaire, and occasionally, from the beginning of 1917, for the simultanist poetry of Paul Dermée. At least in the pages of *Sic,* the avant-garde trend seemed firmly set towards the continuation of pre-war trends, and, with them, the development of yet more brands of dynamic simultanist art to convey the fragmented force of modern experience. But even as early as April 1916 Severini was on the edge of a dramatic change, which was to ally his worship of the mechanical and the modern to an idea of reality and a pictorial style absolutely alien to the Futurist and the simultanist approach.

Among the visitors to Severini's exhibition in January 1916 were Picasso, Juan Gris, and a newcomer to the Parisian avant-garde, the editor of *L'Elan*, Amédée Ozenfant,[53] who was one of those physically unfit for service at the front. By the end of the year Severini was a constant visitor at Ozenfant's studio in Passy, closer than ever before to the supremely un-Futurist Juan Gris,[54] and had rejected the excitement of an art dedicated to the creation of dynamic sensations for an art which shared the quietist precision of Gris, and elements of the Cubist vocabulary of both Gris and Picasso. His conversion was evangelically total and it was concluded at least by September 1916, for that is the date of his 'first woodcut', *La Modeste*, published in the autumn number of *Sic*, a composition whose static figurative theme and calm Cubist balance is already, though still tentatively, in the new vein.[55] He was no longer a Futurist.

The historical importance of Severini's conversion is not at once obvious, since his work was in 1917 and 1918 no more than that of a mildly inventive Cubist follower (Plate 79). It lay in the fact that it left behind no major champion of the dynamic, simultanist idea among the leading avant-garde Parisian painters, and, more profoundly, in the fact that it opened up the possibility of a new, anti-dynamic approach to modern life and the machine in Parisian painting. Severini did not forget his obsession with the machine as *the* quintessentially modern phenomenon; he attempted rather to reshape his idea of the machine and of its relationship with painting along less dynamic, more rational lines. He decided to approach both the machine and painting not as the maker of new, glittering, geometric effects, nor as the accelerator of new fragmented and simultaneous experiences, but as a precise and ordered ideal dedicated to complete efficiency of function. In the autumn 1916 number of *Sic* Albert-Biot anticipated this switch of emphasis with the epigram: 'A work of art should be composed like a precision machine';[56] it was an idea taken to more elaborate ends by Severini himself in an important essay, 'La Peinture de l'Avant-garde', which was serialized by *Mercure de France* early in 1917.

The relationship between the machine and painting is dealt with in the first part of the essay, 'Le Machinisme et l'art', where he takes Albert-Biot's epigram further, writing: 'The process of constructing a machine is analogous with the process of constructing a work of art.'[57] The implication is clear: that the Futurist emphasis on intuition in the creative process is to be replaced by a new emphasis, consonant with the new idea of the machine as an ordered, working system, on the planning of compositions and on their exact technical execution. Severini takes this new approach to its logical conclusion, finding pure aesthetic beauty in the machine itself,[58] declaring that the machine demands the attention of the painter, not because it intensifies for him the experience of simultaneity, but because it is, as a structure in its own right, beautiful. A painting like Severini's 1917 *Nature-morte, Quaker Oats* (Plate 79) may not represent machinery, but in its structure and the precision of its balance it can, for Severini, share with the machine aesthetic qualities which are 'Universal'. His art no longer focused on movement, interpenetration, dissonance and the simultaneous conflict of pure and impure effects, but on unity of pictorial means, precision of statement and equilibrium; it reflected a new view of modern life.

Severini's new position was self-consciously classical. In the second section of his essay, 'Intelligence et sensibilité', he turned to the problem of how reason and intuition should work together in art. He utterly ignored his pre-war Futurist convictions, reinstating reason as the necessary ally of intuition, and he called the rational factor in painting 'architecture' or 'construction'.[59] Pictorial 'construction' was the key to pictorial equilibrium and it was founded on certain constant pictorial principles. It was because of this new faith in constant pictorial principles that he could reject the paranoid Futurist assault on the art of the past. He had already begun to immerse himself in the study of the new mathematical ideas popularized by Henri Poincaré and to contemplate their possible application to Cubism,[60] and here he connects this revived interest in mathematics with the example of Uccello, Andrea del Castagno, Domenico Veneziano, Signorelli, Leonardo and others.[61] He announced his new direction in grand style as early as 1916 by showing at an exhibition organized by Ozenfant in the salon of the *couturier* Madame Bongard, *Maternité*, a portrait of Jeanne his wife and Tonio their child, whose dry, descriptive lucidity he wished to echo that of Tuscan painting in the fifteenth century.[62] His profoundly classical, profoundly anti-Futurist direction was made clear both in word and in public pictorial deed (Plate 140).

By the beginning of 1917 the Parisian avant-garde was the scene of a concerted classical revival, not necessarily allied to the worship of a mechanized modern ideal; Severini's new style and aesthetic was, in fact, merely a part of a new tendency towards order whose pictorial basis was Picasso's daring anti-progressive flirtation with an Ingres-like drawing style and the attempts of both Picasso and Gris at a more economical, incisive Cubism. With Gris more willingly influential than Picasso at its centre, the emergent Cubist classicism involved the pre-war Mexican disciple of Picasso, Diego Rivera, his friend the sculptor Jacques Lipchitz, and the painters Jean Metzinger and André Lhote. Among its energetic supporters were Pierre Reverdy and Paul Dermée (in another new review, *Nord-Sud*), Ozenfant, whose review *L'Elan* occasionally anticipated the trend in 1916, and, as patron, providing both intellectual and financial support, the dealer Léonce Rosenberg, whose galerie de l'Effort Moderne was to provide a centre for discussion and exhibition, and who already bought from Picasso, Gris, Severini and Rivera.[63]

If, however, the trend was clear, the aesthetic position on which it was based was still anomalous and lacking in precision. Severini was willing to draw parallels between machines and paintings, but not to give these parallels more than a generalized shape, nor would he define a clear classical system of laws on which to base working method and pictorial 'architecture'. Yet, perhaps most anomalous of all, the poets who believed in a classical revival were able to continue with a still fundamentally simultanist idea of the way images should combine to create poetic experiences. Paul Dermée is a particularly good illustration of this, for his 1917 *Nord-Sud* articles, 'Quand le Symbolisme fût mort' and 'Intelligence et création' were of some theoretical importance to the new move towards order.

'A period of exuberance and force,' Dermée declared in the first of these essays, 'must be succeeded by a period of organization, classification, of science, that is to say a classical age.'[64] He rejected any suggestion of formulae or of models culled from the past, but went on to cap both Albert-Birot and Severini's epigrammatic statements on the parallel between the machine and the work of art: 'The work of art should be conceived as the working man conceives the manufacture of a pipe or a hat, the position of every part should be determined strictly according to function and importance.'[65] The dry radicalism of these classical sentiments cohabited in Dermée's mind with a still essentially intuitive, simultanist approach to poetry—an approach, shared by Pierre Reverdy, whose origins lay in pre-war Apollinaire. However, the apparently anomalous split between Dermée's faith in a return to order and his continuing dependence on the spontaneity of a simultanist approach, led him to an idea of the role reason should play in art which was clearer than Severini's and, in a sense, as prophetic. He arrived at this idea in 'Intelligence et création'. For Dermée, the task of intellect was not to direct the construction of the work itself, but rather to construct 'an image of the world'—a philosophy or aesthetic.[66] Art might remain almost exclusively the field of intuition in practice, but its aesthetic purpose and its means were to be analyzed and defined by reason: 'A creator is an ardent spirit guided by a cool head.'[67] By implication, the fundamental principles of all the arts could be as firmly and as rationally established as those of the sciences, without undermining the primacy of intuition in the creative act.

Besides Severini's expansive but rather generalized effort, there were before 1918 no sustained attempts seriously to define the terms of a Cubist science of art. However, there were attempts to clarify the relationship between painting and object, attempts which were crucial to the development of Cubism in classical guise. From his Montmartre studio in the rue Ravignan, Juan Gris was an important stimulus behind this particular debate. Amédée Ozenfant recalls in his *Mémoires* regular visits to the studio leading to regular disputes on the possibility and validity of a pure, abstract art, and on the place of the object in painting. According to Ozenfant, Gris 'claimed that his pictures and the forms which composed them resembled absolutely nothing, no object or real-life scene',[68] the implication being that already by 1916 Gris had arrived at his mature concept of synthetic Cubism, according to which pure, coloured shapes were his ideal starting-point rather than the observed qualities of things seen. However, Ozenfant's is but a second-hand reminiscence of Gris' position at that date, and it was not until 1921 that Gris himself was to make a clear statement of his ideas, so that it is only possible to attempt an informed series of guesses as to the way they would have been presented in 1916 and 1917.

The guesses are most helpfully informed by two full and lucid expositions of a synthetic Cubist approach which were published at the time: Pierre Reverdy's brief 1917 essay, 'Sur le cubisme', in *Nord-Sud*, which is particularly relevant because Reverdy was so close to Gris, and a closely related 1916 passage from Pierre Albert-Birot's quasi Socratic 'Dialogues Numiques' in *Sic*. Reverdy began by reasserting the fundamental principle of pre-war Cubism and all its derivatives, including Léger's 'pure painting', that the imitation of appearances in painting was redundant. He went on to present the case for an art whose laws were purely pictorial declaring that the object should be treated as no more than an 'element' detached from the world of appearances for pictorial ends, ends which emphasized what was 'eternal and constant' about it.[69] In a closely analogous way, working from the premise that painting was fundamentally a pure activity, 'Z', the Socratic painter ideal of Albert-Birot's 'Dialogues Numiques', maintained that the artist must progress from a 'qualitative analysis' of reality towards 'synthesis': 'For with these known elements (selected by a process of analysis) the artist goes on to construct his work as an architect builds a house out of stones, iron and wood beams. . . .'[70] Neither Reverdy nor 'Z' went as far as Gris himself in 1921 to suggest that the artist should work from a purely synthetic range of pictorial elements *back* to the objects of reality, but both subordinated the real world to the painting, and Reverdy picked out the constant and the eternal as essential qualities to be possessed by the object in painting. 'The circular form' was considered the type of ideal form that ensured permanence, and it is clear that Reverdy had in mind the extraction above all of forms derived from geometry. As early as February 1916 Ozenfant had anticipated this overtly Platonic concept of the relationship between ideal pictorial form and reality, quoting Plato's eulogy of the straight and the circular, forms drawn by ruler and setsquare, as 'beautiful in themselves'.[71] Where pre-war 'pure painting' had been for Léger synthetic in method but deeply realist in aim, the new, rational synthetic Cubism of Gris and his allies, which in the work of Severini had linked itself to a mechanized notion of the modern world, was to be synthetic in method and deeply, Platonically, idealistic in aim. The raw sensation of things was not to be re-created in painting, but from things were to be extracted 'elements' which, distilled, would produce a pure pictorial perfection.

By 1918, as will be seen, Ozenfant and the young architect Charles-Edouard Jeanneret (Le Corbusier) had taken the implications of the classical Cubist trend as far as a clear grammar and syntax of colour and form, overtly fusing a remodelled idealism with a commitment to the modern and the mechanical. However, in 1916 and 1917 the most explicit evidence of the evolution of a more defined and idealized grammar and vocabulary of pictorial elements, set in the Cubist mould, is contained not in manifestos nor in aesthetic discourses, but in the actual paintings and sculptures of Juan Gris and of the others who believed in a Cubist 'Classical age'. The works themselves are the best demonstration too of just what a Platonic, idealizing approach meant in terms of making works of art.

There is not the space here to examine the development of all those who arrived at an idealizing and ordered Cubist style, nor to unravel the stylistic interrelations between them, but it is possible to demonstrate the nature of the pictorial priorities that came to the fore by concentrating on the centrally influential work of Gris himself. It is perhaps an index of the Spaniard's deepening need for a precisely defined pictorial language, that briefly in 1916 he attempted to ally Cubism to Neo-Impressionist colour techniques seriously re-evaluated, but these experiments did not yield far-reaching results, and he quickly turned to a more subdued and clear-cut use of colour, exploiting dull browns, greys and black in strong contrasts of light and dark. It was as part of the development of this less

77. Juan Gris: *Madame Cézanne (après Cézanne)*, 1916. Pencil, 8¾ × 6¾ ins, galerie Louise Leiris, Paris.

78. Paul Cézanne: *Madame Cézanne dans un fauteuil jaune*, 1890–4. 31½ × 25½ ins, Chicago Art Institute.

diffuse pictorial method that he made, also in 1916, a series of careful pencil drawings after paintings by Velasquez, Corot and Cézanne. The pencil drawing (Plate 77) after Cézanne's *Portrait de Madame Cézanne au fauteuil jaune* (Plate 78) is from this group, and it is closely related to the highly finished painted adaptation from Corot's *Femme à la mandoline*, itself leading to a painted adaptation in 1918.[72]

Gris' *Madame Cézanne (après Cézanne)* drawing demonstrates so well the nature of his emerging pictorial language and of his idealistic approach, because in the current terms of his Cubist painting it makes so clear the distance between the 'model'—Cézanne's painting—and the perfected pictorial image—Gris' projected painting. Yet, Gris' model is itself a transformation of nature, and so his drawing is a transformation of a transformation, and takes its lead from Cézanne's original attempt to 'perfect' the image. A particular passage from Albert-Birot's 1916 'Dialogues Numiques' is recalled: 'The artist aims at creating a whole . . . , but not by a visual representation of the object got by the modification of the subject, rather by a representation, in a sense, of that modification itself.'[73] The blurred distinctions between the lit and shaded surfaces of the head and shoulders in Cézanne's portrait (most resolved of all Gris' transformations) become sharp linear divisions, which extend out into surrounding space. Bust and setting begin to coalesce as a single crystalline structure of flat, angular planes, manifestly alien to the softer solids and broken outlines of

127

79.   Gino Severini: *Nature morte,*
Quaker Oats, 1917. $23\frac{1}{2} \times 19\frac{3}{4}$ ins,
Grosvenor Gallery, London.

the original painted model. Shading is rare and is kept always close to the edges of planes so that the sense of three-dimensions is given above all by a heightened *chiaroscuro,* which lacks any single light source. From Madame Cézanne as seen by Cézanne, Gris begins to extract a crisply defined and perfectly poised pictorial construction. His method could not be described as fully synthetic in the sense given to the term five years later, since he works very clearly *from* a specific subject towards the ideal, but the purity of his idealism is none the less for this. The figure is caught halfway through a process of transformation by which she is to become a purely pictorial creature, her component parts redefined and recombined in ideal formal terms within an ideal pictorial space.[74]

During 1917 Gris continued to work in his new subdued yet clear-cut manner, achieving balance by the equal opposition of dynamically diagonal lines as, for instance, in the exactly resolved *Nature-morte, Le Damier* in the Museum of Modern Art, New York. By winter 1917 he seems to have become dissatisfied with the potential instability of dominant diagonals, and it was further into a style which was, in its *chiaroscuro* clarity and its flatness, both balanced and stable, that he moved during the next months. The orthogonal relationship (of vertical and horizontal) at last became dominant. The 1918 *Nature-morte à la guitare* (Plate 80) combines in ideal harmony all the essential qualities of the perfected style that resulted. In this painting and its 1918 still-life relatives Gris reached the most extreme point in his war-time development towards a Cubist classicism. There is almost no suggestion of recession, the planes of brown, ochre and pale blue being flattened in very shallow relief against the picture surface so that pictorial unity is assured; at the same time there is clarity of formal definition, consistent simplicity of shape and consistent clarity of reference to still-life 'elements', so that, without a hint at mere representation, the relationship between the ideal world of the painting and the real world of objects is made plain. Circles, cylinders, rhomboids, and waving serpentine contours, all under the control of a perfectly stable structural system, become the elements of an ideal guitar, glass, pipe, book and table.

80.   Juan Gris: *Nature morte à la guitare*, 1918. $31\frac{1}{2} \times 23\frac{1}{2}$ ins, private collection, New York.

81.   Pablo Picasso: *Guitare,* 1918. $31\frac{3}{4} \times 17\frac{1}{4}$ ins,
Rijksmuseum Kröller-Müller, Otterlo.

Late in 1917 and during 1918 the pictorial priorities which finally came
to the fore with canvases like Gris's *Nature-morte à la guitare* came to the
fore too with the canvases of Severini, Lhote, Jean Metzinger, and late in
1918 with the first synthetic Cubist reliefs carved in stone to designs by
Jacques Lipchitz. The Cubist classicism which must have seemed imminent
from 1916 on was now conclusively established, Léonce Rosenberg's
galerie de l'Effort Moderne acting as its centre. A group style had emerged.[75]
Amédée Ozenfant and Charles-Edouard Jeanneret were to look back on
the Cubist 'call to order' under the title 'Towards a crystalline state' (*Vers
un cristal*),[76] and, because of the fact that the term 'classical Cubism' has

130

82.   Georges Braque: *Nature morte avec guitare et verre*, 1917. $23\frac{1}{2} \times 36\frac{1}{4}$ ins, Rijksmuseum Kröller-Müller, Otterlo.

already found for itself a firm historical niche, this short-lived style with its accent on clarity, purity and structure might aptly be called 'crystal Cubism'.

By the end of 1917 crystal Cubism was undoubtedly the dominant avant-garde tendency in Parisian painting.[77] Picasso, whose brooding 1915 canvases so comprehensively anticipate the new respect for simple, architectural compositions, led too varied a creative life to be himself called a crystal Cubist, but he also was capable of still-lifes which possess a severe stability the equal of Gris—for instance, the strictly disciplined *Guitare* of 1918 (Plate 81). Yet perhaps most symptomatic of the influence wielded by the style and the purifying approach behind it is the fact that even Georges Braque checked his earlier bent towards a more open and inventive Cubism when he returned from the front. At first, late in 1917, attracted into the circle of Léonce Rosenberg, he painted the profoundly Gris-like *Nature-morte avec guitare et verre* (Plate 82), a work whose economic lucidity is backed by the convictions he expressed in the pages of *Nord-Sud*: 'Limitation of means ensures style, encourages new form, and stimulates creativity.'[78] Left in need of a definite direction by the long aesthetic inaction of the front, Braque could not, it seems, resist the unhesitating classicism that he met at the galerie de l'Effort Moderne.

131

Thus it was that when Léger returned to the Parisian avant-garde from his own war on the front and when he completed the huge *Partie de cartes* to make his new popular realist intentions clear to himself and his old allies, he found at its apex an avant-garde tendency in which the qualities of precision, stability and equilibrium were considered basic to painting, in which the creative process was compared to the process of mechanized manufacture, in which the artist did not aim to convey his raw experience of reality but aspired to an ideal pictorial style whose subject-matter was still the conventional subject-matter of pre-war Cubism—the figure, the landscape and, above all, the still-life—and an avant-garde tendency in which the order of reason had been reinstated as the ultimate guide towards an aesthetic sense of purpose. The simultanist celebration of modern life and the machine still survived in the literary productions of *Sic*, the poetry of Cendrars and a few others, but already it was under pressure from the persuasively pessimistic forces of Dada, and already it was without a major champion in the art of painting. A new classicism— above all in the art of Gino Severini and imminently in the art of Ozenfant and his architect friend Jeanneret—declared the possibility of a new idealistic view of the machine and modern life to be marked by the working precision of still-lifes.

*   *   *   *   *

The theme of Léger's *La Partie de cartes* (Colour Plate 5) has its earliest origins in his pencil sketches of *poilus* at rest on the Argonne front in the autumn of 1915 (Plate 60), and especially in the elaborate pen drawing *Soldats dans un abri* (Plate 62) and the shell-case *collage*, *Les Joueurs aux cartes* (Plate 63). The seated figure on the left of the *collage* is close to the figure on the left of the final painting, but the earliest surviving statements of the compositional idea in full followed a few months later, one of them being the pen drawing *Fragment, Etude pour La Partie de cartes*, made on the Aisne front early in 1916 (Plate 72). These early studies on the theme, all executed while Léger was still a sapper in 'la Cie 4/5 du 1e Génie' on the front, make it clear that the idea was first evolved while he was almost totally absorbed in the lives of the *poilus* and almost totally isolated from the Parisian avant-garde.[79]

As has been seen, it was during a leave of a few weeks, back in his studio at 86, rue Notre-Dame-des-Champs, that Léger painted *Le Soldat à la pipe* (Plate 73). This leave, it is known, was some time between June and Septem- ber 1916,[80] just after Albert-Birot's declaration on art and precision machines and just before his 'Dialogues Numiques' on synthesis, when Gris, Reverdy, Dermée, Severini and Ozenfant were almost certainly deep in the debate on classicism and a more clear-cut idealistic approach to reality. Certainly Léger met Apollinaire on this visit—who else is not known—but, since Apollinaire was actively involved in the circles of *L'Elan* and *Sic*, it is inconceivable that Léger would have returned to Verdun ignorant of the new ideas under discussion.[81] His *dessins de guerre* after the summer of 1916 were not, therefore, produced in total isolation from the Parisian avant-garde and there does seem to have been a move towards a more finite, more precise approach to the pictorial idea as a result of contact.

83. Fernand Léger: *Soldat assis,* 1917.
Pencil, wash and ink on paper,
$20\frac{1}{4} \times 14\frac{3}{4}$ ins, private collection, France.

The drawings behind both *Le Soldat à la pipe* and the *collage, Les Joueurs aux cartes* do not reveal a carefully planned development of compositional ideas, and neither final product gives a precise, finished impression consistent with complete compositional certainty. This lack of planning, of a clear sense of direction towards a definite pictorial end, is also implicit in the early 1916 pen drawings on the *Partie de cartes* theme (Plate 83), for Léger does not inscribe them 'dessins pour La Partie de cartes' but merely 'Fragments'. He remains concerned to develop clear compositional ideas— as here—but his open-ended, flexible approach to their evolution seems to echo his pre-war fear of the finite conclusion, and the flaunted roughness of *Le Soldat à la pipe*, with its coarse patches of grey pigment, echoes that of all Léger's pre-war sorties into 'dynamic divisionism'.

La Partie de cartes is in fact and in effect 'composed like a precision machine'. It *is* given a smoothness of finish which aspires to perfect finality. The studies on the theme of *Les Foreurs* hint at a more planned approach to the process of thematic development as immediate sequel to Léger's summer leave of 1916, but it is not until the drawings for *La Partie de cartes*, probably made in hospital after the spring of 1917, that the hints become conclusive indications of a significant change. Given in general terms by the *Fragment* studies of early 1916 (Plate 72) an idea of the composition— the grouping of the three figures and their postures—he seems to have turned, exactly as was normal in academic practice, to a separate study of at least one of the figures. All the drawings that survive from this phase are for the card-player on the left, one of them being an experiment with a mirror image reversal of pose. This concentration on the left-hand figure seems to have been necessitated by a specific local problem left unsolved by the *Fragment* drawings, since the relationship between this figure and his neighbour had here been confused by the fact that they shared a single downstretched arm. Thus, a study like Plate 83 is in part an attempt to clarify further the solid geometry of head, open tunic and striped vest, and in part an attempt to establish a new position for the card-player's left arm. The solution here is that used in the final painting: the figure raises and bends his arm rather awkwardly to allow the figure in the centre undisputed right to the downstretched arm, in this way involving him more effectively in the game. This ink-and-wash drawing, which is pointedly inscribed 'dessin pour La Partie de cartes',[82] is therefore part of a careful, planned campaign aimed at complete compositional certainty so that few details are left unresolved before work starts on the projected large canvas. A classical method leads to a pictorial conclusion whose technical exactitude and polished machine forms declare with great clarity the current Parisian parallel between the making of a work of art and the manufacture of a machine; not a single *pentimento* is visible.[83]

Yet, however much the mode of conception and execution behind *La Partie de cartes* seems to embrace the mechanized classical values associated through Albert-Birot, Dermée and Severini with crystal Cubism, almost everything else about the work declares its independence from the dominant Parisian tendency in Cubist painting. Where unstable movement is strictly avoided in the still-lives, portraits and landscapes of the crystal Cubists, here, within a firm structure of verticals, there is a strong effect of rotation conveying the potential for dynamic action extracted from the *poilus*; where bright, primary colour is rejected in favour of sober browns, ochres and greens by the crystal Cubists, here strong red, yellow, blue and emerald increase the force of dissonant effect—the yellow of the table being particularly aggressive; where the crystal Cubists never model fully in the round, in order to keep the two-dimensional picture surface unified and intact, here the gleaming volumes of the card-players are so weightly modelled as to detach them from the picture surface in an illusory three-dimensional space; where the rigidly limited range of forms in crystal Cubist painting aids the unity of harmonious relations, here the extraordinary range of forms in conflict excludes the possibility of harmony in the interests of conflict; and then, where the crystal Cubists never refer to the actual appearances of machines, here the metallic shine of figurative surfaces openly mechanize the *poilus*. The differences are many and various, but they share the same profound *raison d'être*: where the crystal Cubists attempt to create a perfect pictorial purity, Léger attempts to create—still as before 1914—the sheer dynamic power of reality as seen in life, and—no longer as before 1914—he declares plainly the subject which is his stimulus. There is significance in the fact that the medals, sergeant's stripes and playing-cards, the insignia which most plainly of all declare the *poilu* identity of his figures, were painted in at the very end and do not appear in the *Fragment* drawings or in the 1917 studies; they were his last-minute attempt to make finally certain that there could be no misinterpretation. The subject counts: Léger was now more than ever a realist. The new brand of Cubism was more than ever idealist.

In the last analysis, although he seems to have taken something positive from the growing classical mood in Paris during 1916 and 1917, Léger returned from the front with a strong and sustained challenge to the dominant classicizing Cubist tendency—a challenge against its most essential principles and aims. *La Partie de cartes* was the first full-scale declaration of that challenge. Public in its scale alongside the intimate scale of the most stable crystal Cubist canvases by Gris the following year (Plate 80), it shares their confident finality, but dramatically asserts the distance between priorities developed within the elite confines of the Parisian war-time avant-garde and priorities developed among the *poilus* in the trenches. For Cendrars, writing in 1919, Léger's new painting announced the transformation, even the end of Cubism—the Cubism of the galerie de L'Effort Moderne. He had no doubt as to the determination of Léger's attack, and the source of its energy: 'the subject'.

*   *   *   *   *

In terms of Léger's own development as a painter, *La Partie de cartes* serves for the post-1918 years, like the *Nus dans une forêt* for the pre-1914 years, as the obvious introduction. It makes the point of Léger's return to the subject more straightforwardly than any other major work of the next two years. From this return was to follow during 1918 and 1919 a confident, almost bullying range of anti-crystal Cubist styles, in which every possible pictorial direction opened up by the *dessins de guerre* was explored.

However, in a sense, for all the novelty of these styles, the period 1918–20 saw the culmination of something, an end: an end to that dynamic dissonant view of reality in whose image Léger's art had been formed since 1911, because in 1920–21 the forces of aesthetic order in the Parisian avant-garde, which had led to crystal Cubism and the idea of classical revival, were finally to converge and discipline his art even as they changed his view of modern life. Ironically, Léger's assault on the classical ideal in 1918 and 1919 was the dramatic prelude to his own 'call to order'.

135

CHAPTER 5
Man and the Machine. Léger's Synthetic Styles, 1917–19

Early in 1919 Léger wrote:

I model uncompromisingly in pure local colour and in hefty volume. I want to get rid of tasteful arrangements, delicate shading and dead surfaces. It is my ambition to achieve the maximum pictorial realization by means of plastic contrasts. I couldn't care less for convention, taste and established style; if there is any of this in my painting it will be found out later; right now I'm going to make some life.[1]

Without any loss of vigour, he assaults—this time verbally—the ideals of harmony and repose, ending with the uncompromisingly realistic remark: 'I'm going to make some life'; yet this statement was published as part of a group of statements sent by Léonce Rosenberg to the Italian avant-garde review *Valori Plastici*—a group of statements which included contributions from Severini, Lipchitz, Braque and other representatives of the galerie de l'Effort Moderne. Paradoxically, Léger's anti-harmonious art was invited into the very centre of the crystal Cubist circle immediately on his return to his Montparnasse studio from hospital, which had occurred by 1 July 1918 when he signed a contract with Rosenberg.[2] In February 1919 it was at Rosenberg's gallery that he was given his first post-war exhibition,[3] so that he became, in a real sense, an aesthetic saboteur working from within—his intended victim being the Cubist good taste of his own sponsor, Léonce Rosenberg.

*　*　*　*　*

The passage quoted above makes a further important point: it demonstrates clearly that not only was Léger's idea of painting still dynamically dissonant, as in 1914, but also that his determination to find his subject in his own time had left his belief in the direct power of pure pictorial effect untouched. The mere representation of modern subjects was not enough; Léger still aimed, as in the *Contrastes de formes*, at 'maximum realization by means of plastic contrasts'. Some years later he was to recall how first, confronted by the machines on the front, he had wanted to copy them, but how later he 'made it' by moving from the pursuit of 'likeness' to the pursuit of 'equivalence'.[4] Away from the insistent presence of the *poilu* and the machinery of war he experienced once again the need to translate reality into the most immediate pictorial terms, and the new pictorial themes which he developed from his *dessins de guerre* on the machine and machine-man subject are emphatically *not* straightforward statements of their subject.

In 1918 *La Partie de cartes* was quick to produce a litter of variants on ideas developed for it, and the revived purity of Léger's pictorial approach is conveyed persuasively by the fact that these variants were developed much as the purifications of landscape and figure were developed to produce the 'pure painting' of 1913. At Biot there is a rough pencil drawing directly related to the large canvas. It is not so much a study for the work as a free variation on the machine-man forms established there. From a fusion of the two lateral card-players Léger arrives at a new and independent pictorial idea, which is given increasing definition and size in a series of oils. The *Etude pour La Partie de cartes* in Stuttgart is one of these (Plate 84), but the most resolved and the largest of all is *Composition (Etude pour La Partie de cartes)* now in Moscow (Plate 85); all the variants (despite the date on the Stuttgart canvas) were probably the product of 1918.[5]

The idea for the new theme seems to have been suggested initially by a mirror-image study for the figure on the left of *La Partie de cartes*, or at least by experiments close to it. Léger fuses the two *poilu* ideas by introducing the crooked arm of the figure on the right so that a metallic blue cylinder can cut across the upward rhythm of red and white triangles adapted from the striped vest of the original figure. Without medals and military tabs to serve as clues, the drawing (Plate 83) is itself far from easy to read as a seated soldier; the Biot pencil *Etude* and the Stuttgart *Etude* are even more 'hermetic'. Thus, in the latter Léger subtracts the *képi* altogether, adds more rungs to the red and white ladder of triangles so that they break out of the figure, and reduces the face to a zig-zag line and two circles, hemmed in on every side by converging cylinders. In these variations it seems that the identity of the subject has ceased to count behind the impact of the painting; the *poilu* figure has been fragmented and reconstructed so that all that is left is the simple pictorial contrast between modelled cylinders and flat planes, and the simple pictorial tension created when strong verticals check an equally strong rotary movement. With the replacement of modelled cylinders by flat colour planes the Moscow variation is given its own new array of contrasts, and with this final purely pictorial development the *Etude* theme moves even further from the subject which had been its starting-point some three years earlier—the card-playing *poilu* in the Forêt d'Argonne. These paintings are part of a group of dynamic rotating themes developed from the machine-man ideas which were given such apparently conclusive form in *La Partie de cartes*; their simple pictorial dependence upon the heavily modelled cylinder as central volumetric component invites the group label, cylinder paintings. So emphatically pictorial were Léger's priorities in the develop-

5. Fernand Léger: *La Partie de cartes,* 1917. $50\frac{3}{4} \times 76$ ins, Rijksmuseum, Kröller-Müller, Otterlo.

6. Fernand Léger: *Composition* (*Le Typographe*), 1919. 97 × 71½ ins, Harold Diamond collection, New York.

84. (left) Fernand Léger: *Etude pour La Partie de cartes,* 1918. $36\frac{1}{2} \times 29$ ins, Staats-galerie, Stuttgart.

85. (right) Fernand Léger: *Composition (Etude pour La Partie de cartes),* 1918. $57\frac{1}{2} \times 45$ ins, Pushkin Museum, Moscow.

ment of the cylinder paintings, so determined his need to disguise their machine-man origins, and so close to the pre-war *Contrastes de formes* was their brand of pictorial brutality, that the question must be asked: were the cylinder paintings in any sense at all the product of a return to the subject? And, if they were, in what way were they different from their close relatives in the period of 'pure painting'?

Just as *La Partie de cartes* produced its own pictorial litter in 1918, so too did *Le Soldat à la pipe* with a series of variants, all far less legible than the war-time painting, for which a very finished pen study survives (Plate 87), the most developed variant being the stupendous *Eléments mécaniques,* finished in every detail with unstinting perfectionism (Plate 86).[6] This latter was touched up, it seems, in 1923, but, like the others in the sequence, was the product of 1918. The questions raised by the purified development of the *Etude* theme can as well be considered with reference to this equally purified pair of cylinder paintings.

The most comprehensive contemporary account given by Léger of his approach to the pictorial purification of machine subjects is in a letter of 11 December 1919 from him to his pre-war dealer Kahnweiler, then still in Switzerland. He writes thus of his post-war phase: 'Then the return to subject-matter, while trying always to set plastic contrasts against one another. I rarely get away from the subject now, not any more. As far as my desire for renewal will allow, I keep it. If I break it up, I do so to get greater intensity.'[7] His emphasis on pictorial effect is the declared drive behind his destruction of the subject by fragmentation, but he is quick to

86. (left) Fernand Léger: *Eléments mécaniques,* 1918–23. 83 × 66 ins, Oeffentliche Kunstssammlung, Basel.

87. (right) Fernand Léger: *Dessin pour Eléments mécaniques,* 1918. Pen and ink on paper, $12\frac{1}{4} \times 9\frac{1}{4}$ ins, Oeffentliche Kunstssammlung, Basel.

point out with equal emphasis that the subject is rarely forgotten—'not any more'—to insist on 'the return to subject-matter'. There is, in fact, both in the process of transformation that leads to a work like *Eléments mécaniques*, and in the nature of the image produced, an essential difference from the pre-war *Contrastes*. Where in 1913 Léger had worked towards pure pictorial effects backed by his feeling for the geometry of aero-engines but moving from the starting-point of a fake subject—a subject of no consequence which could be ignored, here in 1918 he worked towards pure pictorial effect from the starting-point of a genuine subject—the machine-man—a subject of profound consequence whose nature could at no stage be ignored. Where the 1913 subject was largely irrelevant to pictorial effect, the 1918 subject was directly behind pictorial effect. Instead of a pure 'dynamic divisionism', Léger aimed at an impure 'equivalence', and, though the *Eléments mécaniques* does not declare a machine-man identity, it does, far more plainly than the 1913 *Contrastes*, declare a machine identity.

From the need thus to declare a machine identity without resorting to mere 'likeness' follows the essential pictorial differences between the 1913 *Contrastes* and the *Eléments*. Most obviously of all, the *Eléments* has as its central theme a jostling array of cylinders and drums felt from the very beginning as heavy, gleaming, metal solids, their mechanical qualities described, not merely alluded to,[8] and the result is profoundly impure: where the machine qualities of the 1913 *Contrastes* are subdued by the

143

88. Fernand Léger: *Dessin pour Le Poêle*, 1917. Pen and blue ink on paper, $6\frac{1}{2} \times 5$ ins, galerie Berggruen, Paris.

flat, pure violence of colour patches, in the *Eléments* they are accentuated by the impure smoothness of tonal modelling given an unashamedly illusion-istic gleam. The rotating energy of the painting is openly an equivalent of the energy released by machines, and Léger allows nothing to obscure this fact—neither an irrelevant studio model nor a dogmatically pure aversion to illusionistic effect.

It was the reinstatement of descriptive modelling for the sake of the subject that lay behind the final important pictorial difference between the 1913 *Contrastes* and the cylinder paintings. The *poilu*-derived cylinders of the *Eléments* are set in rotating collision course against an array of angular planes which are flat; as Léger put it in his *Valori Plastici* statement early in 1919, he had here rejected altogether 'dead surfaces'. There was a simple attacking pictorial stategy behind this move—a strategy justified by the continued need for dissonant effect following the principles expounded first in the Académie Wassilief lectures of 1913 and 1914. If the central forms of his cylinder paintings were to be robbed of strong, flat colour for the grey of machine surfaces, then the logic of contrast demanded that their setting be given a fresh intensity and a fresh, anti-descriptive flatness. Only in this way could the dynamism of the cylinders be allied to a truly dissonant effect of contrast. Léger, therefore, aims, in the settings of his *Eléments*, at a saturated intensity of local colour effects and an unmodelled flatness more insistent and more pure than he had ever achieved before the war; his angular shaping of planes is far more sharply defined by black contour or clear boundary, and colour planes are filled in from edge to

89.   Fernand Léger:
Le Poêle, 1918.
Solomon R. Guggen-
heim Museum, New
York.

edge to give the greatest possible chromatic strength. A pictorially pure
development takes place in response to a pictorially impure development—
the reinstatement of modelling. Once again, the impetus behind stylistic
change is at root 'the return to subject-matter'.

*   *   *   *   *

La Partie de cartes and *Le Soldat à la pipe* generated a type of *élément
mécanique* theme still closely related to the pure *Contrastes de formes,* but
there was a second group—larger and more varied—which was alien to
their rotating dynamism. The origins of this second group lay in Léger's
most radical and most anti-descriptive *dessins de guerre,* above all in the
gouache *Paysage du front* executed early in 1916 on the Aisne front (Plate
69). Even as he worked on *La Partie de cartes,* with its straightforward
statement of a machine-man subject, he began to explore the possibilities
opened up by this daringly destructive attack on 'likeness', for early
exploratory drawings and even oils survive from his period of convalescence
late in 1917 at the Hôpital Villepinte as well as from early 1918 at Vernon.
His second, apparently alien line of *élément mécanique* development thus
ran parallel with his first.

There is a small precisely worked oil, *Le Poêle* (Plate 89), for which a
mirror-image study survives in blue ink (Plate 88). The oil is dated 'Avril
18' on the back and was therefore probably painted at Vernon, but the
drawing could have been sketched earlier at Villepinte.[9] Here Léger works,

90.   Fernand Léger: *Les Hélices,* 1918. 32 × 25¾ ins, Museum of Modern Art, New York.

91. Fernand Léger: *Le Moteur*, 1918. $63\frac{3}{4} \times 51\frac{1}{4}$ ins, Mme René Gaffé collection, France.

not from memories of guns or aircraft, but from the immediate factory-made facts of his hospital surroundings. His focus is on the ward as a whole, with, in the blue-ink study, an occupied bed, slippers under it, and a chest of drawers clearly visible. In the painting these elements are twisted, scattered, often redesigned, while up the centre of the canvas rises a combination of tall vertical strips to cut over them—Léger's pictorial equivalent of the stove which stood like a monument in the middle of the ward. Léger does not simplify and then adjust the positionings of components to echo the rotary dynamism of *La Partie de cartes*, he fragments what he sees and scatters the remains among an alien, disruptive range of knife-edge planes. As in *Paysage du front*, the subject is totally dismembered to arrive at a dispersed and discontinuous rather than a centrifugal image, a type of image which looks back, not to the *Contrastes de formes* as its ultimate pre-war precedent, but to the anti-dynamic contrasts of *La Femme en bleu*.

At Villepinte and Vernon Léger did not only explore the possibilities opened up by his Aisne front experiments in terms of hospital subjects, he explored them too, as would be expected, in terms of his front-line memories—in terms more specifically of *éléments mécaniques*. The April 1918 number of Pierre Reverdy's review *Nord-Sud* reproduced two of his drawings, both undated but inscribed 'Hôp. Villepinte'. From the idea stated in one of these drawings Léger developed a further pictorial theme, whose emphatically mechanical subject was declared in its title, *Les Hélices*. Possibly while still at Vernon, he painted during May 1918 the smaller oil version, now in Brussels,[10] and then in June he painted the still intimately scaled '2e état' (Plate 90).[11] Working here, it seems, with his memories of aircraft crashed behind the lines on the Aisne front—their broken frames, struts and smashed engines—he arrived at a pictorial image whose scattered, dissonant force is closely analogous with that especially of the 1916 gouache *Paysage du front*. It was from the *éléments mécaniques* of *Les Hélices* that Léger arrived at the most important of his disintegrated machine themes of 1918. This culminated in *le Moteur*, an oil of public scale and conclusiveness (Plate 91).

The links between *Le Moteur* and *Les Hélices* are themselves disintegrated and scattered, but they are unmistakable: the steel screw-propeller elements on the left of centre are obvious mutations of the propeller elements in the smaller canvas, while the wide, flat plane with curved edge, which below centre slices the composition almost in two, is an obvious truncated mutation of the axe-blade device. However, where in *Les Hélices* there is a still strong if constantly interrupted accent on the dynamism of successive rhythms, in *Le Moteur* mobility is checked. The painting is a particularly clear demonstration of a further quality which was the paradoxical outcome of this new, fragmentary mode of arriving 'at maximum pictorial realization by means of plastic contrasts': the quality of firm, balanced structure. Once again, this is a quality anticipated by the prophetic *Paysage du front*, and, once again, it finds an analogy in the alliance between dissonance and structure achieved before the war in *La Femme en bleu*. The disintegrated fragments of engines—tubes, hubs, propellers—are everywhere compositionally disciplined by the balancing of opposed directional forces and by dominant verticals. Large elements, especially the tall propeller-blade on the right, act with vertical rectangular planes both to cut across smaller elements and to build a firmly balanced pictorial architecture. They create at once disruptive pictorial incident and a containing framework of boundaries. Intimations of rotating movement only rarely challenge this framework and thus the forces of pictorial disintegration let loose by the destructiveness of Léger's approach to the subject are checked. Faced with the distinct threat of pictorial chaos—a scattered, incoherent conflict of fragments—Léger turns to a defensive pictorial strategy, and, significantly enough, where the grey but dynamic central themes of his cylinder paintings led him by the logic of contrast to aggressively coloured settings, here the sheer disruptive potential of his central theme led him back to dead background surfaces. He brackets the central field of action between broad areas of recessive darkness where the vertical and the horizontal are even more in control, finally underlining the firm rectangular enclosure of the frame—the discipline of a basically stable structure.

The fact that the scattered elements if not the architecture of *Le Moteur* were arrived at partially by the extraction and mutation of elements from *Les Hélices* makes a further important point—a point which applies also to the cylinder paintings with their comparably free use of elements from *La Partie de cartes*, and which further reinforces the network of links between Léger's pre-war and his post-war attitudes. The point is that the major machine themes of 1918 were the result of a process of 'creative evolution' quite as open-ended and flexible as that which produced the *Contrastes* and the *Escalier* in 1913. No established pictorial theme, however conclusively stated, was, in fact, conclusive—every theme was at every stage open to changes so radical as to create new themes, so that even *Le Moteur* itself could be vandalized, its elements broken apart and rearranged with other, new elements to create the theme *Dans l'Usine*

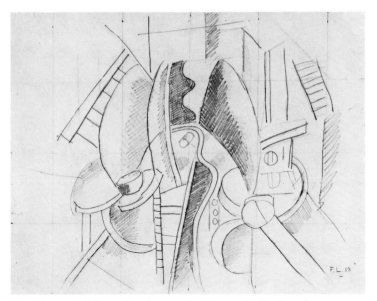

92.   Fernand Léger: *Dans l'usine*, 1918.
$39\frac{1}{2} \times 31\frac{1}{2}$ ins, private collection, France.

93.   Fernand Léger: *Dessin pour Le Moteur,* 1918. Pencil on paper,
$10\frac{1}{2} \times 13\frac{3}{4}$ ins, sold by Sotheby's, London, 8 July 1971.

(Plate 92). The pre-war Bergsonian idea of free creative evolution was not
dead.

Yet the fact remains that *Le Moteur* was *apparently* if not actually conclusive, that for all the freedom with which Léger moved first from his
subject-matter into his 1918 machine themes, and then from one theme to
another, he remained determined to give each theme a finished precision,
which at least, *seemed* conclusive. Where evolutionary change of a radical
kind was essential to the development of so many new *éléments mécaniques*
ideas in 1918, the development of each individual theme as a sequence of
preparatory events, from drawing, to small oil version, to large-scale
statement was designed actually to minimize the opportunities for major
compositional change. Thus, behind *Le Moteur* lay at least one very closely
related pencil drawing (Plate 93) and at least one equally close oil version,[12]
while behind *Dans l'Usine* lay at least one very closely related water-colour
as well as an equally close small oil.[13] Variations from stage to stage in the
process of preparation *never* affected the basic compositional idea. Léger
allowed himself experimental changes of format—there was a change from
horizontal to vertical format in the development of *Le Moteur*—but no
more than fragmentary adjustments of positioning and the introduction
of a few new elements. A similar process of internal development is found
in certain of the pre-war themes—above all in the slight adjustments by
which the *Contrastes de formes* were developed from version to version—
but where in 1913 and 1914 each version was approached afresh without
constriction, by 1918 Léger was so concerned to fix clearly the lines of his
composition, that he began to use the mechanical enlarging process of
squaring-up when for example working from the pencil drawing for *Le
Moteur*. With a deliberate, systematic caution he worked, as if consciously
aware of the analogy with machine-production, towards the highest

possible degree of compositional certainty, aiming again and again at the conspicuous technical perfection achieved in so exemplary a way in *La Partie de cartes.* Smaller preparatory oils did not conceal their exploratory nature, and reveal his indecision over this or that element plainly on the paint surface,[14] but large *états,* like *Dans l'Usine* were presented as complete statements, exposing if possible—as in this instance—not a single mark of indecision.[15] He worked from rough but detailed guide-drawings, drafted on the primed canvas like plans: he was indeed like the worker patiently assembling pipes brought to mind by Paul Dermée.[16]

The classically mechanical sense of completeness achieved in the large *éléments mécaniques* brings back into focus the ideals and the style of the crystal Cubists. In a significant sense the disintegrated style of *Le Moteur* and *Dans l'Usine* was pictorially closer to the harmonious principles behind the new Cubist classicism at l'Effort Moderne than the dynamic style of the cylinder paintings, for not only was it tied to an ordered and deliberate working method, but its stable, architectural mode of construction led to images whose firm poise is stylistically comparable. Moreover, it is worth remembering once again that direct contact with ideas current in the Parisian avant-garde would have been possible at Villepinte, where the foundations of Léger's new disintegrated style were laid.

Undoubtedly the closest that Léger came to crystal Cubism in the disintegrated paintings of 1918 was in one of a pair of still-lifes (Plate 94).[17] Léger's colour range—from rich greens and blues to substantial maroons and violets—is distinctly personal and far from dull, but his subject—a table-top still-life—and his structured treatment of it are not altogether antipathetic to, for instance, Gris' 1918 *Nature-morte à la guitare* (Plate 80). There is the same dominant repetition of verticals and horizontals to build a flattened planar arrangement, and the same tendency to reinforce the material existence of the picture plane by treating solid form as relief—the fully three-dimensional modelling of book and sphere on the left being the exception rather than the rule. Léger disintegrates and rearranges in a perfectly balanced architectural composition the elements of a conventional crystal Cubist theme. Yet even here, so close to what might be thought the archetypal image of crystal Cubism, he achieves a violence of pictorial effect hostile to the emerging, harmonious values of the style. Where Gris avoids sudden cuts from one kind of element to another, Léger seeks them out. Gris' glass and his guitar emerge smoothly from their planar surroundings, as part of a unified pictorial theme, ochre and brown surfaces flowing into the gently moulded forms of objects. By contrast Léger's checkerboard, his rippling newspaper, book and sphere collide with or are cut into by their planar surroundings, everywhere in conflict with them as part of a disjointed pictorial theme. For Léger, the objects even of a studio still-life are the raw material for pictorial drama and, typically, a stable 'architecture' of structural compartments no more than contains this drama, and never subdues it.

Léger's 1918 *Nature-morte* is alien to the clear-cut harmony of *Nature-morte à la guitare* in one further significant way: where Gris states with great lucidity the coordinated structure and identity of his subject, Léger's destructive method of processing the subject for pictorial effect leads him to make only scattered and partial references to its identity. Where Gris

94.   Fernand Léger: *Nature morte*, 1918. 25½ × 32 ins, private collection, Los Angeles.

seeks a clear relationship between the pictorial and the real,[18] Léger's emphasis is so forcefully on pictorial effect that he leaves the relationship between the pictorial and the real anything but clear. Paradoxically, Gris's idealism leads him to a more straightforward statement of his subject, while Léger's realism leads him to a more purely pictorial statement. Once again one is driven to question the nature and significance of Léger's 'return to subject-matter'.

*   *   *   *   *

The sheer strength of Léger's determination to destroy and reshape his subject-matter in the disintegrated paintings, and then his determination to reach a state of manifest pictorial 'equivalence' to a modern subject, was finally demonstrated by means of the most elaborate, most important disintegrated theme of all. A theme whose starting-point was neither the hospital ward nor the machine on the front, but rather the starting-point of the cylinder paintings—the *poilu*. This theme was the sequel to the major disintegrated compositions of 1918—*Le Moteur* and *Dans l'Usine*—and all four versions were executed in 1919. It is *Le Typographe*, of which the major version, one of the most powerful and conclusive canvases painted by Léger in 1918 and 1919, is the *Composition* Colour Plate 6).[19] *Le Typographe, 2e état* (Plate 95) is an early state, and the Philadelphia

95. (left) Fernand Léger: *Le Typographe, 2e état*, 1919. 32 × 25½ ins, Staatsgalerie Moderner Kunst, Munich.

96. (right) Fernand Léger: *Portrait de Philippon,* January 1917. Pencil, brush and water-colour on paper, 14 × 10½ ins, sold by Sotheby's, London, 2 July 1970.

variant (Plate 99) the penultimate one. The title 'Le Typographe' in Léger's hand on the back of the '2e état' seems at first glance to rule out a front-line starting-point for the theme since it probably refers to the typographers with whom Léger worked on the illustrated edition of Cendrars's *J'ai Tué* late in 1918. Yet even though by 1919 the figurative label attached to this newly developed theme—its subject— was a peacetime typographer, the fact is that in its earliest beginnings it was a war-time *poilu*. A change of identity followed from the violence of radical pictorial change.

Recently two *poilu* studies, a water-colour and a wash drawing, passed through Sotheby's (Plates 96 and 97). The water-colour (Plate 96) is in-scribed '17-1-17 Le Godert, Portrait de Philippon', and both seem to be worked up from an earlier sketch which might even have been an original study for *Le Soldat à la pipe*.[20] Léger's pre-war practice of evolving new themes from old ones which he was to take further in 1918, is given here a brief war-time outing. The two 1917 studies of a wounded *poilu* were revisited by Léger in 1919 as the starting-point of yet another new theme; they were the stimulus behind a crude experimental oil, *L'Homme à la roue* (Plate 98).[21] It is here that the machine-man image of Philippon is smashed and put together again in preparation for his return as the peace-time typographer. The two studies had been conceived in unequivocally volumetric terms—colour being used in the water-colour exclusively in a tonal way for modelling. They could, therefore, have provided the stimulus for another rotating cylinder theme, like the Basel *Eléments mécaniques,* but Léger treats only fragmentary parts of the figure in this way—shoulder, arms, hands, and tunic, for instance. The head especially is treated in a discontinuous, disruptive way: it has become the field of action for a series of clashes between the most contradictory of pictorial forces, and these clashes are all suggested, even if no more than tentatively, by the

97. (left) Fernand Léger:
Le Fumeur, January 1917.
Pencil, brush and ink on
paper, $20\frac{1}{2} \times 14\frac{1}{2}$ ins, sold by
Sotheby's, London, 22 April
1971.

98. (left) Fernand Léger:
L'Homme à la roue, 1919.
$36\frac{1}{4} \times 25\frac{1}{2}$ ins, present
whereabouts unknown.

99. (right) Fernand Léger:
Le Typographe, 1919.
$51\frac{1}{8} \times 38\frac{1}{4}$ ins, Louise and
Walter Arensberg collection,
Philadelphia Museum of Art.

1917 studies. The bulky bandages worn almost like a beret become a gleaming, metal eclipse cut into by sharp ridges, and below them the face, split in two by the bandage tied under Philippon's chin, becomes a tripartite sequence of contrasts—dark silhouette profile, flat white dividing plane and metallic cone—while this in its turn is set above a detached rippling surface of metal which was once the scarf around the *poilu's* neck. Dynamic rotation remains here the key to the painting's unity, for the head is fixed as if by spokes to *la roue*—an arc of bands—but with the disintegration of the figure is suggested a decisive move towards the anti-dynamic structures of Léger's disintegrated style.

It is with the '2e état' that Léger gives a confident and almost complete compositional structure to the still experimental idea suggested in *L'Homme à la roue*, and by doing so he finally destroys the *poilu* identity of Philippon. The ridged metal ellipse, once his model's bandaged cranium, and the cone-like element beneath are enlarged to become the dominant central feature, and, beneath them, the rippling surface of maroon, suspended above the canvas base, refers obliquely back to the shoulder of *L'Homme à la roue*. But the crucial clue to the presence of the figure, the dark silhouette profile, is left out, so that the elements synthesized from it become, like the cylinders of the cylinder paintings, no more than pictorial elements to be combined in the most powerful, most strident combinations possible. The profile is not, for Léger, a necessary representational clue, to be left in to establish the presence of a machine-man subject, it is no more than another pictorial component to be dispensed with as required. The accent is unalterably on the force of pictorial effect and so the profile is replaced by a small, cut-out area of relief modelling with a half-coiled length of pipe which is set in conflict against a rich cerise placard plane decorated with dots and dashes and stencilled poster letters. Pictorial clashes are achieved which are even more disruptive than in *L'Homme à la roue*—flat planes of white, yellow and vermilion slicing across the scattered remains of machine and machine-man elements. From a now distant war-time beginning of great descriptive simplicity has evolved a disjointed pictorial statement open to the purest of pictorial developments.

As with the culminating *état* of *Etude pour La Partie de cartes*, the Moscow *Composition* (Plate 85), so with the culminating *états* of the *Typographe* theme Léger moves towards a new range of dissonant effects without altering the established compositional idea, by simply translating much of what is modelled and metallic into flat colour planes. The process of translation is caught in a transitional stage in the Philadelphia canvas. It is complete in the final version (Plate 99 and Colour Plate 6). Here the ellipse has become a brilliant focal area of colour clashes—orange against deep blue against white, white against pale blue against yellow—a focal area at the apex of pictorial activity around which equally strong, flat colour planes emerge from behind and cut in front of austere darker areas and broad expanses of white, creating a floating sensation of spatial depth without perspective. Among this now dominant array of pure pictorial forces the few surviving modelled and metallic machine elements—the half-coiled piping, the solid remains of Philippon's shoulder, a cylinder here and there—are hung like rare and precious trophies to commemorate a long pictorial campaign.

Le Typographe is, then, perhaps the most dramatic demonstration of the continued purity of Léger's pictorial approach to the *éléments mécaniques*— of the determination with which he not only disintegrated his subject, but totally obscured its true identity, its true starting-point in reality. Yet at every stage in its 1919 evolution, including the culminating New York stage, Léger is careful to retain enough fragmentary points of reference to keep touch with the idea of a subject—not a specific *poilu* subject— Philippon—nor even a machine-man subject—*L'Homme à la roue*—but, however generalized, none the less a subject. Thus, in the final *Composition* just enough mechanical 'trophies' remain to serve in the Cubist sense, like the head and hands of *La Femme en bleu*, as clues to a mechanical identity, while the banner-like placard with its bold stencil letters remains to declare a broader modern frame of reference, embracing the dazzling pugnacity of the poster as well as the polished geometry of the aero-engine or 'the breech-block of a 75'.

Less concentrated and less simple in its references to a modern reality, the disintegrated style possessed more than the cylinder style the potential for stating its 'equivalence' to a wide-ranging, all-embracing experience of modern life. The process of disintegration led to a complex variety of pictorial conflicts which, for Léger, seems to have been essential to that all-embracing experience.[22] The modern-life clues of *Composition* do not, in the final analysis, mark the remains of a war-time *poilu* or a machine-man metaphor, but the bustling emergence of a post-war urban reality, a reality which became his new subject, the new power behind his painting.

*   *   *   *   *

Having established the crucial importance of 'the return to subject-matter' in the machine themes of 1918 and 1919, it would be useful to sum up as clearly as possible the essential difference between the deeply felt realism of Léger's search for equivalent pictorial effects, and the deeply pondered idealism of the crystal Cubist search for pictorial perfection.

'The means exist in Cubism,' Pierre Reverdy wrote in 1917, 'to construct a picture using objects as no more than elements.'[23] Léger, too, used the word 'element' in his 1919 letter to Kahnweiler and in certain of his titles, a fact which suggests that he, like Reverdy and Gris, thought of his approach to the subject and its transformation into pure pictorial terms as synthetic; and there is a significant sense in which his machine paintings of 1918 and 1919 were indeed synthetic. In the case of the cylinder paintings an ideal range of geometric solids was extracted from the less than perfect facts presented by *poilus* playing cards, aircraft and by 'the breech-block of a 75', and in the case of the disintegrated paintings a range of especially powerful pictorial contrasts was achieved by the extraction of disparate urban or war-time items from their less forceful daily contexts in life. However, where the idealistic synthetic style of the crystal Cubists extracts from the inconsequential objects of studio reality a perfected harmony of formal relationships, the realistic synthetic style of Léger extracts from the machines, posters and other paraphernalia of front-line or urban reality an intensified dissonance. He does not aim to find in his subject forms which fit an already perfected range of ideal forms: he does not aim to

157

idealize; he aims rather to convey all that is essential to the experience created by his modern-life subjects, whether geometric and perfect, or coarse, clashing and imperfect. In the cylinder paintings he aims to synthesize the experience created by machines in general. In the disintegrated paintings he aims to synthesize the experience created by modern life in general. Thus, the same fundamental realist purpose that so clearly separated the dynamic straightforwardness of *La Partie de cartes* from the synthetic Cubism of Gris' *Nature-morte à la guitare* is the factor that so clearly keeps the Gris painting separate too from the less straightforward *éléments mécaniques* of 1918 and 1919, both the cylinder and the disintegrated compositions.

Still convinced of the violent transience of reality as experienced in modern life, Léger was in 1918, as he had been since 1909, most of all determined to 'realize his sensations', to create an equivalent of what he saw.

CHAPTER 6
A Style for the Modern Spectacle:
Léger's Simultanism, 1918–19

Blaise Cendrars did not, in 1919, feel that Léger's return to the subject was isolated. He believed that, in the general context of the Parisian avant-garde, 'the cube is crumbling',[1] and he prophesied a new kind of painting whose preoccupations would be with colour and content—a kind of painting which would become, like the pre-war pursuit of simultaneous contrasts, a common tendency. The subject of this new painting was to be man: 'man, that is you and I, at work and play, with our everyday things, our enterprise . . .' a subject which was to be celebrated in 'great canvases of great size'.[2] Cendrars was wrong to imagine the imminence of a common tendency which would destroy 'the cube', but he wrote this passage only a few months after Léger had shown his brand new post-war paintings at the galerie de l'Effort Moderne, and the kind of painting that he looked forward to—not only in its subject-matter, but also in its scale and its brilliant colour—was just the kind of painting that Léger, even if few others, looked forward to by May 1919.

The large-scale machine compositions of 1918 and, above all, *Le Typographe* in its culminating 1919 *état* possessed both the dimensions and the chromatic force that Cendrars wrote of, but their elements were not given the power to convey more than a generalized mechanical or modern-life identity—the human subject as such had been transformed beyond recognition. Alongside the synthetic styles of 1918–19, Léger developed a style which *was* capable of celebrating 'man . . . at work and play'—city man in his city surroundings pursuing his city pursuits. Where the origins of almost all the major machine themes lay behind him in his memories of the machine-man *poilu* and the mechanisms of war, this other style was almost always to take as its starting-point the peacetime phenomena of post-war life.

An interesting variation on the theme of *Le Moteur*, is a small, heavily worked oil of 1918, *Le Mécanicien* (Plate 100). Its title is a symptom of the relatively slight yet deeply significant change that Léger has introduced:

from being a painting whose subject is the machine in its modern ambience, it has become one whose subject is the machine and man. For on the right of the machine composition[3] Léger has added a narrow strip in which, as if from behind *Le Moteur,* emerges a figure. The small yet insistent presence of this robot image transforms everything. He is the new point of reference from which the qualities of *Le Moteur* are established as real qualities— from which the sense of 'equivalence' is most of all derived; its fragmented energy is increased by contrast with his static solidity and its scale is swollen to exaggerated proportions by contrast with his diminutive stature, so that an idea is conveyed not only of the generalized power of modern experience, but of its superhuman dominance.

The simple yet always profoundly effective introduction of straight-forwardly legible images, central among them that of the robot man, became during 1918 and especially 1919 the essential factor in the development of Léger's other, more specifically peacetime style. In the Cubist sense, these images acted as further, more specific clues, to attach the intensity of Léger's new range of pure pictorial effects to a more specific idea of a subject—to assert more clearly the nature of their 'equivalence'. The style that emerged combined on occasion the synthetically pure qualities of both the cylinder and the disintegrated machine themes, with a distinctly literary use of the poetic modern-life image. It was in the pre-war Futurist, or more particularly in the pre-war 'Delaunayist' sense a simultaneous style, whose aim was to create a very definite sense of urban or industrial ambience. It was, in short, a revival of the literary simultanism that Léger had so comprehensively rejected in 1913 and 1914. He could not more decisively have asserted his determination to reject pre-war 'pure painting' for 'the return to subject-matter'.

*   *   *   *   *

If crystal Cubism was set firm against the painting of machine elements in the round and the pursuit of a disintegrated pictorial dissonance, it was set even more firm against the impurities of the literary simultanist approach, rejected in such an exemplary way by Severini in 1916. Paul Dermée sums up most uncompromisingly of all the hostility felt against such an approach from within the circle of 'l'Effort Moderne': 'It is dangerous,' he wrote 'to aim at the renewal of one art using the lessons taught by other arts. Literary painting or pictorial literature are the symptoms of decadence. Literary images must not be allowed in painting or sculpture.'[4] When Léger returned from hospital to his studio at 86, rue Notre-Dame-des-Champs in the spring or summer of 1918 he found, therefore, not only no literary simultanist painting of any importance in the avant-garde, but also a strong prejudice against it. Yet, although what survived of simultanist poetry was also on the wane, enough survived to provide a context for his revival of a literary modern-life style, and a closer look at the nature of the decline of simultanism reveals much about the nature of Léger's isolation.

Cendrars made his own important contribution to the survival of a simul-tanist poetry dedicated to the energy of modern experience in two publications of 1916 and 1917: the poem *La Guerre au Luxembourg* and the prose

100. Fernand Léger: *Le Mécanicien*, 1919. 19½ × 26 ins, Munson Williams Proctor Institute, Utica.

poem *Profond Aujourd'hui*, both of which revived with renewed conviction the staccato rhythms and the sudden switches of time and place characteristic of his pre-war writing. *Profond Aujourd'hui*, as will be seen below, was a crucial stimulus for Léger's new simultanist style. But Cendrars was not the only pre-war Parisian poet whose work continued to sustain the simultanist approach to modern life. Behind the anomalous war-time simultanism of Dermée in *Sic* and *Nord-Sud*, lay a deep admiration for the pre-war aims and achievements of Guillaume Apollinaire—in particular his desire to 'conceive a poem simultaneously like a scene from life', and early in 1918 Apollinaire's position as the stimulus behind new simultanist developments was strengthened further by the publication of his collection of poems *Calligrammes*. Among the pieces included were many from before the war whose manner was thoroughly simultanist and thoroughly committed to the immediate facts of modern life—for instance, *Les Fenêtres* and *La tour Eiffel*; and also included, of course, were the poems typographically arranged to create simple graphic images which he called *calligrammes*; strong statements in support of an alliance between poet and painter (Plate 101).

Dermée continued his anomalous pursuit of an intuitive simultanist poetry, but of the newer simultanist poets still receptive to the experiences of modern life in 1918 the most important were Pierre Albert-Birot in *Sic*, and another young admirer of Apollinaire, Philippe Soupault, who

161

POÈME IMAGÉ

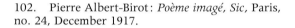

PIERRE ALBERT-BIROT.

101. Guillaume Apollinaire: *Calligramme* from the
catalogue of the exhibition of works by Léopold
Survage at the galerie Bongard, 1917

102. Pierre Albert-Birot: *Poème imagé, Sic,* Paris,
no. 24, December 1917.

from 1917 began to publish in Albert-Birot's review. Soupault perhaps most
derivatively of all concentrated on the immediacy of visual effects treated
with a *parole in libertà* concision and on the pre-war imagery of the modern
world—the Eiffel tower, machinery, and new modes of communication.
Thus, his collection *Aquarium*, published in October 1917, opens as if in
homage to Apollinaire's *Les Fenêtres*, with an evocation of light by colour.[5]
Likewise his poem *Antipodes*, published in the January 1918 number of
Nord-Sud, leaps from place-name to place-name—'Dakar Santiago Mel-
bourne'—to convey the modern shrinkage of distance by new means of
transport and communication much as Cendrars had in *Prose du Transsibérien*.[6] Albert-Birot challenged Soupault's enthusiasm for the imagery of
modern life and the verve of simultanist effects, and even went so far as to
publish in the December number of *Sic* a *Poème-imagé* which combined the
verbal and the graphically visual in complex interpenetrating response to
Apollinaire's *calligrammes* (Plate 102).[7] The poetry these two produced,
careless of the unities of space and time, dipping into the imagery of modern
life, aimed at a composite fusion of the most disparate items, places, evocations and events. Pierre Reverdy was not unsympathetic, and it was he who
in March 1918 summed up the approach basic to the new simultanist modes
of composition. Poetry, for Reverdy, was the creation of images, and

162

images were created by the bringing together of 'distant realities', the more distant, the stronger the image: 'Analogy' was for him *the* fundamental poetic device—'resemblance by rapport'.[8]

Yet, in the notion of a poetic rapport between disparate elements, so lucidly expounded by Reverdy and so fundamental to simultanism in 1918, as in 1914, lay the seeds of the decline of a poetry still dedicated to the energy of modern life. Reverdy himself advocated the avoidance of the 'fantastic', keeping away from an obsessive, singleminded emphasis on the deeper layers of imagination. But the notion he put forward was at root Symbolist, and it could as well justify a poetry of dream beyond the immediate realities of modern life. At the Indépendants of 1914, Apollinaire's Italian *protegé* Giorgio de Chirico had already shown that literary simultanism which was founded on the notion of 'resemblance by rapport', 'analogy', and the fusing of the most disparate of phenomena, could lead to fantastic rather than Futurist conclusions. It was the temptation towards the images of dream and fantasy that most of all challenged the position of modern-life simultanism in 1918.

As always an ambiguous figure, unafraid of contradictions, Apollinaire was instrumental not merely in the survival of simultanism in its pre-war form, but also in the new move towards fantasy. For the performance of his Symbolist drama *Les Mamelles de Tirésias* in June 1917 was an important early pointer and encouragement towards the new trend.[9] And in 1918 Albert-Birot gradually made *Sic* the platform for a poetry of imagination and dream as well as for the simultaneously interpenetrating poetry of modern life. Indeed, it was he who had provided backing for the staging of *Les Mamelles de Tirésias* and his wife, Germaine, who had written the music.[10] During 1918 new poets began to publish in *Sic*, among them André Breton, Luis Aragon and Tristan Tzara (in touch from Zurich), poets who decisively opposed both the development of a more rational aesthetic and the simultanist faith in the power of modern experience. The most conspicuous symptom of the volatile mood created by these new literary forces was the defection in 1918 of Soupault, simultanism's most orthodox supporter. As early as November 1917 he had published in *Sic* a poem of marked irrational, fantastic character, called *Miroir*,[11] and in 1918 this quality became increasingly dominant in the work he published.[12] It was the following year that he and Breton were to collaborate in the early experiments with dreaming as a creative trigger which led to *Les Champs Magnétiques*. In the same year he, Breton and Aragon were to found a new review, *La Littérature*. The trend towards fantasy led first to Parisian Dada and then into Surrealism.

In sum, the 1918 avant-garde situation in Paris was not altogether sympathetic to the revival of a literary simultanist style dedicated to popular modern subjects. Léger was not without the support of continuing parallel efforts, but the attitudes most basic to simultanist poetry were increasingly under attack from a new, and increasingly influential tendency: a tendency utterly opposed to his celebration of the day-to-day facts of modern life. As Luis Aragon put it, the new concern was not with what can be seen, but with 'the shadow', with what is not there, yet in its absence deeply disturbs the poet.[13] Léger dedicated his new style emphatically to what can be seen; he ignored the shadow. Aragon, like Breton and Soupault struck at the very core of his realism—perhaps even more profoundly than the idealism of the crystal Cubists.

*   *   *   *   *

Yet even after the death of Apollinaire in November 1918 one poet continued to resist without compromise the fascination of the shadow—Blaise Cendrars.[14] It was, fittingly enough, with the support of Cendrars' work above all, that Léger developed his literary simultanist painting of modern life during 1918 and 1919. The Swiss poet's faith in Léger's 'return to subject-matter' was built on the respect due to friendship, and on a continuing close alliance of attitudes to art and reality—attitudes whose foundation had been laid before 1914 and deepened by the popular force of their closely related war experiences. Cendrars too felt increasingly isolated in the Parisian avant-garde,[15] and he spent only short periods in the city—a week or two at a time. But he kept in touch with Léger, and worked with him to produce the illustrated 1918 edition of *J'ai Tué*.[16] Many years later Léger was to tell Dora Vallier that he had never read any books by Cendrars,[17] but the latter's enthusiasms and convictions would certainly have been conveyed as much by his talk as by his writing, and his importance as a crucial force behind the painter's simultanist celebration of 'man', in his city surroundings at his city pursuits, cannot be denied.

It is a particularly strong indication of the importance of Léger's alliance with Cendrars to the evolution of his simultanist style, that among his first attempts to apply such a style in 1918 were his illustrations for *J'ai Tué*. The drawings are inscribed 'F. L. Vernon 18', which establishes that they were executed in the spring or early summer of 1918, at about the same time as Léger's hospital ward experiments in the techniques of pictorial disintegration and synthesis.[18] Although literary simultanism was to be, for Léger, a style almost exclusively developed for peacetime subjects, its earliest beginnings still looked back from the not very distant vantage-point of convalescence, to memories of war.

Of the collaborators on *J'ai Tué*, Cendrars was without doubt the one with the most relevant experience to draw on. He had in the previous year collaborated with Zaraga in an illustrated edition of *Profond Aujourd'hui*, but, most important of all, he had in 1913 collaborated with Sonia Delaunay in the production of 'the first simultanist book'—his *Prose du Transsibérien* with a colour accompaniment of 'simultaneous contrasts', and it is clear that in 1918 he carried with him an idea of the potential of literary simultanism in painting still close to the ideas of his pre-war allies the Delaunays. Indeed, though the Delaunays were still not back in Paris, he was in contact with them by letter,[19] and their pre-war pictorial obsessions—pure colour, the disc and the Eiffel tower—are revived as part of the dynamic, simultanist picture of modern life created by *Profond Aujourd'hui*. Again, his views on painting, as expressed in his 1919 *La Rose Rouge* articles, however aptly they apply to Léger's brilliantly coloured 'return to subject-matter', are at root still the ideas which Robert Delaunay had stood for in 1913. Delaunay's major public statements of the pre-war period—*L'Equipe de Cardiff* and *Hommage à Blériot* (Plates 44 and 43)—may have been for most of the Parisian avant-garde in 1918 no more than distant, out-of-date

recollections from past Salons, but for Cendrars the lessons they taught
about the literary as well as the pure potential of painting were very much
alive, and so was the lesson of 'the first simultanist book'. Léger was thus
able, through the medium of Cendrars, to look anew at pre-war Orphism,
and the *J'ai Tué* project enabled him to do so in the context of a working
alliance between poet and painter.

Yet, in fact, the 1918 illustrated edition of *J'ai Tué*, like the 1917 illustrated
edition of *Profond Aujourd'hui*, was not by any means as ambitiously
simultanist as the 1913 'simultanist book' of Cendrars and Sonia Delaunay.
A simple opposition is achieved between the text, printed in red, and
Léger's illustrations, printed in blue, the white of the page acting to separate
and to intensify these unmodulated primaries, but the text does not here
interpenetrate with the illustrations—there is no real interplay between
verbal and visual means of expression (Plate 103). Indeed, the illustrations
do not even refer to particular incidents or images in the text. However,
though not integrated into a fully simultanist book, Léger's illustrations
do contain, as compositions in their own right, the features of the full-dress
simultanist style which was to emerge in his paintings. Thus, the first
illustration in the text, for instance (Plate 103), combines the most disruptive of cutting effects—flat, angular planes slicing across the movements
of volumes—in a characteristically disintegrated composition. But Léger
introduces, far more elaborately than in the 1918 *Le Mécanicien,* a scattering
of easily recognizable images from the war—poplars, French helmets,
signposts, a rifle. They add up to a sum of disparate clues related by analogy

—rapport—which generate the composite idea—war—just as Robert Delaunay's posters, rugger players, and Eiffel tower generate the composite idea of Paris in modern times, in the pre-war versions of *L'Equipe de Cardiff*. A straightforward alliance is announced once again between the power of pure pictorial effect and the capacity of poetic images to convey a subject.

Cendrars gave support to Léger's developing literary simultanism in another, perhaps even more forward-looking way. By 1918 he had a new enthusiasm, the cinema. More than merely a follower of the cinema, he was actively involved in the making of films, and indeed, when he arrived in Paris in November 1918 to help with the final printing of *J'ai Tué*, he was fresh from Nice and the shooting of Abel Gance's *J'Accuse*, in which, if one is to believe his 1952 statement to Michel Manoll, he had been everything from an electrician and assistant set-manager to a corpse in *Les mortes qui reviennent*, the fourth part of the film.[20] He brought with him not only practical experience of film-making, but also newly developed ideas about the nature and the potential of film, which were of obvious and profound significance to the simultanist approach as it was developed by Léger. These ideas can be known with some accuracy, for they are cogently set down in a text called *L'ABC du cinéma*, most of which was written as early as November 1917.[21] Here Cendrars noted two fundamental effects of filming: first, reality was fragmented because of the practice of cutting suddenly from image to image and aspect to aspect; second, David Wark Griffith's invention of the close-up, led to the isolation of objects and aspects of objects outside their usual contexts, thus intensifying the spectator's awareness of, say, an eyebrow or a watch-chain.[22] Léger's disruptive and always sudden pictorial 'cuts' from element to element and image to image in the *J'ai Tué* illustrations obviously paralleled the process of cinematic cutting, while his isolation of images like the helmet and rifle gave them an intensified significance, which obviously paralleled, possibly even echoed with conscious intent, the process of cinematic isolation by close-up. That the new art of film could teach new lessons to the older arts, and, more specifically, that it could underline the essential qualities of the simultanist approach was a point that neither Cendrars nor Léger could have missed. It is a point made by Philippe Soupault in *Sic*, as he hesitated on the edge of simultanism and fantasy: 'Its power,' writes Soupault of the cinema, 'is marvellous, because it overthrows all natural laws; it pays no attention to the laws of space, and time, it upsets the laws of gravity, of ballistics, of biology, etc. . . . Its eye is more penetrating, more precise. It is, then, up to the creator, the poet, to use this power, this richness, until now ignored, for a new servant exists at the pleasure of his imagination.'[23] Léger himself did not yet turn to the making of films, but his new simultanist painting aligned itself closely with the new progressive simultanism of the cinema, it was as much a cinematic as a literary style, and behind both its cinematic and its literary qualities lay the creative support of Cendrars.

*　　*　　*　　*　　*

Léger's first attempt to develop on canvas rather than in print a full literary simultanist theme was the *Remorqueur* of 1918. The subject was not a war

166

104.　Fernand Léger: *Le Marinier,* 1918. 18 × 21¾ ins, Museum of Modern Art, New York (gift of Mr and Mrs Sidney Janis).

subject. It was urban and peacetime and new in Léger's repertoire—the passage of a Seine river barge through an industrial setting of buildings and commercial hoardings. Léger seems to have started on it while still in hospital at Villepinte working on *La Partie de cartes,* because a wash and gouache study dated 1917 survives at Biot, but it probably received its first pictorial treatment on canvas with a small oil, *Le Marinier* (Plate 104), and it reached its culminating point with the precisely finished *Remorqueur,* inscribed on the back 'Etat définitif, juin 1918' (Plate 105), which was painted the month in which he completed the New York version of *Les Hélices.*[24]

Moving with that deliberate sense of planned purpose, seen to be characteristic of his 1918 machine paintings, towards the highest possible degree of compositional confidence, Léger arrived at a painting which is at once immediately legible and in the purest pictorial terms dynamic and dissonant. The purely pictorial force of the idea has its origins, for all the peacetime nature of its subject, in a war-time discovery. With *Le Remorqueur* Léger finds a new, urban identity for the lateral dynamic effect of machine elements in motion which was first given expression, with a crashed aircraft as subject, in the Aisne front gouache *L'Avion brisé* (Plate 68). The cursive flowing motion of wings and fuselage against the angular background fields of *L'Avion brisé* is echoed in *Le Remorqueur* by the rocking lateral motion of steam-barge elements and colour planes against the background of commercial architecture. The interjection of flat colour planes does at certain points disrupt the succession of modelled, mechanical

105.   Fernand Léger: *Le Remorqueur,* 1918. $25\frac{3}{4} \times 36\frac{1}{2}$ ins, Mme René Gaffé collection, France.

106.   Fernand Léger: *Le Chauffeur nègre,* 1919. $25\frac{3}{4} \times 36\frac{1}{2}$ ins, private collection, France.

elements, but Léger retains a strong sense of rhythmic continuity between the shining segments, discs, cylinders and cones, creating a novel dynamic theme. It is related to the cylinder paintings, but in the nature of its movement, the variety of its forms and the sudden sweetness of pink and emerald colour accents it is very much independent of them.

At every stage of the theme's development, Léger's scattered use of easily recognizable images to declare his subject—*le remorqueur*, man and the city—is calculated to attach a definite identity to each group of pictorial elements. In *Le Marinier* a robot figure grasps one of the gleaming metal segments so that it becomes the steering-wheel and the elements rhythmically connected with it become the motor of the barge, while in *Le Remorqueur* itself a similar robot figure is placed to the side to 'steer' the machine volumes of the composition left to right across the canvas. Here too, the markings on the central cylinder turn it unmistakably into a funnel, so that the steam-barge identity of the machine volumes is clear, and the repeated window patterns added to certain background planes turn them unmistakably into buildings, so that the architectural—the city—setting is also clear. The flat planes remain planes and the machine volumes always create the sense of 'equivalence' rather than 'likeness', yet their pictorial qualities, on the one hand of stable angularity and on the other of mobile weight, are defined as the qualities of urban architecture and of a steaming river-barge.

The industry of men in an urban setting was the subject of other pictorial themes during 1918 and 1919—themes which, like the illustrations for *J'ai Tué* and the small *Mécanicien*, were more obviously cinematic in their simultaneity. Being a dynamic rather than a disintegrated theme, *Le Remorqueur* was not a theme in which the staccato use of cutting from element to element was central; it was above all where Léger introduced a poetic accompaniment of easily recognizable images into a disintegrated pictorial context that his simultanism became, in Cendrars' sense of the term, cinematic. *Le Chauffeur nègre* was a theme first explored in 1918, which was carried through in a small scale on canvas in 1919 (Plate 106).[25] Its main components and their positionings suggest a direct link with *Le Remorqueur*—the robot figure on the left, the turning machine elements in the centre, the fanned tubes on the right—but the robot figure (now a stoker) is no longer allowed to 'steer' his pictorial mechanism unchallenged across the picture-surface. A single thick black strip cuts him cleanly off from the metallic centrepiece, whose rotary action of successive forms is itself cut off by a rippling black surface that runs from top to bottom of the canvas. Continuity of movement is prevented in favour of the stable, compartmented structure typical of the disintegrated compositions, with its dominant enclosing features also its dominant instruments of disruption. A structural mode of this kind was obviously especially well suited to Léger's new simultanist aims, for it both isolated the elements and images of his theme so as to concentrate attention on them, and held them into the unified fabric of the painting. Not only had it the power to cut cinematically with decisive force, but it had also the capacity to display its poetic content with uncomplicated clarity and a firm sense of discipline. It was this disintegrated style that was to provide the most common of Léger's new simultanist modes.

169

107.　Fernand Léger: *Le Mécanicien dans l'usine*, 1918. $21\frac{1}{4} \times 25\frac{1}{2}$ ins, private collection, Chicago.

Le Mécanicien, Le Remorqueur, Le Chauffeur nègre and other comparable paintings like *Le Mécanicien dans l'usine* (Plate 107), were all themes whose subject was, in Cendrars's phrase: 'man . . . at work'; in 1918 Léger developed themes too whose subject was modern man 'at play'—themes which celebrate popular pageant and entertainment. Major among the leisure subjects he turned to was the circus. It was a subject with a long pedigree in the Parisian avant-garde stretching from Seurat's *Le Cirque* to the polychromatic *Clown* sculpture exhibited in 1918 by Henri Laurens at the galerie de l'Effort Moderne[26]—a subject which, almost as much as the cinema, absorbed the enthusiasms of Blaise Cendrars.[27] The circus stimulated what is undoubtedly the most poetically illustrative of all Léger's 1918 themes—the gay, brightly coloured oil *Le Cirque Médrano* (Plate 108). The pictorial theme is in general terms dynamic and close to *Le Remorqueur*, its bright variety creating an atmosphere of carnival, but far more comprehensively than either *Le Remorqueur* or *Le Chauffeur nègre* it creates an idea of its subject which challenges the unities of space, time and medium. The trapeze artist, the dog, the clown and the horseman are all brought together by rapport into the same pictorial space and time to create with the verbal fragments 'Medra' and the posted time of the

170

108.   Fernand Léger: *Le Cirque Médrano*, 1918. 22¾ × 37¼ ins, Musée National d'Art Moderne, Paris.

performance '8h ½' an interpenetrating idea of *Le Cirque Médrano*. Word, number, image, colour plane, disc and volume are combined in a single simultaneous whole, each disparate component fixed firmly into the unifying idea of the subject.

Yet Léger felt, it seems, that the illustrative impurity of *Le Cirque Médrano* was too close to 'likeness' for the force of pure pictorial effect to carry unhindered, because it was not a theme that he chose to take beyond a relatively intimate scale. He chose instead to give a more ambitious, more public scale and more definitive treatment to a circus theme which is both more condensed and less elaborately a challenge to the unities of space, time and medium—*Les Acrobates dans le cirque*. *Les Acrobates* was for Léger a major theme—the equal of the major 1918 synthetic themes—*Composition (Etude pour La Partie de cartes)*, *Eléments mécaniques* (1918–23), *Le Moteur* and *Dans l'Usine*. His final version is a large-scale oil (Plate 109), typically unseductive of surface, yet, again typically for a major 1918 statement, finished with thorough precision so that not a single *pentimento* is visible. Indeed, it is the end-product of a planned process of pictorial development whose classical caution is even more conventionally academic than that behind *La Partie de cartes* itself; the *état définitif* following a sequence of three preparatory oils, the first of which is a complete oil *esquisse* and the other two studies of each half of the composition in isolation.[28] Thus, more clearly than the development of the 1918 *Remorqueur* theme towards its *état définitif*, *Les Acrobates* makes the point that Léger's new literary simultanist return to the subject, as much as his *éléments mécaniques* styles, aimed at the completion of definitive pictorial statements both public in scale and precisely perfect in finish.

109.   Fernand Léger: *Les acrobates dans le cirque*, 1918. 38¼ × 46 ins, Oeffentliche Kunstssammlung, Basel.

As a pure pictorial theme, *Les Acrobates dans le cirque* is more condensed, less diffuse than *Le Cirque Médrano,* and yet more varied and more
rich in its conflicting effects, combining in a single composition crucial
features both of the dynamic cylinder paintings and of the anti-dynamic
disintegrated paintings, creating a complex stylistic as well as a simply
declared literary simultaneity with unrivalled success. The structured
setting of plain and patterned planes penetrates the balanced rotation of
the acrobats' metallic limbs, but their rotation continues unchecked as
the central pictorial theme—a cylinder theme—of the right-hand section
of the painting. Yet the vertical of the tent-pole, which cuts the composition
into two spatially disconnected sections, introduces a strong disruptive
note at a crucially central point, and on its left Léger's pictorial theme is
emphatically disintegrated. There is in this way a contradictory collision

which combines the sudden, dissonant force of a cinematic transition with the firm stabilizing effect of the dominant vertical, for the tent-pole does not merely disrupt, it acts too as a structural factor to confront the imminently unstable movement of the acrobats with the threat of pictorial discipline. The coming together on a single canvas of such different modes with such different possibilities lets loose an extraordinary range of pictorial effects, of elements pure and impure, so that Léger achieves for his circus theme a sense of almost anarchistic variety which is yet coordinated. Even within each mode there is an extraordinary variety of detailed effects — thus, the volumes of the right-hand cylinder theme are modelled not only in cool purple, but also in warm red and emerald, while the flat planes of both sections are not only flat in treatment, but also dotted and dashed and checked with patterns. Once again, as in *Le Cirque Médrano*, but with incomparably greater force, the circus subject is the generator of a carnival gaiety in variety, and the 'equivalence' between pictorial effect and subject is absolutely clear. Clown, audience and balancing acrobats present themselves with emphatic clarity, creating nothing like so complete an idea of the circus as *Le Cirque Médrano*, but an idea strong enough to make the sense of 'equivalence' inescapable.

Les Acrobates dans le cirque was almost certainly the first of Léger's literary simultanist themes to be carried through on canvas with a finished decisiveness and on a public scale comparable with that of *La Partie de cartes*. Its emerald and warm red volumes are closely related to the coloured volumes of *Le Remorqueur*, which suggests that it was painted during the summer of 1918. If so, it was the prelude to the evolution in the autumn of 1918 and through into 1919 of two simultanist themes—one perhaps the most cinematic of Léger's simultanist achievements, the other perhaps the most synthetic of them—themes which he expanded to a scale even greater than *La Partie de cartes*—*La Ville* and *Les Disques*. These were just what Cendrars looked forward to in May 1919 'great canvases of great size', given the brilliance of a 'new kind of colour', which declared with expansive optimism: 'a renaissance of the subject'.

*   *   *   *   *

The Seine steam-barge in its industrial setting, the *poilu* machine-man now at work in the factory, the circus as his entertainment with its clowns and acrobats—all these subjects were aspects of a larger, all-embracing modern subject, the city. For Jules Romains and the Unanimists before 1912 the city had been perhaps the most powerful image of the interpenetrating and dynamic Unanimity of modern life, and in 1913 and 1914 it had been endowed with fresh significance, following the Futurist invasion, by the simultanists of the Parisian avant-garde, most decisively in painting by Robert Delaunay, but also by such figures as Henri-Martin Barzun in poetry.[29]

When, therefore, Léger turned to the subject of *La Ville* in order to evolve a comprehensive modern-life theme in simultanist terms, he revived a subject with an extensive pre-war pedigree—a subject which was still a central source of modern-life imagery in the sustained simultanist poetry particularly of Philippe Soupault and Pierre Albert-Birot during

173

1917 and 1918.[30] It is, however, clear that the most important literary stimulus behind his development of the city theme was provided by Cendrars. Cendrars's 1917 eulogy to the dissonant reality of modern life, *Profond Aujourd'hui*, can be read, in fact, as a poet's preface to Léger's *La Ville*, particularly where it throws together the disintegrated images of Parisian life. The clashing of images, certain of the images themselves, and the strong evocation of colour sensations were often to find echoes in the poetic accompaniment and the abrupt cutting effects developed by Léger in the 1919 series. Cendrars writes of a 'multicoloured city', of 'extravagant posters', of trams that squeal and buildings that rise up and over them like flaming incendiaries, of the Eiffel tower transformed by the sun and the clouds:

Watches are set. On every side the transatlantic liners move towards their destinations. There is a semaphore signal. A blue eye opens. A red closes. All is at once colours. Interpenetration. Disc. Rhythm. Dance. An orange and a violet consume one another.[31]

Yet, even as Cendrars's prose-poem looks forward to Léger's *La Ville*, it looks back as well to the pre-war Futurist and simultanist paintings which are Léger's true avant-garde allies, and which are the true stylistic context out of which his literary simultanist style as a whole evolved. Above all, Cendrars looks back very specifically to the modern life imagery, the colours and the discs of Robert Delaunay's *L'Equipe de Cardiff* and *Hommage à Blériot* (Plates 44 and 43), with their prelude, the *Tours* of 1910–11.[32] *Profond Aujourd'hui* acts, therefore, both as a preface to *La Ville* and as a powerful reminder of the pre-war idea of painting and modern life which was the impetus behind Léger's literary simultanism as much as behind his synthetic *éléments mécaniques*.

*   *   *   *   *

The story of the evolution of *La Ville* is a further demonstration of how Léger could turn one established pictorial idea into another, moving in the process to an entirely new subject as well as to an entirely new combination of elements.

The idea at first emerged in the form of a pictorial theme much more purely synthetic than impurely simultanist in the literary sense. This theme exists in three closely related oil versions, each one a preparation for the next—part of a typically deliberate plan of campaign aimed at compositional certainty. The most developed of these, in all aspects worked with the precise care of an *état définitif*, is significantly inscribed on the back: 'La ville (fragment) 3e état' (Plate 110).

The first *La Ville* theme of 1919, which culminates here is, like the large-scale 1918 *Le Moteur,* a convincing demonstration of the creative freedom with which Léger continued to invent his post-war themes, for it too is a pictorial hybrid—a theme in the making of which Léger extracted, further disintegrated, and remodelled, components from other themes. Its major source of pictorial supply was the most important of the disintegrated machine themes—an idea then currently under development as well— *Le Typographe* in its two earliest 1919 *états* (Plate 95). The elements provided

110.   Fernand Léger: *La Ville (fragment)* 3e état, 1919. $51\frac{1}{4} \times 38\frac{1}{2}$ ins, Louise and Walter Arensberg collection, Philadelphia Museum of Art.

by this source are treated with a creative lack of respect almost as un-
predictable as that displayed in the disintegration and transformation of
Philippon, the *poilu* whose portrait was the distant war-time starting-point
for *Le Typographe* itself.

Like *Le Typographe 2e état*, the Philadelphia *La Ville (fragment)* collects
together in a strong central field of force, a clashing complex of metallic
surfaces and flat planes of white or of brilliant colour, framing it with
darkened flanks of blue and black. In more detailed terms, the central
metallic sheet of blue in *La Ville (fragment)* is a mutation of the central
cylinder from *Le Typographe 2e état*; the warm red element hovering solidly
above is a displaced mutation of the modelled maroon element at the base
of *Le Typographe*; and the stave-like rods that rise from the base of *La Ville
(fragment)*, a mutation of the cylinders that rise too from the base of *Le
Typographe*. Moreover, other mutations from the elements of other themes
are visible, for instance the dark central segment and the suggestion of
buildings behind, which look back to *Le Remorqueur*. Thus, the fragmentary
remains of the wounded *poilu* sketched by Léger at Verdun are reshaped
and reshuffled with new fragments to make a disintegrated composition of
modern-life elements, which is for the most part too synthetic for a definitely
urban identity to be conveyed, but the final addition of windows to flat
rectangular planes and a succession of smoke-puffs alongside set the
scene. Finally, the few surviving remnants of Philippon have become the
component parts of *La Ville*.

176

111. (far left)   Fernand Léger: *Dessin pour La Ville*, 1919. Watercolour over pencil on paper, 15 × 11 ins, Société Anonyme collection, Yale University Art Gallery.

112. (left)   Fernand Léger: *Dessin pour La Ville*, 1919. Watercolour on paper, Perls Gallery, New York.

113. (right)   Fernand Léger: *Esquisse pour La Ville*, 1919. 32 × 25½ ins, Mr and Mrs Armand Bartos collection, New York.

After the development of the first *La Ville* theme, Léger moved progressively towards a more elaborately simultanist idea, changing what was already established and constantly adding new elements in a fresh, freely creative spate of invention. The sharpness of his cutting effects and the force of his contrasts were attached more and more to the idea of his urban subject by the addition of an increasing number of scene-setting images. The probable next stage in the sequence of events is represented by two almost identical water-colour studies (Plates 111 and 112) and by an oil development on the basis of these experiments, the *Esquisse pour La Ville* (Plate 113), a canvas slightly larger than the first oil version of *La Ville (fragment)*. The Yale water-colour is squared up for enlargement, an indication of the clear sense of purpose behind the development of *La Ville* even at this relatively free exploratory stage, and here and in the other water-colour most of the remains of *Le Typographe* are eliminated to be replaced among other elements by the cut-out silhouette of a mannekin figure and large stencilled letters in the Yale study, a latticework derrick and framing house-façades in the other. The cut-out mannekin, the smoke-puffs (still there), the derricks, the letters (given strong advertising associations), and the house-façade *repoussoirs* are all brought together in the oil *Esquisse* (Plate 113), and the result is a composition both stronger, because colour is more saturated than in *La Ville (fragment)*, and more clearly legible as a simultanist idea of the city than its predecessors—a fully cinematic idea with an elaborate poetic scenario of images.

177

114. Fernand Léger: *Dessin pour La Ville*, 1919. $19\frac{1}{4} \times 22$ ins, watercolour on paper, Musée National Fernand Léger, Biot.

The final *La Ville* theme was the result of Léger's decision to expand the idea which had been given definition in Plate 113 by adding a whole new section on the right. The process of expansion began, it seems, with an attempt to fill out further the central field by adding new incident, for a careless, experimental water-colour survives (Plate 114) where a new strip is included on the right of the central field complete with the hastily defined shapes of a building, railings, a tree and the walking silhouette of robot city men. All these new images but the city men are gone by the time Léger has reached the next important stage in the evolution of the theme, and at the same time the new right half of the composition is complete in all its essentials. This next stage is an oil sketch (Plate 115). It is the size of the '3e état' of *La Ville (fragment)*, but its heavily worked and reworked surface—the *pentimenti* often left unconcealed—openly declares the fact that it is not an *état définitif*. It is a mark of the lateness of their invention that the most exploratory and least resolved areas are in the centre and on the right flank, in particular the two still lightweight city men and the deep area of black dug into the canvas above them.[33] Both the purely pictorial variety of the theme and the sheer quantity of its images are added to by the extension of the right flank—a new cut-out

178

115. Fernand Léger: *Esquisse pour La Ville,* 1919. 38 × 51 ins, private collection, New York.

mannekin is introduced, a further derrick, a fenestrated white strip and a new sequence of advertising letters—all of which return slightly modified, their pictorial definition as contrasting elements sharpened, in the culminating *La Ville,* the enormous canvas now in Philadelphia (Plate 117). Yet, even still, as he moved into this final stage, Léger was not altogether certain, for not only is the paint-surface typically coarse and unattractive, but, atypically for a work of public scale and ambition, it reveals clear signs of fragmentary change and last-minute addition.[34] At the end of a long, intricate process of evolution, in part deliberately planned, in part freely inventive, he could not conceal the difficulty of the challenge he had set himself—the difficulty of keeping clear compositional control over a pictorial and literary idea so wide in the range of its conflicting incidents and so far flung across so expansive a surface.

The final version of the theme was, like *La Ville (fragment),* a hybrid— a theme which pulled together in mutant form the elements of other, often lesser themes, both simultanist like itself and synthetic. The coloured target disc was, as will be seen, an especially ubiquitous element in Léger's painting. On its right the flat propeller-blade of yellow with polished edge was a simplified extract from *Le Moteur;* the fenestrated strips were reminiscences of the 'architecture' of *Le Remorqueur* seen through the

179

medium of *La Ville (fragment)*; the black depth at the core of the painting with its spilled succession of white letters was an adaptation from the minor simultanist theme so far unmentioned, *L'Echaffaudage*, the vertical strip with decorative bands repeated the disruptive yet stabilizing achievement of the tent-pole in *Les Acrobates dans le cirque* and of the black strip tying top to bottom in *Le Chauffeur nègre*, the blue cylinder with flattened flank rising low in the right corner was a fragment from the Moscow *Composition (Etude pour La Partie de cartes)*, and the robot figures around whom and in relation to whom everything occurs and is given its scale were the relatives of the robot figures of *Le Remorqueur*, *Le Chauffeur nègre*, *Le Mécanicien* and the audience which watches *Les Acrobates dans le cirque*. *La Ville* in this culminating form was, in fact, a simultaneous gathering together of so many disparate elements and images evolved in so many different 1918–19 themes that it can in a real sense be called a simultanist anthology—an attempt at a comprehensive statement of almost the full range of Léger's means and his ends, both pure and impure, attached to the unifying idea of the modern city. Completed early in 1920, it was shown at the Salon des Indépendants in February that year, and its scale— almost seven and a half by ten feet—is a measure of the all-embracing importance which it held for Léger. It was, in sum, his most ambitious public attempt to declare in simultanist terms 'the return to subject-matter'.

*   *   *   *   *

116.   Fernand Léger: Illustration for *La Fin du monde filmée par l'Ange Notre-Dame*, by Blaise Cendrars, Paris, 1919.

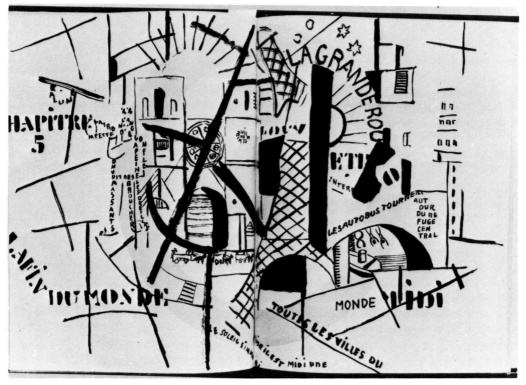

Cendrars did not only provide, with his *Profond Aujourd'hui*, a poet's preface to *La Ville*, he provided also, with another prose piece, its most apposite and most illuminating literary parallel—a parallel which demonstrates conclusively how poetic and how cinematic Léger's painting was. The piece was Cendrars's 1917 'spectacular' *La Fin du monde filmée par l'Ange Notre Dame*.[35] It clearly underlines the alliance between poetry and the style of *La Ville*, because precisely at the moment when the idea of *La Ville* dominated Léger's work, it was the pretext for his second attempt at book-illustration, the edition with his illustrations being published by Cendrars and Jean Cocteau in Editions de la Sirène on 15 October 1919.[36] It clearly underlines the cinematic quality of *La Ville*, because it was written as a film scenario, exploiting that freedom from 'all natural laws' made possible by the cinema, although it was never in fact filmed.

La Fin du monde tells of the vain attempts of God the Father, presented as a cigar-smoking American businessman, to convert the inhabitants of Mars. Before the final cataclysm which ends the world he is driven in his desperation to hold a huge propaganda parade of religious celebrities and, after its failure, to summon as missionary the angel from between the towers of Notre Dame. Unlike his illustrations for *J'ai Tué*, Léger's illustrations for *La Fin du monde* were a genuine attempt, in the first place to illustrate Cendrars's text using specific passages as stimulus, and in the second place to achieve a fully simultanist alliance between the verbal and the visual, an alliance whose interpenetrating closeness comes across especially aptly in an illustration whose subject was the city of Paris itself—the ultimate source in life of every urban experience that Léger celebrated in *La Ville* (Plate 118).

Cendrars sets the Parisian scene with a dazzlingly disruptive, high-speed display of cutting, creating an idea of the city out of a staccato succession of fragments:

Paris. An over-all view.
The Great Wheel; the tower; Sacré-coeur; the Panthéon; the bridges.
Up stream and down stream, the Bois de Boulogne and de Vincennes.
The hillsides of Saint Cloud and Montmorency. In the background, on the Alfortville side, the Seine continues, luminous. Trains. . . .[37]

The ease with which a scenario purpose fits Cendrars' simultanist scorn for the unities of space and time is obvious, and, although Léger brings together only a few of these images, he sets the Parisian scene in the same obviously cinematic way, cutting without transition from visual image to verbal image, to flat colour plane, uniting the scattered and disparate variety of incident into a single, teeming whole. Notre Dame with its sun-disc halo, the Eiffel tower and the Great Wheel are verbally challenged by interjected lines from Chapter 5, which establish with clarity the specific episode for which Paris is the setting; the illustration is thus not merely an evocation or 'equivalent' of Paris, but also a simultanist narrative illustrating that moment—mid-day—when in Cendrars' text 'L'Ange Notre Dame' 'blows his trumpet, that moment when the sun expands and all the cities of the world rise up on the horizon, gliding along railway lines towards the square of Notre Dame'.[38] Literary to the extent of actually telling a story, Léger's illustration goes far beyond the limits so strictly

117.   Fernand Léger: *La Ville*, 1919. 91 × 117½ ins, A. E. Gallatin collection, Philadelphia Museum of Art.

set for artists by Paul Dermée, and, indeed, so close is the alliance between the illustration and the text, between visual and verbal imagery, that Léger even turns to the calligrammatic techniques of Apollinaire, shaping certain of his images—'la lune', 'l'Ange N.D'—with the help of words.[39]

That the impetus behind Léger's *La Ville*—its subject—was above all his simultanist experience of the most dissonant and most modern parts of Paris, is clear. Many years later in a taped conversation with him, Cendrars brought up the question of the painting, recalling their many meetings at the place Clichy. Léger agrees that the place Clichy, site of the largest posters in Paris, of, as he puts it, 'the birth of publicity', had much to do with the painting.[40] The sheer size of the canvas could well itself have been conceived as a challenge to the posters of the place Clichy, but Léger's poetic scenario of images neither specifically refers to it, nor even to Paris—it creates a generalized idea of the city, within which he tells no story. Thus, although cinematically poetic in its simultanism, Léger's big painting has neither a narrative nor more than a generally identifiable city subject, and, perhaps most significantly, it is without either verbal or calligram-matic images. Like the elaborate verbal and visual simultanism of *Le Cirque Médrano* (Plate 108), the even more elaborate and specific illustrations for *La Fin du monde* were *too* illustrative for painting as Léger approached it in 1919; his emphasis was still decisively pictorial and the function of the poetic image was emphatically to declare no more than a generalized 'equivalence', not a specific 'likeness'.

Yet the parallel between Cendrars' poetic mimicry of the film-camera and Léger's staccato use of scene-setting images remains clear and illumi-nating, for *La Ville* is very much a disintegrated composition, dependent upon the sudden dissonance of cutting and the clear isolation of images in a compartmented structure—it is very much a cinematic composition, in Cendrars's sense of the word cinematic. Among the abrupt collisions of flat, hard-edged planes and synthetic elements images, emerge with sharp clarity, displayed in only partial form, isolated from their day-to-day contexts as if by the camera in close-up, acquiring thus, as Cendrars had pointed out in *L'ABC du cinéma*, an intensified significance. The giant advertising letters spell nothing, the smoke-puffs rise from no visible source, the machine-man robots descend their staircase from nowhere to nowhere. For all its lack of specific meaning, Léger's poetic scenario could not be more manifestly and effectively cinematic, nor more clearly urban in its declaration of a subject.

The generalized idea conveyed of Léger's subject, the conspicuous lack of verbal imagery, and the abrupt force of his cuts from image to image, all these factors give to *La Ville*, and the simultanist style that it announced, a pictorial immediacy of impact not equalled by its pre-war antecedents, in particular by Robert Delaunay and his followers. Both Delaunay's Salon statements of 1913 and 1914—*L'Equipe de Cardiff* and *Hommage à Blériot* (Plates 44 and 43)—make this point clearly enough by contrast: they are more literary in every sense and not at all cinematic in the post-war sense. However, it is most decisively in its purely pictorial aspect that with *La Ville* Léger's simultanist 'renaissance of the subject' asserts its individual strength of character—its independence within the literary simultanist tradition of which it was so much a part.

The paradoxical order of the disintegrated mode, with its repeated verticals and compartmented framework, allows Léger to indulge his taste for the grand design without loss of pictorial power, and in this architectural factor lies a basic point of difference between his large canvas and its pre-war antecedents in the work of Delaunay. Only once did Delaunay attempt a grand, stable simultanist painting—*La Ville de Paris*—but the clarity and strength of Léger's structure, not only in *La Ville* but in most of his disintegrated simultanist themes, is utterly alien to the blurred insubstantiality of Delaunay's 1912 composition.

There was but a single peripheral burst of simultanist activity which anticipated the structural firmness of Léger's *La Ville*, the series of inter-pretations of Nice and Monte Carlo painted at the turn of 1915–16 by the Belgian artist Léopold Survage (Plate 118), and these did not go unnoticed because a Survage drawing on the town theme, complete with flat archi-tectural compartmentation and bowler-hatted Chaplinesque inhabitants, was used for the cover of *Sic* in January 1918, and, very significantly,

118.   Léopold Survage: *Nice,*
1915. $39\frac{1}{2} \times 32$ ins, Greer
Gallery, New York.

Survage was the subject of a *Rose Rouge* article by Cendrars.[41] Yet Nice
and Monte Carlo could never have been mistaken for industrial cities in
1915, and the elegant harmony of curves and straight lines typical of
Survage's interpretations, their modishness sweetened by a rich mixture
of softened prismatic colours is a true echo of his subject, quite unlike the
harsh power of *La Ville*. And the harmonious relations of their colours
above all remain far closer to the pre-war simultanism of Delaunay than
to the post-war simultanism of Léger.

   This last crucial difference—of colour—brings us finally to the most
basic difference of all between Léger's post-war style and the pre-war
style that made it possible. The distance between Léger and Delaunay is
most directly and clearly expressed in the contrast between their opposed
attitudes to colour. Even when invaded by the dynamic images of modern
life, as by the tower, the posters and the sportsmen of *L'Equipe de Cardiff*,
Delaunay's painting presented a softened and shifting effect of colour
movement, an effect dramatically opposed to the sudden stridency of
Léger's 1918–19 colour contrasts. Léger may have used the techniques
of Delaunay's literary simultanism in his 'return to subject-matter', but he
remained, as a realist, committed to his own anti-harmonious idea of modern
life. He remained, therefore, in the purest pictorial sense independent, and
his independence is declared brutally and directly by everything that he
produced in the cinematic style which culminated in *La Ville*.

                    *   *   *   *   *

Among the least literary and the purest pictorial elements that survived
from the earliest beginning of *La Ville* through its many stages into the
final version was the target disc. The colours in the final version are

different from those in the first *La Ville* theme, but not its pictorial purpose as an expanding centre of colour incident. The disc is the most direct reference from within *La Ville* to Léger's other major large-scale attempt to develop a simultanist theme—an attempt which in fact anticipated *La Ville—Les Disques*. It is in *Les Disques* that Léger most openly of all declared his debt to the memory of pre-war Delaunayist painting, and at the same time most decisively declared the independence of his dissonant colour contrasts.

The target disc, ringed with rotating 'simultaneous contrasts', was perhaps the central and the purest device invented by the Delaunays for the presentation of their 'simultaneous contrasts', and when Cendrars looked forward in 1919 to a new kind of colour it is altogether possible that he looked forward also to a revival of the disc, for he used the disc himself as a colour image in *Profond Aujourd'hui*.

A blue eye opens. The red closes. All is at once colours.
Interpenetration. Disc.[42]

The image of the disc had dominated the last major public demonstration made by Delaunay and his followers before the outbreak of war, Delaunay's own *Hommage à Blériot* (Plate 43) and Sonia's *Prismes électriques*. It was, therefore, to be expected that the disc should acquire such prominence in the Orphist memories of both Cendrars and Léger.

Les Disques exists in two oil versions: the *Etude pour les Disques* (Plate 119), and the large canvas—almost eight feet high—(Plate 120).[43]

119. Fernand Léger:
Etude pour Les Disques,
1918. $51 \times 38\frac{1}{4}$ ins,
Los Angeles County
Museum of Art.

The dating of the *Etude* '18–19' where the other is dated '18' leaves the chronological relationship with Léger's other major themes uncertain, and all one can be sure about, using circumstantial evidence, is that it was evolved either during or after the autumn of 1918–after *Les Hélices, Le Remorqueur* and probably *Les Acrobates dans le cirque*.[44]

Les Disques is dominated by a pure device, the discs. But it retains just enough recognizable elements and images from the city world for an idea of an urban setting to be created. On the left are the remnants of a pair of helmeted figures, while on the right are the patterns of wrought iron balconies, yet these are no more than vestigial references to a setting in the city and the idea created is not merely generalized as in *La Ville*, but vague and elusive. Indeed, here Léger did not work, as in *La Ville*, from a predominantly synthetic idea towards a more legible cinematic idea, he worked rather from a more legible cinematic idea towards a predominant purity. This is a point demonstrated well by the far more straightforward use of images in the *Etude*, which definitely precedes the large canvas,[45] since here there can be no doubt that the discs expand and jostle among men and buildings. *Les Disques* is, therefore, not merely a theme which announces with great clarity Léger's debt to Delaunay and yet his wilful independence, it is also a theme which demonstrates conclusively how the literary simultanism of his 'return to subject-matter' never subverted the essential purity of his pictorial aims—his need 'to achieve the maximum pictorial realization by means of plastic contrasts'.[46]

Yet, though apparently so unconnected with any recognizable element from the urban world, just how pure were Léger's discs in their origin and their intended meaning? The degree of Léger's emphasis on pure pictorial contrasts is measured to a certain extent by the answer to this question, and at the same time it exposes especially clearly the fundamental differences between the 'new kind of colour' of his discs and the pre-war 'simultaneous contrasts' of the discs that anticipated them in the work of Delaunay. Léger's discs are not loosely formed like the rising sun-disc in Delaunay's *Hommage à Blériot* (the device with heart-shaped segments related to the suns of Delaunay's *Formes circulaires*); they have instead the tight, ringed form of the other discs, and, like them, cut each other into fragments by their overlappings. These tightly ringed discs in *Hommage à Blériot* were endowed with a particular meaning, for in his 1914 text *Du cubisme à l'art abstrait* Delaunay describes the painting as an analysis of the sun at sunset in a deep, clear sky, among countless 'prismes disques'.[47] Echoing in their tightness of form Sonia Delaunay's *Prismes éléctriques*, these discs were clearly meant to expand as the specific equivalents of the light from arc-lamps. As the nature of colour movement from ring to ring created a sensation opposed to the colour movements of the sun 'forme circulaire', so the contrived discipline of the target disc opposed its looseness—the artifical against the natural.

Cendrars implied a precisely electric meaning when he wrote of the disc in his 1917 *Profond Aujourd'hui*, for the blue and red eyes which open and shut in his piece are set in a poetic context of Eiffel tower, transatlantic liners and semaphore, seeming thus to indicate the flashing of signal lamps. Yet it is clear that Léger's discs, for all the manifest impurity of their pictorial and literary antecedents, were free of the limitations which such a specific meaning might impose, because in a significant number of 1918–19 simultanist themes the device is set in a synthetic and poetic context which leaves its identity *un*defined so that it can act only as a point of contrast. It can be a minor, colourless point of contrast, as in the *état définitif* of *Le Remorqueur* (Plate 105), a major colourful point of contrast, as in the preliminary oils for *Les Acrobates dans le cirque*, or it can take the place of a head, as in the large culminating version of *Les Acrobates* (Plate 109);[48] Léger *never* allows it overtly to indicate the spread of light, least of all in *Les Disques* itself—*Les Disques* is a painting of pure colour discs in a city setting, *not* of *prismes éléctriques*.

This fact clearly exposes the fundamental differences between Léger's and Delaunay's approach to colour because once again it underlines the point that Delaunay based his colour contrasts on the observed atmospheric qualities of light in nature (here electric rather than solar) while Léger based his on the pure brute force of colour flat on the canvas. As in the conflict between their approaches before 1914, where Delaunay saw the force of modern life through the softening medium of an atmospheric colour-screen, Léger did not; and therefore, where Delaunay could not but arrive at a naturalistic prismatic harmony, Léger was able to arrive at an anti-naturalistic, unmuted dissonance. Delaunay's experience of modern life was adapted to the flowing movement of a larger, harmonious view of reality as a whole to be captured in the fluxing quality of light; in 1918 both Léger's view of reality as a whole and his experience of modern life were alike still dissonant.

The gap between the colour of Delaunay's *Hommage à Blériot* and the colour of Léger's *Les Disques* was, in sum, dramatic and it is the measure of a fundamental conflict embracing attitudes both to reality and to modern life. Delaunay situates his *prismes éléctriques* in a naturalistic twilight, their outer rings merging by graded degrees into the evening blue sky, but Léger situates his in a stark pictorial structure completely lacking in atmospheric depth, and allows their outer rings to clash without any softening of impact against the white planes and black bands of that structure. Delaunay rejects black and white altogether, placing one colour ring up against the next, often in complementary contrasts, pursuing a chromatic continuity of change, but Léger avoids complementary contrasts and combines both direct colour clashes and clashes between colour rings and separating rings of white or black, pursuing disruption. As before the war, but with a far greater saturation of colour areas, he isolates colour by setting it admist negative grey, white and black thus increasing its intensity and freeing it from all association with the softness of atmospheric effect. Cendrars's pleas for a 'new kind of colour' in memory of pre-war Orphism, coupled with the revival of literary simultanism and even of the disc, none of these persuasive factors could have persuaded Léger to revive the softened transitions of Delaunay's 'simultaneous contrasts'. In September 1921 he wrote thus to Léonce Rosenberg of Delaunay's colour: 'A constant evenness, little variety, as a result of a narrow, tired formula . . . it has light and movement, but little depth or variety.'[49] *Les Disques* was a painting both more purely pictorial than *Hommage à Blériot* and more brutally aggressive in effect; the discs themselves were indeed pure and at the same time, situated as they were among the vestigial images of a

120. Fernand Léger: *Les Disques,* 1918. $94\frac{1}{2} \times 71$ ins, Musée d'Art Moderne de la ville de Paris.

city setting, they conveyed a generalized, all-embracing modern-life significance, their fragmented intensity of impact the equivalent of that fragmented intensity of experience essential to Léger's view of city life.

However, there was a sense in which the pictorial purity of Léger's central theme in *Les Disques* was compromised to underline its generalized modern-life 'equivalence'; the discs may individually declare, by the amplified artificiality of their colour, that they are above all devices applied for pictorial effect, but they suggest too, by the way that they are related

121. Fernand Léger: *Les Deux Disques dans La Ville,* 1919. 25½ × 21¾ ins, Harold Diamond collection, New York.

122. Fernand Léger: *Cylindres,* 1918. Pencil and wash on paper, 13½ × 10¼ ins, present whereabouts unknown.

to one another, strong mechanical associations—associations which conclusively rob them of any specific significance as equivalents of light, either natural or electric, and which give them a more wide-ranging mechanistic significance. There are three major discs, whose halved bulls-eye centres act as focal points in the central field of the composition; these major discs are attached near their centres by a combination of black shaft and metallic rod, as if they are part of a mechanism of spinning wheels, while subsidiary discs with attendant rods suggest a complex gearing system in active support. The machine factor is stronger in the *Etude,* and a small, closely related painting of 1919, *Les deux disques dans la ville* (Plate 121) gives so integral a place to this machine factor that the discs become explicitly rather than merely implicitly mechanistic. Indeed, it is altogether possible that a definitely mechanistic idea lies behind the central theme of *Les Disques,* and that the machine suggestion results from the fact that the complex of attached spinning forms is a translation into flat terms of a more three-dimensional *élément mécanique* idea, like that explored in the gouache *Cylindres* of 1918 (Plate 122).[50]

In the final analysis, therefore, *Les Disques* emerges as a work whose central theme is a pictorially intensified—purified—machine theme, capable still, like the most purified of the cylinder paintings, of conveying a generalized mechanical identity, set among the disintegrated remains of a literary simultanist framework, capable still of conveying the idea of a city ambiance. It brings together in a conflict of disruptive colour forces the synthetic and the simultanist, the pure and the literary, giving control

189

123. Fernand Léger: *Les disques dans La Ville*, 1919–20. 51 × 64 ins, Musée National Fernand Léger, Biot.

in the end to the synthetic purity of the discs. Yet, like the major *élément mécanique* themes, although it may indeed declare the fundamental importance for Léger of pictorial effect, at the same time, with a generalized yet unequivocal insistence, it declares the fundamental importance of attaching the drama of pictorial effect to the idea of a modern-life content: it declares a subject.

*   *   *   *   *

La Ville may be a simultanist anthology fusing almost the full range of Léger's 1918–19 pictorial aims and methods, but an even fuller anthology was arrived at with the merger of *La Ville* and *Les Disques*—a merger of the synthetic and the simultanist yet wider in its references to other themes, where the pure and the impure, the dynamic and the anti-dynamic were given equal pictorial status. This merger was the pretext for what might be called Léger's culminating large-scale theme of the 1918–19 period, *Les Disques dans la Ville*—a culmination which serves as a comprehensive pictorial summing up.

The invention and development of *Les Disques dans la Ville* sums up the combined freedom and discipline of Léger's approach to thematic evolution during these two years. The idea was initiated simply by replacing the central section of *La Ville* with a slightly modified version of the central *Les Disques* theme, simplifying the left flank of *La Ville* and adding images detached from a further theme, *Le Disque rouge*, to its right flank. Once thus established, it was developed with care, a small, preparatory oil surviving, and a large gouache *esquisse* with the rough yet detailed pencil outlining of components (the plan) still clearly exposed. The large oil version (Plate 123) reveals, in conclusion, only a few *pentimenti* of a petty, fragmented kind, far more closely approaching the conspicuous certainty demanded from an *état définitif* than either *La Ville* or *Les Disques*. It is manifestly a finished statement. Dated 1920 on the back of the canvas,[51] this public version was exhibited with *La Ville* itself at the Salon des Indépendants in February 1920, making of Léger's contribution to that Salon a manifesto presentation of his post-war convictions which could not have been more all-embracing.

Yet, more than merely a summing up, *Les Disques dans la Ville* marked for Léger an end: with *La Ville*, the painting took part at the 1920 Indépendants in a display which was in a significant sense the public *finale* of a style, or rather a group of styles. For that spring, after two years in pictorial pursuit of a dramatically anti-order view of modern life, Léger was at the edge of a sudden and apparently complete change of stance. By the end of the next year he had as a painter turned away from his 'renaissance of the subject' openly to reinstate the conventional subject-matter of classicism—the nude, and the pastoral landscape. Moreover, he had turned away from a brutal pursuit of disintegration at the expense of classical clarity for a more measured pursuit of clear-cut figurative and landscape statements, where the qualities of balance and precision were at a premium. Within a very short space of time he had moved from conspicuous isolation to a deep and committed involvement in the 'call to order' introduced by the crystal Cubists, and to an emphatically post-war art. 1920–1 saw Léger at last respond to the convergence of current, classicizing avant-garde pressures, and thus the complete reassessment of those attitudes on which his dissonant realism had been built for over ten years.

CHAPTER 7
Léger's 'call to order': its Beginnings and its Context

Léger's violent assault on the rational, harmonious pictorial values dominant among the other artists of Léonce Rosenberg's galerie de l'Effort Moderne had little effect on them. In particular, Juan Gris, Jean Metzinger and the sculptor Jacques Lipchitz, having been together at Beaulieu-près-Loches during the summer of 1918,[1] continued to work in a crystal Cubist mode during 1919, while Gino Severini took further his interest in the possibility of applying theories of proportion to the visual arts.[2] Rosenberg himself was committed to a deeply classical stance and regularly during 1919 discussed with the Italian the theories of Pythagoras and Plato, as well perhaps as those of Leon Battista Alberti and Charles Henry,[3] the mathematician, once so respected by Georges Seurat, with whom Severini had been in touch since 1917.

Within the circle of 'l'Effort Moderne', as before 1918, until 1920 the most comprehensive demonstration of how clearly defined the language of Cubism could be and how stable its 'architecture', was presented by the actual works of the crystal Cubists. Juan Gris began in 1919 to use the dominant diagonal once again, experimenting with compositions, like *Guitare et compotier* (Plate 124), in which diagonal lines and edges compete about the truncated remains of a vertical axis. He was also tempted by the seductive grace of long curves, here defining the contours of fruit-bowl, guitar and book. But his diagonals always relate in such a way to his rectangular format and vertical axis that stability is assured, and they always by mutual opposition neutralize each other; moreover, he still uses line and *chiaroscuro* contrast with such clarity as to create both a firm pictorial framework and a crystalline solidity of form never detached by fully rounded modelling from the picture surface. In fact, so strong was his sustained classical bias that he was still capable in December 1919 of an image as firm and as anchored to the vertical as *Nature-morte et carafe* (Plate 125). *Guitare et compotier* and *Nature-morte et carafe* do not openly declare any fixed allegiance to a system of proportion, and this is so too of

124. (above left)
Juan Gris: *Guitare et compotier*, 1919. $28\frac{3}{4} \times 21\frac{3}{4}$ ins, Niels Onstad collection, Norway.

125. (above)
Juan Gris: *Nature morte et carafe*, 1919. $28\frac{3}{4} \times 21\frac{1}{4}$ ins, private collection, Basel.

126. (left)   Gino Severini: *Nature morte avec raisins et mandole*, 1919. $17\frac{1}{2} \times 26$ ins, private collection, Florence.

the parallel work of Metzinger and Lipchitz; but during 1919 Severini, supported by his growing knowledge of mathematics, began to declare openly in paintings like *Nature-morte avec raisins et mandole* (Plate 126) the systematic application of ruler, setsquare and protractor to the act of composition. In his painting the new respect accorded to reason in art was made conspicuously a part of the creative process, and to the qualities of architectural construction, crystalline clarity, formal economy, stability and stylistic unity was added, with the minimum of concealment, the quality of mathematical order.

The work of the crystal Cubists may be the most comprehensive demonstration of the developing classical convictions within 'l'Effort Moderne', but there were as well two important verbal statements which in 1919 and 1920 gave intellectual backing to their methods and priorities. The first of these was made by the critic Maurice Raynal in his small 1919 pamphlet 'Quelques intentions du Cubisme', which was the result of a debate held at the gallery during Severini's exhibition there.[4] Raynal had been close to the 'Section d'Or' organizers at Puteaux when in 1912 such figures as Jacques Villon, Raymond Duchamp-Villon, Albert Gleizes and the younger Juan Gris had made the first concerted effort to fit Cubism into an idea of 'the tradition' and to apply proportional systems to Cubist modes of composition, so it is not surprising that he should have reacted positively to the questions raised by Severini's painting.[5] However, avoiding detailed analysis, Raynal does not specifically deal with the question of proportion in painting, but rather with the general question of the function to be given reason and method; he takes a little further the line of argument opened up by Paul Dermée in 1917, envisaging an alliance between the rational and the intuitive by which intuition remains dominant in the creative process. In fact, his more generalized view is closer to the approach of Gris to the rational or 'architectural' factor in painting, with its lack of an openly declared mathematical discipline.[6] For Raynal, a crucial classical quality especially in the art of the French tradition is 'the science of exactitude' (*la science de la mésure*)—but this is nothing so rigidly defined as the science of proportional systems; it is no more than the ability to control the excesses of sensualism. It is a control which comes above all from the strict limitation of 'elements or pictorial means', the kind of limitation coming from an understanding of art in the past used, not imitatively, but intuitively.[7]

The second statement of intellectual support for the classical trend was also published, like 'Quelques intentions du Cubisme', by the Editions de l'Effort Moderne; it was Léonce Rosenberg's own pamphlet 'Cubisme et Tradition', written in 1920.[8] Like Raynal, Rosenberg keeps to a generalized stance closer to Gris than to Severini, but at certain points he suggests a far stronger bias towards the qualities of 'organization', 'classification' and 'science' which Dermée had suggested were essential to 'a classical age'. Thus, after quoting once again Plato's eulogy to geometrical form in *Philebus*, Rosenberg quotes in French translation the American Ralph Waldo Emerson's definition of beauty as that which is simple, without superfluities, bringing together many opposing elements, and goes on himself to declare that Cubism is a return to order by way of 'a hierarchy of values' aimed at 'a new unity', and subject to 'eternal laws of equilibrium'.[9]

Raynal's 'Quelques intentions du Cubisme', Rosenberg's 'Cubisme et Tradition' and the work especially of Gris, Metzinger, Lipchitz and Severini make it clear that between 1918 and 1920 'l'Effort Moderne' deepened its commitment to the revival of reason in art and to the promotion of a new Cubist 'classical age'. Léger's exhibition at Rosenberg's gallery in February 1919, as one of a series which included Gris, Metzinger and Severini, must indeed have seemed outside, even hostile to the 'house style', and there is evidence that both Léger himself and Rosenberg were very much aware of his unremitting isolation. Thus, the first draft of Léger's contract with the dealer (1 July 1918) includes an intriguing protective clause by which Rosenberg retains the right to forbid 'all participation, artistic or not' in the illustration of books representing: 'a tendency clearly hostile to the art for which the galerie de l'Effort Moderne stands'[10]—a clause at least hinting at lack of faith in Léger's then current collaboration with Cendrars on the illustrated edition of *J'ai Tué*. Léger was neither prevented from completing the *J'ai Tué* project, nor from launching into *La Fin du monde filmée par l'Ange Notre-Dame* the following year, but that he felt strongly his isolation as an anti-order and a literary painter is demonstrated by the fact that in the summer or autumn of 1919 he wrote to Rosenberg asking for reassurance.

'Calm down,' the dealer replied, as quoted by Severini, 'I like your painting, but not so much for what it is now, as for what it promises.'[11] The circle of 'l'Effort Moderne' was, it seems, well aware of the alien nature of Léger's work, but Rosenberg, if no one else, saw the potential for something else altogether more sympathetic, and his judgement was, as has been suggested, to be vindicated.

*　　*　　*　　*　　*

Perhaps for as much as half of the year 1920 Léger remained uncompromisingly true to his brash, anti-order convictions, and continued with certain of the subjects and pictorial practices taken to such a pitch the year before. Most significant of all from the point of view of 'l'Effort Moderne' orthodoxy, he continued only to paint stylistically pluralist pictures in which conflicting elements collided with one another and in which the process of disintegration militated against clarity of statement.

This continuing destructive approach, concentrated now especially on the human figure, led in 1920 to the development of a group of new themes in which he explored further the pictorial possibilities of his disintegrated mode.[12] One of these themes was *La Femme au miroir* in a sequence of at least three oils, one stage of which is Plate 127. Léger's subject here is a single figure seen half-length at a dressing-table holding up a hand-mirror whose oval outline cuts across her face, a subject perfectly geared to his destructively ambiguous intentions. Enough legible features are left to announce the essentials of the subject, the eye, the hand and the half cup which are inserted in the *état définitif* being especially recognizable. But these features are dispersed as merely partial clues in a loose, disintegrated array of colour planes, bars, metallic elements, and indeed, the fragmentary use of such clearly recognizable features, much more than the elusive suggestions made in themes like *Le Typographe*, simply serve to intensify the effect of figurative disintegration—of destruction.

127. Fernand Léger: *La Femme au miroir*, 1920. $36\frac{1}{4} \times 25\frac{1}{2}$ ins, Moderna Museet, Stockholm.

128. Pablo Picasso: *L'Arlequin*, 1918. $57\frac{3}{4} \times 26\frac{1}{4}$ ins, Joseph Pulitzer Jr collection, St Louis.

129. Fernand Léger: *L'Homme à la pipe* 2e état, 1920. $35\frac{3}{4} \times 25\frac{1}{2}$ ins, Musée National d'Art Moderne, Paris.

It is perhaps a further comment on the destructive ambiguity of Léger's approach here that *La Femme au miroir* reflects an awareness not so much of the classicizing Cubists of the 'Effort Moderne' circle as of the most self-consciously paradoxical among all the Cubists—Picasso. It invites comparison or contrast not so much with a figure-painting by Juan Gris as with the brighter, more variegated synthetic Cubist figure-paintings of Picasso between 1917 and 1920, for instance the *Arlequin* executed at Montrouge in 1918 (Plate 128). Picasso was still a mesmerizing inventive force for the 'Effort Moderne' artists, impossible to ignore, and his dealer by 1920 was Paul Rosenberg, the brother of Léonce, whose premises were very close to those of the galerie de l'Effort Moderne.[13]

Picasso's fragmentary use of simple signs for eyes, hands and guitar compares with Léger's simplified use of features, and so too does the way his complex, overlapping structure of planes breaks down the figurative coherence of his subject, but this latter destructive process is far more radically violent as Léger applies it. Where Picasso works almost entirely in terms of flat planes, dotted, striped and coloured differently to create a varied but stylistically united result, Léger works in terms both of flat contrasting planes and of modelled elements, using the staccato effects of interruption developed during the previous two years to create a stylistically disunited result. In all three versions the wholeness of the figure is challenged dramatically by the stylistic contradictions out of which it is built: the hair is both a series of corrugations and a dark, sweeping metallic surface, the right arm is a cylinder while the left is an overlapping pair of colour planes. Not even pictorially can the figure be read as a coherent, inter-locking structure, and in the comprehensiveness of its disintegration is conveyed Léger's continuing rejection of stylistic unity altogether.

Yet when Léger initiated his 'call to order' in 1920, it was not towards a sustained unification of style that he moved, but rather towards a simpler, more coordinated presentation of stylistic contradictions, in which a more unified and more clear-cut planar architecture provided the setting for a more unified and more clear-cut presentation of the machine-man figure. An end to ambiguity was allied to conspicuous structural stability. The nature of Léger's next move is most clearly seen in a series of paintings whose subject was an old simultanist concern, man in the city. There are again several versions of this theme, and one of the more finished is the canvas dated 1920 and titled *l'Homme à la pipe, 2e état* (Plate 129). Here the robot city man is, by contrast with the *boudoir* woman of *La Femme au miroir*, a single coordinated structure of head, torso and limbs—a clear figurative statement contained within a stable and equally clear synthetic architecture of flat planes. Stability is ensured by the dominance of vertical and horizontal, and a certain austere strength is achieved by means of the broad, alternating bars of black and white. Yet, for all its stable clarity of statement, violent pictorial conflict remains central to *L'Homme à la pipe*. The metallic solidity of Léger's man and dog strikes so hard against the flatness of their setting because of the clarity with which they are separated from it; thus, although the distinctly classical qualities of clarity and stability controlled by a strengthened sense of pictorial discipline have here come so much to the fore, Léger remains a painter concerned with conflict—with dissonance rather than with harmony.

L'Homme à la pipe is a clear statement of the crucial change that eventually brought about the end of Léger's disintegrated and simultanist view of modern life in 1920. But the change receives its most comprehensive expression, with the machine-man successor to the war-time *poilu* as subject, in a theme which has become since its invention in 1920 the archetypal image of Léger's classical view of man's relationship with the machine, *Le Mécanicien* (Plate 130), the conclusive version of which is the canvas in the National Gallery of Canada at Ottawa.[14] As convincingly as *La Femme au miroir* declares Léger's refusal to compromise with the classical values of his friends in the 'Effort Moderne' circle, *Le Mécanicien* declares his new determination to ally those classical values to a continuing need for pictorial drama, and it declares also his new determination to reconsider in terms of those classical values his idea of modern life. *Le Mécanicien*, no more than months after *La Femme au miroir*—even perhaps at the same time—represents Léger's almost total acceptance of the new common tendency towards a post-war 'classical age'.

The Ottawa canvas is dominated by the mechanic, a figure whose structure is even more stable and coordinated than that of the city man in *L'Homme à la pipe*, set in an architecture of bars and rectangular planes which is even more austerely disciplined. The almost sweet modulated mauves and oranges of *L'Homme à la pipe* are given no place here, and the cooled flesh tones of the figure, with their smoothly finished metallic sheen collide with a stark framework in which black and white is in control relieved only occasionally by mustard yellow and an undiluted, isolated vermilion. Once more, with greater clarity comes greater force of impact, so that Léger's established need for pictorial aggression is not compromised by the new importance of the classical virtues. The mechanic is presented as the creator both of a new, precise mechanical order, and of a violent visual drama.

Léger's remodelled machine-man image manifestly did not yet declare the end of his 'return to subject-matter': it declared a fresh view of a popular modern subject which was not new in his repertoire. As has been seen, the robot figure of *Le Chauffeur nègre* (Plate 106) and *La Ville* (Plate 117) had already in 1918 been identified as *Le Mécanicien* (Plate 100). He was the *poilu* machine-man in civilian life, and indeed his popular and modern appeal had, it seems, aroused Léger's profound admiration as early as 1912. It was the mechanic for whom Marinetti had predicted the evolution of new machine-like features in his 1911 'Le Futurisme',[15] and it was the mechanics themselves as much as the aero-engines on display who had attracted Léger at the Salon de l'Aviation at the Grand Palais in the autumn of 1912. Thus, his memories of that Salon, as set down three years after the painting of *Le Mécanicien*, culminate in an eulogistic passage in praise of the mechanics who accepted his invitation to look at the paintings hung near by in the Salon d'Automne. He recalls above all a sixteen-year-old, with blazing red hair, in a blue checked shirt and orange trousers, his hands stained with Prussian blue, contemplating the gold framed nudes, how the brilliance of the mechanic as a spectacle 'killed the Salon', how, seemingly the child of an agricultural machine, he was, for Léger, the symbol of life tomorrow.[16]

This boy mechanic was not Léger's mature *Mécanicien* of 1920, for the figure of the painting is himself cool and subdued of colour to contrast with his dazzling setting, but, for all that, *Le Mécanicien* is still presented as the symbol of life tomorrow. It is the way that this long-established symbol was changed in 1920 that conveys so comprehensively the depth of the change which took place that year in Léger's idea of modern life—of reality as a whole.

In the figure-paintings of 1913 and 1914 the machine-man image is presented as a fragmented and rotating constellation of gleaming volumes in colours applied straight from the tube (Plates 34 and 74); in *La Partie de cartes* (Colour Plate 4) it is gun-metal grey, but still dynamically rotating and still fragmented; in the 1918 *Le Mécanicien* and in *La Ville* and so many of the other cinematic themes, it is given an unfragmented, robot identity, yet is but a small part of a complex and disintegrated composition, its wholeness violated by the cutting action of adjoining elements and planes (Plates 100 and 117); while, at last, in the 1920 *Le Mécanicien* it has become the unfragmented, unchallenged centrepiece of the composition —a cool construction of volumes utterly devoid of dynamic rotary suggestions. From a presentation of the machine-man image as a disintegrated and dynamic pictorial theme, whose qualities reflect those of a disintegrated and dynamic experience of speed and change in modern life, Léger has moved to a presentation of the machine-man image as an exactly balanced mechanical system, whose qualities reflect the working efficiency of the motors which create speed and change. From a simultanist attempt to convey the place of the mechanic and the machine in a conflicting, many-layered experience of reality, he has moved to a classical attempt to convey the precise perfection of the mechanic and the machine themselves. As Severini had done in very different stylistic circumstances four years earlier, he had replaced an emphasis on the fragmentation of reality by speed, with an emphasis on the unfragmented, the exactly integrated beauty of the machine, here given a human form symbolic of a new, classical order. Moreover, although the Ottawa painting reveals occasional *pentimenti* and late additions,[17] these are carefully concealed from all but the closest scrutiny, and a smoothness of finish is achieved only rivalled during the preceding phase by *La Partie de cartes*, so that the impression of a machine-made perfection is also especially convincing. The result is a work, which, as never before in Léger's art, combines the analogy between the practice of painting and the process of machine-manufacture with an image of mechanical and human order in urban life, and all this without loss of dissonant pictorial power.

Yet perhaps the most striking evidence of the fundamental importance of the change in Léger's idea of painting and modern life is the fact that the figure of *Le Mécanicien* openly courts comparison, not simply with the classicizing styles then current in the Parisian avant-garde, but also with a style from the past. *Le Mécanicien* was painted something over a year after the first Egyptian and Assyrian rooms were reopened at the Louvre following war-time closure, and it is back to the crisply carved structure of the figure as represented in these styles that Léger looks with his new machine-man symbol of 'life tomorrow'.[18] The clear separation and definition of muscles in the arms recalls the musculature of the eighth century BC Assyrian figures in relief from the Palace of Sargon at Kalsabad

130. Fernand Léger: *Le Mécanicien*, 1920. $45\frac{1}{2} \times 34\frac{1}{2}$ ins, National Gallery of Canada, Ottawa.

131. *Winged Spirit,* Assyrian stone relief
from the palace of Sargon at Karlsabad, 8th
Century BC, Musée du Louvre, Paris.

132. Stele. Egyptian, stone, 12th Dynasty, Musée du
Louvre, Paris.

to be seen at the Louvre (Plate 131), while the shallow yet strong modelling,
the frontal posture of the torso, the head set by contrast in profile, the
stiffly placed arms, the use of typical attributes—the tattoo, rings and
cigarette—all these are elements which unmistakably refer to Egyptian
'steles', like the early twelfth dynasty example (Plate 132), also in the
Louvre. Where his *élément mécanique* and cinematic themes of 1918–19
had conspicuously declared their novelty in their lack of contact with
past styles, here Léger's *Mécanicien* conspicuously declares a profound
sympathy with particular past styles. The frozen dignity of Léger's new
machine-man image is given a Hieratic resonance, openly asserting his
belief in the existence of constant pictorial principles to be found as much
in the past as in the present. In this way, like Severini with his 1916
Maternité (Plate 140), Léger allies the change in his idea of man and the
machine to an equally profound change in his idea of the relationship
between the past and the present in art. He adds to his new classicism a
strong sense of tradition.

Not only in terms of its structure and of the ordered image it makes of the mechanized mechanic, but also in terms of its stylistic allegiances, *Le Mécanicien* demonstrates the uncompromising conviction with which during 1920, in the space of less than a year, Léger fully responded to the growing avant-garde pressure on him to classicize his art. It marks for him as a painter an entirely fresh beginning, and it marks too his rejection of relative avant-garde isolation for the more gregarious excitement of a new and growing common tendency—a common tendency at least as broad-based and as influential in the arts as that which had absorbed his energies before the war. *Le Mécanicien* marks the beginning of Léger's own, individual 'call to order'. The quiet persistence of those who believed in a new 'classical age' was in the final analysis more persuasive than his brash post-war aggressiveness.

*　　*　　*　　*　　*

The work of Gris, Severini, Lipchitz and Metzinger between 1918 and 1920, and the ideas disseminated by Léonce Rosenberg and Maurice Raynal under the auspices of 'l'Effort Moderne' were, in fact, responsible for no more than a fraction of the avant-garde pressure put on Léger to classicize his art. The years 1920 and 1921 saw the coming of age of several other developments which in different ways led to the advocacy of clearer, more stable pictorial aims allied on occasion to a deep respect for the classical styles of the past. However persuasive the firm clarity of crystal Cubist painting may have been, there were other forces for aesthetic order released in the Parisian avant-garde which were perhaps more persuasive, more effectively behind Léger's sudden change of stance.

*　　*　　*　　*　　*

Léonce Rosenberg and Maurice Raynal might have avoided the definition of a 'hierarchy of values' or the codification of pictorial laws, but by 1920 there was already under way a concerted campaign which did not avoid these issues. This campaign was led by Amédée Ozenfant and his architect friend Charles-Edouard Jeanneret (Le Corbusier); they called it Purism. Purism was especially relevant for Léger, because, more even than Severini, it stood for a complementary relationship between a newly ordered version of Cubism in painting and a classically balanced view of the machine in the modern world. Its capacity for influence was the direct result of the propagandist energy with which Ozenfant and Jeanneret set out to announce its principles.

From the beginning of 1916 Ozenfant had been actively involved in the avant-garde, and the last two numbers of his review *L'Elan*, whose most radical early contributors had been Roger de La Fresnaye, the Dunoyer de Segonzanc, André Marchand and Luc-Albert Moreau, included such names as Gleizes, Metzinger, Apollinaire, Canudo, Jacob, Salmon, Lhote and Severini. From the December 1916 issue (the last) his course was set as painter and theoretician towards the precise elaboration of a Cubist 'plastic language' without 'parasitic terms'[19]—an elaboration far more closely defined than that attempted by Severini, or Reverdy, or Dermée, or Raynal, or Rosenberg.

Ozenfant built his ideas between 1916 and 1918 on a foundation of knowledge which is remarkable for its impartial breadth—the product of an early combination of studiousness, cultivation and mechanical curiosity. His youthful enthusiasms[20] ranged from the Egyptian rooms, Ingres, Poussin and Chardin at the Louvre, to Georges Seurat, from Debussy to the writings of Kant, Schopenhauer, Bergson and Renan, from the scientific studies of Lucien Fabre (on insects), Haeckel (on evolution) and Jean Perrin (on atoms), to the broader scientific works of Henri Poincaré;[21] and these enthusiasms were complemented by an enthusiasm for the mechanically efficient and the technically new, which derived from his father (an early champion of Hennebique and of reinforced concrete in building), an enthusiasm which had led him as early as 1910 to design with his brother what he later called the first functional sportscar body for their Hispano-Suiza *de grand sport*.[22] The clear logical framework of the Purist aesthetic, as applied to painting at least, came finally of a fusion of his philosophical speculations, his relatively fresh understanding of Cubism in its increasingly crystalline form, his knowledge of the art of the past and the science of the present, and his engineer's bent towards the efficient and the practical; but, before Purism reached maturity as a theory, it needed one further stimulus, which brought with it an equally broad range of ideas and a more highly trained practical expertise, the stimulus provided by Jeanneret.

The young architect met Ozenfant through his former teacher Auguste Perret (an old friend of Ozenfant's father) in May 1917,[23] and his own personal combination of classical idealism and technological faith made for a quick and profound mutual understanding. They discussed aesthetics and corresponded, with Ozenfant, if his *Mémoires* are to be believed, acting as guide to Cubist painting, which hitherto had not concerned his friend.[24] Then, at the beginning of September 1918, Jeanneret came to stay with Ozenfant near Bordeaux, where they painted and drew landscapes of a severe and massive stability, and wrote down the precepts of Purism.[25] In November 1918—the month of the publication of Cendrars's *J'ai Tué* with Léger's simultanist illustrations—the two held an exhibition of paintings and drawings in Madame Bongard's *maison de couture*, renamed for the occasion the galerie Thomas, and published their manifesto, *Après le cubisme*. However, it was not until November 1920 that the aesthetic expounded here provided the editorial foundation for a review capable of making Purism more than a side-issue in the Parisian avant-garde; the review was called *L'Esprit Nouveau*, and its editors at the beginning were Ozenfant, Jeanneret and Paul Dermée.

As has been seen, between 1917 and 1920 Léonce Rosenberg, Severini and Paul Dermée had stood together for the reinstatement of reason as the only instrument by which to fashion an aesthetic and therefore a style. Reason gave intuition a direction, and its most uncompromising product was science. In *Après le cubisme* and their crucial expository articles in *L'Esprit Nouveau*, no. 1 and no. 4 (1920 and early 1921), Ozenfant and Jeanneret echoed this view, declaring that logic alone 'controls and regulates the often fantastic progress of intuition, and allows it to move forward with certainty'.[26] From 1918 on a fundamental axiom for them was that art and science were in an essential sense directed towards the same end: the formation of 'an equation by which to sum up the nature of the universe'.[27] After no. 4, *L'Esprit Nouveau* regularly included articles on such subjects as the atom, Einstein's theory of relativity, organic and inorganic chemistry; their conviction that art and science were essentially parallel activities did not weaken. Science, they believed, was the attempt to arrive at an ordered intellectual idea of the structure of reality, art was the attempt to arrive at ordered structures of a visual, verbal and musical kind which obeyed the same basic laws.[28] Both art and science depended on mathematics—number—and both sought a numerical beauty.[29] For Ozenfant and Jeanneret, 'Number' was, in fact, 'the basis of all beauty', in both science and art, answering a common and constant human need. Yet there was certainly one crucial difference: it lay in the fact that where scientific numerical order answered the needs and therefore reflected the working physiological structure of the brain alone, aesthetic numerical order answered the needs and therefore reflected the working physiological structure of the senses in concert with the brain—in the case of the visual arts, the eye.[30]

The Purists conceived of the artist as a mechanism in his own right—a mechanism which reacted with great precision to the stimuli of the senses and which was invariably drawn, because of its own ordered structure, to ordered conformations of form and colour.[31] Ozenfant and Jeanneret's codification of the Cubist 'plastic language' began, therefore, with an attempt to analyse man's physical and psychological reactions to form and colour, the two kinds of reaction being in their estimation linked. 'From man's point of view,' they write in *L'Esprit Nouveau* no. 4, 'aesthetic sensations are not all of the same value, either in terms of intensity or of quality; it is possible to say that there is a hierarchy.'[32] Implicitly recalling Plato's *Philebus*, they distinguished between 'the brute pleasure of the senses', and sensations which can evoke in man 'that special state, mathematical in kind, which follows, for instance, the clear perception of a great law general in its validity';[33] these latter sensations were capable of creating 'joy', since they carried the beauty of 'Number'. For the Purists, the aim of the work of art was, in sum, to create 'a sensation of mathematical order',[34] and with this aim constantly in view their detailed analysis of colour and form in painting was carried through.

The Purists defined two basic categories of sensation: 'primary' and 'secondary'.[35] The first was created by certain primary forms, such as the sphere or cube, whose effect was identical for all individuals of all races; the second was created by secondary forms whose effect depended on the cultural background of the individual. On this basis invariable laws of pictorial order were established, most clearly and comprehensively in *L'Esprit Nouveau* no. 4. First of all, Ozenfant and Jeanneret declared that painting must contain both a primary formal basis and a range of secondary forms, so that it could have both a constant, geometric validity and a more variable 'human resonance'.[36] However, the organization of these primary and secondary forms was to be controlled by laws of composition, the most important of which were, of course, the laws of proportion. These, significantly, were conceived of as both architectural and pictorial, and they were based on the Golden Section ratio, a coherent relationship between the Golden Section triangle and the picture format being the key to the Purists' compositional method.[37] The Golden Section ensured a

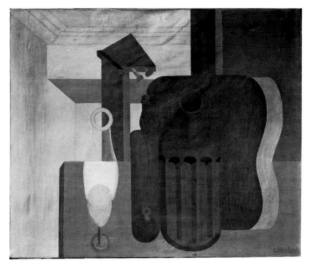

133. Amédée Ozenfant: *Flacon, guitare, verre et bouteille à la table grise,* 1920. 32 × 39½ ins, Oeffentliche Kunstssammlung, Basel.

134. Charles-Edouard Jeanneret: *Nature morte à la pile d'assiettes,* 1920. 32 × 39½ ins, Oeffentliche Kunstssammlung, Basel.

'firm geometry', while 'unity' was ensured by the application to all minor elements of 'modular method', by which every element was proportionally related to every other.[38]

In general terms the Purist attempt, not merely to 'realize sensations' but systematically to arrive at a hierarchy of sensation was analogous with Neo-Impressionism, and it is interesting that among the contributors to *L'Esprit Nouveau* was Charles Henry, Severini's mathematician acquaintance, who had been so admired by Georges Seurat.[39] However, unlike the Neo-Impressionists, the Purists did not concentrate on colour as the crucial factor; following the anti-Impressionist bias of Cubism before 1912, Ozenfant and Jeanneret insisted that colour must be subordinate to form. Yet they still felt it necessary to attempt a brief analysis of colour, identifying three main chromatic scales in painting: 'the great scale'—ochres, reds, earth colours, white, black and ultramarine—colours which promoted unity because they neither appeared to advance nor to retreat, but kept to the picture-plane; the 'dynamic scale'—citrus yellow, orange, vermilions, Veronese green, cobalt blue—colours which challenged unity because they always appeared either to advance or retreat; and the 'transitional scale', all colours which are not full-bodied, which are mere tints. For them, 'the great scale' alone ensured that colour remained subordinate to form in the pictorial hierarchy.[40]

Ozenfant suggests in his *Mémoires* that, although the aesthetic of Purism was virtually formed as a whole by November 1918 with the publication of *Après le cubisme,* the application of its principles to the actual painting of himself and Jeanneret had not yet by that date reached a satisfactory conclusion.[41] It was in 1919 and especially in 1920 that Purism as a style was given confident and comprehensive pictorial form, and in February 1921 canvases from the entire 1918–20 period by both Ozenfant and Jeanneret were shown at the galerie Duret in Paris.[42] Here the paintings of 1920 added to the verbal propaganda of *L'Esprit Nouveau* the far more effective impetus of visual example; among them were Ozenfant's *Flacon, guitare, verre et bouteille à la table grise* (Plate 133) and Jeanneret's *Nature-morte à la pile d'assiettes* (Plate 134).

Style could not more straightforwardly follow theory than in these canvases. Primary forms—the circle and the rectangle for instance—are given 'resonance' by secondary forms—the graceful curves of Jeanneret's opened book and of Ozenfant's flask for instance. Colour is firmly held within the range of 'the great scale', volume being built by the strong *chiaroscuro* use of tonal modelling. And both compositions, stabilized by the dominance of vertical and horizontal, are given a geometric framework by the studied use of the Golden Section triangle—a point made with expository firmness by the illustration of Ozenfant's painting marked out with 'regulating lines' in *L'Esprit Nouveau* no. 17 (Plate 135).

Up to this point in the argument the Purist aesthetic and style have been presented in absolutely pure pictorial terms—as concerned with the ideal order of pictorial effect alone, but these two canvases make it clear that Ozenfant and Jeanneret aimed at more than purity, for, alongside the purified objects of a work like Gris's 1918 *Nature-morte à la guitare* (Plate 80), the weighty sense of physical presence conveyed by the objects they represent seems almost impure. There was, as Ozenfant recalls in his *Mémoires*, a clear difference of opinion between the Purists and Gris over the nature of the ideal and the concrete. Where Gris believed that he could start a painting with the ideal perfection of absolutely abstract forms in mind and then set out to find them in real objects, Ozenfant and Jeanneret believed that they could only legitimately arrive at pictorial perfection by starting with the observed qualities of objects—by starting *in* reality. Thus, where Gris' method sacrificed the physical wholeness of objects to a pure pictorial idea, Ozenfant and Jeanneret returned to a clear-cut analytical Cubist method, giving the object a basic importance as the source of the primary as well as the secondary forms which added up to 'sensation . . .

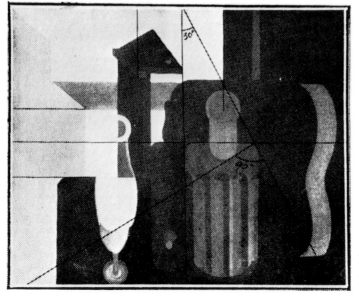

135. Amédée Ozenfant: No. 133 as illustrated in *L'Esprit Nouveau,* no. 17 with 'tracés régulateurs'.

of a mathematical order'. They insisted that the painter should not merely extract a few ideal 'elements' from things seen, but instead should use the Cubist technique of shifting viewpoints to present a complete and truthful sense of things seen, a fact clearly demonstrated by the two 1920 canvases by Ozenfant and Jeanneret at the galerie Druet exhibition.[43] The observed forms of bottles, flask, guitar, plates, etc., are set out in plan and profile to create at once a clear sense of their total physical nature as objects, and a stable composition which follows the laws of Purist pictorial theory. The paintings are ideal in their geometric simplicity and balance, but the impression is given of objects which are in reality ideal. Ozenfant and Jeanneret emerge as idealists with a far stronger bent towards reality than Gris, determined to prove by pictorial example that reality aspires to and occasionally even achieves the ideal. They aimed at the perfected representation of perfect subjects.

It was, thus, logically inevitable that the Purists should complement the idea of a hierarchy of sensations with the idea of a hierarchy of subjects.[44] The subjects at the top of their hierarchy would not, they suggest, merely be perfect in a pure sense, but would convey with particular clarity 'the laws', by which they mean not merely the laws of painting, but the laws on which all reality is based. In 1918 the most important subject with these profoundly significant properties was for them the human figure,[45] but by early 1921 and *L'Esprit Nouveau* no. 4, they had changed their focus to concentrate entirely on still-life as the only possible Purist subject. The reasoning behind this shift of focus to still-life was as always precisely logical. In the first place, they saw condensed and made unequivocally visible in the simple geometric order of certain still-life objects the fundamental principles of evolution and mathematical order basic to life as a whole, and in the second place, they saw the everyday banality of these objects as an advantage, encouraging concentration on their pure qualities of formal order. The Purist idea of the significance of these objects sums up their ordered, idealist view of reality—and at the same time not only clarifies the relationship between their perfected version of analytical Cubism and its timeless still-life subject-matter, but also the basis of its relationship with the reality of modern life and the machine.

The view of Ozenfant and Jeanneret on life as a whole was founded on the premise that man was the product of a strict selective process—'natural selection'—himself becoming a machine perfectly adapted to his situation.[46] This process of selection was considered to proceed from the need to adapt to certain constant circumstances and to fulfil certain constant functions, following the law of 'economy', which was itself the essence of 'natural selection'.[47] The objects which man made directly to answer his functional needs were designed, they continued, of necessity according to the same law of 'economy' according to which man himself was designed.[48] Therefore, the objects most profoundly endowed with human significance were those which were most useful, for they complemented man's perfection. These were the objects of their still-life subjects, which later became known as 'type-objects'. Thus, the apparently mundane subject of Ozenfant's *Flacon, guitare, verre et bouteilles à la table grise* and of Jeanneret's *Nature-morte à la pile d'assiettes* is revealed as, for the Purists, anything but mundane: the perfect simplicity of these ordinary things and their relationship with man were symbolic of an all-embracing idea of the principles governing order in life.

As with Severini's crystal Cubist still-lifes of 1916–20 (Plates 79 and 126), the analogy between the Purist still-life and the modern world— particularly the machine—was not made pictorially plain; Ozenfant and Jeanneret were not tempted illusionistically to mechanize objects. It was, for them, the fact that the objects they painted observed the same laws not only as the human body in its formation, but as machines, that made their still-lifes so simply analogous with the products of engineers. The machine was considered, in fact, to be a particularly complex functional device, which aspired to the perfection of a 'type-object', its parts standard-ized and designed for the greatest possible economy of action and, its function determined by man. It was not considered the ultimate subject for the Purist painting, because no machine could achieve final perfection: a car, a steam-engine, a steam-ship, each was merely a stage in a never-ending process of development: they all would be superseded; but the simple vase, glass, bottle or guitar had reached the ideal and final state of economic efficiency to which it aspired—it was a definitive 'type-object'— a perfect item of reality.[49]

However, as a constantly developing demonstration of the aspiration towards an ideal functional economy, the machine and modern life re-mained of crucial importance behind and alongside the still-life painting of Purism. Later, in L'Esprit Nouveau no. 14, Ozenfant and Jeanneret explained that, for them, the machine was not a subject for the artist but rather 'a lesson for the spirit', 'a lesson of structure', a 'lesson of method' universal in its application.[50] Machines and the constructions designed by engineers (bridges, dams, grain elevators) would, they believed, by the fact of their precision-built presence in the urban environment more and more deepen modern man's awareness of 'the law of selection: economy'— of the order in all things. Thus, far from being the dramatic stimulus behind a dissonant and disintegrated pictorial style, the products of the engineers were seen as the calm, structured stimulus behind an art of order. The machine and the great iron or concrete monuments—dams, factories, bridges and power stations—were presented, not as the initiators of a complex, interpenetrating experience of reality, but as the components of a new geometric world, which aspired to an ideal functional perfection— a modern reality which was more than merely analogous with Purist painting, a positive force behind its precise classicism. Such modern monuments, they declared in Après le cubisme, possessed 'a Roman grandeur'.[51]

In L'Esprit Nouveau nos. 1 and 2, the Purists, signing themselves Le Corbusier and Sanguier, published the first two of three essays called 'Trois rappels à MM.les Architectes', which were in 1923 to form a part of Le Corbusier's manifesto for a new architecture, Vers une architecture.[52] Here they illustrated some of the constructions which so convinced them of a coming esprit nouveau—a new feeling for equilibrium. In no. 1 were American grain elevators (Plate 136), and in no. 2 were factories (Plate 137). Further essays, also signed Le Corbusier-Sanguier, in L'Esprit Nouveau nos. 8, 9 and 10 added the examples of steam-ships, aeroplanes and motor-cars. The pre-war symbols of dynamic simultaneity from Futurist poetry and painting, from Cendrars, Barzun, Delaunay and his followers, were entirely

136. (left)   Grain elevators, illustrated in *L'Esprit Nouveau* no. 1.

137. (below)   Factory, illustrated in *L'Esprit Nouveau* no. 2

redesigned as the symbols of a new, mechanized 'call to order'. For the Purists the most essential modern experience was emphatically not that of accelerated simultaneity, but the experience of order and precision. In modern life, reality, for them, was made more and more ideal.

Far more clearly, comprehensively and persuasively than had Severini in 1917, the Purists examined the analogy between the machine and the work of art, finding that each was an ordered organism constructed according to clearly understood laws, using standardized parts in conformations at once the result of calculation and of intuition, finding that to each economy and precision of action was essential, but finding that where the machine aimed at utility alone, the work of art aimed alone at the beauty of a perfectly balanced sensation. Yet, even more important, they presented an idea of man and the machine in modern life, which far more persuasively and comprehensively than had Severini, promoted the change from a dynamically fragmented to a stable and precise view. In particular, for Léger, as he moved from the fragmented ambiguity of *La Femme au miroir* to the coordinated stability of *Le Mécanicien*, their belief in an *esprit nouveau* attuned to the facts of a newly ordered modern life was especially persuasive, because it so decisively brought a pictorial ideal down to earth. Idealizing though the theory and practice of Purism undoubtedly was,[53] it masqueraded to great effect as the direct product of a new reality, and thus made of the 'call to order' initiated by the crystal Cubists a tendency altogether more in touch with the committed modern-life realism of Léger's approach to painting.

By mid 1921 the link between Purism and Léger was firmly established. Léonce Rosenberg was quick to react positively to the campaign of Ozenfant and Jeanneret, buying several of the canvases exhibited in February at the

138. (above)   Vilmos Huszar: *Stilleven Komposition,*
1918. *De Stijl* vol. 1, no. 3, January 1918.

139. (right)   Piet Mondrian: *Composition,* 1921. Private
collection, Switzerland.

galerie Duret, so that Purism became closely associated with 'l'Effort
Moderne'. Canvases by Ozenfant and Jeanneret were included the same
year in an *exposition de groupe* at Rosenberg's gallery, which included Gris,
Metzinger, Severini and Léger as well as others whose work he admired,
like Picasso and Braque.[54] More important, in 1920, although the exact
date is not known, Léger met Jeanneret himself;[55] and early in 1921 *L'Esprit
Nouveau* no. 4 contained a republication of an essay on Léger by Maurice
Raynal—the most important critical assessment of his work to date.
Indeed, even Blaise Cendrars was involved, for a chapter of his prose piece
L'Eubage appeared in no. 7.

From certain crucial points of view *Le Mécanicien* conveys an approach
to painting and to modern life which is emphatically hostile to Purism as
formulated theoretically and pictorially in 1920. Léger's violent use of
vermilion seems almost specifically judged to reject the Purists' conviction, expressed a few months later, that 'the use of burnt ochres' can
be more powerful in effect than that of vermilions.[56] He combines the
dulled solidity of what the Purists called 'the great scale' with the forbidden
vigour of the 'dynamic scale', aiming at a pictorial cacophony of contrasts
which is as alien to the harmonious quiet of the Purist still-life as it is
to that of Gris' crystal Cubism. He does not, as has been seen, sacrifice
his need for dissonant power to the requirements of the 'call to order'.
Again, the precise balance of his composition is not the result of an exacting
series of geometric and modular calculations, so that the intuitive factor in

the creation of his pictorial theme is not sacrificed to the rational factor with the kind of careful emphasis advocated by the Purists. Finally, his subject is not the 'type-object' still life, but the machine-man, and by means of the machine-man he does not celebrate the designer of machines or modern constructions—the engineer—but, instead, the working man who fabricates and maintains them—the mechanic. Yet the fact remains, starkly and unequivocally declared by the smooth perfection of his mechanic, that Léger's view of what was essential to reality in modern life gave a central importance to the qualities of precision, economy and equilibrium, that these were qualities which for him were found both in the machine and in man, that, in the constructions and the motors of the new industrial environment, in the Salon de l'Aviation and the industrial suburbs of Paris, there was for him an *esprit nouveau*—a common drive towards a forceful yet balanced perfection.

*   *   *   *   *

Among the works shown at Léonce Rosenberg's *exposition de groupe* in 1921 were paintings by Piet Mondrian, and one of these was the 1921 *Composition* (Plate 139). Mondrian's contribution to the exhibition was rather perfunctorily dismissed by the critic Waldemar George in *L'Esprit Nouveau* no. 9,[57] and it is clear that his particular pictorial declaration in favour of a new ordered style committed to the classical virtues of precision, clarity and equilibrium was of little interest to the Purists. Without the slightest hint of compromise, *Composition* and its neighbours in the galerie de l'Effort Moderne stood for an art of absolute purity, utterly devoid of all references either to 'type-objects' or to modern life; if Ozenfant considered Juan Gris' synthetic Cubism too pure, it is clear that he could not have tolerated an approach as extreme as this, and nor, it would seem, could Léger. However, from his return to Montparnasse in 1919 Mondrian had been accepted by Léonce Rosenberg,[58] and there can be no doubt that his work was of considerable significance in Léger's 'call to order'. For Léger, the collision of opposites was to be sought, and so opposing forces of order—the order of Purism and the order of Mondrian—were by no means mutually exclusive.

Yet, as telling an influence towards abstraction was the Amsterdam review *De Stijl*, to which Mondrian contributed major articles. It was certainly known in the circle of 'l'Effort Moderne' within months of its 1917 foundation, and remained important through 1918 and 1919.[59] However during 1919 the aesthetic and philosophical theories for which *De Stijl* stood could only have been comprehended by artists like Léger in the simplest terms, since only on rare occasions were essays or statements published in anything but Dutch. Thus, before 1920 *De Stijl* could act in the Parisian avant-garde as no more than a limited influence—above all the supplier, by means of its usually poor illustrations, of shadowy photographic hints.

It was perhaps an injustice to the importance of van Doesburg and Mondrian as formative forces within *De Stijl* that during the 1917–20 period the strongest impact made by the review in purely visual terms was

211

made by the Hungarian painter Vilmos Huszar. From the first number until January 1921 the cover design was his, and in January 1918 the review illustrated in colour as a double-page layout his *Stilleven Komposition* (Plate 138).[60] At this point *De Stijl* did not promote a static pictorial flatness uncomplicated by spatial evocations, as did Mondrian's 1921 *Composition*. It announced in strong chromatic terms relatively dynamic and dissonant possibilities, in tune with the flat planar settings of, for instance, Léger's 1919 *Composition (Le Typographe)* (Colour Plate 5), whose suspended rectangles may even be a direct response. It could not yet tempt him away from his violent, disintegrated approach to painting and to reality.

During 1920 and 1921 Mondrian's presence in the circle of 'l'Effort Moderne' itself made him, far more than any other *De Stijl* artist, a force within the Parisian avant-garde. By the end of 1920 his ideas were available in the clumsy French of the pamphlet 'Le néo-Plasticisme', which was published by Léonce Rosenberg, and, although van Doesburg's 'Classique-Baroque-Moderne' was also published in French that year,[61] Mondrian's ideas were given added point by the fact that his painting could be seen at first hand. His mystical promotion of an 'abstract' reality was obviously opposed to Léger's realist resurrection of the subject,[62] but the stark and stable clarity of the style which he developed during 1920 and 1921 held out equally obvious attractions among the converging stimuli which pushed Léger towards a more classical mode of composing.

It is in the stable structure of black bands and white spaces and sudden, vivid planes of primary colour, the setting for *Le Mécanicien*, that Léger finds a place for pictorial effects in sympathy with Mondrian. He is as sparing with his positive elements (primary colour) as Mondrian, and as shy of the spatial ambiguities caused by overlappings, and he too achieves an austere strength by the clarity of his contrasts—red or yellow against black, black against white. Yet the point must be made that Mondrian's *Composition* was *later* in date than *Le Mécanicien*, and that these very close comparisons do not merely indicate the influence of Mondrian on Léger, but also the influence of Léger on Mondrian. The synthetic structure of the settings for *Le Mécanicien* and *L'Homme à la pipe* (Plates 130 and 129) has its origins in the grids of black lines, often frilled and patterned, found in Léger's own cylinder and disintegrated paintings as early as 1918 (Plates 84 and 90), long before Mondrian's paintings could have acted directly as an influence. Moreover, during 1920 Mondrian did not produce a single composition whose linear clarity and chromatic force approaches either that of the settings for these two Légers or that of his own 1921 *Composition*.[63] It seems probable, therefore, that on the one hand the sheer simplicity of Mondrian's painting in 1920 and the strictness with which he used the vertical and horizontal helped Léger towards the stabilized simplicity of *Le Mécanicien*'s pure setting, while, on the other hand, the brutal strength of Léger's primary colours and black barred scaffolds helped Mondrian towards the power of his 1921 *Composition*.

In the final analysis, the two paintings declare a mutual willingness on the part of Léger and Mondrian to learn from each other, coupled with a mutual determination not to compromise their independence. Mondrian's *Composition* is absolutely pure, Léger's *Le Mécanicien* denies absolute purity —its pure setting being violently opposed by the impurity of its subject.

Mondrian was thus a significantly positive factor in the body of pressure that so persuasively pushed Léger towards a more stable, precise and economic art, but he could only provide partial lessons, helping to reshape the peripheral areas of Léger's paintings—their setting rather than their substance.

*   *   *   *   *

The Mondrian and *De Stijl* approach to the history of art was dynamic. They saw their pure style as lying at the end of a development, a view comprehensively expounded in French by van Doesburg in his 'Classique-Baroque-Moderne' published in 1907 by 'l'Effort Moderne'. For van Doesburg, the purity of *De Stijl* completely separated it both in spirit and in form from the representational impurity of classicism; in effect, therefore, the art of the past was irrelevant—it could never validly influence the pure art of the present.[64]

'Nevertheless,' wrote Maurice Raynal in 'Quelques intentions du Cubisme', 'I continue to believe that Knowledge of the Masters, right understanding of their works, and respect for tradition ought to provide strong support.'[65] By 1920 van Doesburg's view of the past was very much a minority view in the classicizing Parisian avant-garde; Raynal's acceptance of the past represented a strong and broadly based body of opinion which affected more than merely the settings of Léger's paintings. The lesson of Severini's 1916 *Maternité* (Plate 140) with its open admission of debts to the past, had prefaced a widespread reaction against Futurist *anti-passéisme*, at the centre of which was 'l'Effort Moderne'. Raynal's pamphlet was a 'l'Effort Moderne' publication, and Léonce Rosenberg's pamphlet, 'Cubisme et Tradition' (1920) dwelt too on the importance of 'respect for tradition', by which he meant, like Raynal and Severini, the continuation of certain pictorial principles which were constant.

The Purists may have considered *l'esprit nouveau* to be the product of exclusively modern experiences, but they were amongst the most active champions of the past, believing too in the existence of constants. Thus, not only in *Après le cubisme* did Ozenfant and Jeanneret find a sense of order in the new bridges and factories and dams, which looked forward, but also 'a Roman grandeur', since the laws on which that order was based—mechanical and proportional—applied as much to Roman as to modern constructions. The experience of the twentieth century and the innovations of the Cubists might have produced new forms and new modes of representation, but Purism was still based on the same fundamental laws as lay behind what for Ozenfant and Jeanneret were the great styles of the past: the Hieratic styles of Assyria and Egypt, the classical styles of Greece and Rome,[66] and, after Raphael, of Poussin, Chardin, Ingres, Corot, Cézanne and Seurat—those styles in which the human figure or a simplified concept of landscape and still-life was central, and in which the qualities of stability, precision, economy and equilibrium were at a premium. More specifically, the Purists revived the idea of the French tradition, which Gleizes above all had stressed before the war, publishing between *L'Esprit Nouveau* nos. 1 and 9 illustrated essays on Seurat, Fouquet, Ingres, Poussin and Corot in an attempt to show how the constant laws of pictorial order

213

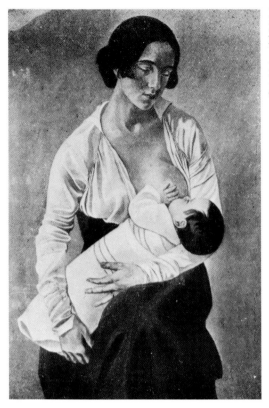

140. (left)   Gino Severini: *Maternité,* 1916.
$36\frac{1}{4} \times 25\frac{1}{2}$ ins, Jeanne Severini collection,
Paris.

141. (below)   André Derain: *L'Eglise de Vers,*
1912. 26×37 ins, National Museum of Wales,
Cardiff.

had been given especially clear support by the French. Purism, for them, was a style both detached from the past by modern conditions and deeply rooted in it.

Léonce Rosenberg began 'Cubisme et Tradition' by insisting that to retain merely the 'familiar appearances' of past styles was to escape the new and to conserve 'ancient heresies'.[67] Neither he nor Raynal nor the Purists took their belief in tradition so far as to advocate the imitation of past models. In imitation, Rosenberg wrote, 'tradition is lost'.[68] The example of Gris' transformation of models from Cézanne (Plates 77 and 78) and Corot was the guide: the modern painter retained the basic values of tradition, he never copied the forms of the past. Yet Severini's *Maternité* (Plate 140), although it accompanied paintings of an irreproachably Cubist character when first exhibited in 1916, had already announced the possibility of an altogether more radical return to the past, concerned not simply with the recognition of constant traditional values (laws), but with the actual revival of past forms, and his evocation of Tuscan memories was complemented by a return to conventional representation.

Severini's conspicuous attempt at the revival of representational styles from the past was neither isolated nor the first of its kind in the Parisian Cubist avant-garde. Even before 1914 André Derain had arrived at a prophetic alliance between the modern primitivism of the Douanier Rousseau, a simplistic version of early Cubism, and reminiscences of early Tuscan painting,[69] in for instance a work like *L'Eglise à Vers* (1912, Plate 141). Derain spent much of the war at the front, but he was in contact with Ozenfant's *L'Elan* in 1915, and his work was included in the exhibitions which Ozenfant and André Salmon organized in 1916.[70] At this stage his was a return to styles which were both highly simplified and perspectively primitive by high Renaissance standards, not to styles which were considered by the Cubists retrogressively representational, and it was left to Picasso to take the first step backwards from synthetic Cubism into such a style. Picasso took this step in 1915 with a series of portrait drawings whose point of departure was Ingres, but it was his February 1917 trip to Italy with Cocteau and the Ballet Russe that really led him back, for the experiences given him, especially of the antique, in Rome, Naples and Pompeii were the stimuli behind a sustained exploration of classical representational styles during the next six years. It was an exploration which has been shown to have embraced not merely the frescoes from Herculaneum in the Naples Museum and Ingres' portraits,[71] but also the sculpture of the Parthenon frieze,[72] the Greek white figure vases of the Louvre, the peasant drawings of Millet,[73] and the late nudes of Renoir.[74] Though still, of course, an active and revered exponent of synthetic Cubism, by 1920 it was Picasso who most persuasively stood for the revival of classic representational styles from the past. Works like the large *Femme assise lisant* (Plate 142), with its reminiscences of Ingres' London *Mme Moitessier* and of antique fresco,[75] were in themselves a convincing enough argument for a radical reassessment of the relationship between past and present styles, between pictorial form and representation. Moreover, such works, though apparently inviting retrogression fitted easily within the progressive context of the 'call to order', presenting as they did so grandiose a classical ideal of economy, equilibrium and stability.

142.   Pablo Picasso: *La Femme assise lisant (La Liseuse),* 1920. $65\frac{1}{4} \times 40\frac{1}{4}$ ins, Musée National d'Art Moderne, Paris.

The phrase 'the call to order' has thus far been used without specific acknowledgement. It was, in fact, the invention of Jean Cocteau, who in 1926 published a collection of his writings under that title.[76] Besides turning Picasso's energies in the direction of the ballet with *Parade* which took the painter to Rome, Cocteau was from 1917 Picasso's constant ally in the return to past styles and to an art of order. For him, Picasso was part of a broad 'call to order'—a common tendency which even before 1920 involved not only the visual arts, but literature and music. His own book of poems, *Vocabulaire*, a journal of his months with Picasso and Diaghilev in Italy, returned openly to the classicism of Ronsard,[77] and in 1918 he published *Le Coq et l'Arlequin,* an assault by aphorism on Romantic and Impressionist music, in which he advocated a return in music to the classical qualities of simplicity and order. The hero of *Le Coq et l'Arlequin* was Erik Satie, whose music had accompanied Picasso's sets and costumes in *Parade*, and whose chamber cantata *Socrate* seemed to announce the coming of a new classicism in music. *Socrate* was a setting to music for a single voice of three fragments from Victor Cousin's translation into French of Plato's *Dialogues*. Satie described it as 'a musical reading'[78] and its spare, clear balance, so overtly linked to the rational idealism of Platonic philosophy, obviously paralleled the idealism of the crystal Cubists. Like the painters, Satie did not revive past styles, but significantly Cocteau was tempted in *Le Coq et l'Arlequin* to compare the lucidity of his melodic line with the line of Ingres.[79] Satie and a small, loosely knit circle of composers, most of whom admired his work—Georges Auric, Louis Durey, Arthur Honnegger, Francis Poulenc, Germaine Tailleferre and Darius Milhaud—became, with Picasso, the centre of Cocteau's particular idea of 'the call to order', accompanied after 1919 by the precocious poet and novelist Raymond Radiguet. The musicians quickly became known as 'Les Six'.[80] From Cocteau's many writings of the period (1918–23) in defence of himself, of Picasso, Satie, 'Les Six', Radiguet and any others who seemed in sympathy with them, an idea can be formed of the attitude to the relationship between past and present styles which lay behind Picasso's return to antique and post-Renaissance classical styles. It is an idea constructed from necessarily oblique glances and suggestions, and therefore by no means comprehensive, but Picasso has himself provided verbal evidence of a more direct kind, in the form of his 1923 statement to Marius de Zayas—a statement of great explicitness.[81]

'Imagine,' said Cocteau in 1923 while considering Radiguet, 'how boring it would be to have works which were deliberately direct, deliberately comprehensible, deliberately blank, deliberately sober, deliberately like everything else.'[82] Radiguet, like him, was an admirer of Ronsard and he too had consciously modelled his novel *Le Diable au corps* on past models, but for Cocteau a return to narrative clarity and to form in the novel did not mean a denial of paradox, and in the same way neither did a return to representation in painting. Indeed, it seems possible that it was at least partially out of a sense of paradox that Picasso turned against the anti-representational dogma associated with Cubism, to revive Ingres in 1915; certainly, in an article in *L'Esprit Nouveau* no. 3 on Roger de La Fresnaye (by 1921 a neo-classicist too), Cocteau suggests that where audacity had become convention—as in the Parisian avant-garde—the resurrection of old modes could create a special kind of novelty: that by looking backwards the artist could even more dramatically move forward.[83] There is no direct evidence that Picasso consciously aimed to create such a paradox, but the fact remains that his 1915 portrait drawings would have profoundly disturbed more orthodox Cubists like Metzinger, that by turning back he did achieve novelty, and that his perverse development of synthetic Cubist and representational styles alongside one another between 1917 and 1921 was calculated to throw the paradox implicit in his progressive move backwards into the highest possible relief.

Yet it was not most profoundly this sense of paradox that so clearly distinguished the return of Picasso and Cocteau to past styles from the return of Cubists like Gris, and the Purists; rather it was their attitude to style in general. In 'Le Secret professionnel', written during the summer of 1921, Cocteau considered at length the question of style and of styles, though mainly with reference to literature. Here he dismissed the cultivation of a single manner, of what he calls 'a "tic"', that is, saying it does not matter what in a certain manner', in favour of an altogether more flexible notion of style.[84] 'Style,' he writes, 'does not know how to be a starting-point. It is a result . . . A Stendhal, even a Balzac . . . above all tries to hit the bulls-eye. They make it nine times out of ten, no matter how. It is this no matter how, easy for them, adopted according to the results obtained, this way of shouldering the gun, aiming, and firing quick and true,·that I call style.'[85] Later, when writing of Baudelaire's *Paradis artificiels*, he makes it clear that what matters is that the manner should 'exactly follow from the object of his [Baudelaire's] scrutiny'[86]—should adapt itself to the particular content of the work. In a lecture of 1923 he concludes: 'In sum, here is what I propose: the absence of a style. To have style rather than to have a style.'[87]

That for Cocteau Picasso's return to the styles of the past proceeded from a parallel attitude, is made plain when he comments thus in 'Le Secret professionnel': 'Picasso, nourished by the masters, extending further their territory, knows the meagre prestige of the arabesque, and of touch' (touch and the arabesque being for him the equivalent of a literary 'tic').[88] It is clear from Picasso's 1923 statement to de Zayas that his attitude was indeed that of his ally: 'If the subjects I have wanted to express,' said Picasso, 'have suggested different ways of expression I have never hesitated to adopt them. . . . Different motives inevitably require different methods of expression.'[89] His work between 1917 and 1921, ranging as it did from a gay synthetic Cubism to a sober classicism repeatedly confirmed the irrelevance for him of having 'a style', and the relevance for him of Cocteau's idea of 'style'. The bright colour planes of Cubism are right for the carnival brilliance of the 1918 *Arlequin* (Plate 128), the sheer figurative weight of Roman fresco painting and of Ingres's *Mme Moitessier* was right for the monumental stability of *La Femme assise lisant* (Plate 142); the implication was that any style, old or new, could be adapted to Picasso's needs, could be made subject to his will.

The basic distinction between the approach of Gris, the crystal Cubists and the Purists to past styles, and that of Picasso is that, where the former used the evidence provided by the past to prove the objective existence of laws underlying all art, Picasso used the past merely as a prolific supplier

143. (left) Pablo Picasso: *Mère et enfant*, 1921. $56\frac{1}{4} \times 63\frac{3}{4}$ ins, Chicago Art Institute.

144. (above) *Juno*, Roman copy of a 5th Century Hera, Museo Nationale, Naples.

of different modes. He provided an uncompromisingly individualistic alternative, an alternative whose individualism is summed up by Cocteau in his 1921 study of his friend when he declares that there are no schools of painting: 'there are only strong men'.[90]

A further distinction made clear by Picasso's 1923 statement is that, where the Purists in particular thought of style as progressive, and their own version of Cubism as the end-product of a long evolutionary development, Picasso thought of every style that he revived as complete in its own right and therefore outside evolutionary developments. 'Variation,' he said, 'does not mean evolution.'[91] It was for this reason that he did not, like the Purists, consider old styles to be superseded, and it was for this reason that he was able to indulge his sense of paradox still further, for his individualism led him on occasion, as has been seen, dangerously close to imitation. The need 'to hit the bulls-eye' allowed him to purloin literally *all* the essentials of a relevant style without any attempt at concealment. So confident was he in his strength as an individual that he was unafraid of parody.

The most monumental of Picasso's neo-classical figure paintings were executed in Fontainebleau and Paris during the summer and autumn of 1921. *Mère et enfant* (Plate 143) is one of them. Picasso was capable of mocking classicism by distorting its figure styles, but here there is no mockery. The poses are harmonious and static, relating closely to Maillol's *Méditerranné*. Head and limbs are modelled with a simple and full sense of solidity close to the Roman frescoes of Herculaneum, to such antique models as a Roman copy of a fifth-century Greek *Juno* in the Naples Museum (Plate 144), or to the late figure style of Poussin's *Elizieh and Rebecca at the*

145. Nicolas Poussin: *Elizieh and Rebecca at the Well*, 1648. Musée du Louvre, Paris.

Well (Plate 145). An elementary space made up of separated horizontal planes for land, sea and sky provides a setting reminiscent of Puvis de Chavannes. To achieve a balanced grandeur Picasso arrived at a complete neo-classical style presented with uncompromising simplicity: poses, figure and spatial illusion all of a piece. Without copying any specific model, he brought off not merely a petty theft of attractive postures but a complete stylistic robbery.

Not only does the individualism of Picasso and Cocteau suggest an approach to the past very different from that of the Purists and the crystal Cubists, but also a very different attitude to the pursuit of order. Where the Purists advocated a concerted attempt to find an objectively valid aesthetic order, Picasso and Cocteau, like Maurice Raynal, believed in a 'call to order' without rules. Thus, in 1923 Cocteau could write of 'a general disorder, formed from individual kinds of order', which, in the guise of anarchy, was directed towards a return 'to law', an *'esprit nouveau'*.[92] Yet, however alien this anarchistic pursuit of order may have been to Purist objectivity and logic, there can be no doubt, in the final analysis, that Picasso's and Cocteau's 'call to order' aspired to aesthetic qualities and an idea of order which in general terms *was* in tune both with 'l'Effort Moderne' and *L'Esprit Nouveau*. As early as 1918 in *Le Coq et l'Arlequin* Cocteau could expound an approach to order in art and in modern life extraordinarily close to that expounded by the Purists in *Après le cubisme*. Thus, he demands economy in art with the maxim: 'A POET ALWAYS HAS TOO MANY WORDS IN HIS VOCABULARY, A PAINTER TOO MANY COLOURS ON HIS PALETTE, A MUSICIAN TOO MANY NOTES ON HIS KEYBOARD';[93] and, even more in the Purist vein, he compares American constructions with Greek architecture, finding in them 'a grandeur stripped of irrelevancies'.[94] He remained an individualist, but aimed for economy and precision in art, aware that these qualities reflected those of a new industrial reality designed for efficiency. Picasso certainly would have been aware of these views, and, though his work never underlined the background presence of a mechanized *esprit nouveau*, canvases like the Cubist *Arlequin* of 1918 or the neo-classical *Mère et enfant* demonstrate how important the qualities of economy and precision were for him too. It is finally, therefore, clear that at least in this general sense the Purist, the crystal Cubist and Picasso's individualist return to past styles were each part of a wide-ranging 'call to order'—a new, post-war tendency in which a fresh and vital importance was attached to 'knowledge of the Masters, right understanding of their works and respect for tradition'.

Between 1918 and 1921 Léger was constantly kept aware of Cocteau, Picasso and their musical allies' 'call to order', even briefly, though no more than tangentially, becoming involved himself. First of all, Cocteau, Satie and 'Les Six' were in close touch with 'l'Effort Moderne'. As early as the turn of 1916–17 Gris and Severini had been members of a non-sectarian avant-garde organization called 'Lyre et Palette' which put on exhibitions of a wide range of artists accompanied by *matinées* presenting the poetry of, among others, Cocteau, and the music of, among others, Satie;[95] while by April 1919 Léonce Rosenberg was sympathetic enough to organize his own *matinée* as accompaniment to the Gris exhibition, in part dedicated to Cocteau's poetry and in part to Georges Auric's music.[96] Secondly and perhaps even more significantly from Léger's point of view, Cocteau, Satie and 'Les Six' made contact, not only with 'l'Effort Moderne', but with Blaise Cendrars, and it was through this connection that Léger became tangentially involved. Cendrars too had been active in 'Lyre et Palette', and in November 1917 had read his *Profond Aujourd'hui* at a *Soirée de Poésie et de Musique* given by Paul Guillaume, where Satie and Auric had provided much of the music.[97] These contacts led to a friendship between Cocteau and Cendrars out of which came active collaboration. According to Cendrars, Cocteau was present at the December 1918 *Matinée de Poésie* which launched the illustrated edition of *J'ai Tué*, and showed the degree of his support by paying 100 francs for a single one-franc copy.[98] The following year they came together to launch the Editions de la Sirène, and Léger was quickly pulled into the venture with the illustrations for *La Fin du monde filmée par l'Ange Notre-Dame*. It was a testimony to the anti-dogmatic individualism of all three that the violence of Cendrars's scenario and the rugged inelegance of Léger's illustrations could be promoted with the help of perhaps the most elegantly stylish of all the champions of a new classicism. Finally, Léger could add to a deepening awareness of the 'call to order' and the revival of past styles announced by Cocteau, a deepening awareness of what must have been the most persuasive classic-izing force of all, the pictorial revival of past styles which was brought to a new, monumental stage during 1920 and 1921 by Picasso, for the paintings, gouaches and drawings which declared his more and more paradoxical commitment to classical representation were to be seen at first hand, it will be remembered, not far from the galerie de l'Effort Moderne, in the gallery of Léonce Rosenberg's brother, Paul.

It is, therefore, not surprising that in 1920, with *Le Mécanicien*, Léger should have arrived at an image of the machine-man, which combined the precise balance of the Purist approach to man and the machine with the uncompromising dignity of a figure style from the past. The Hieratic Egyptian manner applied here was a manner which was specifically to be mentioned by Picasso in his 1923 statement to Marius de Zayas, and Hieratic styles had already received respectful attention in Léonce Rosenberg's 'Cubisme et Tradition', Raynal's 'Quelques intentions du Cubisme' and Ozenfant's and Jeanneret's *Après le cubisme*. Though not an antique or post-Renaissance classical style, it was a style which ensured for Léger a new representational clarity in figure-painting, and thus, like Picasso's neo-classical figures, his Hieratic *Mécanicien* marked at once a step back into the past and back towards representation. Moreover, as has been seen, in pose, in the manner of its muscular development and the manner of its relief modelling Léger's figure, like Picasso's, took over the essentials of a past figurative style as a whole, in this way daring to approach the past much more closely than Gris or the Purists. Yet the total effect of the revival declared by *Le Mécanicien* was altogether different from that declared for instance by Picasso's *Femme assise lisant* of 1920, because Léger placed his Hieratic figure not in a backward-looking Hieratic setting, but in a conspicuously modern and pure planar setting—a setting, as has been seen, almost the equal in its modern purity of Mondrian's art. He achieved in effect both a stylistic collision and the coming together of styles across time, conveying both the distance between the Hieratic styles of the past and the pure styles of the present, and the basic aesthetic qualities held in common by them—the unifying qualities of stability, economy, precision and equilibrium. In this way, he conveyed an awareness of the Purist belief both in the fundamental difference between past and present stylistic conditions, and in the existence of constant pictorial principles of order—beliefs utterly alien to the anarchistic individualism of Picasso. Finally, and most effectively of all, he asserted his independence both from Picasso and from the Purists' 'call to order' by the sheer visual force of the stylistic collision that he achieved between past and present, because in this he conveyed the force of his continuing need to seek out dissonance rather than harmony, even within the context of a stable Hieratic monumentality. Léger could not, like Picasso, have been satisfied with the theft of a single style in its entirety—the substance *and* the setting. He needed the violence of stylistic conflict even as he had needed it without reference to the past in 1918 and 1919. As Cocteau might have put it, he needed more than one stylistic shot to 'hit the bulls-eye'.

*   *   *   *   *

In the end, it is clear that the simplicity of *Le Mécanicien* is the result of a complex fusion of responses to a wide-ranging and very powerful combination of classicizing pressures, all of which were especially persuasive in 1920, all of which converged on Léger from his immediate avant-garde surroundings, and all of which had been active on him for at least two years. Isolated as he was in his pictorial advocacy of a dissonant, disintegrated approach to painting and to modern life, and faced with so broad-based and so compulsive a movement towards order in music and literature as well as in painting, it was perhaps only ever a question of time before Léger's pursuit of a fragmented violence in the *éléments mécaniques* and the cinematic compositions of 1918 and 1919 would give way to his own violent yet definitive 'call to order'. The period 1918–19, for all the appearance it gives of a new post-war beginning, was indeed for Léger a final gesture. The sheer destructive force of his war experience, by recharging his old convictions and bringing them so effectively back down to earth, delayed the end, but in 1920 it came with what, in a truly profound sense, was for him a new approach to painting based on a new approach to modern life and to reality as a whole.

CHAPTER 8
Léger as a Classical Figure-painter, 1921–4

During 1921 Léger established several possible lines of development, but most ambitiously and most publicly of all he did so with the theme that culminated in the large-scale *Le Grand Déjeuner* (Plate 146)—a canvas whose size is comparable with that of *La Partie de cartes* or *La Ville*. Where *Le Mécanicien* was a remodelling of a decisively modern subject, the *Déjeuner* theme was a remodelling of the most decisively backward-looking classical subject of all, the decorous female nude posed for harmonious effect—the subject given such status by Ingres and Renoir and which was so much a part of Picasso's 'call to order'. A year after Léger's vigorous call for a modern 'return to subject-matter' with the showing of *La Ville* and *Les Disques dans la Ville*, he declared his return to the archetypal subject of tradition with the showing of three paintings of nudes at the 1921 Salon des Indépendants: certainly two of them—*La Femme couchée* and *Les deux femmes et la nature-morte*—were stages in the pictorial evolution which culminated in *Le Grand Déjeuner*.[1]

The story of the development of *Le Grand Déjeuner* follows the stages of Léger's move from a mechanical to a classical figure style, and from an occasionally unstable ambiguity to an always stable clarity of statement. Perhaps the earliest oils directly related to *Le Grand Déjeuner* are a pair of reclining nudes, of which the small *Femme couchée* dated 1920 is one (Plate 147). The simple clash between flat rectangular planes and curved metallic surfaces modelled in relief repeats the simple, forceful theme of *Le Mécanicien*, but as yet Léger does not overtly refer by the shaping of his figurative forms to a classical past and he sets his hefty mechanical nude, like the barges of his 1918 *Remorqueur* paintings, in rolling lateral movement across the verticals and horizontals of her scaffolded surroundings. *Femme couchée* is by no means in repose and she is by no means classical either.

Before the end of 1920 Léger brought the dynamism of his *Femme couchée* idea to rest and rooted it deep in the past. He brought the idea to

146.   Fernand Léger: *Le Grand Déjeuner*, 1921. $72\frac{1}{4} \times 99$ ins, Museum of Modern Art, New York.

rest by introducing a vertical figurative element and he made contact with the past by his remodelling of every figurative component, achieving both ends in the smoothly finished *Deux femmes et la nature-morte*, dated 1920 (Plate 148).[2] The evenly modelled weight and the generous amplitude of these two females make them the direct relatives of Picasso's most monumental female inventions, and the single line joining nose to brow, which cuts into the spherical head of the reclining nude, seems specifically to refer to the antique mode of simplification found, for instance, in Picasso's *Femme assise lisant* of 1920.

The theme given such precise shape in the Wuppertal painting was taken to a conspicuously definitive state in the large oil version sometimes titled *Les Odalisques* (Plate 149). This canvas is also dated 1920 and could well be the *Deux femmes et la nature-morte* shown in 1921 at the Indépendants, its size testifying to a possible public intention. Here every hint at a blurring of distinctions is gone. Looking forward to the definitive classicism of the final *Déjeuner* theme, Léger weds his weighty sense of the classical tradition, as redefined by Picasso, to an unequivocal clarity of figurative statement. Where the nudes of the Wuppertal version are both modelled in the same

224

147.   Fernand Léger: *La Femme couchée,* 1920. $24\frac{1}{2} \times 36\frac{1}{2}$ ins, galerie Beyeler, Basel.

148.   Fernand Léger: *Des Deux Femmes et la nature morte,* 1920. $28\frac{3}{4} \times 36\frac{1}{4}$ ins, Von der Heydt Museum, Wuppertal.

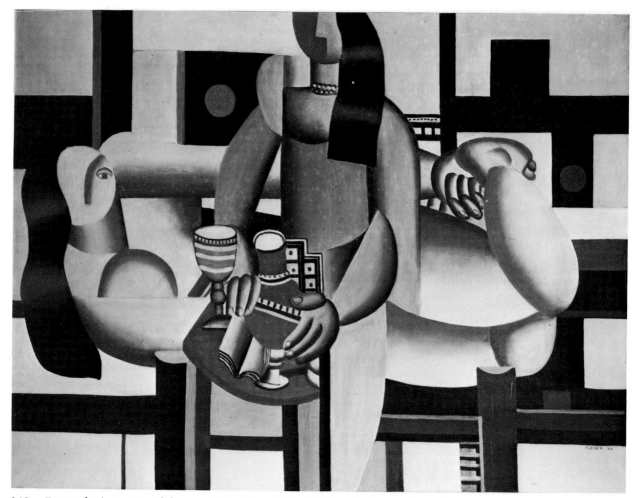

149.   Fernand Léger: *Les Odalisques*, 1920. Mr and Mrs William A. M. Burden collection, New York.

steel grey so that the relationship between them is not always distinct,
here the grey of the reclining nude is set in clear contrast against the
dark, earthy ochre of her standing companion; and again, where the still-
life glass of the Wuppertal version is modelled grey like the nudes, sharing
in their subtle blurring of distinctions, here it is striped orange and white,
allowing not even the smallest area of uncertainty. A careful clarification
of detailed relationships leads Léger to an utterly distinct and utterly
stable grouping of female nudes—a figurative statement which in the
most classical of senses declares his commitment both to 'the call to order'
and to the revival of tradition, in particular the tradition of Poussin, David
and Ingres.

It was as the obvious complement to the thorough classicism of *Les
Odalisques* and of the *Déjeuner* theme which came afterwards, that Léger
took to a new pitch of exactitude the analogy first established in *La Partie
de cartes* between the work of art and 'a precision machine'. Far more than
the careful development and finish of *Les Odalisques*, the final planning
and completion of *Le Grand Déjeuner* establishes this fact. The *Déjeuner*

theme took at once to clearer and to more complex conclusions the basic notion put forward in *Les Odalisques* of a balance between vertical and horizontal elements, both pure and figurative. The introduction of two new figures in the place of the standing nude coupled with the intricate remodelling of the surrounding scaffold, created so many fresh pictorial possibilities that Léger felt himself compelled to launch into a long series of fresh investigations before attempting a further large-scale definitive statement. Thus, behind the painting there lay separate oil studies for the reclining nude alone and for each half of the composition,[3] as well as at least four full oil studies for the whole composition, two of which are the *Petits Déjeuners* (Plates 150 and 151).[4] Most tellingly of all, however, it is the minute attention that Léger paid to the least important of details as he moved from the smallest of the *Petit Déjeuner* paintings to the final one that betrays the now almost obsessive degree of his perfectionism—the care with which every component was tested before being passed for final use.

In the Minneapolis *Petit Déjeuner* Léger worked, probably with the routine aid of squaring, from a detailed pencil outlining.[5] As yet unconcerned with finish, he filled in his design at speed, making only a few fragmentary changes. So clearly defined were the main lines of the idea at this stage that already he seems to have been concerned with no more than minimal adjustments of detail, and it is only adjustments of this kind that are revealed by the *pentimenti* of the Connecticut painting. Thus, the table is purged of its fussy decoration and the diamond floor-pattern is established as green and white; thus too, where the head of the reclining nude in the Minneapolis version is almost spherical, here the rippling sheet of black hair is broadened at a late stage to cut across it far more emphatically, and where the vase behind the reclining nude in the Minneapolis version is softly curvacious, here it is painted out in favour of something more solid and round. Léger's method of procedure, working with careful guide-drawings from preparatory canvas to preparatory canvas, is essentially the same as that which led to the major compositions of 1918 and 1919, most of all as that which led to *Les Acrobates dans le cirque* (Plate 109). But the self-discipline with which he avoids the addition or subtraction of important elements to concentrate on the perfecting of details reveals a newly intensified feeling for mechanical precision, which inevitably leads to a work whose smoothness of finish is, for its great size and complexity, unprecedented. *Le Grand Déjeuner* emerges as both a classical composition of unequivocal clarity, and an exact pictorial statement, impervious in its finality.

What, then, was the nature of Léger's new classical figure-painting as stated by *Le Grand Déjeuner*? What was the attitude that it declared towards tradition in the resuscitated classical nude, towards the question of representation and of pure pictorial effect, and, most important of all towards modern life—*l'esprit nouveau*—towards reality as a whole?

That Léger's emphasis remained on pure pictorial effect, is made clear by his continued insistence in a letter of March 1922 to Léonce Rosenberg on the need to achieve 'maximum pictorial realization by means of plastic contrasts'.[6] He goes on here to declare that 'the primitives' had shown how the clear presentation of a subject need not necessarily militate against the invention of pictorial forms for pure pictorial effect: the pre-Renaissance

150.   Fernand Léger: *Le Petit Déjeuner,* 1921. 25½ × 36¼ ins, private collection, Minneapolis.

painters (*les avant-Renaissance*), the douanier Rousseau, Ingres ('sometimes'), Poussin ('often'), the Le Nains ('sometimes'), Clouet, Fouquet ('almost always'), Cézanne—all were most essentially, for Léger, inventors, not imitators of nature. By looking so openly back to the figure styles of David and Poussin, Léger did not therefore declare a new tolerance towards representation, he declared the continuing vitality of their figure styles considered in the purest pictorial terms. Moreover, his emphasis on pictorial innovation, for all his acknowledgement of the masters of the past, leaves him, like Picasso, with his stylistic independence uncompromised. He is free creatively to revive a classical figure style without being obliged to keep to it.

Both Léger's continuing sense of stylistic independence and his emphasis on pictorial innovation are conveyed, in a way significantly comparable with the example of Picasso, by the fact that he did not develop his classical style in isolation. Alongside it he took further the implications of the disintegrated and ambiguous style explored earlier in *La Femme au miroir* (Plate 127), arriving at results which were more strictly stable and therefore which were more in tune with 'the call to order', but which were

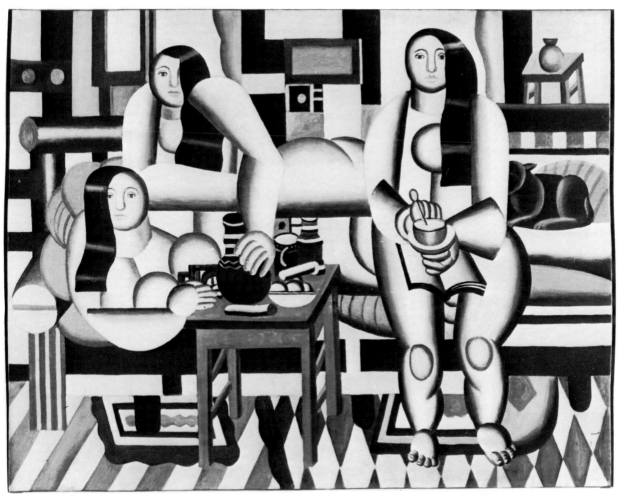

151.   Fernand Léger: *Le Petit Déjeuner,* 1921. 40 × 53 ins, Mr and Mrs Burton Tremaine collection, Connecticut.

none the less neither classically traditional nor figuratively clear. Thus, probably late in 1920, as he worked on *Les Odalisques,* he painted *Trois figures* (Plate 152), looking here not to Picasso's neo-classical figures as stimulus, but to Picasso's gay Cubist gouaches depicting *Comoedia del Arte* subjects executed at Juan-les-Pins in the summer of 1920 (Plate 153).[7] For Picasso, the playful variety of the *Comoedia del Arte* gouaches was a genuine alternative to the monumentality of his large classical compositions, and they led a year later to the enormous *Trois musiciens* paintings; for Léger, the *Trois figures* theme was in a sense no more than a foil and it led to no such large-scale sequel, but the fact remains that for him too the continuing pursuit of an anti-traditional figure style was a continuing reminder that his aim, as Cocteau was to put it in 1923, was to have style rather than 'a style', that he was free of stylistic restrictions even as he turned back to the most apparently restrictive classical styles of all.

In the nature of his approach to the classical styles of the past and in the nature of the figure style that he evolved for *Le Grand Déjeuner* Léger's debt to the example of Picasso could not be more transparent, and yet, of

229

152.   Fernand Léger: *Trois figures,* 1920. $36\frac{1}{4} \times 28\frac{3}{4}$ ins, Joseph Müller collection, Soleure.

153.   Pablo Picasso: *Pierrot et arlequin,* 1920. Gouache on paper, $10\frac{1}{2} \times 8\frac{1}{4}$ ins, private collection, New York.

course, he could not, like Picasso, borrow both a figure style and a setting from his memories of Poussin, David and Ingres. As in *Le Mécanicien,* his need for contrast was too strong to allow so complete a theft. However, unlike the flat, modern setting designed for the Hieratic figure of *Le Mécanicien,* the setting that Léger designed for the classical nudes of *Le Grand Déjeuner* is neither flat nor specifically modern, for he has introduced clear perspectival elements and, with these, clear reminiscences of a further, utterly separate style from the past. The painters who first concerned Léger as pictorial innovators in his letter of March 1922 to Léonce Rosenberg were 'the primitives', by which he meant 'the pre-Renaissance' painters, and among the painters he named as pictorial inventors 'almost always' was Jean Fouquet. It was back to the paintings, tapestries and illuminated books of the fourteenth, fifteenth and early sixteenth centuries in France and the Netherlands, that Léger looked when he remodelled the still flat setting of *Les Odalisques* to open up the strong, conflicting perspectives of *Le Grand Déjeuner.*

Like the classical figure style of the nudes, their setting, replete with its 'pre-Renaissance' reminiscences, was the end-product of a stylistic development which involved other, lesser themes. A painting whose interior setting closely relates to that of *Le Grand Déjeuner* is the intimately scaled yet carefully prepared *Mère et enfant* (Plate 154). Though undated, affinities with works undoubtedly of 1921—not least *Le Grand Déjeuner* itself—

indicate that it was part of the background of pictorial exploration out of which the large painting emerged, and it has the advantage over *Le Grand Déjeuner* of pointing to the possible stimulus of a specific 'pre-Renaissance' composition. One of the most comprehensive and most impressive collections of early Renaissance art to be seen in Paris was in the Musée de Cluny, not far from Léger's studio, and during the autumn of 1920 it was reopened after war-time closure and reorganization.[8] Among the French fifteenth-century tapestries to be seen there was *L'Arithmétique* (Plate 155), whose grouping of figures about a table with a dog at its foot, though more crowded, seems in general terms close to *Mère et enfant*. Léger's polished, tubular woman and child and his stark architectural structure of black bars with sudden, intense planes of colour, are perhaps far from the fifteenth century, but the perspectival conflict between tilted central table-top and patterned floor beneath, coupled with the uncoordinated recession of planes behind, is closely akin. Moreover, objects placed on side tables as well as on the central table—a loaf, vases, a bowl of fruit—are displayed by Léger with a naïve simplicity, at once geometric and descriptive, which is in this context strikingly 'pre-Renaissance', obviously recalling not only *L'Arithmétique* but a wide range of precedents—the Merode Altar-piece by Campin, Jean Fouquet's miniatures in the Bibliothèque Nationale or his Book of Hours for Etienne Chevalier, and much else besides. The nature of Léger's perspectival and naïvely descriptive reminiscences are always partial and no more than generalized, so the importance of specific precedents should not be overstressed, but there can be no doubt that, both in *La Mère et enfant* and in *Le Grand Déjeuner*, these reminiscences are so strong as to add an incongruous and yet unmistakable 'primitive' flavour to the central classical theme.

Léonce Rosenberg, Maurice Raynal and the *L'Esprit Nouveau* no. 5 article on Fouquet all make it clear that the inventive revival of a pre- or early-Renaissance European style was in tune with the current 'call to

154. Fernand Léger: *Mère et enfant*, 1920–1. $25\frac{1}{2} \times 36\frac{1}{4}$ ins, present whereabouts unknown.

155. *L'Arithmétique*, French 15th century tapestry, Musée de Cluny, Paris.

order';[9] and in 1921 interest in these periods seems to have reached a new pitch among those concerned with order in art. Not only was the Musée de Cluny reopened late in 1920, but so too, among the other French rooms in the Louvre were the French fifteenth-century rooms, and the Purists report that it was above all to those rooms that the young artists went, admiring especially *L'Homme au verre*, then attributed to Fouquet.[10] For Rosenberg and the Purists, as for Gleizes in 1913, Fouquet, Clouet and the 'pre-Renaissance' painters were a part of that tradition, whose central values were purity, lucidity and balance, which embraced too the great classical figure-painters—Poussin, David and Ingres. So *Le Grand Déjeuner* attached itself, both in setting and in substance, not merely to a classical idea of tradition, but to a current idea of tradition far wider in its comprehensiveness which gave equal status to the 'primitive' and the classical.

Yet attached though they are to a single idea of tradition, the classicism of Léger's nudes and the primitivism of their setting collide with one another; they are opposing pictorial systems which create contrasts of an altogether new kind. The monumental unity of the post-Renaissance figurative ideal is challenged on all sides by the clear-cut, contradictory perspectives of the 'pre-Renaissance' painters, the latter reinforced by a post-Cubist feeling for paradox, and in the conflict is conveyed not only the idea of a single, stable tradition committed to order, but the distance between the style of one time and of another. Léger reveals his commitment to the new 'call to order' and at the same time his continuing commitment to the dissonant power of pictorial—of stylistic—contrast. His nudes in themselves generate a sense of conflict, for they are not merely classical but modern, so that an awareness of tradition strikes against an equally powerful awareness of the mechanically new. The polished sheen of their surfaces may recall the cool modelling of David, but it recalls too the photographically touched-up illustrations of engines and machine parts common in 1920–21 motor magazines like *Omnia* (Plate 159); the rounded geometry of their limbs may recall the Poussin of *Elizieh and Rebecca at the Well*, but it looks as well to the grandiose geometric volumes of the grain elevators illustrated in *L'Esprit Nouveau* late in 1920 (Plate 136). Moreover, not only were the nudes of *Le Grand Déjeuner* as conspicuously modern and mechanical as traditional, but their setting too, though not mechanical, was both primitive and dazzlingly new, containing its own internal conflict between the past and the present. Thus, the sudden thrusts of contradictory perspective and the sudden solidity of 'primitive' objects themselves conflict with the synthetic Cubist overlappings of flat planes, and the stark simplicity of Léger's architectural scaffold. Altogether, both in its figurative substance and in its architectural setting, *Le Grand Déjeuner* is at once traditional and new, a complex fusion of contradictory statements and conflicting pictorial effects. As in *Le Mécanicien* the previous year, and as in *La Femme en bleu* and the *Nus dans un paysage* over a decade before, Léger conjures up the past in order not merely to situate himself in a tradition, but to confront tradition with the sheer power of modern life and modern painting. Early in 1921, as he worked on the *Déjeuner* theme, Léger was involved in the completion of Abel Gance's film *La Roue*, and we know that Gance's original hope had been cinematically to oppose 'modern machinery and antique art';[11] Gance was prevented by circumstances from realizing this aim, but Léger was not, and in his own way, in paint, he achieved it.

Classical, primitive and modern, attuned to tradition and to *l'esprit nouveau*, precise and ordered yet violently dissonant, *Le Grand Déjeuner* declared, it seems, a comprehensive 'call to order', which was at root still realist however ideal its apparent perfection. But the fact remains that with it Léger rejected the modern subjects of 1918–19 and appeared to return to the subject-matter of a conventional traditionalism rather than a popular realism. The question therefore remains: how far did Léger's acceptance of the prevailing 'avant-garde' approach to the machine and modern life in figure-painting constitute a rejection of the popular realism of 1918–19 for an 'elite' style? How far did his return to a realism attuned to a broad avant-garde tendency lead him to forget the allegiance to popular concerns which had been the prime result of his life with the *poilus* on the front?

Surprisingly, the fact is that Léger's decision to return to the styles of the past reflected as much an increased popular as an increased avant-garde enthusiasm for the art of the past. The progressive reopening of the Louvre, starting in January 1919 with an Egyptian and an Assyrian room and culminating late in 1920 with the French rooms, combined with the reopening of the Musée de Cluny was responsible for this new enthusiasm, and something of its intensity can be gathered from the attention these events aroused in the press. 'The opening of the Louvre dominates opinion,' reported *L'Intransigeant* in January 1919, 'it symbolizes the return to peace.'[12] For a short while, the masterpieces of the museums were brand new again, and the sense of a revived link with the past after half a decade of chaos must have been irresistible.

Yet at least as important was the fact that Léger's central decision to revive the classical nude was a reflection as much of a popular as of an avant-garde tendency. So too was his attempt to fuse figurative equilibrium with the precise perfection of the machine. The idea of the human figure as at once classically and mechanically perfect received strong support from two articles contributed by Jeanneret's brother Albert to *L'Esprit Nouveau* nos. 2 and 3. Albert Jeanneret was Professeur de Rythmique at the Conservatoire Rameau in Paris, and there and in these articles he set out to teach a system of physical and musical education called Eurhythmics, which had been pioneered before 1914 by Jacques-Dalcroze. The basis of his approach was a frankly mechanical concept of the human body. His aim was to achieve a precise harmony between body and 'spirit', the human body considered as a 'rhythmic machine'.[13] He believed that music released through dance a complementary mental and muscular sense of rhythmic proportion, so that, in the coming together of music, dance and gymnastics, there could be consumated a genuine marriage of his mechanical and his classical ideal of beauty.

Using the popular illustrated magazines as evidence, it is clear that by 1921 Albert Jeanneret's ideas situated him right in the centre of a broad popular movement. A particularly influential force behind this movement was lieutenant Georges Hébert and his Collège d'Athlètes feminin de la Palestra. Hébert had already formulated his ideas on physical education before 1914, expounding them in his *L'Education physique* and his *Code de la force*, but the need for physical education created by the war ensured

156. 'Fresque de Puvis de Chavannes animé', Lieutenant Georges Hébert's course as taught at Deauville, *L'Illustration*, August 1919.

more successful activities after 1918. Like Jeanneret, he aimed in the *course naturelle* taught at his college to achieve an alliance between the mechanical beauty of the human body and a classical ideal, and something of the manner of his teaching is conveyed by the aptly captioned *Fresque de Puvis de Chavannes animé,* a double-page illustration of his course in action which appeared in August 1919 in *L'Illustration* (Plate 156). Between 1918 and 1921 several other such courses sprang up in Paris, so that by September 1921, writing in the new review *La Danse,* D. Strohl could mention courses in gymnastic dancing run by Irène Popard, Jeanne Ronsay and a Monsieur Paysée as well as the Dalcrozian school and Hébert's college.[14] The popular appeal of the movement was fast-growing and very wide: thus, late in 1919 Charles Gémier produced at the Cirque d'Hiver *Oedipus Rex* in French translation, and a feature of his production was an 'athletic interval' in which two hundred athletes from clubs all over France combined to express, as Gémier put it: 'one of the principal manifestations of life in antiquity: athletic beauty';[15] thus again, in April 1920 Marshal Pétain attended huge displays of gymnastics at Nice and Antibes; and thus once more, in May 1921 an equally large display was held as the *fête de Printemps* at the Stade Pershing in Paris.[16] No doubt a common stimulus behind these activities were the performances, of Isadora Duncan, but her passion had been replaced by something more cool, more controlled and more profoundly classical, in which the body at its most mechanically balanced and developed stood once again for a rational, proportionate ideal of beauty. It was perhaps a symptom of the coming mood that in November 1919 the female nude was allowed onto the Parisian music-hall stage for the first time, in the Casino de Paris review *Paris qui danse*, and that the event could successfully have been defended on the grounds of the chastity of the classical ideal.[17]

The massively static nudes of Léger's *Le Grand Déjeuner* were hardly athletic, but they were perfectly balanced, they were mechanical and they generated a sense of power, so that in the end it is clear that with this painting Léger declared not only his commitment to an elite, avant-garde 'call to order', but his awareness of a popular enthusiasm for the mechanical in physical perfection. With his return to the nude decorously posed for harmonious effect, he may have rejected his modern subjects of 1918–19, but he did not reject the popular for the avant-garde—the nude presented in the ideal terms of the classical tradition *was* a popular subject. Significantly, the popularist lesson of the war was still very much in Léger's mind when he wrote in March 1922 to Léonce Rosenberg, and it was here that he admitted, as he continued to move his new classical way, that: 'The war made me mature. . . .'[18] It was, in the final analysis, both an avant-garde and a popular view of modern life—of reality—that led him eventually away from the brutal anti-order vision of *La Ville* and *Les Disques dans la Ville* to the balanced traditionalism of *Le Grand Déjeuner*. *Le Grand Déjeuner* declared Léger's continuing realist determination to realize by contrasts on canvas the dissonant force of experience, but declared too his conviction that modern life in popular experience was neither fragmented nor alien to the classical values of order, but aspired to the qualities of precision and balance, its power illuminating rather than obscuring the importance of tradition. Even when so close to idealism and to the past, the Purist notion of a developing, ordered *esprit nouveau*, the product of a new, ordered reality and new classical enthusiasms, allowed him to remain a modern realist with popular aspirations.

*   *   *   *   *

Yet though the traditional artificiality of the posed nude may have attained for Léger a popular pungency in *Le Grand Déjeuner*, during 1922 he was drawn as a classical figure-painter towards subjects which were both less artificial and more realist in a more contemporary sense. He attached his new mechanized classical ideal of the human figure more directly to the facts of everyday existence. The theme in which he made this move on the grandest scale was *La mère et l'enfant*, a theme whose development from oil study to oil study was at least as careful as the development of *Le Grand Déjeuner*, and which culminated in a canvas almost as large and even more exactly finished (Plate 157).[19] It was either this painting or one of the oils related to it that he sent to the Salon d'Automne of 1922 as his major public statement of the year.[20]

Among the painters who, for Léger, in his March 1922 letter to Léonce Rosenberg, were 'inventors' (sometimes) were the brothers Le Nain, and between 1919 and 1923 the Le Nains were the focus, like Poussin, David and Ingres, of much interest, popular and elite. It was early in 1919 that Louis Le Nain's monumental celebration of the ordinary, *La Famille de paysans dans un intérieur* (Plate 158), entered the Louvre to be exhibited as one of the stars among the recent acquisitions,[21] and in January 1923 the enthusiasm for the work of the Le Nains came to a head with an ex-

157. (above) Fernand Léger: *La Mère et l'enfant*, 1922. $67\frac{1}{2} \times 94$ ins, Oeffentliche Kunstssammlung, Basel.

158. (left) Louis Le Nain: *La Famille de paysans dans un intérieur*, circa 1642. $44\frac{1}{2} \times 62\frac{5}{8}$ ins, Musée du Louvre, Paris.

hibition of twelve paintings at the galerie Sambon which was considered important enough to be given expansive front-page space in *L'Intransigeant* with a laudatory article by Maurice Raynal. 'The subject', Raynal wrote, 'is chosen without research. Always it is peasant in essence,' yet, these 'luminous . . . variations on popular themes' were always submitted to 'a taste for order and economy of means' in the interests of compositional balance, a purely pictorial classicism.[22] It was as cool classicist and popular realist that the reputation above all of Louis Le Nain rose between 1919 and 1923, paintings like the *Famille de paysans* standing as proof that an ordered, a 'French' sense of pictorial structure could root itself in the simple depiction of everyday life.[23] There was, therefore, every reason for Léger to shift his attention at least partly to the Le Nains in 1922, and that is what he did with the development of the *Mère et l'enfant* theme.

The two figures of the painting have still that smooth tonal modelling which looks back to David, that largeness and weightiness of limbs which looks back to Poussin and classical antiquity, but they are not timeless nudes set in a timeless space (at once modern and traditional); they are modern figures in a modern interior through whose windows can be seen a French landscape. With deliberate clarity Léger declares a simple everyday subject as the excuse for a monumental figure-painting, a subject which is emphatically the 1920s equivalent of Louis Le Nain's peasant family subject, and the curious combination of authentic informality and stiff, slightly self-conscious posing, the feeling of figures who have frozen at the painter's request right in the middle of the most ordinary domestic moment is precisely that of the Louvre *Famille de paysans*. Here too a classic monumentality emerges from the most ordinary of popular themes, and it is worth pointing out that it was in 1922 that Léger began his retreats with Jeanne his wife to the countryfied suburban calm of his little house at Fontenay-aux-roses so that the subject could well have been extracted from the calmer moments of his own daily routine, from the small-scale comforts of his own life.[24]

Yet, though imbued with the classic simplicity of Louis Le Nain, Léger's *Mère et l'enfant*, like his *Grand Déjeuner*, did not conceal its modernity and did not mute the force of his view of modern life. Working with this new, popular subject, Léger arrived at a new compound of the contradictory elements that had given such power to *Le Grand Déjeuner* and thus at a pictorial result hostile to the unbroken calm of the seventeenth-century *Famille de paysans* in just the same sense that *Le Grand Déjeuner* is hostile to the Poussin *Elizieh and Rebecca at the Well*. The setting is once again not only post-Cubist in its pursuit of complex overlappings and modern in the stark clarity of its contrasts, but primitive or 'pre-Renaissance' in the stressed conflicts of its perspective and in the naïve presentation of its still-life objects on their tilted table-tops. What is more, the figures themselves generate just that same sense of conflict between the classically traditional and the mechanistically up-to-date as the nudes of the 1921 canvas, their impassive machine perfection robbing them of the individuality still so strongly stated by each one of Louis Le Nain's peasants.

La Mère et l'enfant may more openly situate Léger's 'call to order' within a popular realist tradition, taking its subject from the most ordinary aspects of contemporary life, but Léger does not allow the intimacy and warmth

7. (above) Fernand Léger: *La Lecture*, 1924. 45 × 57½ ins, Musée National d'Art Moderne, Paris.

8. (right) Fernand Léger: *Nature morte au chandelier*, 1922. 45½ × 31½ ins, Musée d'Art Moderne de la Ville de Paris.

inherent in such a subject to rob him of the mechanized anonymity essential to his classical approach. At the same time he does not allow the harmonious calm of the Le Nains to rob him of his feeling for the power of contrasts. It is evidence of a fundamentally unchanged approach that at least one response to the version of *La Mère et l'enfant* shown at the 1922 Salon d'Automne could as well have been provoked by *Le Grand Déjeuner*: 'Léger,' wrote Marcel Hiver in Montparnasse, 'would you like to live in the world your paintings evoke, that crystalline, metallic world, which has the frozen emptiness of planets without atmosphere, where living beings, like (inanimate) things, exist petrified in the precise, mechanical stillness of a film suddenly stopped. Why do you treat a human face exactly like that porcelain pot . . .; why those arms in pressed steel?'[25]

*   *   *   *   *

La Mère et l'enfant did not announce the end of the classical figure subject in favour of the popular figure subject. It was in Léger's continuing treatment above all of the neutral classical nude, that the ideas already so intensively explored in *Le Grand Déjeuner* realized their full potential during 1923 and 1924.

1923, however, was not for Léger a year of intensive activity as an easel-painter, and the cause of this is easy to find, for that year saw him divert his energies into other new and demanding areas of activity. In February 1923 he combined with the 'Effort Moderne' sculptor Csaky to produce an architectural ensemble for the Indépendants, his first excursion into painting for architecture. Already early in 1922 he had become involved as a costume and set designer with Rolf de Maré's Ballet Suédois, working as designer for Ricciotto Canudo's ballet *Skating-Rink*.[26] Arthur Honnegger, one of 'Les Six', had composed the music for *Skating-Rink*, and it was another of the group, Darius Milhaud, who composed the music for the ballet that absorbed his energies during the late summer and autumn of 1923, Blaise Cendrars's *ballet nègre*, *La Création du Monde*. This was produced in November with Léger's mobile yet austere set the foil for the dancers in their far from austere costumes,[27] and it is not surprising that there was no major contribution by Léger to the Salon d'Automne of the same month. What is more, 1923 saw Léger's interest in the cinema turn into participation, with his designs for the notorious laboratory and the opening *élément mécanique* sequence in Marcel L'Herbier's film *L'Inhumaine*, which was made, as *La Création du Monde* was being rehearsed, during the late summer and autumn.[28] These activities outside easel-painting, in mural-painting, theatre and film were complemented by a growing amount of theoretical activity—of lecturing, debating and writing. On 1 June 1923 Léger delivered an important lecture, 'L'Esthétique de la machine', as part of a series organized by Dr Allendy at the Collège de France; it was 'enthusiastically applauded'[29] and was then published later in the year in *Der Querschnitt* the most comprehensive of several statements to be published that year.[30] Altogether 1923 was for Léger the year of so much else that it could not be the year of major developments in his painting. His discoveries especially in film did have an effect on his future as an easel-painter, but they had no clear-cut effect on his future as a classical figure-painter, and from that point of view they were a diversion.

240

There was, however, one major classical figure-painting produced by Léger in 1923, and with it one significant innovation. The painting was the large, heraldic *Nus sur fond rouge* (Plate 161) behind which lay at least one smaller oil (Plate 160) plus a carefully squared-up drawing, both dated 1922.[31] It made no attempt to overlay its traditional classicism with the costumes and the attributes of a contemporary subject. It was a conventional arrangement of two nudes, its subject openly in line with academic practice. The innovation that the painting declared seems to have come of a desire to replace the spatial complexities of *Le Grand Déjeuner* and *La Mère et l'enfant* with something simpler and yet something as powerfully set against the modelled weight of the figures. The conflicting perspectives and tilted table-tops of the 1921–2 interiors gave way to a flat intensely red ground plane on which the polished components of the nudes were hung, their steel grey chilled by contrast with the warmth of the red surround, their rounded weight even more emphatic against its unrelieved flatness. The major effect of this innovation was to concentrate all attention

159. Illustration from *Omnia*, Paris, 1922.

160. Fernand Léger: *La Femme*, 1922. $25\frac{1}{2} \times 18$ ins, Perls Gallery, New York.

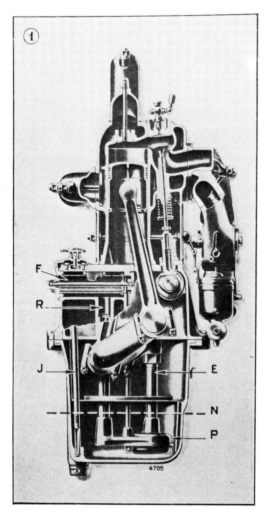

on the central figurative theme: on the precision and the complex equilibrium of the figurative components, on their cold anonymous perfection, and on the conflict they carry within themselves between the modern image of the machine and the traditional image of the nude. There is no concession made to the warm flush of skin tones in the painting of their surfaces and so the sense of the mechanistic is even stronger than in *Le Grand Déjeuner*, but at the same time the styling of nose and brow makes even more emphatic contact with the classical past through Picasso, and the decision thus to isolate the nude with such clear definition on an undifferentiated ground plane itself makes direct contact with the antique, recalling the reproductions of the Roman mosaics from the Baths of Caracalla published in *L'Esprit Nouveau* nos. 12 and 13, early in 1922 (Plate 162).[32] After the many distracting complications created by the paintings of 1921 and 1922, Léger uses the simple clash between red ground and figurative centrepiece to concentrate interest on the central figurative conflict between the traditional and the modern, the classical and the mechanical.

Nus sur fond rouge was the only classical figure-painting of any importance produced by Léger in 1923, but it was the prelude to a series of monumental figure-paintings completed during the first half of 1924, and it was in these large ambitious compositions that the ideas comprehensively set out in *Le Grand Déjeuner* finally realized their full potential. The best-known is the utterly undemonstrative yet grand canvas *La Lecture* (Colour Plate 7). Léger had finished it by July 1924[33] and behind it lay a planned development even more exact and even more painstaking than that which lay behind *Le Grand Déjeuner* and *La Mère et l'enfant*. Not only was each figure, taken separately, the subject of individual compositions as minutely and smoothly painted as the *état définitif* itself, but there were also elaborate and exact pencil drawings executed with obsessive care, one for the whole composition, one for the reclining and one for the standing nude.[34] Even more than *Le Grand Déjeuner* and *La Mère et l'enfant*, *La Lecture* presented itself as a precision machine.

Neither *La Lecture* itself nor the canvases that lay behind it announced a single new direction in Léger's classical figure-painting and they contained not a single pictorial innovation; indeed, the clear-cut clash which is engineered between the hefty metallic females and their flat Mondrian-like setting looks right back beyond *Le Grand Déjeuner* to the 1920 *Les Odalisques* (Plate 149) and ultimately even to *Le Mécanicien* (Plate 130). But its setting is more austere, more strictly defined, and its females are both more mechanistic and more classical: its significance lies not in its novelty but in the degree of definition it reaches. It is the statement of an extreme.

1924 might have seen a marked increase in Léger's activity as an easel-painter—the drawings and paintings leading up to *La Lecture* were no more than a part of his total production—but at the same time it saw little slackening of his efforts in other directions. Yet though his theatrical and cinematic activities took him deeper into circles he had not entered until after 1921—the circles above all of Jacques Hébertot and Rolf de Maré at the Théâtre des Champs Elysées—even so he remained deeply involved in the avant-garde circles which had been the context for the 'call to order', which had led him initially to the uncompromising traditionalism of *Le*

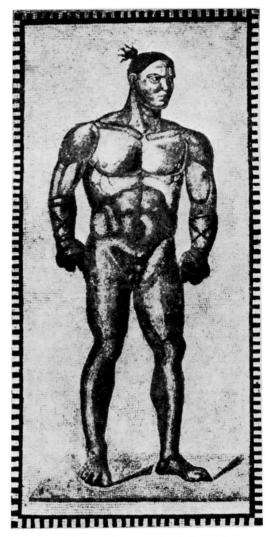

161. Fernand Léger: *Nus sur fond rouge*, 1923. $57\frac{1}{2} \times 38\frac{1}{2}$ ins, Oeffentliche Kunstssammlung, Basel.

162. Romain mosaic, from the Baths of Caracalla, as reproduced in *L'Esprit Nouveau* no. 13.

Grand Déjeuner. His painting was positively unpopular with the small but growing group of 'modern art' buyers, yet Léonce Rosenberg remained loyal, buying his work, publicizing it in his new *Bulletin de l'Effort Moderne* begun in 1924, and publishing his ideas too. Indeed, they were close enough that year to travel together during August in Italy as prelude to a September visit by Léger to the important Viennese theatre exhibition. What is more, during 1923 and especially 1924 Léger's relationship with Ozenfant, Le Corbusier and *L'Esprit Nouveau* became increasingly close, and a revealing symptom of this is the fact that when in 1924 he decided to open a school for the dissemination of his ideas, he did so in his Paris *atelier* at 86, rue Notre-Dame-des-Champs, with Ozenfant.

Still very much a part of the 'Effort Moderne' and the Purist Parisian *milieu*, within which a commitment to order, precision, to the lesson of the

243

engineer and the machine, to the classical tradition was still unchallenged, it was not surprising that Léger's own commitment to a classical 'call to order' should have both deepened and become more clearly defined by 1924. *La Lecture* is evidence of this fact, as too is the uncompromising clarity with which his now ordered ideas on painting and on modern life are expressed between his letter of March 1922 to Léonce Rosenberg and his articles of 1923–24, above all his lecture 'L'Esthétique de la machine', which, significantly, was first published in French by the *Bulletin de l'Effort Moderne* in January and February 1924. In 1922, Léger had written to Rosenberg:

We are bound to our environment . . . I am a firm believer in a slow and continual inroad brought about by the *manufactured object* which holds the secret of any renaissance we may have. A man living for a long time in the environment of these stern geometric forms will unconsciously find himself won over by them . . . The contemporary environment is clearly (dominated by) the manufactured and 'mechanical' object; this is slowly subjugating the breasts and curves of woman, fruit, the soft landscape— inspiration of painters since art began.[35]

He finds his own words here for the Purist idea of *l'esprit nouveau*, which so crucially supported the popular aspect of the mechanized nudes of *Le Grand Déjeuner*, and it is the Purist idea of *l'esprit nouveau*—of a modern, machine-made environment whose precise order must deepen the aesthetic need for order—that is elaborated in a very personal way by Léger in 'L'Esthétique de la machine'. But, though 'L'Esthétique de la machine' contains echoes of the approach to tradition elucidated in the 1922 letter, it concentrates almost entirely on 'the manufactured and "mechanical" object' alone. The idea so crucial to Léger, in his letter to Rosenberg, of a conflict between 'the breasts and curves of woman . . . inspiration of painters since art began' and the 'mechanical' object had certainly been expressed by the nudes of *Le Grand Déjeuner*, but with *Nus sur fond rouge* and even more in 1924 with *La Lecture* it received more concentrated, more definite expression. So polished, so precisely balanced, so impassive are the females of *La Lecture* that the image of woman survives with difficulty the dominant image of the machine. Where the sense of traditional classicism was perhaps dominant in *Le Grand Déjeuner*, however strongly challenged, here in 1924 the sense of mechanized modernity is dominant, and the lack of 'primitive' perspectival side-issues intensifies the effect.

Already in *Le Grand Déjeuner* the clear definition and hardly varied standardization of Léger's figurative components gave his nudes the appearance of products assembled on a conveyor belt—the products, like the Voisin aeroplanes and Ford cars praised by Le Corbusier in *L'Esprit Nouveau*'s early numbers, of the still new methods of mass-production.[36] As the figures of *La Lecture* are more effectively machine-like in shaping and in finish, so they are more obviously composed of standardized components, and more obviously, as has been seen, the mechanically carried out product of a plan, a plan which it seems could have been executed by any technician trained in oil painting. There is absolutely no feeling of individual touch.

The pursuit of the typical element and the celebration of standardization in mass-production had been from the beginning, of course, a central theme in *L'Esprit Nouveau*, so that Léger's pursuit of the mass-production effect in *Le Grand Déjeuner* did take place within a well-defined Purist context. Indeed, so interested was Léger in the idea of mass-production that it seems he was actually tempted by Gleizes's 1921 plan to mass-produce paintings, only being dissuaded by the terms of Léonce Rosenberg's galerie de l'Effort Moderne contract.[37] Yet, significantly, as Léger's relationship with Ozenfant and especially Le Corbusier became closer late in 1923 and during 1924, and as he moved through the carefully planned pictorial phases that led to *La Lecture*, Le Corbusier's ideas on standardization were sharpened and at last were put to the test of practical application in building. In November 1923 Le Corbusier received a letter from a major industrialist based in Bordeaux, M. Frugès, asking him to design a small housing scheme to settle the workforce of a saw-mill. Frugès was a convert to the ideas on mass-production housing so persuasively put in Corbusier's *Vers une architecture*, published that summer,[38] and this was the architect's first real chance to apply them in more than isolated individual villa commissions. During the first half of 1924, up to the July completion of the experimental 'type A' house, the so-called *maison du Tonkin* at Bordeaux, Le Corbusier was, therefore, deeply involved in the attempt to convert his ideas on standardization and mass-production in building first into plans and then into actual structure.[39] From the outset the aim had been to use the Frugès saw-mill for the pre-fabrication of standardized doors, windows and floors, and in July 1924 Corbusier arrived at the proportions of his standardized reinforced concrete structural skeleton, the basic design-unit of what in the next two years became the *cité ouvrière* of Pessac.[40] The forms of Le Corbusier's Pessac housing are perhaps no more than distantly related to those of Léger's *La Lecture*, but the ideas on mass-production so sharply placed in focus by the commission are profoundly in tune.

Le Corbusier gave these ideas pungent expression in March 1924 with 'Construire en série', an article which first appeared in a Czech review.[41] Standardization, he announced here, 'leads to perfection'; from the machine, from 'selection', from standardization came 'a style'; and he introduced these statements with a passage which might be applied almost directly to *La Lecture*: 'Machines replace hand-work; spheres are smooth, regular and perfect; cylinders are absolute . . . : the machine without faltering, turns out the most exact of surfaces.' What is more, as Le Corbusier planned his different residential types on the basis of standardized units repeated in varying combinations, so Léger moved from the figurative grouping of *Nus sur fond rouge* to that of *La Lecture* by simply combining anew the same standard components—the same eyes and lids, the same noses, the same forearms and hands and fingers. By 1924 he had very nearly if not quite absolutely standardized the units out of which he built his figure-paintings, and in December that year Georges Charensol interviewed him for *Paris-Journal*, extracting the telling statement: 'When my drawing is finished my painting is three quarters done. I mass-produce my canvases always; so at the moment I'm working on a dozen simultaneously, after the drawings you see here.'[42]

If in its precise equilibrium and its standardized components *La Lecture* took to an extreme the mechanistic factor already so strong in *Le Grand*

Déjeuner, it took to an extreme also the popular character of the approach *Le Grand Déjeuner* declared. For there can be no doubt that, like the mechanistic classical idea of the human body, the Purist idea of the machine as an exact, perfectly coordinated instrument of efficiency, and the Purist enthusiasm for mass-production reflected strong popular concerns. The extensive reports on the Salon de l'Aviation and especially on the Salon de l'Automobile which appeared every autumn in the newspapers and the wide-circulation magazines like *L'Illustration* and *Le Monde Illustré* between 1919 and 1925 provide much evidence of this. The emphasis is repeatedly placed on purely technical innovation and on the increased efficiency of the engines, gearing, suspension, etc., of the exhibits, rather than on questions of style;[43] and this reflects the emphasis placed on the making of mechanical points in the presentation of aircraft or cars stripped down, as for instance in the presentation of the 10 HP BSA chassis at the 1922 Salon de l'Automobile illustrated in *Le Monde Illustré* (Plate 163). The advertising of the popular French manufacturers in the newspapers and illustrated magazines—of Renault, Citroën and De Dion Bouton, also provides convincing evidence: they aimed to appeal as much to the mechanic as to the stylist in the consumer. Thus, as early as 1919 the 10 HP Citroën advertisement in *Le Monde Illustré* (Plate 164) describes the motor as the heart and lungs, the 'essential organ' of the motor-car, and right from 1918 to 1924 the Citroën advertisements carried the boast—'first mass-produced motor-car in France'.[44] The idea of mass-production as well as the ideal of functional efficiency were current enough and popular enough to be good publicity. Indeed, of such current concern were the aims of the American apostles of efficiency F. W. Taylor and Henry Ford—both much admired by Le Corbusier—that the front page of *L'Intransigeant* could carry an elaborate satire on 'Taylorization' in April 1923,[45] and during 1924 *Le Quotidien* could serialize the memoirs of Ford, culminating in their French

163. 10 HP BSA chassis, Salon de l'Automobile, Paris, 1922. As illustrated in *Le Monde Illustré,* November 1922.

164. 10 HP Citroën advertisement, *Le Monde Illustré,* 15 November 1919.

Le splendide châssis 10 HP, B. S. A. sans soupapes.

165. Fernand Léger: *Trois figures,* 1924. Josef Müller collection, Soleure.

publication as *Henry Ford, ma vie et mon oeuvre.* By 1924 there was indeed evidence to support the Purist belief in an *esprit nouveau*, and therefore to endow the mechanical efficiency of *La Lecture* with a popular flavour.

If the Paris *La Lecture* took to an extreme the mechanistic, popular aspect of Léger's classical figure-painting, there was another canvas completed during the first half of 1924 which was as large, as highly finished, as carefully planned and mechanistic yet at the same time more emphatically traditional in its use of the artificially posed nude, which took to an extreme both the machine factor and the classical factor—this was the exactly square, robustly unlovely *Trois figures* (Plate 165).[46] Here the female nude given early form in the 1922 *Femme* (Plate 160) and then so precisely in the large nude of the *Nus sur fond rouge* (Plate 161), reappears, her parts slightly readjusted and her hairstyle changed, with new companions constructed out of the same standardized components. The setting is flat, but unlike the red ground of *Nus sur fond rouge* it is utterly neutral—a cool blue-green—and there is no attempt at all, as there is in *La Lecture*, to make a pretence at naturalness—no books, no flowers, no accessories of daily life, but only a staff and a roll of paper, the undisguised accessories of the life class.[47]

Léger's elevation here of the classic life-class nude, its artificial origins undisguised, to the level of the machine or the 'manufactured object', takes to an extreme and therefore brings into focus, perhaps more effectively than *La Lecture*, an aspect of his classical figure-painting present right from the late 1920 preparations for *Le Grand Déjeuner*, an aspect which is the corollary of both its classicism and its mechanization—its total lack of sexuality, its impersonal even inhuman coldness. In his 1922 letter to Rosenberg Léger rejects out of hand the seductive beauty of woman as painted by Raphael, Leonardo and Renoir. Of Renoir he writes: 'Ultimately, his "fruity" women started off the rot. Sensuality is taken to excess.'[48] The Purists certainly, right from the beginning, echoed his horror of the sensual subject sensually treated, and it runs as a strong undercurrent not only through Léger's classical figure-painting between 1921 and 1924, but also through the approach to dance, theatre and to film that he developed in these years, coming to a head, alongside *La Lecture* and *Trois figures*, in the articles on theatre and film first published in 1924. As Elie Faure's essay on Chaplin in *L'Esprit Nouveau* no. 6 demonstrates, much of the considerable appeal that Chaplin had for the Purists and their allies came of his ability to seem almost to depersonalize gesture and expression, using them in and for themselves on the screen.[49] Chaplin had been since 1916 an enthusiasm of Léger's, and in 1920 Léger had illustrated Ivan Goll's *Die Chaplinade*, a small personal homage. It is therefore not surprising that Chaplin should have been, for him, *the* example of the film actor most capable of exploiting the anti-literary, anti-individualistic potential of film, a point clear in Léger's early 1924 essay 'Le Ballet-Spectacle, l'objet-spectacle'. For Léger here, the actor in film or theatre 'becomes a mechanism like everything else . . . he becomes a means',[50] just as the figures of *La Lecture* and the 1924 *Trois figures* are no more than pictorial mechanisms—pictorial means used for pictorial ends. 1923 and 1924 were years when Léger spent much time in the dance-halls with his theatre and film friends,[51] and it was this experience that lay behind his ideas on popular dance as set out in 'Les Bals populaires' which was published early in 1924 with 'Le Ballet-Spectacle, l'objet-spectacle' in *La Vie des Lettres et des Arts*, ideas which played down the sexuality of popular dance just as he played down the personality and sexuality of the film actor. In 1971 Armand Lunel recalled visiting a dance-hall on the rue de Lappe with Darius Milhaud, Paul Morand, Léger and Jeanne, Léger's wife; it was an evening in December 1923. The story he tells is perhaps the most revealing of all demonstrations of the utterly asexual, impersonal way in which Léger approached the human figure, above all the female figure, in 1923 and 1924. Lunel tells how they sat and watched the dancers; Léger fixed on one female in particular, 'the least sophisticated' but a figure 'marvellously well constructed'. 'Look at that woman,' he whispered, 'she's beautiful! Like a gas-meter!'[52]

Yet, in the final analysis, the nudes of *Trois figures* are impersonal and asexual not most fundamentally because of their standardized, mechanistic polish, but because for Léger their ultimate *raison d'être* is purely pictorial. Chaplin, the dancers of the Ballet Suédois and of the popular dance-halls are considered asexually, impersonally, because personality and sexuality are, for Léger, irrelevant to the pure dynamic equilibrium of their *visual* effect; and in the same way these qualities were, for Léger, irrelevant to the pure static equilibrium of his nudes. It was most essentially because their sensuality led them to imitate the appearance of the nude at the expense of pure formal 'invention' that Léger rejected Raphael, Leonardo and Renoir. His nudes were above all the means towards compositional ends, ends which had nothing to do with the femininity, masculinity or humanity of the figure. Thus, when Rosenberg, horrified at the hairlessness of the standing female in *La Lecture*, asked him to add some hair, Léger could not do it because he needed 'a precise, round form' just there.[53] Thus too, in *Trois figures*, the fingernails and toenails are given as much importance as the glintless eyes; and thus again, Léger creases the hip of the kneeling nude on the left, even though the representational origin for the creasing, the sash tied round the hips of the 1922 *Femme* (Plate 160), has been forgotten, the formal need for an echo of the fingers that hold the staff being justification enough. Léger's realistic variant on the Purist notion of *l'esprit nouveau* meant that his classical idea of order was inevitably associated with the machine and the manufactured object, since these created the feeling for order special to the time, but ultimately that feeling for order remained a question of form, a pure question of composition.

Behind the classical figure style of *Le Grand Déjeuner*, of *La Mère et l'enfant*, of *Trois figures* and of *La Lecture* there lay the desire to declare his commitment both to the machine as an image of order and to the stylized nude as the image of tradition. But the mechanical classic nude remained for him essentially the vehicle of formal effect, of a pure asexual power held in check by an exact, modern, sense of structure. Between 1921 and 1924 Léger arrived at more than one kind of painting with a central figurative theme, but all his classic figure-paintings are held together not only by the constant themes of contrast, precision, standardization and tradition, but also by the recurrence of basic formal characteristics and a basic formal sense of priority. It is this unity of formal concern that gives unity as well to the many other kinds of painting that followed from Léger's 'call to order' between 1921 and 1924—to the *Paysages animés*, the object-paintings and the architectural paintings which are the subject of the next two chapters.

CHAPTER 9
Léger and the Purist *esprit nouveau*, 1920–5

Léger's 'call to order' was certainly at its most overtly traditionalist in the classical figure-paintings of 1920–4—it was in these paintings that the clash between the past and the present was most striking, because it was in them that the forms of the past were most uncompromisingly recalled. But Léger's 'call to order' was pursued too through landscape, townscape and still-life, and it was in these themes that his ordered idea of the *esprit nouveau* created by modern life was most elaborately developed, because it was in them that he could declare most effectively his firm conviction that an environment of 'stern geometric forms' would in the end win modern man over.[1]

Though *Le Grand Déjeuner* was Léger's grandest and most ambitious theme in 1921, it was not the only one. There was also a further, very different line of development established by a group of modern landscapes, the *Paysages animés*, whose subject was the conflict between figures, buildings and countryside in rural Normandy, where Léger spent the summer (Plate 168). However, just as *Le Grand Déjeuner* was the conclusion to a development whose beginnings lay in 1920, so the *Paysages animés* and the landscapes with figures related to them were the sequel to pictorial ideas explored the year before. In this case the ideas in question were taken to very elaborate lengths in two large well-worked canvases, the *Pont du remorqueur* in the Musée National d'Art Moderne, Paris, and the *Remorqueur* (Plate 166).

The Grenoble *Remorqueur* is less than the Paris painting a development from the 1918 *Remorqueur* theme (Plate 105). But in general pictorial terms the connection is clear. What is more, the robot figures and the patterned balcony grille look back also to the simultanist paintings of 1919. Yet as a modern landscape with figures it occupies a transitional position in the same way that the 1920 *L'Homme à la pipe* occupies a transitional position as a figure-painting. It both looks back to the dynamic and the disintegrated compositions of 1918–19 and forward to the precisely controlled equilibrium

166.　Fernand Léger: *Le Remorqueur,* 1920. 41 × 52 ins, Musée de peinture et de sculpture, Grenoble.

of 1921. The stable containing structure of rectangular planes is more expansive, more clear-cut and therefore more dominant, but the distinctions between the component parts of the composition are far more sharply defined, so that within a firmly constructed pictorial scaffold everything is altogether less fragmentary and therefore more legible. The bright, flat arrangements of planes, with their intense yellows, reds, greens and blues, clearly declare themselves as the equivalents of *remorqueur* and architecture, the modelling only rarely obscuring the issue by being applied to barge or building elements. The three figures and the dog are all heftily constructed from metallic grey volumes, each one of them treated as a co-ordinated whole; while, neatly contained within a rectangular frame, the less mechanistic, freer, curves of a landscape are unfolded behind the soft outline of a single tree. Finally, the rather thin and sometimes summary way in which large areas of the composition have been painted reveals a broad yet definite squaring-up system and a rough yet detailed pencil outlining as the preparatory basis. Léger's mode of planning is by no means yet exact and his pictorial components are certainly not yet so well defined as those that made up *Le Grand Déjeuner* in 1921, but the 'call to order', with its consequent clarification both of technique and of pictorial means, has evidently begun.

Léger was extremely prolific in his production of *Paysage animés* and related landscape with figure themes, although not one of them even approaches the public scale of *Le Grand Déjeuner*. With these paintings, however, he did commit himself as completely as in *Le Grand Déjeuner*. *Les Pêcheurs* (Plate 167) is a relatively small canvas, thickly, even roughly, painted, but the certainty with which each area is filled in with hardly a single change of mind is evidence of a care in the planning process comparable with that which led up to *Le Grand Déjeuner*. Thus, a careful pencil outlining, far more precise than that which shows through in the Grenoble *Remorqueur*, acted as strict guide in the execution of the composition, and the sureness with which this was drawn onto the primed canvas as blueprint was the result of a sequence of preparatory studies in pencil and oil.[2] In its own small way *Les Pêcheurs*, like every one of the more finished versions of the *Paysages animés* (Plate 168),[3] is as much a mechanically planned and perfected product of Léger's new classical approach as *Le Grand Déjeuner*, and, significantly, it is inscribed on the reverse 'Etat définitif'.

Moreover, there is a clarity of distinction between the constituent parts of *Les Pêcheurs* that gives it both sharper definition and easier legibility than the *Remorqueur*—the bottle-green boa-constrictor trees stand up each so separate against the sky with its bulbous arrangement of clouds, and the fishermen, grey in the centre, brown on the flanks, counter so clearly the flat planar architecture of man-made structures, while on the right the countryside rolls away layer after well-defined layer, studded with emerald-green bushes. The total outdoor space of the scene is not unified, the trees acting to disrupt that unity, but the space within each compartment of the composition is opened up without ambiguity and a restricted range of tones from muted browns and greens to grey ensures a unified sense of atmosphere and place. There is too a vague yet unmistakable feeling of contact with the past, with the 'primitive' and classical tradition recalled much more overtly by *Le Grand Déjeuner*, a reminiscence of Poussin in the crystal clarity with which each landscape element, however distant, is defined, a reminiscence of the landscape backgrounds of the Maître de Moulins in the simple overlapping of landscape layers studded with bushes, and perhaps also, anticipating the 1922 *Mère et l'enfant*, a vague reminiscence of the Le Nains in the grouping of the figures and the everyday ordinariness of the scene. No specific comparisons could be made, but there is a feeling for tradition not even vaguely to be found in the *Remorqueur*.

Yet, in a couple of crucial respects, *Les Pêcheurs* is not like the *Paysages animés* proper: landscape is not dominant and the flat planar architecture of man-made structures neither reads as buildings in the countryside nor makes its pictorial point with the help of primary colours. *Les Pêcheurs* is therefore not typical of Léger's 'call to order' as a landscape painter, where a well-developed *Paysage animé* like *L'Homme au chien* is (Plate 168). Here Léger's anonymous robot men with their dog are very much subordinate to a green and brown Norman landscape the near unity of whose space is sharply interrupted by flattened polychromatic buildings. This painting too, like *Les Pêcheurs*, is painstakingly prepared,[4] stable of structure

167.   Fernand Léger: *Les Pêcheurs*, 1921. 24 × 36 ins, galerie Beyeler, Basel.

168.   Fernand Léger: *L'Homme au chien*, 1921. $25\frac{1}{2}$ × $36\frac{1}{2}$ ins, Nathan Cummings collection, Chicago.

—the vertical and horizontal in control—and possessed of a simple legibility. It brings together as well the essentials of Léger's pictorial 'call to order'. But it sets man, architecture and countryside against one another in a strikingly new way, a way so far unprecedented in Léger's work and revealingly symptomatic of his emergent idea of modern life, *l'esprit nouveau*.

As an initial stimulus the half-timbered patterns of the farm-buildings so common in the Norman countryside may have had an effect, but the architecture of these paintings never even vaguely recalls such a stimulus. Occasionally it recalls the new suburban villas around Paris and the towns of Normandy, but most of all it is a pure pictorial invention whose origins lie in the black lined grids, the broad white rectangles and sudden primary colours of Léger's earlier figurative work—the flat architectural settings of *L'Homme à la pipe, Le Mécanicien* and *Les Odalisques* in 1920 (Plates 129, 130 and 149). His port-holed buildings often flat roofed and strongly coloured had never been seen before; their justification was at once purely pictorial—their flat, bright angularity so vigorously in conflict with the dull, rolling earthiness of the landscape—and prophetic, casting, as they did, a glance sideways at the possibility of a new architecture declared by Le Corbusier's 'Trois rappels à MM. Les architectes', and more directly at the polychromatic architecture anticipated by Mondrian's pamphlet 'Le néo-Plasticisme'.[5] So pure and modern an architecture in so impure and so traditional a landscape could not but strike hard, and the near unity of the outdoor space, the simplicity with which the countryside is unfolded layer by layer to the horizon, the clarity with which each cloud and tree and hummock of ground are modelled and the solid stability of the whole (far less vaguely than *Les Pêcheurs*) bring to mind the landscape backgrounds of the Maître de Moulins, or the Poussin landscapes of the 1640s, or the Corot, so much admired by *L'Esprit Nouveau*, of the sturdy little Roman landscapes from 1826–29.[6]

There can be no doubt that, as in *Le Grand Déjeuner* so in the *Paysages animés,* Léger pursued his contrasts between flat and modelled, bright and muted, most essentially for pictorial effect; but, just as the contrasts of *Le Grand Déjeuner* expose a significant and very special approach to the relationship between tradition and pictorial progress, so the contrasts of the *Paysages animés* expose a significant approach to the relations between things in modern life, in the changing environment of the time. 'Architecture,' wrote Mondrian, 'is an aesthetic and mathematical presence, therefore *exact* and more or less abstract.'[7] For him, the *abstract* reality of art and therefore of architecture set it necessarily against the material reality of nature, and, though Léger would never have echoed the mystical beliefs so fundamental to the Dutchman's idea of art, architecture and nature, the clarity of the opposition between 'abstract' architecture and natural countryside in the *Paysages animés* does seem, at least superficially, linked to it. Yet, both more obviously and more profoundly, the character of the hostile relationship that Léger develops with such clarity in canvases like *L'Homme au chien*, not only between buildings and landscape, but also between buildings, landscape and mechanized man, reflects the Purist view of the world—the view of the relationship between the major creators of the *esprit nouveau* celebrated by Ozenfant and Jeanneret (Le Corbusier) between 1918 and 1921. The *Paysages animés* are too concerned with the imperfect realities of modern life, too dissonant however stable, for them ever to be labelled Purist, but they do reveal a new and strong undertow of Purist attitudes, an undertow as strong as that revealed by the standardized precision of the classical figure-paintings.

Nature, for the Purists, was a paradox. 'Superficially experienced or observed, nature,' they wrote in *Après le cubisme,* 'seems like a magma of continually changing and variable incidents.' It gives the appearance of formless chaos. 'But, carefully studied or seriously experienced, nature seems not like an unplanned fairyland, but rather like a machine.'[8] Beneath its surface lay a complex and precise balance of forces governed according to laws defined by 'physical geometry and mathematics', but this order it effectively disguised. Architecture, in the Purist view, far from disguising its kinship with mechanical order had a duty to recognize it actively and openly. And, significantly, it was in 1920 that Le Corbusier arrived at his fundamental model for the mass-produced house, the *Maison Citrohan,* the year before he first put into print the provocative claim: 'A house is a machine for living in.'[9] Nature, therefore, in the Purist idea of the modern world, was set at least visually against the overt rational and proportionate order of architecture; and man, as at once a work of nature, a machine and the constructor of architecture, was situated neatly in between, while all three in a very profound sense were brought together as elements in a single perfectly balanced order.[10]

Léger almost certainly did not aim consciously to load his *Paysages animés* with the weight of Purist doctrine, but the relationship he declares between man, nature and architecture reflects with uncanny exactness the simple essentials of the Purist view. Architecture and landscape are the two opposing pictorial poles, while between them, geometrically rigid like the buildings yet heftily modelled like the rolling earth and the trees, the robot figures act as pictorial intermediaries. This simple sequence of relationships is clear enough in *L'Homme au chien,* and it is repeated, with only minor variations in every single one of the 1921 *Paysages animés.* It is difficult to believe that so clear-cut a statement of the relations between the man-made, the natural and man himself, could have been arrived at without the impetus of Ozenfant and Le Corbusier. As comprehensively as *Le Grand Déjeuner* but more directly in response to the realities of 1921, these paintings reveal a view of modern life which is no longer necessarily simultanist and fragmentary and tied to the experience of speed and change, but a view which is coherent and which implies the existence of constant relationships between things in a fundamentally ordered world.

It was most significantly of all with the development of the *Mère et l'enfant* and related domestic themes that Léger explored further in 1922 the pictorial possibilities opened up by the conflict between the natural, the man-made and the figure in the 1921 *Paysages animés,* although here, as has been seen, the figure was dominant and the interior settings were far more based on actuality than on architectural fantasy. However, he did not entirely forget the theme of outdoor conflict between the natural and the man-made, because a careful water-colour survives on the 1920 *Remorqueur* theme, and Léger seems to have painted a *Paysage-animé*-sized oil on this basis in the same year.[11] This return to the *Remorqueur* theme in the light of the *Paysages animés* was the prelude to the composition which brought to a climax the line of development opened up by the 1921 landscapes, the composition which most ambitiously of all coordinated the range of architectural and landscape contrasts established in them and which most expansively declared Léger's new view of *l'esprit nouveau* in town and country. The composition it led up to was the *Grand Remorqueur*, finished in 1923 as Léger absorbed himself in his new theatrical, cinematic and mural painting enthusiasms (Plate 169).

Le Grand Remorqueur is bigger than either *La Mère et l'enfant* or *La Lecture* or *Trois figures*; it is finished without a single suggestion of uncertainty; and it was prepared with the aid both of squaring-up and of an exact pencil outlining. The robot figure has disappeared and Léger's subject here is the machine—the Seine river-barge. But the curving and rocking coloured planes with their rows of port-holes and their single funnel form do not dominate the painting as they do in the versions of 1920. Instead they are set within the contradictory context of a hummocky riverside landscape, itself contradicted by industrial buildings translated into flat pictorial terms. The controlled yet energetic motion of the Seine barge has been placed within an industrialized *Paysage animé*.

Once more, as in the *Paysages animés*, the clarity with which Léger manages the pictorial conflict between flat and modelled, bright and muted, angular and cursive is the corollary of a sharp distinction between the man-made and the natural, but the decision to focus on the mechanical movement of a river-barge within an industrial rather than a rural landscape reveals even more clearly the Purist character of his approach to modern life. The Corbusian analogy between the machine and architecture is picked up at least implicitly in the pictorial alliance between the flat brilliance of the steam-barge components and that of the industrial buildings;[12] and the industrial buildings themselves, their forms so simply described, specifically connect with the architecture of the engineers celebrated by Le Corbusier two years before. As has been seen, it was late in 1923 that the Pessac commission gave Le Corbusier the chance to apply his standardized mass-production ideals, ideals in part evolved from his admiration of the constructions designed by engineers; it was also in 1923, in the summer, that Le Corbusier's celebration of the American grain elevator and the factory in the 'Trois Rappels à MM. les Architectes' was republished as part of *Vers une architecture*.[13] And it was to these industrial buildings that Léger looked when he painted the industrial architecture of *Le Grand Remorqueur*, recalling both the grain elevators (Plate 136), and, on the right, the most repetitive of the factory façades illustrated in *Vers une architecture* (Plate 137). Such buildings did exist (though not grain elevators) set incongruously in the greenery along the industrial suburban banks of the Seine from Bilancourt, through Courbevoie to Asnières, so the landscape of *Le Grand Remorqueur* does relate to the industrial reality Léger knew at first hand. But it is deeply significant of his close adherence to the Purist view of *l'esprit nouveau* that he should have selected structures so much in tune with Le Corbusier's well illustrated preferences. Behind the pictorial power of contrast and behind the firm over-all order of *Le Grand Remorqueur* lay a view of the relationships between the man-made and the natural, industry and the countryside which was fundamentally

169.   Fernand Léger: *Le Grand Remorqueur*, 1923. $49\frac{3}{4} \times 74$ ins, Musée National Fernand Léger, Biot.

Corbusian. It is a painting which declares more plainly and more forcibly than any Purist still-life the take-over of the environment by the geometry of modern structures, the rise of *l'esprit nouveau* in daily life. 'There arise everywhere,' the Purists had written in 1918, 'the constructions of a new spirit (*esprit nouveau*), the embryos of an architecture of the future; in them already harmony reigns . . .'[14] 'Modern life,' they wrote early in 1924, 'has with its machinery perfected our eye. The spirit itself, as a direct consequence, has developed its taste for perfect order.'[15] Léger's *Le Grand Remorqueur* made the apparently irresistible workings of this process plain.

Yet *Le Grand Remorqueur* could never have been called Purist, however Purist-like the view of the world it revealed. Not only has it a pictorial pugnacity alien to the painting of Ozenfant and Jeanneret (Le Corbusier), but it also declares Léger's debt to the facts of the modern world—to the river-barge, the industrial buildings and the invaded landscape of Bilancourt or Courbevoie—with a straightforwardness equally alien to Purism. Léger did not need to disguise the most potent stimuli behind his new, precise, ordered mode of painting by depicting only the regulated curves of the guitar or the simple geometry of the litre wine bottle; and so *Le Grand Remorqueur* could make the connection between his art and his view of modern life explicit. His convictions as a realist committed to the popular subject demanded that he should.

If 1924 brought no new developments in Léger's work as a classical figure-painter, producing in *La Lecture* and *Trois figures* only what had been established earlier but taken to an extreme, the year did bring new developments in his work as painter of the environment and man within it. *Le Grand Remorqueur* was indeed the climax of a sequence of pictorial events, for it had no sequel. Instead, on Léger's return from his trip with Léonce Rosenberg to Italy and to Vienna he produced a series of drawings and a painting on the theme of city man in his city surroundings which were very different.[16] The painting in question is a small but exactly worked *Paysage animé* (Plate 170). The title was certainly contemporary, since it is captioned thus in the *Bulletin de L'Effort Moderne*, but the distance between this and the Normandy *Paysages animés* of 1921 is very considerable. What is more, what is new about the later *Paysage animé*, underlines Léger's willingness to respond to all kinds of visual stimuli, not merely to those encouraged by the Purists, and ultimately therefore his independence as a painter of the modern world.

The most obvious difference between the 1921 *Paysages animés* and the later one is, of course, the latter's complete lack of rural forms; but the most profound differences lie in the treatment of figures and urban forms—architecture. Léger's new city men are not the generalized robot mechanisms of 1921, but far more specifically they are the stiffly formal inhabitants of city suits, their impersonal 'neo-classical' heads topped by neat city hats. They are, in fact, the men of urban routine for whom Le Corbusier with the 'Voisin Plan' was designing a new ideal Paris along the rational lines of a machine late in 1924.[17] Then too, the architectural setting within which Léger has placed them is not uncompromisingly flat and anti-perspectival, as was the fantastically progressive architecture of 1921, instead perspectival depth is repeatedly suggested, while the chimney on the right and the railings below are firmly modelled. A sense is created of a compressed, claustrophobic space, part Cubist, part perspectival, articulated by the forms of buildings which are not fantastic or progressive, but lifted item by item from the actual and ordinary building forms of Paris.

There is, however, one elaborate pencil drawing directly related to the Philadelphia *Paysage animé*, which does have a few apparently fantastic elements attached rather arbitrarily to the architecture of its setting—a post to which is fixed a strange rhomboidal shape and a placard bearing a cryptic sign, with a segmented circle behind (Plate 171). These incongruous additions suggest the existence of a new and equally unexpected source of visual supply for Léger—the 'metaphysical interiors' and collections of ordinary and extraordinary objects produced by Giorgio de Chirico especially before 1919.

The Rome-based avant-garde review *Valori Plastici* had been in touch with Léonce Rosenberg and the galerie de l'Effort Moderne in 1919, and the review had badly reproduced *12 Opere di Giorgio de Chirico* in a small publication of that year. But 1924 saw a perceptible rise in the Italian's Parisian reputation, Rosenberg and 'l'Effort Moderne' taking an active part in the process. The Surrealists had naturally also been much interested in the one-time protegé of Apollinaire and in 1923 Paul Eluard travelled to Rome to see him, to buy earlier paintings from him and to commission a copy of *The Disquieting Muses*. In June 1924 the *Bulletin de l'Effort Moderne*

170. (above) Fernand Léger:
Paysage animé, 1924. $19\frac{1}{2} \times 25\frac{1}{2}$
ins, Philadelphia Museum of Art.

171. (right) Fernand Léger:
Deux hommes dans la ville, 1924.
Pencil on paper, $8\frac{1}{4} \times 9\frac{3}{4}$ ins,
Musée National Fernand Léger,
Biot.

no. 6 announced a public sale of the 'Collection Eluard': it included, besides Braque, Ernst, Picasso and Metzinger, works by de Chirico, and was billed for 3 July. That August Rosenberg visited Italy with Léger, and, according to Léger their twenty-five days together took them to 'Florence, Rome, Venice, Ravenna and the whole of Northern Italy'.[18] De Chirico was then based on Rome and it seems very possible that they visited him, for by April 1925 Rosenberg had bought enough de Chiricos to hold an exhibition at the galerie de l'Effort Moderne. It was not until this exhibition that the Surrealists turned against the Italian,[19] and late in 1924 he was very much in vogue, the designer of the sets for Pirandello and Casella's *La Jarre* performed by the Ballets Suédois in December and the subject of an important article by Pierre Maville and Benjamin Perret in *La Révolution Surréaliste*.

It is not, therefore, altogether surprising that Léger should have responded late in 1924 to the 'metaphysical' mode of de Chirico, and if the curious signs of the drawing for the *Paysage animé* are almost specific in their references, the *Paysage animé* itself conveys a generalized yet strong kinship, which is perhaps even stronger in the variation produced early in 1925 (Plate 172) and in the early 1925 theme *Le Viaduc* (Plate 174). In the stiff statue-like figures, weighed down by their formal clothes, and in the irrational, pressurizing perspective of their setting, the *Paysages animés* recall such canvases as de Chirico's 1915 *Joy of Return* (Plate 173),[20] while in the repeated arches of *Le Viaduc* are recalled the arcades so common in the de Chirico of pre-1914.

Yet, thus turned by his position within the 'Effort Moderne' circle towards a painter never mentioned by the Purists whose art seems, at least through the eyes and minds of the Surrealists, so alien to the classical

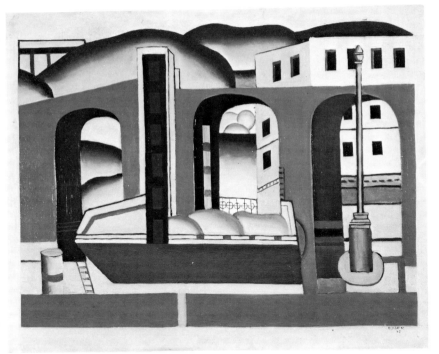

172. (far left) Fernand Léger: *Les Visiteurs*, 1925. $36\frac{1}{4} \times 25\frac{1}{2}$ ins, Mr and Mrs Leigh B. Block collection, Chicago.

173. (left) Giorgio de Chirico: *Joy of return*, 1915. $33\frac{1}{2} \times 27$ ins, private collection, California.

174. (right) Fernand Léger: *Le Viaduc*, 1925. $19\frac{3}{4} \times 24\frac{1}{4}$ ins, Perls Gallery, New York.

'call to order' of the early 1920s, Léger's approach to painting, to man and the city remained fundamentally uncompromised. His strong planes of colour are emphatically un-Chiricoesque, his viaduct arcade and his black window parallelograms or rhombuses do not suggest concealed mystery and neither do his clean-cut city men; he has adapted from de Chirico a figurative type, made very much his own (up to date and real) and aspects of a type of architectural setting, again made very much his own by combination with the flat overlapping planes of his earlier work. And he has adapted these elements not for their psychological but for their purely pictorial value. As early as 1919 André Salmon had taken a purely formal line, writing of de Chirico's ability to 'express his time . . . according to the rule of a composition so rigorous, so measured that it allies itself with the classical'.[21] The Italian could be thought of, especially as he moved in an emphatically traditional direction after 1919, as part of the 'call to order', and it was thus that late in 1924 Léger could make him part of his personal 'call to order'.

Novel in their architecture and their inhabitants, the Philadelphia and Chicago *Paysages animés* of 1924–5 retained, as has been said, the approach to man and the man-made, so Purist in character, first comprehensively revealed by the paintings of 1921. Léger's view of modern life did not change late in 1924, and this fundamental unity of approach which links not only his classical figure-painting of 1924 to his classical figure-painting of 1920–1, also links his 1924 attempts to situate man in the modern environment with those of three or four years earlier. This fundamental unity of approach is a point perhaps best made by another canvas probably completed late in 1924,[22] a painting free of de Chirico which looks back beyond the 1921 *Paysages animés* to *Le Mécanicien—L'Homme au chandail* (Plate

261

175. Fernand Léger: *L'Homme au chandail,* 1924. 25½ × 36½ ins, Mme S. Frigerio collection, Paris.

175). The profile turn of the head and the frontal placing of the torso give it that Hieratic quality so crucial to *Le Mécanicien,* and the treatment of the head especially has that cool precision essential to the fusion of traditional past and progressive present so effectively achieved in that painting, while the clash between flat, angular pictorial architecture, here straight-forwardly associated with real architecture as in the *Paysages animés,* is repeated. Léger's rigidly controlled vision of the cyclist—as much man of his time as the mechanic—both set against and placed in pictorial con-junction with his urban environment has not basically changed; and *Le Viaduc* early in 1925 makes it clear that neither had his vision of the relationship between the man-made and the natural. He remained, for all the independence of his pictorial means, the convinced exponent of a *L'Esprit Nouveau* view of *l'esprit nouveau.*

*   *   *   *   *

Revealing as it may be of Léger's fundamentally Ozenfant-and-Corbusian view of modern life, the fact remains that his treatment of man outside in the cityscape and landscape of the modern world avoids the pictorial subject central to Purism—still-life. And at the same time, the fact remains that for Léger himself it was not man or architecture or the structures of the engineers in the countryside and the town that most insistently threatened 'the breasts and curves of woman, fruit, the soft landscape', but 'the manu-factured and "mechanical" object'—the inanimate contents of the modern still-life.

It is, therefore, perhaps surprising that as Léger established his new ordered approach to painting in 1921 with *Le Grand Déjeuner* and the

Paysages animés he should for a while have totally ignored still-life and all that it stood for in the avant-garde view of the French tradition—the tradition embracing Chardin, Cézanne and Cubism. In fact, it was not until 1922, and then seemingly almost as a 'spin-off' from the *Mère et l'enfant* theme, that he began to apply his new approach to tradition, to pictorial order and to pictorial clarity in terms of still-life. He produced that year a significant group of such paintings. Most commonly these are so closely related to the 'primitive' settings and 'primitive' yet Cubist still-lifes of the *Mère et l'enfant* paintings that they stand apart from the Purist still-lifes exhibited at the galerie Duret in 1921.[23] But there is one, the grandest and most carefully finished of all, which is far more comprehensively attuned to the Ozenfant and Jeanneret of 1920–1: *Nature-morte au chandelier* (Colour Plate 8). The pale warmth of the painting, with its intense central note of red for the cup against deep grey-blue, is hardly Purist, and neither is the incisive way the central sharp-edged plane cuts off the hemisphere of the cup, but the clear Cubist analysis of the candlestick, and the way in which the tilted table-top with its objects are contained by the strict verticals and horizontals of the planar surround, these factors are profoundly Purist, and profoundly unlike the variety and the perspectival complexity of the settings for the 1922 *La Mère et l'enfant*.

It was further towards the precisely planned, perfectly finished stability of the Purist still-life that Léger moved with the few but again significant still-life themes developed in 1923. The most stable and the most clear-cut of these is the *Nature-morte* (Plate 176). Here too there is none of that dramatic conflict between tilted perspectives and flat overlapping planes so forceful in the setting of the *La Mère et l'enfant*. The discreet angling of the left edge of the table, which suggests its recession, is comfortably absorbed by the stable architecture of flat planes, its stabilizing verticals and horizontals stressed by thick black bars. Again, the objects of the subject are simply described, the distortions of Cubist analysis always used both for formal effect and for descriptive lucidity, and the objects themselves—though perhaps not the fruit—are the 'type-objects' given such elaborate evolutionary significance by the Purists. Though neither so complex nor so ambitious in scale it is closely comparable with the contemporary painting especially of Le Corbusier (as Jeanneret), for instance his much praised contribution to the Indépendants of 1923, the *Nature-morte aux nombreux objets* (Plate 177). The São Paolo *Nature-morte* makes the point, made more elaborately by *Le Grand Remorqueur*, that 1923 saw a marked deepening of Léger's commitment to the Purist view of life and art, adding the point that the year saw as well the development of a more directly appreciative response to Purist painting.

In 1922, in *L'Esprit Nouveau* no. 14, Ozenfant and Jeanneret reiterated 'Les Idées de L'Esprit Nouveau', and their attitude to painting was unchanged from that expressed in nos. 1 and 4.[24] 'Hierarchy is the law of the organized world,' they wrote in *L'Esprit Nouveau* no. 20, early 1924, 'natural as much as human.'[25] Their basic idea of that hierarchy as found in art did not change between 1923 and 1925. They remained committed to the Golden Section and to modular proportion, to the stability created by the dominant vertical and horizontal, to the concept of primary and secondary sensation, and it was in 1923 and 1924, as Le Corbusier's ideas

176.   Fernand Léger: *Nature morte,* 1923. $31\frac{1}{4} \times 39$ ins, Museu de Arte de São Paolo.

177.   Charles-Edouard Jeanneret: *Nature morte aux nombreuses objets,* 1923. $45 \times 57\frac{1}{2}$ ins, Fondation Le Corbusier, Paris.

on standardization were deepened by practical experience, that the concept of the 'type-object' was given really clear definition.[26] Their painting certainly had evolved towards a slightly greater complexity, slightly more freedom from the duties of analytical representation and a slightly richer range of colour, but, as Léger's view of the world and his painting of still-life moved closer to the theoretical and pictorial approach declared by the Purists in 1920–21, Purism stood conveniently still.

Yet there remains much about the São Paolo *Nature-morte* that is special to Léger, much that makes it far from a doctrinaire Purist painting. The composition is not organized according to any repressive proportional system; colour is used with the stark vigour characteristic of Léger's polychromatic *Paysage animé* or *Grand Remorqueur* architecture—the intense red of the *compotier* and of the half discs on the left striking hard against black contours or white surrounds; and, although Jeanneret approaches an analogous contradictory combination of flat planes, sometimes undescriptive, and modelled object elements always descriptive, there is a compulsion with which Léger cuts off every object in his still-life, to present fragments, which is very personal, a pursuit of the fragmentary which looks back, in fact, beyond *Nature-morte au chandelier* to 1918–19, and is yet prophetic.

'The manufactured object', the modern yet traditional subject of still-life was not alone the major creator of *l'esprit nouveau*. In Léger's 1922 letter to Rosenberg he added as well 'the "mechanical" object'. In 1922 Léger had, in fact, supported this conviction by painting a couple of classicized *Eléments mécaniques*, one of which, an adaptation from the 1919 simultanist composition *Le Mécanicien dans l'usine* (Plate 107), acted as the basic plan for a relatively large and impeccably handled canvas, inscribed on the reverse 'Elément mécanique' and dated '24' (Plate 179). With this painting and with a sequence of three other *Eléments mécaniques* loosely adapted from the 1918 theme of *Les Disques*, the *état définitif* of which is in the Paris Musée National d'Art Moderne, Léger declared more overtly even than in *La Lecture* the analogy between the work of art and the precision machine (Plate 178).[27]

It has been stressed that the Purists' admiration for the machine did not lead them to advocate the machine as the subject of painting, and their rejection of the overtly mechanical subject remained a tenet of *L'Esprit Nouveau*. Yet their own less direct, more sophisticated belief in the analogy between the work of art and the precision machine led them to tolerate, even to admire, painters who allowed the machine into their work. Among these naturally was Léger himself, but also there was the German painter, already influenced by Léger's art, Willy Baumeister, and the Belgian Victor Servranckx. In 1924 Baumeister travelled to Paris specifically to see both Le Corbusier and Léger, and there are close links between Léger's Paris *Eléments mécaniques* and Baumeister's 'Maschinen-bilder' of 1922–4 which at least hint at the possibility that Léger responded positively to the German's work known either in fact or in photograph. Servranckx too seems to have provided visual stimulus, though more behind the smooth almost silkily finished surfaces and sweet yet metallic colours of the Zurich *Elément mécanique*. He exhibited at the Indépendants in February 1924, Maurice Raynal commenting on his compositions as 'good gram-

265

179.   Fernand Léger: *Elément mécanique,* 1924. $38\frac{1}{4} \times 57\frac{1}{2}$ ins, Kunsthaus, Zurich.

180.   Victor Servranckx: *Opus 47,* 1923. $40\frac{1}{2} \times 82$ ins, Musées Royaux des Beaux Arts, Brussels.

178. (left)   Fernand Léger: *Eléments mécaniques,* 1924. $57\frac{1}{2} \times 38\frac{1}{4}$ ins, Musée National d'Art Moderne, Paris.

matical exercises' in *L'Intransigeant*;[28] and in *L'Esprit Nouveau* no. 22, also early that year, the Purists paid their tribute by reproducing five of his paintings. His *Opus 47* of 1923 (Plate 180), is closely related to two of the paintings illustrated there, and, although Léger was working on a long established compositional basis in his Zurich canvas, the affinities it shares with the Servranckx are obvious.

Yet, if the connections between the Zurich *Elément mécanique* and Servranckx's *Opus 47* demonstrate Léger's openness to the most Purist of all machine painters in 1923–4,[29] just as the connections between the São Paolo *Nature-morte* and Jeanneret's *Nature-morte aux nombreuses objets* demonstrate his openness to the Purist still-life, it is again most forcibly of all Léger's independence that is demonstrated by the 1924 precision-machine compositions. Significantly, Servranckx himself was to write the following year of Léger as an incorrigible individualist.[30] The seductive polish of the Zurich painting, almost verging on slickness, was in fact unique among Léger's products of the time; it was the closest he ever came to the Belgian, and, therefore, in the final analysis the Paris *Elément mécanique* is far more representative of his approach to the machine in painting during the early months of 1924.

It has been noted that Baumeister's 'Maschinen-bilder' may be connected with the Parisian composition, but the connection must certainly have been more limited than that between the Zurich composition and *Opus 47*. Here, as in the Zurich composition, the fundamental elements of the pictorial structure had been established long before, but, more significant, here the pictorial conflict between flat red ground plane and cool central grouping of machine forms has its origins not in Baumeister but in an innovation which was unquestionably Léger's own—the innovation so forcibly announced in 1923 by *Nus sur fond rouge* (Plate 161). Again, the cool metallic sheen and sharp-edged elements of the central machine theme refer, far more strikingly than to Baumeister, to the heightened modelling and touched-up clarity of the engine sections, and machine parts illustrated in, for instance, the car magazine, *Omnia* (Plate 159), and in advertising (Plate 164). There is a forcefulness in the way that Léger's *éléments mécaniques* slice across each other, a stridency in the clash between red surround and central forms, and a sense of contact with popular sources that declares the independence of his pictorial equivalent of machine order and machine energy.

Alongside his celebration of the 'mechanical' object, Léger took further his idea of the 'manufactured' object in the modern still-life, painting a series of still-lifes as accompaniment to the *Eléments mécaniques* and the classical figure themes of 1924. Almost certainly the earliest of these still-life themes was the composition very carefully prepared by means of at least one highly finished drawing, and one small oil whose most definitive version is the *Nature-morte* (Plate 181).[31] Probably a late product of the year is *Le Siphon* (Plate 185), the care of whose preparation is again demonstrated by a smaller oil version very closely related, while the equally dry, equally precise *Nature-morte* (Plate 183) seems to have been the product of the middle of the year.[32]

The most Purist of all these still-lifes is without doubt the composition from the early months of the year (Plate 181). It is, indeed, more austere

181.   Fernand Léger: *Nature morte,* 1924. $31\frac{3}{4} \times 45\frac{3}{4}$ ins, galerie Beyeler, Basel.

182.   Juan Gris: *Guitare et compotier,* 1921. $24 \times 37\frac{1}{2}$ ins, private collection, Basel.

and more clear-cut than the 1923–4 still-lifes of the Purists themselves, looking back to the most Puritan compositions of 1920 and 1921 (Plates 133 and 134). Objects, table and background are perfectly locked into the most rigorous of structures; the range of colour is, but for the brief interference of the two triangles of bright yellow, the ideal pictorial range of the Purists as set out in *L'Esprit Nouveau* no. 4; and the objects themselves conform to the strict doctrine of types, the bottle in particular being precisely a Purist bottle. There is just a hint of aggression in the way that the modelled neck of the bottle gives way to a flat black silhouette and the way the bottle-silhouette then cuts off the stand of the candlestick, and, of course, no repressive proportional system dictates the dimensions of every detail. But this is as close as Léger came to a doctrinaire Purist still-life, and even its most apparently independent characteristic, the grouping of still-life and interior elements so that they hang as it were on a pale grey ground plane has its origins in still-lifes which, though not Purist, were deeply admired by Ozenfant and Jeanneret, in, for instance, Juan Gris's 1921 *Guitare et compotier* (Plate 182) and Picasso's 1922 *Tapis rouge* (Plate 184).

The strictly limited colour, the simply described objects locked into the stable pictorial structure, the classical fluting of the coffee-percolator, all this gives to the other still-life (Plate 183) perhaps even more the appearance of 1920–1 Purism. But there is in the choice of objects a distinctly undoctrinaire character. The adjustable lamp and the light-bulb are 'type-objects' in the sense that they answer very basic human needs, but they have not that traditional quality essential to the 'type-objects' of Purist painting—that capacity by reference to a long evolutionary process to convey the concept of evolution towards a typical end; they are the brand new products of mass-production. The lamp reappears in *Le Siphon*, combined with a glass and a syphon; these new items are more obviously connected with the past, but their treatment is—it will become clear— emphatically modern and popular, manifesting an approach to the object utterly unconcerned with its evolutionary significance.

The Purists may have painted nothing but 'type-objects' charged with a backward-looking significance; yet they as much as Léger saw the cheapest of mass-produced objects as important stimuli behind the developing, ordered *esprit nouveau* of the 1920s. Le Corbusier's investigation of mass-production and standardization late in 1923 and through 1924 covered far more than the questions of reinforced concrete construction, of wall-infilling, doors, windows, etc., raised by M. Frugès's *cité ouvrière* commission at Pessac; it reached as far as the smallest aids to daily living. From December 1923 through 1924 Le Corbusier published a series of articles in *L'Esprit Nouveau* on the Exposition des Arts Décoratifs planned for 1925. They demanded a new anti-decorative, functional approach to interior design, according to which all furnishings and fittings were treated as 'tools' and nothing more, and they extended the 'type-object' idea to include all the most fundamentally useful, most formally Purist of *modern*, mass-produced products—lamps, typewriters, filing-cabinets, etc.[33] In this sense the straightforwardly efficient mass-produced objects of Léger's mid-1924 Beyeler *Nature-morte*, and his *Siphon*, were 'type-objects', however lacking in traditional flavour. They are very much the kind of

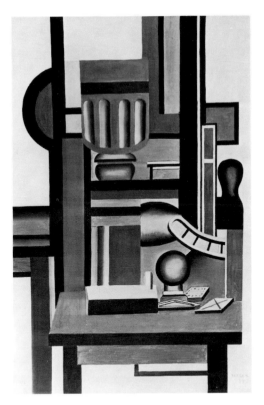

183. (right)   Fernand Léger: *Nature morte,*
1924. $36\frac{1}{4} \times 24$ ins, galerie Beyeler, Basel.

184. (below)   Pablo Picasso: *Tapis rouge,* 1922.
$31\frac{1}{2} \times 45\frac{1}{4}$ ins, private collection, London.

185. (left)   Fernand Léger: *Le Siphon,* 1924.
36 × 23½ ins, Mrs Arthur C. Rosenberg collection, Chicago.

186. (right)   Campari advertisement, *Le Matin,* Paris, November 1924.

thing illustrated by Le Corbusier to support his argument in *L'Esprit Nouveau* nos. 23 and 24—very much akin to the sports equipment, the pipes, straw-boaters and cigarette cases taken from department-store advertising (Plate 187). So, in the final analysis, though not dogmatically Purist, Léger's selection of 'manufactured objects' for the ordered requirements of his still-lifes does reflect a profoundly Purist approach to the modern world, to *l'esprit nouveau* in the broad sense of the term.

Yet, as already suggested, the way in which Léger presents the objects of his subject especially in *Le Siphon* demonstrates an approach to their depiction which is modern and popular, and unconcerned with the evolutionary philosophical significance of the 'type-object' idea. Thus, in December 1924 Léger said to Georges Charensol: 'I am inspired by diagrams or mechanical elements, sometimes even the stereotypes of advertising, like in this drawing of a syphon, which I found in *Le Matin.*'[34] And he referred here to a simple black-and-white graphic of hand, syphon and glass used for a Campari advertisement in the Parisian newspapers of 1924, which is the source for the major elements of the Chicago painting (Plate 186). It was not merely the syphon and glass as such that took his eye, but their simplistic representation in *Le Matin*; it was not merely the mass-produced 'type-object' that mattered, but its character as mass-produced popular image in advertising. As striking as the objects is the severed hand, brother of the ubiquitous signpost pointing hand, the specific invention of advertising.

The exaggeratedly naïve depiction of things in *Le Siphon,* so clearly derived from advertising, effectively sets the painting apart from the Purist still-life, for it does not use the distortions of analytical Cubism crucial to Ozenfant and Jeanneret; it uses instead the undistorted forms of the object itself, lifted out of context, simplified, and ruthlessly deprived of individual blemishes. This frank isolation of the ordinary mass-produced object or the figurative fragment, simplified and used for formal effect against the flat planes of a pure pictorial setting, was prophetic; it looked forward to a kind of object-painting which, though still rigorously ordered

273

187. Cigarette cases. *L'Esprit Nouveau* no. 24.

and precisely executed, could never be called Purist, a kind of painting which was without any doubt Léger's own invention. The undistorted, faultless perfection of the pipes of *Les trois pipes* (Plate 189) is the 1925 sequel to the glass and syphon of *Le Siphon,* and the heightened modelling of these objects finds a pictorial application for that of the photographically touched-up consumer products illustrated by Le Corbusier (Plate 187) or by the catalogues and the popular advertising of the big department stores.

If this simple response to the manufactured object as popular image is the result of an approach to the object-subject different from that of the Purists, what was special about Léger's approach? That he should have gone to the raw material of *l'esprit nouveau* in its most popular, its most 'debased' form is, of course, typical of his realist's determination to find his images of clear-cut order in the most available aspects of everyday life; but there is more to it than this, and his still anti-idealistic approach to modern life and most particularly to the 'manufactured object' as raw material for art is very fully expounded, first in his June 1923 lecture 'L'Esthétique de la Machine' and then in his 1924 texts on *le spectacle.*

'L'Esthétique de la Machine' was given a significant subtitle: 'L'Objet fabriqué, l'artisan et l'artiste'. It was written as much in praise of the ordinary 'artisan' and his products as to elaborate an aesthetic. It begins by insisting, as Léger had insisted in his letter of 1922 to Rosenberg, that 'plastic beauty in general is totally independent of sentimental, descriptive and imitative qualities' and that things are 'beautiful' therefore not because of the associations they arouse but because of their formal qualities alone. The claims of the 'manufactured object' had not weakened his ultimately Cubist emphasis on form, and that his idea of 'plastic' value was now deeply Purist is clear, for he defines the beautiful as 'when the relationships of the lines which define volumes are balanced in an order equivalent to those of earlier architecture'.[35] What is more, it is clear too that his idea of *l'esprit nouveau* is indeed as Purist as *Le Grand Remorqueur* suggested, his text for the lecture being: 'More and more, modern man is living in an order geometrically directed. Every man-made mechanical and industrial creation is dependent on geometric forces.'[36] But this conviction in the capacity of the manufactured object by its purely 'plastic' beauty to beautify,

geometrically to order the environment led him to celebrate the manufactured object and its maker in a way that was too simple, too philosophi-
cally unsophisticated to be called Purist. He utterly dismissed the tendency,
so fundamentally Purist, to classify all things hierarchically—especially
the subject-matter of art. His hero, significantly, as in the *Mécanicien* of
1920, was not the engineer or the great industrialist but the working man.
And he did not surround the 'beautiful' objects of modern life with the
battery of concepts—natural selection, mechanical selection, economy,
etc.—essential to the Purist 'type' idea of the object; he simply noted their
beauty as a fact which is in itself enough. For him, 'the manufactured object
(is) inherently beautiful',[37] the artisans are 'the real artists', and the exhibitions most worth seeing are the displays of the window-dressers and
the machine salons. The useful objects of Léger's 1924 still-lifes may,
therefore, closely conform to the 'type-objects' of the Purists, but they do
so without the accretion of theory that made the 'type-object' Purist.

Léger may have insisted on the *inherent* beauty of so many manufactured
objects in his June 1923 lecture, and this certainty is the conviction that
lies behind his simplistic use of the object in *Le Siphon* and its 1925 suc-
cessors, but he also made the dogmatic statement: 'A beautiful thing should
not be imitated or copied, it should be admired and that is all.'[38] He remained opposed to the mere depiction of the object as he had been since
1918, and he gave to the artist a role that went far beyond this. The artist,
for him, was to treat nature and the products of the artisan as 'raw material'
to be absorbed and ordered in the mind and then on the canvas.[39] Certainly,
in *Le Siphon* and in *Les trois pipes* the object is absorbed into a pure pictorial
structure, but however 'plastically' it is used the fact remains that it is
straightforwardly presented in and for itself. Before the approach to the
object as raw material expounded in 'L'Esthétique de la Machine' could
become the approach to the object as subject declared in these paintings,
a significant change was required in Léger's approach to the pictorial
potential of the object.

Popular advertising had for years isolated the graphically simplified or
photographically touched-up object against a neutral ground as one of its
most usual modes of consumer persuasion,[40] so this of itself could not have
initiated the change late in 1924. The decision thus to use the object or the
figurative fragment frankly depicted without distortion as the creator of
pure pictorial incident was, in fact, backed most effectively by something
else, it was backed by Léger's ideas on film and his experience of filming,
which reached a climax in 1924. It was film more than advertising that
freed his still-life compositions from the look of Purist painting.

When Léger gave his lecture on 'L'Esthétique de la Machine' at the
Collège de France he accompanied it with a small exhibition of works by
'the artisans of the machine' (it would be fascinating to know what), and
a showing of so far 'unshown reels' from Abel Gance's film *La Roue*.[41]
Léger had, it will be remembered, been creatively aware of film at least
since his return from hospital to Paris in 1918, and *La Roue* had been his
first practical experience of the 'seventh art'. *La Roue*, at great length for
the time, told the story of a railway mechanic, Sisif, who brings up a small
orphan girl—'Rose du rail'—marries her off to an engineer but cannot
suppress his love, thus initiating disaster. The Locomotive sequences,

which last only a few minutes, were shot by Gance at the *gare des marchandises* in Nice between December 1919 and June 1920. The final part of the shooting took place in the Alps, and was completed by February 1921.[42] The film was released in 1922 at the Gaumont, place Clichy, with a poster by Léger advertising it,[43] and when it was shown again early in 1924 *Paris-Journal* remarked that the involvement of Léger and Cendrars (who was 'assistant') explained the special power of the machine sequences.[44] Certainly Léger acted as an advisor during the editing process in 1921, and Descargues has even suggested that he was involved in the shooting itself.[45]

With the release of *La Roue* Léger set down what, for him, was the film's importance in an essay published in *Comoedia*. He ignored the 'dramatic' and 'sentimental' themes, whose existence he did however acknowledge, to focus on the 'plastic' theme contained almost exclusively in the first sections of the film in no way suggesting that anyone but Gance was responsible for them. For Léger, film is not theatre, and its significance therefore is not literary but is found in 'the projected image'—that alone is its *raison d'être*; and Gance's achievement in the machine sequences of *La Roue* is to realize the power of the machine as image-maker, turning the locomotive into the leading actor. He is the first successfully to use the object as actor in film, just as Chaplin was, for Léger, the first to turn the actor into an object.[46] He then goes on to the nature of Gance's purely 'plastic' images, anticipating much of what was to concern him in film and then in his object paintings for the next three or four years: the mobility of Gance's images, the balancing of mobile and static, the effect of the human figure as a whole or of a hand against 'a geometric mass, of discs, abstract forms, play of curves and straight lines', the sudden clarity given to an eye, a finger, a fingernail by fragmentation and by enlargement on the screen so that it becomes 'an absolute whole, dramatic, comic, plastic . . .' far more compelling than the actor in the 'theatre next door'.[47]

Gance himself had begun in the theatre and, interviewed by Jean Mitry in the spring of 1924, rejected a purely visual approach to the image on the screen, insisting on its expressive capacity to convey ideas as its major value. For him, the passages picked out of *La Roue* by Léger were simply 'moments' in a film whose prime concern was 'psychological nuance'.[48] Such an approach was profoundly opposed to Léger's, and, though the painter was too loyal to say so in his essay, it is significant that in 1923 he wrote of only 'partially' being interested in *La Roue*.[49] Léger's focus on the machine sequences of the film and his lack of interest in its longwinded literary development was, however, not isolated. Between 1922 and 1924 the progressive Parisian film-critics almost to a man—Jean Epstein, René Clair, Léon Moussinac, Boisyvon—agreed on the importance of *La Roue*, but rejected the sentimentality of its screenplay to praise the energy and sheer originality of the machine sequences.[50]

There was, in fact, a context for Léger's approach to film as it developed after his involvement in *La Roue*, for the cinema had its own avant-garde in Paris, an avant-garde intimately connected with progressive theatre, literature and painting, and between 1922 and 1924 Léger became deeply involved in it first as observer, then as set-designer for Marcel L'Herbier's *L'Inhumaine* in 1923 and finally as film-maker himself with *Ballet mécanique*.

It had been Blaise Cendrars most of all who had first promoted Léger's interest in film in 1918–19, and it was, of course, he who involved the painter in *La Roue*. In July 1920, while working on *La Roue*, Cendrars was visited in Nice by a young writer deeply interested in film, Jean Epstein, who brought with him a substantial text much indebted to the Swiss poet, *La poésie d'aujourd'hui. Un nouvel état d'intelligence*. The next year Cocteau and Cendrars published it in Editions de la Sirène, together with a book of *poèmes libres*, *Bonjour Cinéma*; Epstein himself arrived in Paris in July 1921, having published a little review called *Promenoir* at Lyons over the previous few months.[51] He was already aware of Léger for he had shown a painting by him at his Lyons premises and published a text too in *Promenoir*, and during the years 1922–4, as Epstein became more and more prominent in film-making and film-punditry, he made a vital contact for the painter in the film avant-garde, so that in March 1923 Léger could name him with Gance and Cendrars as one of the important men of the future in the cinema.[52]

L'Herbier, with whom Léger worked on *L'Inhumaine* during the summer and autumn of 1923, was, of course, a further vital contact, but perhaps not as vital from the point of view of the development of his film ideas as either Epstein or another young critic-film-maker, René Clair. From December 1922 Clair was editor of *Film*, the cinema supplement to *Le Théâtre et Comoedia illustré*, which was a review put out with *La Danse* and *Paris-Journal* by the extraordinary cultural entrepreneur Jacques Hébertot, director of the Théâtre des Champs-Elysées and Paris patron of Rolf de Maré's Ballet Suédois. Clair's offices were in the theatre and he would, therefore, have been quickly aware of Léger, whose work on *Skating-Rink* in 1922 had so deeply involved him in the Ballet Suédois circle. Significantly, Léger was one of those to whom he sent an *enquête* on attitudes to film, his reply being published in *Film* in March 1923; and André-L. Daven reports in the October 1923 issue that Léger was one of many—including Rudolph Valentino, Hébertot and Philippe Soupault—to visit the Joinville studios for the shooting of scenes from Clair's first film, the comic fantasy *Paris qui dort*.[53] It was in June 1924, as Léger worked on *Ballet mécanique*, that Clair began work (play?) on Francis Picabia's single-page scenario for the short film *Entr'acte*, whose performers included—apart from Duchamp and Man Ray—Jean Borlin, the leading male dancer of the Ballet Suédois as well as the *corps de Ballet*, and which was designed to fill the gap between acts for Picabia's *Relâche*.[54] *Entr'acte* and *Relâche* opened to the public at the Théâtre des Champs-Elysées in December 1924; Léger was there,[55] and included an enthusiastic piece on René Clair's film in his article 'Vive Relâche' published by *L'Action* on 18 December.

What made the Purist view of the world so persuasive for Léger was the fact that it was presented as the result of an experience of order open to all, a reality of significance in a popular sense; perhaps it was the fact that film was a popular art, even for its most avant-garde Parisian exponents, that convinced him of its importance. René Clair maintained in *L'Intransigeant* that with all its innovations the cinema reached 'the masses . . . the screen masterpieces are almost always its great successes'.[56] Chaplin was the proof of that, and indeed, so impressed was Marcel L'Herbier by its power as a popular art, that in 1924 he wrote of the cinema as a political

188.   Still from the film *L'Inhumaine* directed by Marcel L'Herbier, 1923 (laboratory set here by Fernand Léger).

tool capable of persuasively underlining the need for Socialism internationally.[57] There was a political point to be made by the fashionable luxury of the *femme fatale*'s life in *L'Inhumaine* and the triumph of science, given visual expression in Léger's science-fiction laboratory, which provides the film with its climax (Plate 188).

Yet, if the mass-appeal of the cinema must have attracted Léger, what he focused on was, as has been seen, its pure 'plastic' potential, and his emphasis on cinema as a 'pure' art, free of the theatre, found strong support in the film avant-garde. As early as 1921 in his *Poésie d'aujourd'hui. Un nouvel état d'intelligence* Epstein had insisted on the freedom of the cinema from the theatre,[58] and in a wonderfully pungent lecture, 'De quelques conditions de la photogénie', given at the 1923 Salon d'Automne he specifically released it from all 'historical, educational, fictional . . . geographical or documentary' subject-matter. 'The cinema,' he said, 'must seek little by little to become at last uniquely cinematographic . . . to use only photogenic elements. Photography is the purest expression of cinema.'[59] His view—so close to Léger's celebration of 'the projected image' in his 1922 essay on *La Roue*—was echoed above all by Clair, who in February 1924 was provoked by the banal plot of Epstein's own film *Coeur fidèle*, to note that the subject of a film is of no more importance than the subject of a symphony.[60]

As important to Léger in his *La Roue* essay as the nature of the object or fragment imaged on the screen was its mobility, that too was so of Epstein, Clair and the other progressive commentators on cinema. 'In a film,' Clair wrote in 1923, 'the public loves movement,' and he singles out as the most rare pleasure 'action graded by the disposition of images'. He later clarified his meaning 'MOVEMENT, I do not say movement registered by the image itself, but the movement of images one in relation to another.'[61] He means the rhythm created by the succession of images, each projected for differing lengths of time, the rhythm created by cutting from one image to another at a measured speed—the kind of movement for which *La Roue* was commonly taken as *the* exemplar. Clair's first film, *Paris qui dort*, was above all about movement, the fantastic idea of a Paris put to sleep by mysterious rays—horses frozen with hooves lifted, dancers in mid-shimmy—being essentially a device to create juxtapositions of mobile and static images in rhythmic sequences. As he wrote in 1924: '*Paris qui dort* had as its theme the opposition of immobility and movement.' And movement considered rhythmically was also a central concern of Epstein's from his 1921 *Poésie d'aujourd'hui* (where he pointed out the English use of the word 'movie') onwards. He too dwelt on the measured cutting from image to image as key to rhythm in his Salon d'Automne lecture of 1923, and, as Clair noted in reviewing *Coeur fidèle*, demonstrated his 'pre-occupation with the question of rhythm' throughout this important film which was released in January 1924, using 'images recalled' rather as a poet might use 'assonance or rhyme'.[62]

Léger's views on 'pure' cinema and cinematic movement were closely in tune with the views of Clair and Epstein and progressive film-critics. How close was their view of the image as such? It was precisely because of their belief in the power of the figure, figurative fragment or object as image that a strong resistance existed against 'décor' in film, a resistance persuasively expressed by Epstein in a short article on 'Le Décor au cinéma' published in *La Revue Mondiale*, March 1923. And this led to the few hostile opinions of Léger's décor for *L'Inhumaine*, which was in fact a critical as well as popular success on its 1924 release. Thus, very much in line with the ideas of Epstein and Clair, the critic of *L'Action*, Jacques Parsons, commented perceptively that the desire to create 'a machinery of the imagination' for the laboratory had produced a pictorial invention 'infinitely less photogenic and less moving than real elements would have been mobile in space' (Plate 188); and he added pointedly: 'Fernand Léger would not contradict me on this point.'[63]

René Clair and *Film* were repeatedly emphatic as to the power of the object or figurative fragment as such, enlarged on the screen. 'Let us praise the cinema,' Clair wrote in *L'Intransigeant* (16 June 1923), 'for having revealed to us the existence of the object itself, of the animate detail and of the object. On the screen an insect has the same individual value as a mountain. A door knob which turns can arouse the most dramatic emotion.' As René Bizet noted of *Paris qui dort*: 'All is images, and nothing but images, without useless intellectualism,'[64] and the same could have been written of *Entr'acte* with its dancing field-gun, its spinning ballerina seen from below, its eggs on jets of water, and its slow-motion funeral *cortège*. Yet this concentration on the capacity of the cinema to isolate and to fragment and to enlarge by close-up had of course already been pointed out by Blaise Cendrars in *L'ABC du Cinéma*, who had named Griffiths as its inventor, and it was Epstein, following Cendrars, who gave it early elaboration in his 1921 *Poésie d'aujourd'hui* the year before Léger's essay on *La Roue*. Epstein too made practical use of these techniques in his

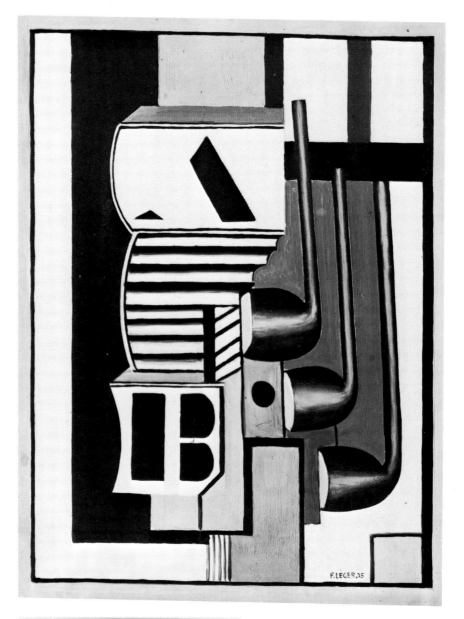

189. (above)   Fernand Léger: *Les Trois Pipes,* 1925. $25\frac{1}{2} \times 18$ ins, galerie Louise Leiris, Paris.

190. (left)   Still from the film *Ballet mécanique* directed by Fernand Léger, 1923–4.

documentary *Pasteur*, which was released in December 1922 the very month of Léger's essay's publication, where dramatic close-ups of the hypodermic syringe caused appreciative comment in *Film*. He, like Clair, in his 1923 Salon d'Automne lecture stressed: 'that quasi-divine importance which figurative fragments (and) the coldest elements from nature take on when enlarged. A revolver in a drawer,' he went on, 'a bottle broken on the ground, an eye circumscribed in an iris, are raised by the cinema to the status of personalities in the drama. Being dramatic, they seem alive . . .'[65]

The 'pure' visual character of film, the creation of rhythm in the measured succession of images and of contrasts between the mobile and the immobile, the exploitation of fragmentation, isolation and enlargement—all these themes were touched on, as has been seen, by Léger's essay on *La Roue*, but were by then already established in the cinematic thinking of Cendrars's protegé Jean Epstein above all and were quickly given clear expression during 1923 by the criticism of René Clair, his first film *Paris qui dort*, and by the writing of other progressive film-critics. It is not surprising, therefore, that supported by this strong avant-garde trend, Léger should have further clarified his own approach in 1923 and 1924. That the process was well under way by March 1923 is clear from his answer to René Clair's *enquête* published that month in *Film*, but the process did not come to a head until he had turned his dabbling and his theorizing into practice with *Ballet mécanique*.

According to Léger himself, he and the American cameraman Dudley Murphy, made *Ballet mécanique* in '1923–4',[66] and it seems to have been a project that occupied him for almost a year, though the result lasts hardly more than fifteen minutes. Most, it seems, was complete by July 1924, because the text by Léger on the film which appeared in *L'Esprit Nouveau* no. 28 is dated July, and a reel was shown in September during Léger's visit to the Vienna theatre exhibition.[67] However, there is one strong indication that additions and adjustments were made on his autumn return to Paris, because the sequence in the film which arranges and re-arranges the words 'On a volé Un collier de perls de 5 millions' seems to have been inspired by a story headlined 'Un collier de 5 millions. On l'a volé naturellement' which appeared in *L'Intransigeant*, 10 September 1924. And the film was first shown in Paris in November, giving time for additions.

'The other day,' wrote Paul Achard in *L'Action,* 3 November 1924, 'before a group of the initiated, the painter Fernand Léger showed a short experiment in technical innovation, with the title *Ballet mécanique*. There passed by in eighteen minutes all the means of expression of that art for tomorrow the cinema, put together in logically combined rhythms, which turned upsidedown the clichés of today.' *Ballet mécanique* never got beyond the 'initiated'; it was not a popular film as *L'Inhumaine* had been, much to the regret of Léger in later years. But it did make a certain mark in the avant-garde, and it did condense into a very short space and with great force an extraordinary range of novel effects, every one in tune with the most important progressive concerns of the day.

Léger underlined its purity by declaring in his *L'Esprit Nouveau* statement: 'No scenario. The interactions of rhythmic images that is all.' And

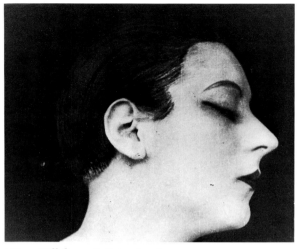 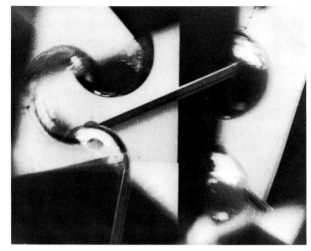

191.   Still from *Ballet mécanique*.   192.   Still from *Ballet mécanique*.

it was most significantly an experiment in the controlled creation of movement using: 'Figures, fragments of figures, mechanical fragments, metallic (fragments), manufactured objects, enlargement with the minimum of perspective';[68] using the photographic image, mobile or static, as the basic unit in a series of measured rhythmic sequences. Like Epstein in *Coeur fidèle*, Léger uses the repetition of images;[69] several of the images which appear at the beginning of the film—the seried wine bottles (Plate 190), the straw-boater, the isolated smiling lips, the pendulum (Plate 192)—reappear again and again; but most of all he uses combinations of contrasted or analogous images—pulsing metallic discs lead into the sudden contrasting image of a cockatoo reflected three times in mirrors, the sequence on the *collier de perls* leads into the sudden analogous image of a horse's harness. There are sequences of pure shapes—flat circles, squares and triangles—but, as Léger insisted in *L'Esprit Nouveau*, 'This film is objective realist and in no sense abstract'; for him, what mattered was the quality of his images in themselves—of his bottles, typewriter, metal discs, working mechanisms, of the eye opening and closing or the profile of a man smiling enlarged many times on the screen (Plates 192 and 191). He used a technique related to the earlier 'vortograph' which multiplied his images in complex ways by means of mirrors (Plate 192) and which was the invention, according to himself, of Murphy and Ezra Pound,[70] but always the hero was the object, the figure or the figurative fragment filmed, these often static images made dynamic by the rhythmic use of cutting (Plate 190). *Ballet mécanique* put into practice the convictions, so deeply in sympathy with those of Epstein and Clair, which Léger had most clearly expressed in his March 1923 reply to Clair's *enquête* in *Film*: 'The detail of an object, a complete whole projected in enlarged form, is a personality; the human fragment projected enlarged is a personality . . . The nature of an eye, a figure, a finger, a hand are ignored. The screen must seize them, individualize them and from them extract every possibility.'[71]

Yet in Léger's idea of the figurative fragment or object as cinematic image there was a crucial element which was not shared either by Epstein

193.   Still from the film *La Roue* directed
by Abel Gance, 1920–1.

194.   Still from *Ballet mécanique*.

or Clair or their avant-garde allies. They might have advocated the end
of the theatrical plot in order to focus on pure cinematic rhythm and the
photogenic image as such, but in the final analysis their idea of the image
was not Léger's. Epstein and Clair might not have agreed with Abel Gance's
preservation of the elaborate theatrical plot in pursuit of 'psychological
nuance', but they would have agreed with Gance's conviction that the
cinematic image should not merely be visual in its impact but should carry
with it a psychological charge. Epstein made just this point when talking
to Jean Mitry about *La Roue* in the summer of 1924,[72] and the fantastic
factor so strong in the imagery of *Entr'acte*, shown the month after the
first showing of Léger's film, demonstrates Clair's concurrence. Significantly,
when Clair tried to sum up the nature of the imagery in *Entr'acte*, writing
for *La Danse* (November–December 1924), he quoted André Breton's
Surrealist plea for an imagery 'freed from its duty to signify'. The ideas of
Breton could not have been more foreign to the straightforward 'plastic'
emphasis on the object or figurative fragment so central to Léger's approach
and therefore to *Ballet mécanique*; this pure, visual emphasis is what gives
his film its independence, and nothing could more effectively underline
this emphasis than the studied way in which it keeps its distance from the
'psychological' values of Gance and *La Roue*. As has been seen, for Gance,
length was a function of involvement with 'psychological nuance'; 'A
spectacle', Léger remarked in his 1924 text 'Le Spectacle, Lumière, Couleur,
Image Mobile, Objet-Spectacle', 'must be fast, its unity does not allow of
it more than fifteen to twenty minutes,'[73] and *Ballet mécanique* gave this
conviction point. Even more emphatically, the opening and closing
sequences of Léger's film are dominated by a particularly sentimental
image from *La Roue* (Plate 193), a pretty girl (Gance's 'Rose du rail') sim-

pering on a swing (Plate 194), but used utterly without sentiment to contrast with the interjected images of wine bottles, boater and pendulum—the 'psychological' image purified.

How then did Léger's immersion in the film avant-garde between 1922 and 1924, and his experience as film-maker with *Ballet mécanique* actually affect his painting? The answer is obvious: the experience of discovering through the actual process of film-making the sheer wealth of formal potential contained in the figure, the figurative fragment and the manufactured object enlarged on the screen finally convinced him that the conventions of Cubist distortion were no longer necessary in painting, that the manufactured object in particular could be used simply as itself to create pictorial incident. Typically, it was not until he himself could test the validity of the idea by making his own film that it acquired the force to affect his approach to the object in painting; only when theory had been translated into visual facts projected on the screen was he deeply enough convinced. It was, therefore, with the backing of a substantial and persuasive body of avant-garde film theory underlined by the lessons learned in the making of *Ballet mécanique* that he moved at the end of 1924 into a kind of object-painting finally freed from the look of the Purist still-life. The glass, syphon, and severed hand of *Le Siphon* may have been lifted from the pages of *Le Matin*, but the decision so straightforwardly to use a simple representational image here and for instance in *Les trois pipes* could not have been made without *Ballet mécanique* and all that led up to it in the Parisian avant-garde of the cinema.

Yet there is another less obvious, even negative, sense in which Léger's experience of the cinema and his thinking on film seems to have affected his painting. For Cendrars, for Gance, for Epstein and Clair, as for Léger, what most essentially distinguished the cinema from the other arts was, of course, its particular character as a mobile, rhythmic art. Theatre—especially dance in the theatre—could also be visually dynamic in a compelling way, but the special capacity of film to create dynamic rhythm not only by the mobility of images filmed in movement but also by the effect of cutting from image to image gave it even greater potential as an art of movement. This fact must have thrown into strong relief the essentially static nature of the immobile arts, most obviously of all easel-painting, and, although a causal connection could never be proved, it is perhaps not an accident that Léger should have moved so decisively towards the stable easel-painting principles of his 'call to order' precisely as he discovered at first hand the sheer dynamic force of film; that he should have worked towards the stable grandeur of *Le Grand Déjeuner* and all that it heralded through the last months of 1920 and into 1921, precisely as Abel Gance and Blaise Cendrars were consulting him on the machine sequences of *La Roue*.

Certainly, the avant-garde and popular elevation of traditional classic values and the persuasive theory and practice of the 'Effort Moderne' artists, of such as Raynal and Rosenberg, and of the Purists, converged to shove him into his 'call to order'; and certainly he could not, would not, have made the move without the backing of a more clear-cut, a more ordered, a more Purist approach to modern life, the emphasis on the balanced structure of things rather than on the vacillations of experience. But the fact is that such classicizing tendencies, avant-garde and popular, and such a view of the modern world had been there for him to absorb ever since his 1918 return from the trenches to Paris, and, though the increase in their persuasiveness already noted as so marked in 1920–1 must have had its effect, his opening first-hand experience in film as a creative art— *La Roue*—must have helped him realize the essential inadequacy of easel-painting as an expression of the dynamic, changing aspect of modern experience, the essentially *stable,* structural character of painting.

This suggestion is made more convincing by the fact that Léger's personal adaptation of the Purist view of *l'esprit nouveau* as the basis for his more classical painting represented a *deepening* of his view of modern life, not, as the *volte face* in his easel-painting suggests, a total change. For the texts Léger published between 1923 and 1925 make it unmistakably clear that he did not reject his dynamic view of the new world when he took on his ordered view of its structures: he evolved instead a two-level approach, remaining capable of celebrating speed even as he celebrated the geometrical precision and the balance of the things around him. 'Speed,' he wrote in 1924, 'is the law of the modern world . . . everything becomes mobile.'[74] His involvement in the cinema, and his experience in theatre in 1922 with *Skating-Rink* and in 1923 with *La Création du Monde* gave him a dynamic means of communicating his dynamic experience of modern life; and it is significant that the sets and costumes for both his theatrical experiments took further his dynamic pictorial methods of 1918–19. A two-level view of the modern world found expression in two levels of creative activity, one dynamic—the theatre and, more mobile still, the cinema—one static, painting; and, as the dynamic side of Léger's activities came to its climax in 1924 with *Ballet mécanique,* so too his painting achieved a stable firmness thus far unprecedented with *La Lecture, Trois figures,* the Paris *Eléments mécaniques* and the 1924 still-lifes. *Le Siphon* and its sequel, the object-paintings of 1925, like *Les trois pipes,* owed their straightforward use of the 'manufactured' object as such to the experience of *Ballet mécanique,* but, where the figurative fragments, the straw-boaters, bottles, travelling clock, saucepans and working machine parts of Léger's film, even when not moving are set in the most dynamic arrangements, often made more dynamic by the mirror technique, the objects of the object-paintings are always firmly contained within the most static of architectural structures. These compositions may be freed from the look of Purist painting, but their standardized, mass-produced subjects, their careful planning and execution, and their precisely stable sense of balance remain the product of an ordered view of modern life, simpler and less sophisticated than the Purist view but closely related to it. They, like all the achievements of Léger's 'call to order' as an easel-painter, convey only a part of his response to the modern world, but by 1924 it was only this, his reponse to the ordered, 'classical' *esprit nouveau,* that was for him attuned to the essentially stable nature of easel-painting.

CHAPTER 10
Painting and Architecture: Léger's Modern Classicism and the International avant-garde

On 23 April 1924 Le Corbusier and Pierre Jeanneret's office sent a summary plan, section and elevation of their proposed Pavillon de L'Esprit Nouveau to the Direction des Services d'Architecture, Section Française, of the Exposition Internationale des Arts Décoratifs to be held the following year.[1] It may perhaps be remembered from the beginning of this book that the Pavillon proposed was a single 'Citrohan house' (Plates 1 and 2) slightly rearranged as a specimen apartment from Le Corbusier's 'Immeubles Villas', which were in themselves conceived of as but single appartment blocks among the many contained within his ideal vision of a 'Contemporary City for three million' and of a rebuilt central Paris.

On 10 September 1924 a letter from Fernand David, the 'commissaire générale' of the Exposition finally accepted Le Corbusier's proposals, after much difficulty, and allotted L'Esprit Nouveau a cramped site in the shadow of the Grand Palais, impossibly hemmed in by trees whose every branch was sacrosanct.[2] The Exposition was due to open in April 1925 and many of the pavilions were already nearing completion, so the project was under pressure from anxious officialdom from the start.[3] But Le Corbusier had other difficulties with contractors and with money, and work did not actually begin until mid February 1925, by which time Fernand David had very nearly succeeded in giving the site to another exhibitor. The structure was almost complete by the opening of the Exposition late in April, but there was much left to do in the fitting out and painting of the building, and this was carried out through the early summer against a battery of coolly worded but vigorously hostile official letters threatening action over the lopping of trees, forbidding the passage of lorries to and from the site, and even at one point in May threatening to wall in the Pavillon as punishment for its lateness.[4] Then at last on 10 July all was finished for the opening, and there to attend it was the Ministre de l'Instruction Publique et des Beaux Arts, M. de Monzie himself—a powerful and much appreciated defector from the Establishment, with the industrialists M. Frugès, and

195.   Le Corbusier and Pierre Jeanneret: *Pavillon de L'Esprit Nouveau,* the living room (sculpture on balcony by Jacques Lipchitz; painting Colour Plate 1), 1925.

M. Mongernon and Gabriel Voisin of Voisin, alongside such as Picasso, Braque, Ozenfant, Lipchitz, Gris and Léger.[5] Le Corbusier's house-as-machine was complete, and beside it were the plans and drawings for his ideal city and his reconstruction of Paris—the Voisin Plan—most effectively of all advertised by two huge, painstakingly painted dioramas, ninety square metres each. Inside the living room of the house itself, of course, with sculpture by Lipchitz and painting by Le Corbusier and Ozenfant, was Léger's contribution, probably *Le Balustre* (Plate 195 and Colour Plate 8). The Pavillon de L'Esprit Nouveau brought to a climax Purism and Léger's involvement in it, but, as it did so, Le Corbusier and Ozenfant brought Purism to an end.

It is perhaps not surprising that the Pavillon was built in the teeth of official hostility, for not only was it not completed within the deadline, but also it was a criticism of the entire attitude behind the enormous operation. It was a sermon directed against the regional quaintness of the 'Village Française', the modish luxury of Ruhlmann's interiors of the 'Hôtel d'un riche collectionneur', and the extraordinary extravagance of for instance Sauvage and Wybo's *Pavillon de Primavera*; it was Le Corbusier's conclusion to the series of *L'Esprit Nouveau* articles with which, in 1924, he had attacked the very idea of decorative art as alien to the precise logic of a functional approach. Only Auguste Perret (vice-president of the architecture jury), with his Exposition theatre and his violent attack on the superficiality of the approach to ornament typical of the Exposition in

287

L'Amour de l'Art (May 1925), Tony Garnier to a limited extent with his Lyons and St Etienne pavilion, and to a fuller extent Robert Mallet-Stevens with his hall for the ideal French embassy and his tourist information office, were in any way in tune with Le Corbusier; and Perret's continuing allegiance to the paired-down remnants of classical forms set even him against the Purist pavilion.[6]

From the beginning designed as a subversive statement made in a hostile setting to a hostile audience, it is not surprising also that the Pavillon and its visionary city schemes should have made so uncompromising, so extreme and so ambitious a declaration of the more Puritan, more functionally 'Taylorized', machine and mass-production side of Purism. Questions of interior colour and of proportion were crucial but subordinate to the primary questions which were planning, standardization down to the smallest detail, adaptability to mass-production on a vast scale, and application of the most up-to-date ideas in engineering.

Le Corbusier's much publicized dependence on the patronage of industrialists was in itself a means of demonstrating a possible working alliance with the leaders in the field of mass-production themselves. Pessac was by late 1924 well under way, and M. Frugès, besides prefabricating the window frames at his saw-mill there provided essential financial backing for the Pavillon. Voisin, of course, gave its backing to the Voisin Plan and all it entailed—the *Salle des dioramas* and the dioramas themselves, while there is evidence that Le Corbusier approached André Michelin of Michelin as well.[7] Then every aspect of the Pavillon was a further demonstration of the possibilities that existed for standardized design, committed to economy and precision, to exploiting the potential of engineering and industry. The reinforced concrete frame was standardized as at Pessac. The walling and flooring was a light yet rigid and well-insulated synthetic material called 'solomite', ordered in standard rectangles, and rendered externally by means of the new Ingersoll-Rand cement-gun.[8] The doors were flush-fitting and metal, manufactured by the office-suppliers Roneo, and they, with the window-frames prefabricated at Pessac, and the fitted cupboards and storage units, also hurriedly supplied by Frugès after the failure of a Czech firm to complete the order, fitted precisely within a modular proportional system which was the key to the unity of the whole design.[9] Even the metal staircase was a standard fitting; and the strict emphasis on efficiency throughout is perhaps summed up by the fact that the dining table was ordered from L. Schmittheissler, specialists in hospital furniture,[10] while, on the larger scale of his city plans, Le Corbusier's determination to make even his most visionary buildings seem in touch with current engineering is perhaps summed up by the fact that he wrote to the engineer Freysinet, celebrated designer of the hangars at Orly, for advice on the foundations of his projected office skyscrapers.[11]

Pessac was too real to have been ideal. The Pavillon, a temporary exhibition building without an actual client, was just far enough from the restrictions of reality and yet just tangible enough as a built fact to make the Purist ideal environment on the scale both of a single housing unit and of a city seem possible. It was the closest the ideal Purist environment came actually to existing, and so directly involved was Léger that it is no wonder that 1925 saw his 'call to order' in easel-painting attain its most stable, most simply standardized and yet most original form.

The Exposition of 1925 was emphatically an international event, and, though the end-product of a French development whose beginnings had occurred in the isolated avant-garde of war-time Paris, the Pavillon de L'Esprit Nouveau set Purism in an international context. Ozenfant and Le Corbusier had, in fact, turned *L'Esprit Nouveau* increasingly in an international direction during 1923 and 1924. In 1923 the review had published the first French article on new developments in Russian art, with the painter Ivan Puni as author.[12] But, more significant, these years saw the development of a clear-cut international alliance between *L'Esprit Nouveau* and the Bauhaus. At first the Purist response to Bauhaus advances was cool, but by no. 23, early in 1924, the decisive move by the Bauhaus after the Weimar exhibition of the previous year towards a more functional and industrially orientated stance had been noticed. And in no. 27 Walter Gropius himself was included as a contributor, providing an article which comprehensively underlined the closeness of the Bauhaus to the Purist approach. He too insisted that the artist should work within industrial limitations, he too rejected the idea of applied ornament as alien to 'the sense of the object, which alone can count', he too wrote of 'the aesthetic of the engineer', yet he too allied his belief in functionalism to a belief in the 'laws of proportion' and a demand for the scientific investigation of the physiological response to colours and forms.[13]

What is more, Léonce Rosenberg through the galerie and the *Bulletin de l'Effort Moderne* developed an emphatically international orientation for his 'call to order'. In November 1923 he held a profoundly influential exhibition of *De Stijl* at the gallery, and in 1924 was negotiating to put on an exhibition of El Lissitzky;[14] while in the *Bulletin* he repeatedly published articles which stressed the idea of a 'collective style', a style based on universal principles (as, of course, Purism held itself to be), which ignored national boundaries. Thus, in no. 4, April 1924, he published an extract from Theo van Doesburg's 'Classique-Baroque-Moderne' under the title 'Vers un style collective', while in no. 9, November 1924, the fifth *De Stijl* manifesto 'Vers un Construction collective' appeared, and then in nos. 16 and 19 (June, November 1925) there appeared extracts from Servranckx's internationalist lecture 'Les Voies nouvelles de l'Art Plastique', all these statements sharing the conviction (again shared by the Purists and by Gropius) that so constant were the effects of colour and form if considered in purely pictorial, sculptural or architectural terms, that the foundation existed for an art whose meaning would be proof against all cultural and linguistic divisions, a genuinely international art.[15]

Moving within the circles of the galerie de L'Effort Moderne and *L'Esprit Nouveau*, Léger too became increasingly aware of his involvement in a modern movement which was much more than merely French, a movement much more coordinated than the pre-1914 attempt that had involved him with the Futurists and sent his *Contrastes de formes* to Berlin. In 1923 he and Ozenfant were invited to contribute lithographs to a Bauhaus portfolio, and significantly, too, 'L'Esthétique de la machine' was first published by *Der Querschnitt* in Berlin, late 1923; and in November that year his deep appreciation of what could be gained from outside France

196. Robert Mallet-Stevens: Entrance hall of the Ideal Embassy at the Exposition Internationale des Arts Décoratifs, Paris, 1925, with *Peinture murale,* 1924–5 by Fernand Léger. From *L'Amour de l'Art,* August, 1925.

was expressed in a letter written to the newspapers violently protesting against the decision to hang the Salon des Indépendants alphabetically and by nationalities. 'As to the foreigners,' he wrote. 'their contribution is excellent for French art . . .', and he ceased to show at the Indépendants in order to underline his antagonism to national divisions.[16] The next year, 1924, his links outside France became even stronger: he provided the cover for Paul Westheim's *Europa 1925*, put together in 1924; he was visited, as has been seen, by Baumeister; and he was invited on the initiative of Friedrich Keisler to the Vienna theatre exhibition in September. There he gave his lecture 'Le Spectacle, Lumière, Couleur, Image Mobile, Objet-spectacle', and his designs for *Skating-Rink* and *La Création du Monde* were seen in company with a dazzling international array including contributions from Lissitzky, Moholy-Nagy, Ludwig Hirschfeld-Mack (from the Bauhaus) and the abstract film-makers Hans Richter and Viking Eggeling, all set within a space knowingly articulated as an 'international' new space by Keisler.[17] Léger's knowledge of what had happened since 1917 in Russia had been much increased by the return to Paris in 1923 of Alexandra Exter, an old friend, and the sheer breadth of his sense of international involvement is emphasized by the fact that when in November 1924 his pupils from the 'Atelier' held a little exhibition at the 'Maison

Watteau', foreigners were dominant, especially the Scandinavians with Otto Carlsund, Erik Olson and Franciska Clausen.[18]

International though the 1925 Exposition Internationale des Arts Décoratifs was always intended to be, it had at first been decided to exclude for political reasons both the Germans and the Russians, a decision which in 1924 provoked a great deal of protest from journalists sympathetic to the idea of an international avant-garde and aware of how significant German and Russian developments were.[19] The Russians were in the end invited, and produced Melnikov's pavilion, its interior laid out by Rodchencko; and this, with Keisler's *cité dans l'espace*, was the foreign contribution most relevant to the subversive anti-decorative declaration made by the Pavillon de L'Esprit Nouveau. Le Corbusier's 'Citrohan house' apartment was itself of interest to the Russians, for Tugendhold, who was in Paris as a member of the USSR section and staying with Exter, wrote to the architect asking for photographs to publish in Moscow and for a meeting with him.[20] What is more, there was an obvious and close alliance between Le Corbusier's approach to housing—his emphasis on economy, on industrial means of production, on the worker as client and on the city— and the approach outlined by the architect M. L. Ginzburg in his official article on architecture which appeared in *L'Amour de l'Art* (October 1925). As Waldemar George had pointed out in the August number of *L'Amour de l'Art*, what most fundamentally of all singled out the Pavillon de L'Esprit Nouveau from the luxuriant and luxurious confections typical of the Exposition was the fact that it was designed for the ordinary man; it was this that made Le Corbusier's building, with Perret's theatre, the two Mallet-Stevens pavilions and the Russian pavilion: 'the only building in the entire exhibition which could be termed modern'.[21] And Keisler's contribution too, though less down to earth, was concerned with the problem of the city, with the newest possibilities opened up by engineering, and reflected an approach not unaffected by the sterner, more materialist side of Lissitzky, which emphasized the fact that in his *cité dans l'espace*, 'the processes of daily life are mechanized'.[22]

Yet, however much Léger's contribution to the Pavillon de L'Esprit Nouveau involved him in an approach to the architecture of an industrial society whose emphasis on planning for machine-production was international, the fact remains that what most endowed the paintings he showed at the Exposition with international significance was their purely 'plastic' relationship with architecture. They retained the mass-production associations which had been a feature of Léger's painting since late 1920, but the way that they were consciously integrated into an architectural setting was new, and reflected a change of approach to the relationship between painting and architecture directly initiated by the growing influence of the international avant-garde outside France. This certainly is so of the painting hung in Le Corbusier's Pavillon, but it is perhaps even more so of the strictly architectural painting so carefully placed in Mallet-Stevens's entrance-hall to the ideal French Embassy (Plate 196), Léger's other contribution to the 1925 Exposition. It is Léger's new approach to the relationship between painting and architecture—and his answer to the question of abstract art—that sets his 1925 achievement in its international context.

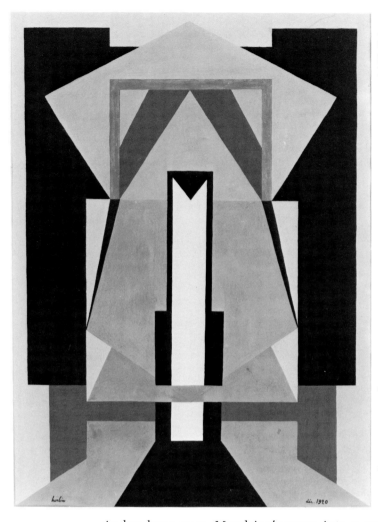

197. (left) Auguste Herbin: *Peinture,* December 1920. Gouache on paper, 21 × 15 ins, sold by Sotheby's, London, 11 December 1969.

198. (right) Fernand Léger: *Ie état graphique, projet fresque,* 1922–3. Ink on paper, Musées Royaux de Belgique, Brussels.

199. (far right) Fernand Léger: *Fresque (extérieur) pour un Hall d'Hôtel,* 1922–3. *L'Architecture Vivante,* Paris, autumn/winter 1924.

As has been seen, Mondrian's move into a mature geometric abstract style in 1920–1, though noticed by Léger himself, attracted to him neither avant-garde praise nor avant-garde followers when the results were shown at the group exhibition held by Léonce Rosenberg in the galerie de l'Effort Moderne in 1921. The Purists with their interest in the 'type-object' as subject were not sympathetic, and avant-garde painting in general, dominated as it was either by the rise of traditional classical modes or by attitudes whose origins lay in Cubism, could not accept its extreme purity. There were, in fact, compositions seemingly as abstract as Mondrian's in the 1921 'l'Effort Moderne' exhibition—the *Peinture* on cement by Auguste Herbin, most notably, to which the gouache (Plate 197) is closely related— but Laura Miner in an unpublished thesis has established that Herbin arrived at his *Peinture* as a result of a basically 'synthetic' process of selection and simplification, a tree being his initial *motif*, and that his purpose here was emphatically decorative, as was the other abstract contributor to the exhibition, Lambert's.[23] According to Gino Severini, he himself, Rosenberg and the architect Auguste Perret were deeply interested in the possibility of a new decorative style at this time, and Herbin's elaborate symmetrical

compositions seem to have been the result of an allied aim.[24] There was no question here of rendering all relationship between painting and the world of appearances obsolete—no question of a development at all comparable with Mondrian's abstraction. Something that neared abstraction was allowed, but only as an embellishment to architecture, and only as a kind of art so separate that it in no way challenged easel-painting.

There had always been after 1917 a marked decorative quality in Léger's treatment of the flat, planar architecture of his compositions—a tendency to embellish borders with frills and patterns of dots or dashes (Plates 90, 109 and 157), a quality that was held in control but not scotched in the 1921 development of *Le Grand Déjeuner*. So it is not perhaps surprising that he should have been drawn to the idea of painting as an embellishment of architecture—as decoration; especially since Rosenberg, Severini and Herbin had been very much aware of the popular potential of decorative art in their discussions of 1919–21.[25] In the Musées Royaux de Belgique, Brussels, there are two closely related pen-and-ink drawings, one of which is inscribed on the reverse: 'le état graphique, projet fresque 1922, exposé Salon Indép. 22' (Plate 198). It refers, in fact, to an architectural arrangement of shaped panels by the 'Effort Moderne' sculptor Joseph Csaky which were painted by Léger and shown at the 1923 Indépendants in February of that year (*not* 1922); and these drawings, with a colour illustration captioned 'Fresque (extérieur) pour un Hall d'Hôtel' which appeared in *L'Architecture Vivante* (Plate 199), are the only surviving indications, besides verbal accounts, of what it looked like.[26]

293

In a sense, the backdrop of Ricciotto Canudo's *Skating-Rink,* designed by Léger for the Ballets Suédois early in 1922, had been an enormous wall-decoration, and Léger's approach to the painting of Csaky's panels for the 1923 Indépendants was clearly very similar. The wall was treated as a surface to be made dynamic by means of the oblique, the flat jostling disc and, as Maurice Hiver put it in *Montparnasse* (1 March 1923), by 'the violence of pure colours', the clashing red, blue, green and yellow of the illustration in *L'Architecture Vivante* giving an idea of the quality of this violence. The illustration, with the Brussels drawings, make it clear that Léger's contribution was indeed powerful enough to effectively challenge whatever architectural qualities Csaky's arrangement might have had, and this point is underlined perhaps most of all by the hostile remarks made by Waldemar George in *L'Amour de l'Art* (February 1923). 'The ensemble project for a hall by Joseph Czaky (sic),' he writes, 'has been spoilt by Fernand Léger's polychromy . . . Instead of animating it, the painter punches holes, cuts it up, fragments and destroys the flat harmony of the wall surface.' Léger's decoration does not seem to have enhanced the architecture it embellished, it seems rather to have taken control by force of shape and colour: the ammunition of *Les Disques* had found a new target. As a painter for architecture, Léger's stance seems to have changed little from the stance he had established as an easel-painter in his *Valori Plastici* statement of 1919: 'To me, "the opposite of a wall" is a picture, with its verve and movement.'

The February 1923 Indépendants mural project backed a definite attempt

200.   Fernand Léger: *L'Architecture,* 1923. $25\frac{1}{4} \times 36\frac{1}{4}$ ins, private collection, France.

by Léger to involve himself more with the problems of painting for architecture. Marcel Hiver's *Montparnasse* report on the project and the mention of a 'fresque (extérieur) pour un Hall d'Hôtel' in *L'Architecture Vivante* indicate that the Indépendants decorations were not only for the inside but also for the outside of an imaginary building. The polychromatic fantasy architecture of the 1921 *Paysages animés* had, of course, looked forward to a dazzling transformation of the outside of buildings, and it was perhaps an expression of Léger's strengthened faith in such an idea that he developed a pictorial theme whose subject was polychromatic architecture alone, during 1923: the theme of *L'Architecture* (Plate 200). During the summer and early autumn of 1923 Léger experienced two major fresh stimuli towards the development of a dynamic approach to large-scale environmental painting: his involvement as set-designer in Blaise Cendrars's and Darius Milhaud's *La Création du Monde* (which opened in early November), and in Marcel L'Herbier's film *L'Inhumaine* (completed about the same time). The broad, obliquely angled moving planes of Léger's *Création du Monde* set,[27] must have seemed to open up altogether new possibilities in mural-painting as well; and so too must the more complex, more elaborate laboratory set designed for *L'Inhumaine* (Plate 190). Yet the actual mobility and the constantly changing light-effects of these two sets were obviously not adaptable to the more limited potential of architecture, and indeed they may even have helped underline the point made by Waldemar George in criticism of the Indépendants project—that dynamic effects were altogether alien to architecture.

This latter point, with its corollary—that architectural ornament should be static and architecturally contained—would perhaps have been underlined further by the approach of a new architect acquaintance introduced to Léger while he was working on L'Herbier's *L'Inhumaine*, Robert Mallet-Stevens. It was Mallet-Stevens who designed the exterior of the building in which Léger's laboratory was supposed to be. He had not yet built a single real building of any importance, but by the end of 1923 his activity as designer, for instance, of the Magasin du Costumier Rossignol interiors and especially as Salon exhibitor had made a big enough reputation for him to start a small school disseminating an approach which emphasized the potential of reinforced concrete, encouraged geometric simplicity and a sense of linear or cubic composition strongly reminiscent of the Vienna Secession.[28] His most notable success to date had been a life-size model control-building for the aero-Club de France shown at the new architecture section of the 1922 Salon d'Automne (Plate 201), a design whose combination of science-fiction and simple geometric decorative effects would have appealed greatly to the designer of the laboratory in *L'Inhumaine*. But here, as in all his current interior designing, Mallet-Stevens had clearly subordinated all decorative embellishment to the broad requirements of his total architectural composition, so that, for instance, a sequence of long vertical stained-glass panels are included but firmly contained within the stable vertical and horizontal grid of glazing-bars. Decoration is emphatically the servant of architecture.

It was not further in the architecturally destructive direction announced by the Indépendants project, but rather in the direction of an harmonious alliance between painter and architect that Léger moved at the end of

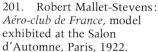

201. Robert Mallet-Stevens: *Aéro-club de France,* model exhibited at the Salon d'Automne, Paris, 1922.

1923. And the impetus without any doubt came from abroad, from the fast growing international movement towards a 'collective style' embracing architecture, sculpture and painting; it came from the exhibition of three villa projects with attendant plans and axonometric projections by Theo van Doesburg and Cor van Eesteren (aided by Gerrit Reitveld) at the galerie de l'Effort Moderne: the *De Stijl* exhibition of November 1923. Van Doesburg treated the wall planes of the villa projects as flat rectangular planes of primary colour, of grey or of white. *De Stijl* had found a role for colour in architecture so crucial and so integrated with the essential nature of the wall that it could become in itself a primary architectural element rather than a factor in applied decorative design. The painter in a sense had become part architect, working in space with elementary colour planes. Léger, it is known, was instantly and profoundly impressed by what he saw at the galerie de l'Effort Moderne, and the nature of the lesson he learned is fortunately there to be read in an interview with a certain 'M.X' (almost certainly Le Corbusier) published at the time in *L'Esprit Nouveau* no. 19. 'M.X' is sternly opposed to the effects destructive of a simple volumetric statement created by exterior polychromy, but feels that the interior use of the Dutch 'formula' has great potential. 'There you are, that is the problem that excites me,' says Léger. 'Ah! thus to give architecture to a bank, by planes of colour.' M.X then asks him if he now is convinced that unbroken planes of colour are in themselves enough and if therefore he now rejects the decorative approach behind his collaboration with Csaky at the 1923 Indépendants. 'Precisely,' replies Léger, 'there is the mistake; the walls must be complete wholes which are involved as units in the equation.'[29] Painting in architecture, for him, was no longer set dynamically against architecture, and the breakthrough had been made possible by the international activism of Theo van Doesburg in alliance with Léonce Rosenberg.

At the end of 1923 Le Corbusier was just beginning on the Pessac scheme,

202. Fernand Léger: *Peinture murale,*
1924. $70\frac{3}{4} \times 31\frac{1}{2}$ ins, Musée National
Fernand Léger, Biot.

had just arrived at the final designs for his double villa in Auteuil for
Raoul La Roche and Albert Jeanneret, and was still involved in building
Ozenfant's studio-house near the parc Montsouris.[30] Both outside and
inside he still thought in terms of the white wall. As Richard Francis has
established, it was in the summer of 1924 that he sent instructions to the
contractor engaged on completing the Atelier Ozenfant giving details for
the colouring of the internal walls and in March the following year the
internal colour-scheme for the walls of the Villa La Roche-Jeanneret was
arrived at too.[31] 1924 was the year when Le Corbusier and Léger in close
collusion worked out their new approach to the relationship between
painting for architecture and architecture. Parallel with Le Corbusier's
coloured interior for the Atelier Ozenfant, Léger produced two *Peintures
murales* (Plate 202), both now in Biot, and a considered statement of his
ideas, 'L'Architecture polychromie', published in the autumn/winter
number of *L'Architecture Vivante*.

With the 1924 *Peintures murales* and 'L'Architecture polychromie'
Léger completely rejected that idea of painting for architecture which
necessarily aligned it with the destructive dissonance of his easel painting.

297

Painting in architecture, he now believed, fulfilled man's need for 'live surfaces', but had to be completely in harmony with architecture: the architectural painter's aim was 'to create a calm and anti-dynamic atmosphere, a coloured "plastic" order inside or outside', and he was to remain always aware of the power of pure colour to command a far greater area than the area it actually covers.[32] In the Atelier Ozenfant and later the Villa La Roche-Jeanneret Le Corbusier worked with entire wall planes or anyway large surfaces of a single colour, where Léger restricted himself to the far smaller surfaces of easel-painting and broke these up with still smaller planes, but both worked with a subdued range of 'Purist' colour—ochre, earth browns, dull greens and white—and just as the vertical and horizontal was dominant in Le Corbusier's interior compositions, so they were too in Léger's *Peintures murales*. What is more, Léger's murals, though they were no more than simplified and subdued adaptations from the 'architectural' planar settings of his classical figure and object paintings, altogether rejected the frilled and dot or dash patterns which had so characteristically embellished these settings before 1924. There was no longer any association in Léger's mind between decorative art and mural-painting—the mural was itself considered a basic architectural element, possessed of the same classical qualities— stability, repose—as architecture itself (architecture, that is, according to Le Corbusier's definition of the term). It was working with these convictions that Léger made his contribution to the architectural achievements of Le Corbusier and Robert Mallet-Stevens at the 1925 Exposition, and placed his art thus in an international context.

As has been suggested, Léger's contribution to Mallet-Stevens's hall for the ideal French Embassy at the Exposition was more strictly an architectural painting than his Pavillon de L'Esprit Nouveau contribution (Plate 196). Photographs of the installation show clearly that, although Léger did not specifically design the painting for this particular ensemble, it perfectly tuned in with its setting. The asymmetry of the composition acted with perfect tact against the strict symmetry of the space as a whole, the simplicity of the flat colour planes and their playful spatial implications finding echoes in Mallet-Stevens's use of architectural elements, the overlapping of planes finding an echo, for instance, in the superimposed hanging planes of the central light-fittings. M. Paul Léon, the director of the Beaux-Arts, was so antagonized by Léger and Delaunay's additions to Mallet-Stevens's hall that he actually had them taken down the day after the opening of the Embassy (they were replaced in response to loud protests later); but, showing an extraordinary blindness to the one obvious quality that Léger's composition certainly possessed, Léon was not antagonized by the sheer simplicity or the absolute abstractness of the 'pure' *Peinture murale*, but rather by the conviction that both Léger's and Delaunay's canvases were out of tune with their architectural surroundings.[33]

Up to this point it has repeatedly been suggested that when the Pavillon de L'Esprit Nouveau opened the composition by Léger that hung above the dining table was 'probably' *Le Balustre* (Colour Plate 1). Such a probability is supported by the fact that almost all the photographs of the Pavillon living room published at the time, notably in the *Almanach d'Architecture Moderne* (1926), and those later included in the *Oeuvres Complètes* of Le Corbusier show this painting in position. Photographs are available—

again notably in the *Almanach* and the *Oeuvres Complètes*—of almost every other wall surface in the Pavillon, and, if one accepts them as convincing evidence of how the building was fitted out, this was the only position given to Léger by the Purists. However, it has often been stated that Léger painted abstract murals (more than one) for the Pavillon, and *Le Balustre* is neither an abstract mural nor more than one painting.[34] In a statement of 1950 Léger himself merely notes: 'I worked at this time (the time of the 1925 Exposition) with Le Corbusier on large mural compositions in pure colours without any subject,'[35] making no specific reference to the Pavillon, and there is persuasive eye-witness evidence in support of all the photographic evidence that murals were not hung in the building.[36] Yet, intriguingly, when he wrote to Le Corbusier in November 1925 about the collection of his work from the Pavillon, he mentioned 'mes oeuvres' (implying more than merely *Le Balustre*),[37] and it is tempting to speculate that the Biot murals may in fact have been painted for the project and then for some reason not actually hung—their strictly Purist range of colour and their date is so exactly right. But the truth is probably a little less as one would expect, for there was a single photograph of the living room published at the time, a view published in the winter 1925 number of *L'Architecture Vivante*,[38] which shows that for a while at least—when and for how long it is impossible to say—another Léger hung above the table in place of *Le Balustre*, a painting which was far closer to the absolute abstraction of the Mallet-Stevens mural and yet not quite completely a mural itself, the expansive, aptly sombre *Composition*, dated '24' (Plate 203). Not only *Le Balustre*, but this painting too, both considered as part of their architectural context, made up therefore Léger's contribution to the Pavillon de L'Esprit Nouveau at the 1925 Exposition.

The 1924 *Composition* was, like the Zurich *Elément mécanique* of that year (Plate 179), a simplified reworking of a pictorial theme whose origins went back beyond 1920, for there exists a small oil version on paper dated '22' which included a disc *motif* and is obviously connected with the early disc and Armistice-day themes of 1918.[39] It has therefore a variety of pictorial incident, a richness, not shared either by the mural Léger painted for the Embassy hall or by the 1924 Biot murals or by the new pure murals completed in 1925 and 1926, for instance the canvas, tall and narrow like the Mallet-Stevens canvas (Plate 204). These latter paintings are more strictly expressive of Léger's 1924–6 approach to painting for architecture, and it is, therefore, more aptly by looking at these that one can ask how his approach related to the ideas internationally promoted above all by Theo van Doesburg through *De Stijl*.

The axonometric projections of the villa designs shown at the November 1923 *De Stijl* exhibition made it clear that van Doesburg's intention here was colouristically to separate his wall planes into large often undifferentiated areas of white or primary red, blue and yellow. The flat unity of the wall plane was not to be challenged, as it was challenged by the smaller-scale planar arrangements of Léger's *Peintures murales* which were, of course, still easel-paintings hung *on* the wall. There was, however, another *De Stijl* exhibition in 1923, which presented an alternative *De Stijl* approach to the wall-surface, an approach more obviously in tune with that developed by Léger the following year. In Berlin Gerrit Reitveld

203. (left) Fernand Léger: *Composition*, 1924.
51 × 39 ins, sold by Parke-Bernet, New York, 1974.

204. (right) Fernand Léger: *Peinture murale*, 1925.
82¾ × 31¾ ins, Josef Müller collection, Soleure.

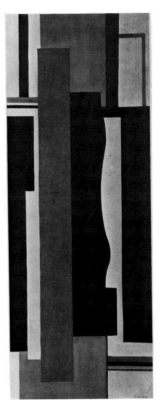

designed an exhibition room furnished with his own painted wooden furniture, its walls coloured by Vilmos Huszar. This room, seen from three viewpoints, was given a two-page spread of illustrations in the autumn/ winter 1924 number of *L'Architecture Vivante*, precisely the number which contained Léger's 'L'Architecture Polychromie', and the black and white photographs were retouched in blue, yellow and red where the wall planes were coloured, the colours keyed down to something close to the muted range of the Biot murals (Plate 205). Huszar did challenge the separate rectangular unity of the wall here, his flat planes floating on their neutral grey ground (in the photographs) not only overlapping to imply space as it were *in* the wall, but also turning corners to destroy the distinction between one wall and another.

'For him (Huszar),' wrote Jean Baldovici in his commentary on the Berlin room, 'the aim is to create an abstract space in a given concrete space with combinations of different colours.'[40] And Baldovici, commenting on Léger, was equally certain that his aims as a painter in architecture were essentially spatial.[41] In this respect certainly there is a link between Léger's murals and Huszar's, for they both attempt at once to harmonize with architecture by working in flat, stable pictorial elements and to challenge the wall by opening up a pictorial space within it. Thus, for all the uncompromising flatness of his planar vocabulary, Léger continued in his murals to play the games with overlapping elements and advancing or retreating colours which he had played for years as a Cubist, but with a

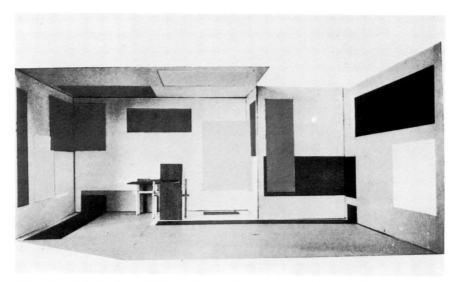

205. Gerrit Reitveld and Vilmos Huszar: Room designed for an exhibition, Berlin, 1923. *L'Architecture Vivante,* Paris, autumn/winter 1924.

new simplicity keyed to the breadth of their implied architectural environment. To the left of the Biot *Composition murale* (Plate 202) a thick black line drops down the edge of the canvas; it runs alongside a brown rectangle, at first seeming to lie behind it, then abruptly it comes to an end so designed as to seem to *over*lap the rectangle. Then again Léger evokes an ambiguous 'abstract' space by letting the white pass apparently beneath all planes as the ground plane of the painting and then bringing it forward in front of them all by isolating between grey and deep green a single white rectangle. Yet though this ambiguity is not in tune, the basic intention to open up an 'abstract' space within a 'concrete' space is in tune with Huszar's wall painting, and it is an intention as clearly pursued in the murals of 1926 as in those of 1924.

However, Léger's decision to contain spatial incident within the confines of easel-painting led to differences of effect and followed from differences of approach to the relationship between painting and architecture which were profound, separating him from Huszar and Rietveld as well as from van Doesburg and van Eesteren. The creation of new 'abstract' spaces was perhaps *the* central aesthetic concern which bound together the artists and architects of the international avant-garde between 1923 and 1925, not least van Doesburg with Huszar with El Lissitzky, Keisler and, though rather uncomfortably, with Moholy-Nagy at the Bauhaus. But space was not considered in isolation, certainly not by Moholy, van Doesburg, Keisler and the rest of *De Stijl*. 'The "new architecture",' declared van Doesburg in his 1924 manifesto 'Towards a Plastic Architecture', 'reckons not only with space but also with time as one of its characteristics.'[42] The spaces of the villa projects exhibited at the 'Effort Moderne' were designed to be moved through, their corners opened up to encourage movement, so that the experience of 'concrete' and 'abstract' space created by the over-lappings of coloured wall planes constantly changed, introducing the factor of time as a crucial element. In the same way Reitveld's Berlin exhibition room was designed to be moved in, and so Huszar's colour planes were kept free of enclosure, turning corners to encourage the movement of the eye from one wall plane to another as well as to destroy all sense of fixed enclosure. By concentrating all spatial play within the closed rectangle of an easel-painting, Léger discouraged movement of this kind, excluded the factor of time and reinforced the sense of the wall as a fixed enclosing plane, however effectively holed by the illusion of depth. The distinction between the dynamic media of film or theatre and the static medium of painting was, it seems, too clear in his mind for him directly to involve painting in a dynamic experience of space along the lines advocated by *De Stijl*.

Léger's murals are 'frontal' compositions and they are related therefore not only three-dimensionally to the space of the room, but also—and as importantly—two-dimensionally to the wall on which they hung, from which followed concerns altogether irrelevant to van Doesburg or Huszar as painters for architecture. For Léger in 'L'Architecture polychromie', it may be remembered, an area of pure colour could command an area far greater than that it actually covered, and so the proportions and intensity of, for instance, the central red slat which dominates the Soleure mural were ideally to be judged in relation to the proportions and the colour of the wall on which it was placed as well as the room it confronted. But the radiant power of a mural—its capacity harmoniously to command a wall—depended on more than merely the proportions and strength of its colour planes, it depended as much on their positioning in relation to the picture-edge, on the supplementary potential of line to direct the eye away from the painting and, of course, on the framing of the canvas as a whole. The murals therefore focused Léger's attention in a new way on the peripheries of the composition.

The photograph of the Pavillon de L'Esprit Nouveau living room in the winter 1925 *L'Architecture Vivante* shows that the 1924 *Composition* was hung, like *Le Balustre*, in an emphatically enclosing frame. The murals proper, however, were almost certainly not intended to be enclosed thus, for the photographs of the Mallet-Stevens Embassy hall show that Léger's composition was framed if at all very unobtrusively, while the Soleure mural, according to Josef Müller was sold to him by Léger in the 1920s framed, as it is now, with a thin moulded strip of wood painted dull green, which creates no more than the flimsiest of visual boundaries. The edges of the murals therefore seem to have been judged to relate almost directly to the walls on which they were placed—white walls in the case of the Embassy hall, but theoretically, if Le Corbusier were the architect, any colour in the Purist range that he might choose. For this reason, Léger's decision in the Biot *Composition murale* (Plate 202) to drop that black bar down the left edge of the canvas is significant in two as well as in three dimensions, closing off as it does the left side of the composition from the wall surface; while his decision to allow horizontal bars of black, ochre and green to strike the right edge of the canvas unhindered is equally significant, encouraging a sense of expansion as it does on the other side. The colour range of Léger's murals and their lack of bounding black lines for planes distinguish them from the compositions of Mondrian—they are too muted and too spatially active to sustain close comparison—but in this factor at least, in the care with which they are considered as expanding

303

centres of force flat on the wall they are not out of tune with Mondrian.

Léger developed his approach to painting for architecture during 1924 and 1925, firmly convinced of the essentially stable nature of painting as a medium; and he developed it in close collusion with Le Corbusier, for whom the unity of the wall surface, whether coloured or not, as a separate two-dimensional element in a three-dimensional experience of space was sacrosanct. That he kept to the relatively small rectangle of the easel-painting as a part of the larger rectangle of the wall, thus reinforcing the wall's identity, and avoiding the more complex space/time concerns of the international modern movement is not, therefore, surprising, and in this he retains his Paris-based identity as a painter. Yet even so the fact remains that the development of the murals placed his art in a new and more direct relationship with the international avant-garde, gave it an international identity. They stood, like van Doesburg or Huszar's painting for architecture, as declarations of an alliance between painter and architect in which the painter became part-architect, his work an integral, non-decorative element in architectural design. Though strictly circumscribed in their architectural function, they declared the validity of pure abstraction as simply as did the painting of De Stijl or of Lissitzky. And finally, though unconcerned with time, they were as deeply concerned with the relationship between an 'abstract' and a 'concrete' space as the international activists would have wished them to be.

'We declare,' wrote van Doesburg and van Eesteren in their 1923 manifesto, 'that painting without construction (i.e., easel-painting) has no further reason for existence.'[43] Léger's murals may have been abstract and may have declared a new alliance with architecture ('construction'), but they did not thereby declare non-architectural, non-abstract easel-painting invalid. In one further crucial way his approach to painting for architecture differed from that above all of van Doesburg and the artists of De Stijl: he did not see the experience created by such a marriage of colour and construction as self-sufficient. His murals and the walls on which they might hang were no more than a setting for the main drama, created above all by people—the figure—and the manufactured object. The dissonant action of modern life remains even still the focus of attention however firmly contained by its coloured architectural setting. 'In this new environment,' Léger wrote in L'Architecture Polychromie', 'a man can be seen, for the eye is not distracted by dispersed qualities. Everything is arranged. Against these big calm areas, the human face assumes its proper status. A nose, eye, foot, hand or jacket button will become a precise reality.'[44] The interest for Léger lay in what happened in front of the wall, not on it, and the painting which celebrated in pictorial terms the objects and figures of the main drama retained still 'the right to a place in this organization'.

Yet Léger's deepened awareness of the relationship between painting and architecture as an harmonious relationship, and the development between 1924 and 1926 of his mural-painting style did have its effect on his development as classical figure-painter and composer of object-paintings, providing the impetus behind important aspects of the mature and stable style that brought his 'call to order' to its climax in 1925–7, endowing it with a new identity as part of the international modern movement. And perhaps the most effective way of demonstrating this is to pause and look again at the two paintings which Léger sent as his contribution to Le Corbusier's Pavillon de L'Esprit Nouveau with its international audience, the 1924 *Composition* and the 1925 *Le Balustre*.

The 1924 *Composition*, as has been seen, had as its starting-point a compositional idea whose origins went back to the *Disques* compositions of 1918–19. With so dazzling a parentage, the severe clarity and the sobriety of colour of the painting is extraordinary. In the Pavillon it hung opposite an earth-brown wall with which it would have struck up a quiet rapport at once, even though itself set in a dark frame on a pristine white surface. Though still more complex than the murals, the quality of its spatial suggestions, the calm of its dominant browns, ochre and greys, and the flat, clear-cut simplicity of its dominant elements were all perfectly in sympathy with the room in which it hung. Even though not a mural it could act as an architectural element in an architectural composition, and the reason is obvious: with the subject so distant, its remnants so few, the painting has become virtually all architectural setting, and it was of course the architectural settings of Léger's object- or figure-paintings that were affected by the experience of the murals. Their colour was muted, their spatial activity was made more definite and they were progressively purged of their decorative borders and all other embellishments—a point clearly made by the settings of *La Lecture*, the mid-1924 galerie Beyeler *Nature-morte* and the later *Le Syphon*. It is an indication of where Léger was moving both to and from, that the one major change visible on the carefully brushed surface of the 1924 *Composition* is the painting out of a strong zig-zag pattern, originally included as embellishment to the wedge of orange at the foot of the long curving band that falls from the top of the canvas—the zig-zag pattern had been a central feature in the small 1922 version.

Le Balustre (Colour Plate 1) was not even nearly a mural, and the bright flat scarlet of its vase on the left would not have toned quietly in with the brown of the wall opposite; it was one of the brand new, post *Ballet-mécanique* object-paintings, and entirely the product of 1925. Yet, significantly, the central object-*motif*, the ballustre, is architectural, and the theme seems to have developed as sequel to a pictorial idea developed during the first three or four months of 1925 with architecture as its sole concern, the theme of the *Composition à l'escalier* (Plate 206). *Composition à l'escalier* is put together from standardized architectural parts, the building from the right of the *Paysage animé* (Plate 170) on the right, the staircase from a little canvas completed also early in 1925 in the centre, and on the left architectural motifs in flat strips, taken, according to Blaise Cendrars, from the court of the modern apartment block where he lived on the rue Nordmann.[45] By June 1925 Léger had completed a new composition known now as *Composition au poteau* (Plate 207). Here he lifted the ballustre-post out of *Composition à l'escalier*, gave it a polished metallic sheen like a photographically touched-up sparking-plug (Plate 208), and hung it on a black ground beside a flat vase within a new setting of flat planes. This *Composition* is the close relative of *Le Balustre*, which is in fact a simple variation on the idea it states; *Le Balustre* itself would probably have been complete for the July opening of the Pavillon.

What is so striking about *Le Balustre* by comparison, say, with the gay carnival bustle of the 1923 *L'Architecture* (Plate 200) is its sheer simplicity. The new importance given the object as object by the film experience of 1924 demanded a consequent playing down of all competitive pictorial activity in the setting, and the murals showed the way. There had been instances before 1924 when the grand simplicity of the planar setting for *Le Balustre* was anticipated—the 1922 *Nature-morte au chandelier* is perhaps the most impressive, most relevant of all (Colour Plate 8)—but they were the prophetic exceptions and did not equal the extreme reached in 1924–5. The machine-finished steel-grey ballustre, firmly contained by its rectangular black surround hovers before a structure of flat planes far more colouristically forceful than the murals, but in every other respect mural-like. The focal collision on the canvas is that between the black ballustre-supporting plane and the scarlet of the vase, and aptly enough along the line of their meeting Léger plays with special relish the simple yet ambiguous game with spatial suggestion so typical of the murals. Midway up the dividing edge the black juts into the red of the vase seeming to overlap it, the way that the vase shapes are cut off above enhancing this effect, but at the base the black plane juts unmistakably *under* the red, reversing the illusion. Again, as in the murals, Léger exhibits great care in the way he positions colour areas and linear accents in relation to the canvas edge, allowing strong, unchecked linear thrusts above, but none beneath, and part closing, part opening the composition on the right by the siting of the rich blue bookcover-like plane which implicitly continues outwards even as visually it repeats the enclosing vertical of the frame. Finally, Léger allows only a single short passage of dots to embellish the architecture of the whole. *Le Balustre* would indeed more violently than the 1924 *Composition* have challenged the flat identity of the wall on

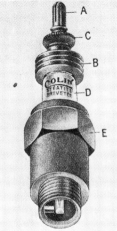

206. (above left)   Fernand Léger: *Composition à l'escalier*, 1925. 25¾ × 36 ins, private collection, France.

207. (above)   Fernand Léger: *Composition au poteau*, 1925. 36 × 28¾ ins, Oeffentliche Kunstssammlung, Basel.

208. (right)   'Colin' sparking-plug, *Omnia*, Paris.

which it hung in the Pavillon de L'Esprit Nouveau, but in no way would it have opposed the stable simplicity of Le Corbusier's architecture.

It was the architectural firmness—the sense of an harmonious rather than a hostile relationship with architecture—and the clear-cut spatial articulation of the settings Léger designed for the figures, figurative fragments and manufactured objects of his painting in 1925 that set it so emphatically within the international context of the 'modern movement'. As has been seen, the idea of the figure and of the object that it stood for was in no sense the product of an international development, but the planar architecture that contained them was. This is so not only of *Le Balustre*, of *Composition au poteau* and of their relative *Les trois pipes* (Plate 188), but even of the direct descendants of the traditional still-life themes, for instance the 1925 *Compotier* (Plate 209).

In the living room of the Pavillon de L'Esprit Nouveau, as part of the ensemble which came closest to making the proportionally harmonious, strictly rational, mass-production ideal of the Purists seem a possible reality, as product itself of an approach to modern life which was at least in part a simplified version of the Purist approach, Léger's painting brought his 'call to order' towards a climax, and did so within an avant-garde whose range of activity was international, linking Paris with Amsterdam, Berlin, Dessau, Vienna and even, it must have seemed, Moscow. Probably in the latter half of the year Léger produced a series of paintings which could not more openly have celebrated this new sense of international involvement; the best-known of them is the 1925 *Composition* (Plate 210).[46] *Composition* is, in fact, an object-painting; its subject, as other versions of the theme make clear, is an 'anglepoise' lamp, the broad brown disc being the shade seen from behind, the black and white bars being the poised structure of metal rods. So modern, so utilitarian a mass-produced object as subject ensures for the painting a definite Purist identity. Le Corbusier

209. (left) Fernand Léger: *Le Compotier*, 1925. $23\frac{1}{2} \times 36$ ins, James J. Shapiro collection, New York.

210. (right) Fernand Léger: *Composition*, 1925. $51\frac{1}{4} \times 38\frac{1}{2}$ ins, Solomon R. Guggenheim Museum, New York.

had illustrated a very comparable piece of equipment—from a dentist's surgery—to support his arguments for the modern 'type-object' in *L'Esprit Nouveau* no. 24. Yet thus transformed into a composition of flat bars set obliquely against a broad brown disc in an infinite grey 'space', and thus attended by hovering circles of black, the 1925 *Composition* seems almost rhetorically to declare Léger's allegiance to the international offspring of Malevich's Suprematism. It looks back to Lissitzky's 'prouns' and very specifically recalls one of the water-colour studies for his 'Electro-Magnetical peepshow' *Victory over the Sun*, seen by Léger at the Vienna theatre exhibition, reflecting the deepened sense of contact with Russian ideas no doubt promoted by the Russian effort at the 1925 Exposition. In doing so it seems to acknowledge, not only Léger's awareness of his international position as a painter, but his awareness of the Russian foundations so crucial to the international avant-garde he had now joined—to van Doesburg and *De Stijl*, to Moholy-Nagy at the Bauhaus, to Keisler and so many others. The 1925 *Composition* is the painting of an artist profoundly conscious of an international role to be played in an international scenario.

EPILOGUE
Four Paintings

Between 1925 and 1927 Léger produced a series of masterpieces. Each was preceded by a careful preparatory sequence of drawings, gouaches and often smaller oils; they were large, stable, utterly self-assured and marked the final maturity of the ordered, classical approach which he had developed from the last months of 1920. They are the product of a pictorial idea of the figure or object whose brutal 'plastic' simplicity is personal, but which is the product of an approach to the realities of modern life indelibly tinged with the idealism of *L'Esprit Nouveau*, an approach which remains stubbornly 'realist' but whose highly selective vision of the world picks out the most useful, the most geometrically 'pure', the most precisely finished of its manufactures, and subjects even the nude or the figurative fragment to the mass-production yet 'classical' values thus extracted. And in their grand, harmonious architecture with its clear articulation of spatial incident, these paintings are at the same time the product of an international avant-garde. Even now, in a decade which seems profoundly out of tune with the optimism that greeted accelerating technological progress during the 1920s, the grand classical qualities and sheer self-confident force of these paintings remains convincing. Their assurance and the conviction they carry is founded on more than fifteen years of faith in what was then most modern about the industrial world, of openness to what was most new in the avant-garde and of experiment in book illustration, theatre and film as well as in painting. Four compositions demonstrate their maturity and, by acknowledging the imminent arrival of new styles in 1927, make an end.

Composition 7 of 1925 (Plate 211) is closely related to the Pavillon de L'Esprit Nouveau painting, *Le Balustre*, and sums up all that was at once Purist, international and personal about the style that Léger evolved in 1925. Its central collision is between a deep cerise and a warm buttercup yellow, with a white planar intrusion to heighten both colours (the cerise of the vase, the yellow of the lettered plane), and, as in *Le Balustre*, there

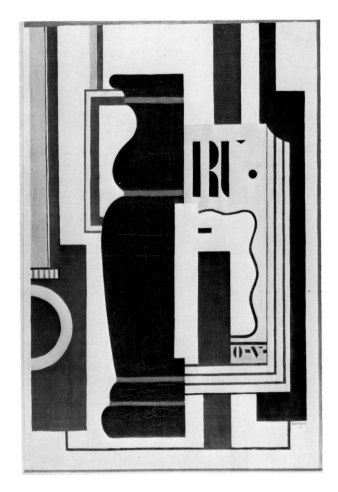

211. Fernand Léger: *Composition
7*, 1925. 51½ × 34¼ ins, Société
Anonyme collection, Yale
University Art Gallery, New
Haven.

is great spatial interest generated here. The cerise vase hangs on a ground
of white planes, the white becoming 'space', but a neat effect of ambiguity
is achieved when white is used for the intruding area between vase and
yellow plane, for here the white overlaps and is a flat surface *in front*;
yet even this effect is not quite what it may seem at first, because the white
overlapping surface itself is rendered 'spatial' by the long blue bar with
tiny dash-like accompaniment which hovers within it. The force of the
collision between red and yellow is utterly typical of Léger's search for
dissonant contrast, and the Cubist flavour of the ambiguities is personal
too, but the clarity of the spatial play, and the broad surfaces of the elements
involved set *Composition 7* in its international context, as the choice of vase
as central object-*motif* sets it in its Purist context. Vases figured discreetly
but significantly in the Purist Pavillon, and Ozenfant's pictorial contribution, which hung opposite *Le Balustre*, took a vase as its central feature,
its volume sacrificed to its two-dimensional profile just like the vase of
Composition 7, for the vase was a 'type-object' of special importance to
Ozenfant and Le Corbusier—its ideal alliance between formal simplicity
and utility achieving a particular perfection—and in Le Corbusier's
Almanach on the Pavillon it received the accolade of a passage all to itself:
Des Pots . . .[1]

311

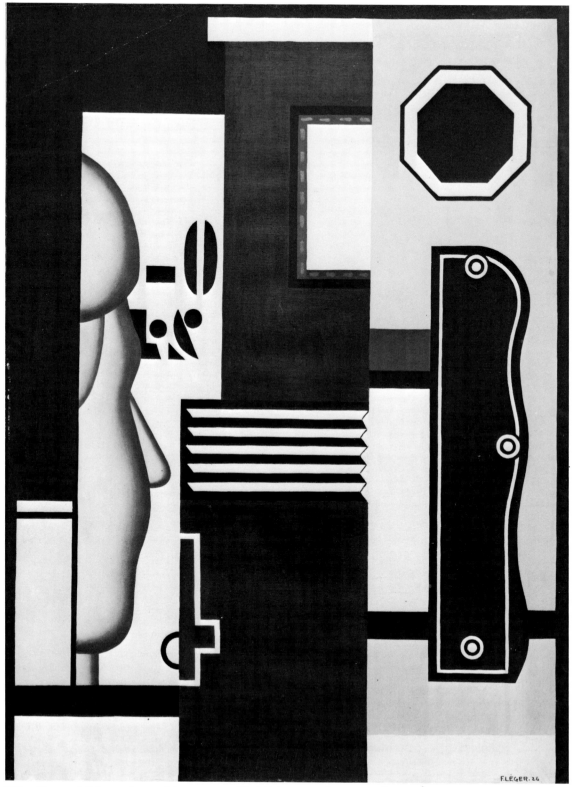

212. Fernand Léger: *Composition avec profil,* 1926. 51 × 38¼ ins, Fondation Le Corbusier, Paris.

Composition avec profil of 1926 (Plate 212) was owned by Le Corbusier himself until his death, yet it throws into relief not so much Léger's Purist-like view of the world he painted, but rather his independence as an artist— the independence particularly in object-painting which followed from the crucial experience of *Ballet mécanique*. It is the mirror-reflection of a carefully prepared series of smaller oils and is exactly finished in the image of the standard mass-produced object, the door-handle and finger-plate on the right themselves being simplified versions of mass-produced fittings.[2] Its muted range of colour, its severely stable structure, and its spaciousness would have found it a place in the ideal Corbusian interior even more harmonious than that found for *Le Balustre*. But the conjunction of door mechanism, of stencil signs in mirror reversal and especially of disembodied profile, eyeless and cold, this is startlingly original. Both in 'Les Bals populaires' and in 'L'Architecture polychromie' Léger had written of the profile thus discovered as a purely 'plastic' fact,[3] with an enthusiasm comparable to the enthusiasm he had felt in 1914 for smoke seen against roofs; it was a discovery of special importance to him, underlined by the part it played in *Ballet mécanique* (brief but as heroic as the straw-boater and the wine bottle). Integrated into the architecturally well-trained activity of flat overlapping planes Léger brings together the products of his new cinematic approach to the figurative fragment and the manufactured object, an approach which ensured the survival of the unexpected, the personal in his painting however stable, however classical it became.

The mural-paintings and the grand yet so often personal object-paintings of 1925–7 were certainly dominant during these years, but Léger produced a few equally grand, equally pugnacious and personal figure-paintings, the sequel to *La Lecture, Trois figures* (Plate 165) and *Nus sur fond rouge* (Plate 161). They establish a strong and true sense of continuity with the beginnings of Léger's 1920s 'call to order', and not the least expressive of this link is the single *Nu sur fond rouge* of 1927 (Plate 213). The idea is precisely that of the *Nus sur fond rouge* of four years earlier, the modelled steel-grey of the figure in collision with the flat intense red of the ground-plane. The female herself has no exact predecessor in the Basel painting, and the positioning of her arms is taken from a new theme developed between 1924 and 1927 where the hands hold a vase, but the standardized components of her eyes, brows, nose, mouth, breast, fingers and falling lock of hair, and the polished finish of her surfaces all look back very precisely to 1923, and beyond to the impassive mechanized women of *Le Grand Déjeuner*. The point is made that in the decision to treat the classically simplified image of the figure as an inanimate mass-produced object lay the seeds of the decision to treat as plastically self-sufficient the undistorted, simplified image of the mass-produced object itself; for the object-paintings made possible by the experience of *Ballet mécanique* may have rendered obsolete the conventional still-lifes of 1923 and early 1924, but they could not render obsolete the conventional figure-paintings that were their contemporaries.

If Léger could, with a painting like the *Nu sur fond rouge*, look from the vantage-point of 1927 right back to the classical figure-paintings which had announced his 'call to order' six or seven years before, he could too in 1927 make object-compositions which looked forward to a new change,

213.   Fernand Léger: *Nu sur fond rouge,* 1927. $50\frac{1}{2} \times 30$ ins,
Hirschhorn Museum and Sculpture Garden, Washington.

a change which would bring his 'call to order' to a close within a few months.
The superb *Nature-morte* of 1927 (Plate 214) is such a painting, holding in
tension qualities both from the immediate classical past and to be developed
further in the immediate, far freer, future. The simplistic, photo-like
rendering of compass and sardine-can — both suitably useful mass-produced
objects — is perfectly in tune with the pipes of the 1925 *Trois pipes* and the
syphon of the 1924 *Le Siphon*. But, though these objects are firmly contained

214.   Fernand Léger: *Nature morte*, 1927. $44\frac{3}{4} \times 57\frac{3}{4}$ ins, Kunsthaus, Bern.

within their architectural setting—powerful, unexpected incidents of conflict in a stable structure—across the architecture of the painting, completely free of it, float the capricious forms of leaves and flowers. They too are coolly and clearly defined, but they are neither geometrically simple nor the standardized products of mass-production. In their curvacious outlines and their freedom from containment are the seeds of Léger's future as a painter, and the beginning of the end for the phase which had reached maturity only two years before, at the Exposition Internationale des Arts Décoratifs. Within a year Léger had rejected the precisely balanced idea of modern life which had been the foundation of his art for half a decade, and his painting, therefore, had moved on yet again.

Bibliographical Note

On Fernand Léger a very extensive bibliography is found in Douglas Cooper, *Fernand Léger et le nouvel espace*, Geneva–Paris, 1949, which, with Pierre Descargues, *Fernand Léger*, Paris, 1955, is the most important early monograph on Léger. This bibliography is supplemented in Katherine Kuh, *Léger*, Art Institute of Chicago, 1953; in the catalogue of the exhibition *Fernand Léger*, Musée des Arts Décoratifs, Paris, 1956; in Robert Delevoy, *Léger*, Geneva, 1962; and in the very full 'Bibliographical Guide to Léger' in Fernand Léger, *Functions of Painting* (The Documents of 20th Century Art), London–New York, 1973. The latter includes most significant publications up until 1972. Important omissions from these bibliographies are: Jean Cassou and Jean Leymarie, *Léger, dessins et gouaches*, Paris, 1972 (a very lavish selection with much comparative material from related oil paintings); *Fernand Léger, sa vie, son oeuvre, sa rêve*, Milan, 1972 (a fascinating collection of photographs and documents the latter reproduced often in facsimile); *Hommage à Léger, XXe siècle*, Paris, Special Number 1972 (which includes a crucial 1919 letter to D. H. Kahnweiler, previously unpublished, in the essay 'Un Grand Normand roux'). I have used other material unmentioned in these bibliographies, mostly newspaper articles and most importantly Georges Charensol's report of an interview with Léger 'Chez Fernand Léger', *Paris Journal*, December 1924. This material can be extracted from the notes to this book, as can extensive bibliographical information on the avant-garde in Paris between 1909 and 1927. So wide is the range of subjects involved that a bibliography devoted to the avant-garde would have been too highly selective to have served any useful purpose here.

Notes

Introduction.

1. See Le Corbusier, *The City of Tomorrow*, London, 1929, pp. 107–26; translated by Frederick Etchells from *Urbanisme*, Paris, 1925.
2. *Art et Décoration*, Paris, July–December, 1903, p. 390.
3. See P. Reyner Banham, 'Machine Aesthetic', *Architectural Review*, London, 1955.
4. For more information on this, see pp. 288 and 289, below.

Chapter 1.

1. E.g. Wilhelm Uhde, Roger Dutilleul and Hermann Rupf; see D-H. Kahnweiler: *My Galleries and Painters*, London, 1971, pp. 37–8.
2. The contents of 'Salle 41' are described by Albert Gleizes; see *Souvenirs 1, Le Cubisme 1908–14*, privately published by Les Soins de l'Association des Amis d'A.G., 1957, p. 18.
3. Ibid., pp. 6–7 and 11.
4. See Daniel Robbins: 'From Symbolism to Cubism: The Abbaye of Créteil', *Art Journal*, 1963–4, pp. 111–16; Cf. M-L. Bidal: *Les Ecrivains de l'Abbaye*, Paris, 1938, pp. 8–11.
5. See Gleizes: op. cit., p. 12.
6. Ibid., p. 4.
7. Dora Vallier: 'La Vie fait l'oeuvre de Fernand Léger; Propos de l'artiste recuellis par Dora Vallier', *Cahiers d'Art*, Paris, 1954, p. 150.
8. Gleizes: op. cit., p. 13.
9. Gino Severini: *Tutta la vita di un pittore*, vol. 1, Rome–Paris, 1946, p. 172.
10. Gleizes, op. cit., p. 18.
11. Dora Vallier: op. cit., p. 149.
12. Ibid., p. 149.
13. First Académie Wassilief lecture, May 1913, in *Fonctions de la peinture*, Paris, 1965, p. 12.
14. Ibid., p. 14.
15. Cf. John Golding: *Cubism, a History and Analysis, 1907–1914*, London, 1968, pp. 147–8.
16. See M-L. Bidal: op. cit., pp. 33–4, 39–43.
17. Walt Whitman: *Feuilles d'herbe*, trans. Léon Bazalgette, Paris, 1909; Cf.

M-L. Bidal: op. cit., pp. 54–6.

18. See Georges Duhamel: 'Charles Vildrac et les hommes', *Vers et Prose*, January–February–March 1911, p. 105.

19. *Vers et Prose*, July–August–September 1911, pp. 122–9. *Vers et Prose* was edited by Paul Fort, a friend and mentor of the Abbaye poets, who was a leading personality at the Closérie des Lilas.

20. 'Paroles devant la femme enceinte', *Vers et Prose*, April–May–June 1911, pp. 125–36; 'Paroles devant la mort du juste', *Vers et Prose*, October–November–December 1911, pp. 120–8.

21. *Revue Indépendante*, September 1911, pp. 162–72.

22. Georges Duhamel: 'Jules Romains et les dieux', *Vers et Prose*, July–August–September 1910, pp. 114–15; 'Charles Vildrac et les hommes', *Vers at Prose*, January–February–March 1911, pp. 104–5.

23. Dora Vallier: op. cit., p. 149.

24. D-H. Kahnweiler: op. cit., p. 46. He wrongly dates the exhibiting of the *Nus* to 1910. Cf. Douglas Cooper: *Fernand Léger et le nouvel espace*, Geneva–Paris, 1949, p. 36, and Pierre Descargues: *Fernand Léger*, Paris, 1956, p. 28.

25. See Gustav Vriesen and Max Imdahl: *Robert Delaunay: Light and Colour*, Cologne–New York, 1967, p. 22.

26. Cf. John Golding: op. cit., p. 149.

27. A particularly telling comparison is between Léger's *Le Pont* of 1909 (Sidney and Harriet Janis collection, New York), and Braque's L'Estaque landscapes of 1908.

28. Orthon Friesz exhibited two other relevant works, both large and ambitious, at the Indépendants and the Salon d'Automne of 1908: *Travail d'Automne* and *L'Eté*.

29. The first two books of *Terrestre Tragédie* were published by the Abbaye de Créteil in 1907.

30. The book entitled *Le Bras* is given a third section entitled *La Force*, which begins: 'Invisible, elle court, ardente, les Espaces,/elle fait la lumière et tourne les Soleils,/Maîtresse universelle aux pouvoirs sans pareils,/elle forge les lois qui regissent les Masses./Invisible, elle court sans cesse les Espaces.'

31. 'Les bûcherons portèrent sur eux la trace des corps que leur cognée laissait aux arbres . . .' Guillaume Apollinaire: *Les Peintres cubistes, Méditations esthétiques*, Paris, 1965, p. 85. (1st edn, 1913.)

32. Cooper quotes Apollinaire as his justification; see op. cit., p. 35; Cf. Pierre Descargues: op. cit., pp. 23–6.

33. Cf. the French translation by Bazalgette, *Feuilles d'herbe*, Paris, 1909, vol. 1, p. 256.

34. The importance as a stimulus of the Cézanne *Baigneuses*, though several of these feature male bathers, suggests the possibility that Léger's nudes were female in origin, and this notion is supported by the treatment of the pelvic region in the standing nude on the left and by the long hair of all three nudes. However, Kahnweiler describes the painting thus: 'Es stellte dar Männer, zwischen Baumen,' and Léger makes so little of the sex of his figures that they are in effect adrogynous. See D-H. Kahnweiler: *Der Weg sum Kubismus*, Munich 1920, p. 47.

35. Gleizes: op. cit., p. 27.

36. I have been unable to discover the identity of the sitters.

37. The date of the move is disputed by Dr Virginia Spate, see n. 53 below.

38. The *Tour* exhibited in the 'Salle 41' was exhibited again in December 1911 at the first Blaue Reiter exhibition in Munich, where it was sold. It has since been destroyed. See Vriesen and Imdahl, op. cit., pp. 30, 36–8.

39. As theirs was a Cubism dependent on the earlier inventions of Picasso and Braque, it is legitimate to talk of the Cubism of Le Fauconnier, Gleizes, Metzinger, Léger, Delaunay (until 1912), Villon, Duchamp and de La Fresnaye as second-phase Cubism.

40. Cf. *La Vie Unanime*, Paris, 1908, as quoted by Virginia Spate: 'Orphism', unpublished Ph.D. thesis, 1970, p. 425.

41.　For a particularly striking account, see: Blaise Cendrars: Text published in *Aujourd'hui*, Paris, 1932.

42.　See John Golding: op. cit., p. 149.

43.　Albert Gleizes and Jean Metzinger: *Du Cubisme*, Paris, 1912, p. 12.

44.　Cf. Albert Gleizes: 'Jean Metzinger', *Revue Indépendante*, no. 4, September 1911, pp. 165–6: 'A la vérité purement objective, il veut ajouter une vérité nouvelle, née de ce que son intelligence lui aura permis de connaître. Ainsi qu'il le dit, lui-même. A l'*espace* il joindra la *durée*.'

45.　Tancrède de Visan: 'La Philosophie de M. Bergson et le Lyrisme contemporaine', *Vers et Prose*, April–May–June 1910, p. 125; Cf. M-L. Bidal: *Les Ecrivains de l'Abbaye*, Paris, 1938, p. 114.

46.　'La durée est le progres continu du passé qui ronge l'avenir et qui gonfle en avançant.' Henri Bergson: *L'Evolution créatrice*, Paris, 1927, p. 5.

47.　Ibid., p. 42.

48.　See George Heard-Hamilton and William C. Agee: *Raymond Duchamp-Villon, 1876–1918*, New York, 1967, p. 56.

49.　Jules Romains: *Mort de quelqu'un*, Paris, 1911. The novel takes as its central theme the theme of Henri Bergson's *Matière et mémoire* (Paris, 1896)—the living force of memory in the present. The novel describes the death of an obscure railway mechanic, and his continued life in the memories and consciences of those who knew him.

50.　Georges Duhamel: *René Arcos et Ce qui naît, Vers et Prose*, April–May–June 1911, p. 81.

51.　See Virginia Spate: op. cit., p. 204.

52.　Cf. Brian Petrie, 'Boccioni and Bergson', *The Burlington Magazine*, March 1974, pp. 140–7.

53.　The St Louis version was given as a wedding present to André Mare, and the late 1910 date of Mare's wedding has led Golding to postulate a late 1910 date for the canvas (see John Golding: op. cit., p. 152). This date Golding links with Léger's reported move in September 1910 to 13, rue de l'Ancienne Comédie from which studio the view was painted. However, Spate has demonstrated that there is at least a possibility that he did not move to this studio until 1911, and has pointed out that a lost version very close to the St Louis painting is reproduced in the first edition of Apollinaire's *Les Peintres cubistes* with the date 1911 (see Spate: op. cit., Chapter 4, note 20). Spate's suspicions seem to be borne out on stylistic grounds.

54.　For a fuller account, see Vriesen and Imdahl: op. cit., p. 34.

55.　Georges Duhamel: 'Jules Romains et les dieux', *Vers et Prose*, July–August–September 1910, p. 115.

56.　Emile Verhaeren: *Les Villes tentaculaires*, Paris, 1895, p. 114.

57.　Ibid., p. 211.

58.　Cf. Entretiens de Fernand Léger avec Blaise Cendrars et Louis Carré sur *Le Paysage dans l'oeuvre de Léger*, Paris, 1956, p. 21.

59.　This group of drawings is separated by style from another group of figure-drawings, some dated 1910 or 1911, also executed in thick-nibbed pen or quill on paper. Where the drawings of the other group are geometrically simplified, these drawings retain something of the organic complexities of the figure as observed and further complicate things by the use of mobile perspective. The preposterous dating of several drawings in the group (dates ranging from 1902 to 1905) have caused doubt about their position in the sequence of events, since the dates accompany signatures which could well be from the pre-1914 period. However, the problem does seem to have been solved by the sale at Parke-Bernet in New York in 1969 of the drawing (Plate 17), which is, as is explained below, a truncated version of *Femme nu* (Plate 16), and which has all the stylistic chracteristics of the group. The fact that this drawing was illustrated in the first edition of Gleizes and Metzinger's *Du Cubisme* with the caption (surely applied with Léger's knowledge) *Etude pour un abondance* indicates that it was made after the showing of Le Fauconnier's *L'Abondance* at the spring 1911 Indépendants. But, even more persuasive is the fact that the combination of bananas and pears at the side of the fruit-bowl are extracted almost unchanged from *Les Fumeurs*, a painting indisputably of 1911 or early 1912.

60.　Léger, Gleizes and Metzinger were all reported to have been visitors at Puteaux during 1912; Cf. Heard-Hamilton and Agee, op. cit., p. 589.

61.　In *Vers et Prose,* July–August–September 1911, pp. 125–30.

62.　Ibid., pp. 128–9.

63.　See Bergson: op. cit., p. 139.

64.　For the dating of this painting in relation to *La Noce,* see p. 43, below.

65.　These elements cut by means of line, and Léger's method is calculated to emphasize line. For *Les Fumeurs* he first lays in vital contours with the brush, and then painstakingly works up the broader, softer areas (smoke, clouds, curtains), so that they push against the outlines defined. Finally, where strategically necessary, these are separated as clear black accents, sometimes strengthened at the last moment.

Chapter 2.

1.　Having at an early date completely misunderstood and misrepresented the information she had given me, I feel a special debt of gratitude to Angelica Rudenstine of the Solomon R. Guggenheim Museum for her generosity in letting me see her information on *La Noce* and the 1912 Indépendants. It was she who pointed out that when *La Noce* was exhibited at Zurich in 1933 the Kunsthaus catalogue noted an inscription then visible on the reverse—'Composition avec personnages'; very convincing evidence. The first person to have suggested, on grounds of size and subject, that *La Noce* was the *Composition avec personnages* shown at the Indépendants was Virginia Spate. See 'Orphism', unpublished Ph.D. thesis, 1972, pp. 208–12.

2.　Léger's working method here, with the late strengthening of strategic linear accents, is very close to that of the *Fumées* and *Les Fumeurs*.

3.　*Table et fruit*, the relatively small still-life in the Minneapolis Art Institute, is another painting that announces Léger's move away from descriptive painting, its angular setting of planes having no overt descriptive purpose.

4.　Umberto Boccioni: *Gli scritti editi e inediti*, Milan, 1971, p. 7.

5.　Ibid., p. 7.

6.　Pär Bergmann: *Modernolatria e Simultaneitè*, Upsala, 1962, pp. 37–47.

7.　Marianne Martin points out that Marinetti wrote enthusiastically about the Abbaye in *Poesia*, 2, October–January 1906–7, p. 24; See Marianne Martin: 'Futurism, Unanimism and Apollinaire', *Art Journal*, Spring 1969, p. 259.

8.　See Marianne Martin: *Futurist Art and Theory, 1909–1915*, Oxford, 1968, p. 30.

9.　Ibid., p. 110.

10.　Ibid., pp. 109–19.

11.　*Archivi del Futurismo*, Rome, 1958, vol. 1, p. 106.

12.　Ibid., p. 108.

13.　Ibid., p. 105.

14.　Ibid., p. 106.

15.　Marianne Martin: 'Futurism, Unanimism and Apollinaire', *Art Journal*, spring 1969, pp. 265–7.

16.　Towards the close of *Mort de quelqu'un*, Romains exploits both a funeral and a riot as interpenetrating Unanimist images. The psychological force generated by the funeral *cortège* finally absorbs the physical force generated by the riot. See *Mort de quelqu'un*, Paris, 1923 (first edn, Paris, 1911), pp. 114–16.

17.　*Archivi del Futurismo*, Rome, 1958, vol. 1, p. 104.

18.　Ibid., p. 105.

19.　Gleizes in his *Baigneuses*, Delaunay in *La Ville de Paris*. Delaunay's painting in particular both uses the nude and is overtly allegorical. See Spate: op. cit., p. 140.

20. For a fuller discussion of the 'maison cubiste', see George Heard Hamilton and William C. Agee: *Raymond Duchamp-Villon, 1887–1918,* New York, 1967, pp. 65–9; and Marie Noel Pradel, 'La Maison Cubiste en 1912', *Art de France*, 1, 1961, p. 177.

21. For a fuller discussion of the 'Section d'Or', see John Golding: *Cubism, a history and analysis, 1907–1914,* London, 1968, pp. 159–63.

22. Ibid., pp. 161–2.

23. *Montjoie!* no. 1, 10 February 1913, p. 4.

24. For a fuller discussion of this subject, see Heard Hamilton and Agee: op. cit., pp. 59, 69; and William A. Camfield, 'Juan Gris and the Golden Section', *Art Bulletin*, March 1965, pp. 128–34.

25. My thanks are due to John Golding for having pointed out this parallel.

26. *Archivi del Futurismo*, Rome, 1958, vol. 1, p. 104.

27. Guillaume Apollinaire, 'Du sujet dans la peinture moderne', *Soirées de Paris*, no. 1, April 1912, p. 2.

28. Cf. Guillaume Apollinaire, 'Les trois vertus plastiques', in *Chroniques d'Art (1902–1918),* with a preface by L-C. Breunig, Paris, 1960, pp. 56–80.

29. This letter is quoted by Vriesen; see Gustav Vriesen and Max Imdahl, *Robert Delaunay. Light and Colour,* Cologne–New York, 1967, p. 38.

30. Cf. Virginia Spate: op. cit., pp. 150–8.

31. 'Du sujet dans la peinture moderne', op. cit., p. 4.

32. It is on this visit that Picabia is reported to have pointed out that a circle, triangle, volumes and colours are as intelligible as a table or a cup. See Gabrielle Buffet-Picabia: 'Recontre avec Apollinaire', *Le Point*, Paris, 1937, p. 189.

33. Dora Vallier: 'La Vie fait l'oeuvre de Fernand Léger; Propos de l'artiste recueillis par Dora Vallier', *Cahiers d'Art*, Paris, 1954, p. 150.

34. Guillaume Apollinaire: *Montjoie!* no. 3, 18 March 1913, p. 4.

35. See André Warnod: 'Fauves et Cubistes', *Comoedia*, 18 March 1913, pp. 1–2. I am very grateful to Angelica Rundenstine of the Solomon R. Guggenheim Museum for having indicated that *Le Modèle nu* was in fact shown, and to Dr Virginia Spate for having pointed out this article by Warnod.

36. The *Paysage*, now in the Vienna Kunsthistorisches Museum, and *Pasage à niveau* now in the Musée National Fernand Léger, Biot, both probably painted in the summer or autumn of 1912.

37. This landscape is closely related to the series of wash and gouache studies which culminate in *Le Modèle nu dans l'atelier* (Plate 30). These are definitely late 1912 and early 1913, since *Le Modèle nu* was painted for the spring 1913 Indépendants. See p. 53, below.

38. The *Nus descendant un escalier no. 2* had been rejected by the Indépendants earlier in 1912, largely, it seems, because its Futurist successive approach to movement offended anti-Futurist Cubist feelings, especially those of Gleizes. Cf. Pierre Cabanne and Marcel Duchamp: *Dialogues with Marcel Duchamp*, London, 1971, p. 31; and Arture Schwarz: *The Complete Works of Marcel Duchamp*, New York, 1969, p. 16.

39. Fernand Léger: 'Les Réalisations picturales actuelles,' *Soirées de Paris,* no. 25, 15 June 1914; in *Fonctions de la peinture,* Paris, 1965, p. 26.

40. Cf. *Marie Wassilief*, Galerie Hupel, Paris, June–July, 1969, and Andrei B. Nakov, *Alexandre Exter*, Galerie Jean Chauvelin, Paris, May–June 1972, p. 11. The Académie was at 21, avenue du Maine.

41. Fernand Léger, 'Les Origines de la peinture et sa valeur représentative', *Montjoie!*, 29 May and 14–29 June 1913; in Fernand Léger: op. cit., p. 11.

42. It is more likely that the study was adapted from the Biot than from the Basel version, since the wedge plane introduced from above to the right of the head is found in the Biot and not the Basel version, as are other features.

43. This process of geometric simplification is closely related to the process of simplification found in Léger's drawings from the nude made at the Académie de la Chaumière in 1909 and 1910.

44. Léger seems to have developed a type of study from the nude which ac-

centuated form at the expense of surface and line at this time. A good example is the 1913 drawing *Deux figures* (Ayala Zacks collection, Toronto), where rubbed pencil shading is used to accentuate the effect of three-dimensional volume.

45. Robert Delevoy: *Léger*, Paris–Geneva, 1962, p. 48.

46. Fernand Léger: op. cit., p. 11.

47. Ibid., p. 15.

48. The other oil related to *Les Maisons sous les arbres* is in a Chicago collection.

49. The ten oil versions of the 'kite device' theme known to me are in the following locations: Galerie Beyeler, Basel (1971); Galerie Rosengart, Lucerne; the Louis Carré collection, France; the Heinz Berggruen collection, Paris; the Museum of Modern Art, New York (Colour Plate 2); the Solomon R. Guggenheim collection, New York; the Rupf collection, Bern; the Arensberg collection, Philadelphia Museum of Art; Sotheby's, London, 1974; and the Kunstsammlung Nordrhein-Westfalen, Düsseldorf.

50. There are two major exceptions, the *Contrastes de formes* now in the Musée National d'Art Moderne, Paris, and the *Eléments géométriques* in a Parisian private collection. See *Fernand Léger*, Musée des Arts Décoratifs, Paris, 1956, p. 102, no. 17, for the latter.

Chapter 3.

1. 'Nous arrivons, j'en suis persuadé, à une conception d'art aussi vaste que les plus grandes époques précédentes: même tendance aux grandes dimensions, même effort partagé par une collectivité . . . La plupart des mouvements littéraires et artistiques français se sont, en général, manifestés de la même manière.' Fernand Léger: 'Les Origines de la Peinture et sa Valeur représentative', *Montjoie!*, 29 May 1913, and 14–29 June 1913; in *Fonctions de la Peinture*, Paris, 1965, p. 16.

2. Gustav Vriesen and Max Imdahl: *Robert Delaunay, Colour and Light*, Cologne–New York, 1967, p. 65.

3. *Montjoie!* no. 1, 10 February 1913, p. 1.

4. Cf. Vriesen and Imdahl: op. cit., p. 60.

5. Henri-Martin Barzun: 'La Génération des temps dramatiques et la "beauté nouvelle"', *Poème et Drame*, vol. 2, January 1913, p. 41.

6. Cf. Fernand Léger: op. cit., p. 16.

7. *Poème et Drame*, July 1913, p. 62.

8. That Delaunay himself was convinced is made clear by the notes he collected during the summer of 1912, which were published by Apollinaire in *Soirées de Paris*, December 1912, under the significant title 'Réalité—peinture pure'.

9. Cf. Guillaume Apollinaire: *Les Peintures cubistes, Meditations esthétiques*, Paris (Editions Figuière), 1913; Introduction by L-C. Breunig and J-Cl. Chevalier, Paris, 1965, p. 57.

10. The bare bones of Delaunay's colour theory and usage have been very cleary elucidated by Max Imdahl; see Vriesen and Imdahl: op. cit., pp. 71–85.

11. Robert Delaunay: 'La Lumière', in Vriesen and Imdahl: op. cit., p. 6.

12. Spate has established that a study of Leonardo da Vinci's *Trattato della Pittura*, then recently translated into French, supported Delaunay's rejection of successive effects, for Leonardo insisted that the factor essential to painting was that it makes its impact all at once. See Virginia Spate: 'Orphism', unpublished Ph.D. thesis, 1970, pp. 151–6.

13. Early in 1911, as part of its programme of experimental *matinées*, Georges Duhamel's play *La Lumière* was put on by the Théâtre de l'Odéon; it was serialized in *Vers et Prose* in the summer and winter of 1911, and late in 1911 was the subject of much discussion. The coincidence of titles linking the play to Delaunay's text 'La Lumière', seems to be significant, since the play deals with a theme so profoundly in tune with Delaunay's ideas: the basic conflict between light as a mere sensation, and light as understanding. Anticipating with remarkable aptness Delaunay's

Fenêtres, he uses as the culminating visual image of the first two acts of the play, a window, through which the light of a mountain landscape pours. However, Duhamel does not share Delaunay's faith in the *sensation* of light, for the final part of the play demonstrates the superiority of the conception of light as understanding over the conception of light as sensation.

14. Vriesen and Imdahl: op. cit., p. 6.

15. Ibid., p. 62.

16. Ibid., p. 61.

17. This roughness of preparation and execution is a feature of *all* the variants, whatever their size, and so the point made is generally applicable.

18. 'Je voulais arriver à des tons qui s'isolent: un rouge très rouge, un bleu très bleu.' Fernand Léger, quoted by André Verdet in *Fernand Léger, Le Dynamisme pictural*, Geneva, 1955.

19. See 'Entretiens de Fernand Léger avec Blaise Cendrars et Louis Carré sur *Le Paysage dans l'oeuvre de Léger*', Paris, 1956, p. 66.

20. For a fuller discussion of this topic, see Robert Goffin: *Entrer en poésie*, Paris, 1948, and Michel Decaudin: 'Le Changement de front d'Apollinaire', *Revue des Sciences humaines*, November–December 1966, pp. 255–60.

21. Cf. Pär Bergmann: *Modernolatria e Simultaneità*, Upsala, 1962, pp. 376 and 257.

22. According to André Billy, *Fenêtres* was one of the first *poèmes conversations*, taking extracts from a conversation between himself, Pierre Dalize and Apollinaire. Ibid., p. 394.

23. For a fuller discussion of this problem of links between the poems, see Pär Bergmann: op. cit., pp. 311–12, and Scott-Bates: *Apollinaire*, New York, 1967, chapter 5, note 4, pp, 181–2.

24. By the end of 1912 it seems that Cendrars had met Apollinaire. Cendrars himself suggests the early summer of 1912; see Michel Manoll and Blaise Cendrars: *Blaise Cendrars vous parle*, Paris, 1952, p. 137; Delaunay implies late 1912, see 'Du Cubisme à l'art abstrait', ed. Pierre Francastel, Paris, 1957, p. 111.

25. Blaise Cendrars: *Prose du Transsibérien et de la petite Jehanne de France*, in *Du Monde entier*, Paris, 1967, p. 40.

26. Cf. 'Une vieille paire de chaussures jaunes devant la fenêtre/Tours/Les tours ce sont les rues/Puits/Puits ce sont les places/Puits.' Guillaume Apollinaire: *Les Fenêtres*, in *Calligrammes*, Paris, 1966, p. 25.

27. Perhaps this is why in *Journal*, written in August 1913, Cendrars could look back over the previous year and remark with perceptible dissatisfaction: 'J'ai même voulu devenir peintre.' In *Du Monde entier*, p. 69.

28. See Delaunay: op. cit., p. 111.

29. Cendrars: op. cit., p. 33.

30. The idea of *parole in libertà* was first expounded by Marinetti in his technical manifesto of Futurist literature (May 1912); see *Opere di F. T. Marinetti*, Milan, 1968, vol. 2, pp. 40–54.

31. See Vriesen and Imdahl: op. cit., p. 56.

32. Guillaume Apollinaire: *Montjoie!*, Supplement no. 3, 18 March 1913, p. 4.

33. See Fernand Léger: op. cit., p. 20.

34. Ibid., p. 20.

35. Ibid., p. 21.

36. Ibid., p. 25.

37. Cendrars later recalled that they met in 1911, but his memory seems a little uncertain, and it is unlikely that they met before Cendrars met Delaunay in the second half of 1912. See Léger, Cendrars and Carré: op. cit.

38. Blaise Cendrars: *Tour,* in *Du Monde entier*, p. 73.

39. Sebastien Voirol: *Le Sacre du Printemps, Poeme et Drame*, vol. 6, September–October 1913, p. 15, and 'A propos du *Sacre du Printemps*', *Poème et Drame*, Paris, vol. 6, September–October 1913, pp. 28–9.

40. Igor Stravinsky: 'Ce que j'ai voulu exprimer dans *Le Sacre du Printemps*', *Montjoie!* no. 8, May 1913, p. 2.

41.　It was in the autumn number that the first extracts of Polyphonic ('Drama-tiste') poetry appeared. The controversy that followed, involving Apollinaire, Cendrars and Barzun, was fought in the pages of *Paris-Journal, Gil-Blas* and *Soirées de Paris.*

42.　Henri-Martin Barzun: *Poème et Drame,* vol. 2, January 1913, p. 39.

43.　In *Poème et Drame,* vol. 3, March 1913, p. 24.

44.　Carrà's letter is dated 12 June 1913; in *Archivi del Futurismo,* Rome, 1958, vol. 1, p. 271. Spate mentions the letter and attempts an extensive comparison between *Le Modèle nu* and *Simultaneità,* the 1912 figure painting by Carrà. See Spate: op. cit., pp. 225–6.

45.　See Marianne Martin: *Futurist Art and Theory, 1909–15,* Oxford, 1968, p. 143, note 3.

46.　See Gino Severini: Preface to the catalogue of the exhibition of Severini, Marlborough Gallery, London, April 1913.

47.　See Gino Severini: 'Tutta la vita di un pittore', pp. 187–92.

48.　Umberto Boccioni: *Gli scritti editi e inediti,* Milan, 1971, p. 53.

49.　Marinetti continually returned to the theme of conflict: in December 1911 he acted as enthusiastic war correspondent in Libya, and his first attempt at *parole in libertà* was *Battaglia Peso – Odore,* written in August 1912 and inspired by the war in Libya. See Bergmann: op. cit., pp. 90–2.

50.　Cf. Fernand Léger: op. cit., p. 26.

51.　Fernand Léger: 'L'Esthétique de la machine: l'objet fabriqué, l'artisan et l'artiste' *Der Querschnitt,* vol. 3, 1923, and *Bulletin de l'Effort Moderne,* January 1924; in *Fonctions de là peinture,* pp. 61–2.

52.　Dora Vallier: op. cit., p. 140. Léger did not exhibit at the Salon d'Automne between 1912 and the publication of his essay 'L'Esthétique de la machine' in 1923. This means that the recollection in this essay is certainly 1911 or 1912. Léger is not mentioned in the catalogues of either the 1911 or the 1912 Salon d'Automne as one of the *membres de bureau* assisting in organization and hanging, but there was good reason for him to be involved in installation work at the 1912 Salon, since it was here that the *maison cubiste* was built. Both he and Marcel Duchamp were contributors, and it was an elaborate enough installation to have required the help of contributors. That the recollection included in the Dora Vallier inter-view also refers to 1912 is suggested by Duchamp's reported remark on seeing the wooden propellors: 'C'est fini la peinture. Qui ferait mieux que cette hélice,' for it is a remark very much in tune with *Broyeuse de chocolate No. 1,* his contri-bution to the Salon d'Automne of 1912, but not with *Portrait, Dulcinea,* his con-tribution to the Salon d'Automne of 1911.

53.　Not only do all the variations on the 'kite device' theme closely related to the Philadelphia *Contrastes* reveal telling differences, but Léger did make at least two attempts to transform the theme dramatically, in a variant recently exhibited at the Galerie Beyeler, where wholesale colour changes are made, and in the *Variations de formes* recently exhibited at the Lefevre Gallery, London, where colour changes are accompanied by formal changes which follow from a horizontal rather than a vertical format.

54.　The major variant on this theme is *L'Escalier, 2e état,* dated '14' on the re-verse (Harold Diamond collection, New York).

55.　There are further versions in the collection of Dr Emil Freidrich, Zurich, and the Museum of Modern Art, New York. The latter is known as *Exit les Ballets russes.*

56.　This is one of a group of gouaches, one a study for the other *Escalier* theme, all of which are dated '13'. They have a quick, decisive technique, an initialled signature, and the title in pencil. They are all inscribed 'dessins'.

57.　In view of Léger's remark in the second Académie Wassilief lecture that Cézanne need not actually have set out his objects for his still-lifes, the probability is that these still-lifes were painted from memory. See Fernand Léger: op. cit., p. 13.

58.　Dora Vallier: op. cit., p. 151.

59. It should be added that brown primer is often used instead of grey. With this qualification, the present writer knows of *no* painting from the spring 1913–August 1914 period not executed as described.

60. See Virginia Spate: op. cit., p. 189.

61. Ibid., p. 349.

62. *La Pittura futurista, Manifesto tecnico* (11 April 1910), in Umberto Boccioni, op. cit., p. 11. Also note the importance given to intuition in the creation of force-lines in the Bernheim-Jeune catalogue. *Archivi del futurismo*, Rome, 1958, vol. 1, p. 107.

63. Quoted from 'Revisione del futurismo' by Pär Bergmann: op. cit., p. 114.

64. Henri Bergson: *L'Evolution créatrice*, Paris, 1927, pp. 191–2.

65. Cf. Georges Duhamel: 'René Arcos et *Ce qui naît*, *Vers et Prose*, April–May–June 1911, p. 81.

66. F. T. Marinetti: *Le Futurisme*, Paris, 1911; in *Opere di F. T. Marinetti*, Milan, 1968, vol. 1.

67. Henri Bergson: op. cit.

68. René Gillouin: 'Bergson et Anti-Bergsonisme', *Montjoie!* no. 4, 29 March 1913, p. 6.

69. Examples of groups of gouache *dessins*, which show themes in an early unformed state, are the *dessins* for *La Femme en rouge et vert*, and for *L'Escalier*. These are often inscribed in pencil: 'dessin pour', followed by the title of the theme.

70. Fernand Léger: op. cit., p. 15.

71. Ibid., p. 21.

72. I know of only two exceptions: one recently in the galerie Beyeler, Basel, and one in the Kunstsammlung Nordrhein-Westfalen, Düsseldorf. Both are variations on the 'kite device' theme.

73. Fernand Léger: op. cit., p. 25–6.

74. Ibid., p. 26.

Chapter 4.

1. Blaise Cendrars: 'Modernités 6, Fernand Léger', *La Rose Rouge*, 3 July 1919, in *Aujourd'hui*, Paris, 1931, p. 121.

2. Ibid., pp. 121–2.

3. Cendrars and Léger were close at this time, see pp. 163–66, below. The reference to 'la culasse du 75' exactly echoes the image first used by Léger when writing his *Pensées* for Léonce Rosenberg, see Fernand Léger: 'Pensées', *Valori Plastici*, Rome, February–March 1919, p. 3.

4. Fernand Léger: 'Correspondance', March 1922, *Bulletin de l'Effort Moderne*, no. 4, April 1924, p. 10.

5. Cendrars maintains that he was completely isolated from the avant-garde while on the front, see *La Main Coupée*, Paris, 1946, p. 287.

6. Douglas Cooper in *Fernand Léger, Dessins de guerre*, Paris, 1956.

7. The documents known to me are reproduced in *Fernand Léger, sa vie, son oeuvre, sa rêve*, Milan, 1972.

8. Cooper: op. cit., no page number.

9. Its position relating to the front, on the main route, indicates this, as does the title of the shell-case *collage, Les Chevaux, dans le cantonnement*, 1915, private collection, France, which is inscribed 'Le Neufour Sept. 15'. For illustration, see *Fernand Léger*, Musée des Arts Décoratifs, Paris, 1956, p. 113. The term 'first line' used here means the foremost line in the front.

10. See General J. Roquerol: *La Guerre en Argonne*, Paris, 1937, pp. 127–83.

11. Ibid., p. 155.

12. Ibid., p. 10.

13. That the 'A' stands specifically for 'Aisne' is indicated by a gouache study closely related to those thus inscribed and exactly the same size, which is in-

scribed more fully: 'front de l'Aisne'; see illustration in Maurice Jardot: *F. Léger, Dessins et gouaches, 1909–55,* Paris, 1956, Plate 7.

14.   General J. Roquerol: *Le Drame de Douaumont,* Paris, 1931, pp. 92–102.

15.   Cf. Dora Vallier, 'La Vie fait l'oeuvre de Fernand Léger, propos de l'artiste recuellis par Dora Vallier', *Cahiers d'Art,* 1954, p. 140.

16.   *Fernand Léger, sa vie, son oeuvre, sa rêve,* no page number.

17.   This is indicated by the generally peaceful nature of the studies executed on 24 October. The attack involved four front-line divisions, three second-line and two reserve divisions. See Rouquerol: op. cit., p. 111.

18.   Quoted in Cooper: op. cit., no. 42.

19.   Dora Vallier: op. cit., p. 140.

20.   See Henri Barbusse: *Le Feu,* Paris, 1916, pp. 134–5.

21.   Ibid., p. 232.

22.   *Fondazione e Manifesto del Futurismo,* February 1909; in *Opere di F. T. Marinetti,* Milan, 1968, vol. 2, p. 10.

23.   Ibid., pp. 291–3.

24.   Ibid., p. 282.

25.   Ibid., p. 287.

26.   It was French military practice at Verdun to keep units in the first line for no more than three or four days at a time. See B. H. Liddell-Hart: *History of the First World War,* London, 1970, pp. 285–301.

27.   Cendrars makes it very clear that he was not averse to action; see *La Main coupée,* Paris, 1946, pp. 32–42 and 213–23.

28.   Barbusse: op. cit., p. 20; cf. Cendrars: op. cit., p. 29.

29.   Cendrars quotes himself in conversation with a general who was surprised at his highly irregular photographic career, and it is here that he outlines the range of subjects given above. See Cendrars: op. cit., p. 199.

30.   *Le Miroir,* 8 October 1916, p. 11.

31.   *Le Miroir,* 16 July 1916, p. 12. Including one photograph of the rue Mazel, a subject drawn by Léger.

32.   *Le Miroir,* 8 October 1916.

33.   Curiously enough, this comparison between the subjects of the war photographers and of Léger was first suggested to me in the course of conversations with John House of the University of East Anglia about Monet.

34.   See Blaise Cendrars: op. cit., pp. 223–4.

35.   *Le Miroir* published the following notice every week: 'Le Miroir paie n'importe quel prix les documents photographiques rélatifs à la guerre, présentant un intérêt particulier,' which indicates a broad base of soldier photographers, like Cendrars.

36.   Barbusse: op. cit., pp. 19–20.

37.   Cendrars: op. cit., p. 283.

38.   *L'Elan,* no. 6, 1 July 1915, no page number.

39.   In this instance the overlappings of coloured pieces of paper indicate that the white pigment was added before the colour, not, as in the 1913–14 paintings, after the colour. This is also the case in the *papier-colleé, Les Chevaux dans le canton-nement,* 1915, which is inscribed 'Le Neufour/Sept 15/F.Léger.' Illustrated in *Fernand Léger,* Musée des Arts Décoratifs, Paris, 1956, p. 113.

40.   The text of the postcard is quoted Cooper, op. cit., no page number.

41.   Cooper groups one of these drawings with others executed between July 1915 and January 1916. However, the often legible inscriptions (cf. Plate 66) dating closely comparable drawings to December 1916 coupled with the fact that Verdun was not bombarded until after February 1916 make it probable that in this instance he is mistaken. Ibid., no. 12.

42.   Blaise Cendrars, *J'ai Tué,* Paris, 1918; in *Aujourd'hui,* Paris, 1931, p. 26.

43.   Cf. *Opere di F. T. Marinetti,* pp. 84–92.

44.   See Cooper's dating of the group, Cooper: op. cit., no page number.

45.   There is a second version of this study, also in pen, the same size and inscribed 'Fragment F. Léger'; see the catalogue of the Christies' sale, 4 July 1969.

46. *Opere di F. T. Marinetti*, vol. 1.

47. Cendrars: op. cit., pp. 32–3.

48. Léger's starting point was the quick on-the-spot pencil sketch, and several of these survive; that the series came to its culminating phase in December is demonstrated by the fact that the water-colour study in the Museum of Modern Art, New York, is inscribed December 1916.

49. Dora Vallier: op. cit., p. 151.

50. See Gino Severini: *Tutta la vita di un pittore*, vol. 1, Rome–Paris, 1946, p. 235.

51. For an account of the circumstances in which the war paintings were executed, see ibid., pp. 236–7.

52. *Sic*, no. 2, February 1916, p. 5.

53. Gino Severini: op. cit., p. 242.

54. See Ibid., pp. 242, 243, 259, 260. It was Gris who introduced Léonce Rosenberg to Severini in 1916; see Gino Severini: *Tempo de l'Effort Moderne. Tutta la vita di un pittore*, Nuovedizione Enrico Valecchi, 1968, pp. 22–3.

55. That autumn Severini marked the death of his old Futurist companion Boccioni with a commemorative article in *Sic* accompanied by a portrait, straight-forwardly representational, which retained in its clarity a reminiscence of Ingres. See *Sic*, no. 8–9–10, August–September–October 1918, p. 3.

56. Ibid., p. 10.

57. Gino Severini: 'La Peinture de l'Avant-garde', *Mercure de France*, June 1917; in *Témoignages; 50 ans de reflexions*, Rome, 1963, p. 58.

58. Ibid., pp. 58–9.

59. Ibid., p. 62.

60. According to Maritain, it was in 1917 that Severini met Charles Henry; see Jacques Maritain: *Severini*, Paris, 1930, p. 8. Severini also himself writes of their friendship; see *Tempo de l'Effort Moderne*. pp. 196–8.

61. Ibid., pp. 66–8.

62. See Severini: *Tutta la vita di un pittore*, vol. 1, p. 249.

63. See 'Curiculum Vitae de l'Effort Modern', *Bulletin de l'Effort Moderne*, no. 1, January 1924, p. 3.

64. *Nord-Sud*, no. 1, March 1917, p. 3.

65. Ibid., p. 3.

66. *Nord-Sud*, no. 7, August–September 1917, p. 6.

67. Ibid., p. 5.

68. Amédée Ozenfant, *Mémoires*, Paris, 1968, p. 91.

69. Pierre Reverdy: 'Sur le cubisme', *Nord-Sud*, no. 1, March 1917, pp. 6–7.

70. *Sic*, no. 11, November 1916, p. 6.

71. Ozenfant quotes from Plato's *Philebus*, in *L'Elan*, no. 9, February 1916, no page number. The reference given here is: 'Platon. *Oeuvres complètes*, Charpentier, IV.517 SQ.'

72. The oil is not dated, but on stylistic grounds 1918 seems the right date.

73. *Sic*, November 1916, op. cit., p. 6.

74. There can be no doubt that *Madame Cézanne (après Cézanne)*, drawings and 1918 painting, was also a declaration of allegiance to the French tradition as written about before the war by Metzinger and Gleizes.

75. According to Léonce Rosenberg, Severini became a L'Effort Moderne artist in 1916, Metzinger in 1915. See 'Curriculum Vitae de l'Effort Moderne', *Bulletin de l'Effort Moderne*, no. 1, January 1924, p. 3. Lhote was not a l'Effort Moderne painter, but he contributed to *L'Elan* no. 9, and attended l'Effort Moderne openings; cf. Pierre Albert-Birot; *Chroniques quelquefois rimée, Vernissage, Sic*, Paris, no. 28, April 1918, p. 2. He is relevant in this context because he lived at 86, rue Notre-Dame-des-Champs, Léger's new Montparnasse studio address.

76. See *L'Esprit Nouveau*, no. 25.

77. The capricious synthetic Cubism with strong decorative qualities that Picasso practised alongside his more severe Cubist experiments, influencing in particular Serge Férat, was not backed by a clear and coordinated sense of purpose,

while Picasso's exploration of representational styles was as yet in its early stages and had attracted few allies.

78. Georges Braque: 'Pensées et réflexions', *Nord-Sud*, no. 10, December 1917, p. 3.

79. The only Paris leave mentioned by commentators who had access to Léger is that in which *Le Soldat à la pipe* was painted; see Douglas Cooper: *Léger et le nouvel espace*, Geneva–Paris, 1949, p. 52, and Pierre Descarques: *Fernand Léger*, Paris, 1956, p. 38. He could only have kept the most tenuous contact with his friends by postcards and letters.

80. The date of this leave was some time between Apollinaire's return in June 1916 and Léger's postcard to Jeanne of 15 September announcing his departure for the autumn counter-offensive at Verdun, for he recalls a visit while in Paris with Apollinaire to what was his first Chaplin film. Cf. Robert Delevoy, *Léger*, Geneva–Paris, 1962, p. 59.

81. Apollinaire contributed to *L'Elan* nos. 9 and 10 (February and December 1916), and to *Sic* nos. 7, 8, 9 and 10 (July–October 1916).

82. One should perhaps be careful not to invest this inscription with too much importance as a symptom of a changed approach, since 1913–14 themes like *La Femme en rouge et vert* were also backed by studies described 'dessins pour . . .'.

83. The work was completed at the hôpital Villepinte, only a few kilometers from Paris, where renewed contact with friends in the avant-garde would not have been difficult.

Chapter 5.

1. Fernand Léger: 'Pensées', *Valori Plastici*, Rome, February–March 1919, p. 3.

2. See *Fernand Léger, sa vie, son oeuvre, sa rêve*, Milan, 1972, no page number.

3. This exhibition is wrongly dated in *Léger and Purist Paris*, Tate Gallery, London, 1970, p. 40. A short criticism in *L'Intransigeant*, 17 February 1919 fixes the date to that month.

4. See Roger Garaudy: *Pour un réalisme du XX siècle. dialogue posthume avec F. Léger*, Paris, 1968, p. 48. Quoted from an unpublished manuscript.

5. A 1918 date for the Stuttgart version is indicated by the many *pentimenti* visible. These all represent changes away from formal combinations which are not found in the Moscow *Composition* towards formal combinations which *are* found there. As the Moscow *Composition* is dated '18' and as there is no other cylinder painting known to me which was not either executed or at least begun in 1918, it seems clear that the painting is wrongly dated; cf. *Léger and Purist Paris*, p. 38. Another oil variant on the theme is the *Cylindres colorés* (Louis Carré collection).

6. Related oils are the *Contrastes de formes* dated 1918 (Armand P. Bartos collection, New York), the *Contrastes de formes* of 1918 (Daniel and Eleanor Saidenberg collection, New York), and the *Eléments mécaniques* dated 1918 (Joseph Hazen collection, New York).

7. Quoted in D-H. Kahnweiler, 'Un Grand Normand roux', *Hommage à Léger*, Paris, numéro speciale de *XXe Siècle*, 1972, p. 4.

8. That Léger thought in fully three-dimensions from the outset is demonstrated by the very sketchy preliminary oil on the theme of the Basel *Eléments* now in the Musée National Fernand Léger, Biot, where a *chairoscuro* treatment of volumes is already evident. This painting is dated 1913 in *Fernand Léger*, Staatliche Kunsthalle, Baden-Baden, 1967, no. 3. However, the date on the canvas can equally easily be read as '18', and the tonal treatment of volumes plus the close relationship with the 1918 Basel *Eléments* theme convincingly support such a reading.

9. Such sketches were made at Villepinte, e.g. the study for *Le Pot à tisane* (Chicago Art Institute) which is signed and dated '17'.

10.   See *Fernand Léger*: Grand Palais, Paris, December 1971–January 1972, p. 9.

11.   The canvas is inscribed on the reverse: 'Les hélices/2e état. Juin 18. F. Léger.'

12.   A horizontal format is also found in another oil version, now lost, reproduced in D-H. Kahnweiler, *Der Weg zum Kubismus*, Munich, 1920, as Abb. 36, and captioned 'Der Moteur' with the date 1919.

13.   The watercolour is now in the Musée de peinture et sculpture, Grenoble.

14.   I have been able to study few early *états* of disintegrated themes; however, certainly the *Typographe, esquisse* of 1919 (Kröller-Müller museum, Otterlo), and, among the cylinder paintings, both the Stuttgart *Etude pour La Partie de cartes* (Plate 83) and the *Eléments mécaniques* (Joseph Hazen collection, New York) are coarsely worked and expose their *pentimenti* without attempted concealment.

15.   Other examples known to me where a comparable smoothness of finish is seen, are: *Composition, Le Typographe*, 1919 (Harold Diamond collection) (Colour Plate 5), the Basel *Eléments mécaniques* of 1918–23 (Plate 85), and the simultanist *états définitifs*: *Les Acrobates dans le cirque* (Plate 109) and *Le Remorqueur* (Plate 105), both 1918.

16.   The most obvious example of this is the oil *Cirque Médrano* (Plate 108), where both the rough speed of the guide-drawing and its detailed completeness is clear. Other 1918 examples are the *état définitif* of *Le Remorqueur* (Plate 105), and the study for *Les Acrobates dans le cirque* (private collection, Paris): Léger has superimposed a grid for squaring-up over the latter.

17.   Another variant was sold as Lot 99 in the Drouot sale of 6 February 1928. The catalogue notes measurements of 65 × 54 cm., and the title and date inscribed on the reverse: *Le Damier jaune*, 11–18. The work is now lost.

18.   The relationship between object and painting is not at all clear in the paintings of late 1917 and earlier 1918, for instance *Compotier, pipe et journal* (Basel Kunstmuseum, inventory number G 1956.24), dated 11–17. or *L'Homme au violon*, Moderna Museet, Stockholm, 1918.

19.   Katherine Kuh accepts the 1917–18 dating of this painting provided by the canvas itself, see *Léger*, The Art Institute of Chicago, in collaboration with the Museum of Modern Art, New York, and the San Francisco Museum of Art, 1953, p. 25. However, the evidence suggests persuasively a 1919 date. The less faded white paint of the date on the canvas indicates that it was added later, and it is known from the present owner that the work remained with Léger until after his arrival in New York when it was sold to Mrs Meric Callery, so the addition could have been more than twenty years later. More important, though, is the *Composition*'s relationship with the Philadelphia version; this is larger than either of the 1919 dated versions in Otterlo and the galerie Moderner Kunst, Munich, and its solids are only partially flattened as if representing a halfway stage between these smaller versions and *Composition*, suggesting for both a later 1919 date. The date given in *Léger and Purist Paris*, p. 98, is therefore probably mistaken too.

20.   The possibility that it might have been the study from which Léger worked on *Le Soldat à la pipe* is indicated by the fact that in the 1916 painting an alternative hand emerges from beneath the wrist of the raised arm treated and positioned exactly as the hand is in Plate 97.

21.   It is listed as having been in the collection of Mrs Meric Callery in Douglas Cooper, *Fernand Léger et le nouvel espace*, Geneva–Paris, 1949, p. 190.

22.   Cf. Letter from F. Léger to D-H. Kahnweiler, quoted in 'Un Grand Normand roux, *Hommage à Léger'*, p. 4.

23.   Pierre Reverdy, 'Sur le cubisme', *Nord-Sud*. no. 1, March 1917, p. 6.

Chapter 6.

1.   Blaise Cendrars: 'Modernités, I, Quelle sera la nouvelle peinture?', *La Rose Rouge*, 3 May 1919; in *Aujourd'hui*, Paris, 1931, p. 98.

2.   Ibid., pp. 99–100.

3. *Le Moteur* itself is presented here in a horizontal format, closer to the pencil study (Plate 93) than to the oil version in the Gaffé collection (Plate 91).

4. Paul Dermée: 'Un Prochain Age classique', *Nord-Sud*, no. 11, January 1918, p. 3.

5. The October publication of *Aquarium* was announced in *Sic*, no. 21–2, September–October 1917.

6. Cf. the use of mechanical and communications imagery in *Rose de Vents*, published in *Nord-Sud*, no. 14, April 1918, and the use of the Eiffel tower image in, for instance, *Escalade*, published in *Sic. Paris*. no. 29, May 1918, with the last line: 'La Tour Eiffel lance ses rayons aux îles Sandwich.'

7. *Sic*, no. 24, December 1917, p. 4. A particularly striking instance of his purely verbal simultanism is *Métro*, in *Sic*, no. 14, February 1917.

8. Pierre Reverdy, 'L'Image', *Nord-Sud*, no. 13, March 1918, p. 2.

9. The play opened on 24 June 1917 at the théâtre Maubel. *Sic*, no. 18, June 1917, was a special number devoted to it.

10. Cf. Blaise Cendrars and Michel Manoll: *Blaise Cendrars vous parle . . .*, Paris, 1952, p. 237.

11. In *Sic*, no. 23, November 1917, p. 2.

12. Cf. 'Note I sur le cinema', *Sic*, no. 25, January 1918, pp. 2–3, and '23 heures', *Sic*, no. 35, December 1918.

13. Luis Aragon, on Pierre Reverdy's *Les Ardoises du toit. Sic.* no. 29, May 1918, p. 5.

14. Cendrars was close to Apollinaire just before his death. He visited him while he was ill, attended his funeral (with Léger), and it was he who corrected the proofs of *Le Flaneur des deux rives*; see Cendrars and Manoll: op. cit., p. 254, and Blaise Cendrars: *Bourlinger*, Paris, 1948: Paris, Port de Mer, note 17.

15. See Blaise Cendrars: *L'Homme foudroyé*, Paris, 1945, p. 173.

16. Cf. Cendrars and Manoll: op. cit., pp. 246–7.

17. Dora Vallier: 'La Vie fait l'oeuvre de Fernand Léger; propos de l'artiste recuellis par Dora Vallier', *Cahiers d'Art*, Paris, 1954, p. 149.

18. It is possible that he was in contact with Cendrars at this time, since he was certainly in contact with Paris, a fact demonstrated by the April 1918 publication of his two Villepinte drawings in *Nord-Sud*.

19. Information given by Sonia Delaunay to the present writer in answer to a questionnaire. It seems that Cendrars had the key to the Delaunay's studio at 3, rue des Grands Augustins, though the large canvases of 1913–14 were not stored there.

20. See Blaise Cendrars and Manoll: op. cit., p. 254.

21. In *Aujourd'hui*, Paris, 1931. Fragments in: *Les Hommes du jour*, 8 February 1919; *La Rose Rouge*, 12 June 1919; *Promenoir*, Lyon, May 1921; *Cosmopolis*. Madrid, September 1921; *Les Environs Revins*, 1926; *Der Querschnitt*. Berlin, 15 January 1931. It is dated by Cendrars 7 November 1917 and 21 April 1921.

22. Ibid., p. 57.

23. Philippe Soupault: 'Note I sur le cinéma', *Sic*. no. 25, January 1918, pp. 2–3.

24. There is another version, very close in treatment to *Le Marinier*, in the Walraf-Richartz Museum, Cologne, *Le Remorqueur rose*.

25. No other versions are known to me.

26. The Laurens exhibition was held in December 1918.

27. Cendrars had even travelled with a circus during 1916, accompanying his gypsy friend from the front, Sawo; see Blaise Cendrars, *L'Homme foudroyé*, p. 171.

28. The *Esquisse pour les Acrobates dans le cirque* is in a French private collection; there is also a study for the left part of the composition, and the oil *Les Deux Acrobates dans le cirque* (Norman Granz collection, Geneva) is a study for the right part. That the *Esquisse* came first in the sequence, and did not immediately precede the final *état*, is indicated by the fact that the clown's head is still fragmented and the disc remains a major element as in the study for the left part of the composition. This use of a rough oil *esquisse* as the first stage in the final

process of development was, of course, conventional academic practice, and so too was the use of studies to investigate particular parts of the composition.

29.   Especially, of course, in Delaunay's Unanimist allegory *La Ville de Paris*. For Barzun, see Henri-Martin Barzun, *Voix et Acclamations de la Ville* in *Poème et Drame*, vol. 6, September 1913.

30.   Cf. Pierre Albert-Birot, *Métro. Sic.* Paris, no. 14, February 1917.

31.   Blaise Cendrars: *Profond Aujourd'hui*, Paris, 1917; in *Aujourd'hui*, pp. 10 and 13.

32.   His trams threatened by buildings recall Boccioni's *Le Forze di una strada* of 1911, while the image of the Eiffel tower distorted by clouds recalls Delaunay's 1910–11 *Tours*, and the discs recall Robert Delaunay's *Hommage à Blériot* and Sonia Delaunay's *Prismes électriques*, both exhibited at the 1914 Indépendants.

33.   The changes in the central area as follows: a disc is overpainted, and the vertical sequence of the stencilled letters has been changed, being overpainted too and then repainted while the black was still wet. The robot city men are sketched in very quickly and thinly, their forms as yet left ill-defined.

34.   Visible changes are as follows: the white area on the right edge of the canvas with a derrick has been repainted to exclude a more complex pattern of derricks and windows. The white quarter disc below is painted over a ringed disc, closer to the Schoenborn study. The original quarter disc had three rings—a green centre, then red and white. Within the placard of the green cut-out mannekin two red dashes have been painted out, and also on the rectangular white field a dark square. The letters in the central black field have been changed, and the zig-zag, top right, is a late addition.

35.   See Cendrars: *L'Homme foudroyé*, p. 173.

36.   The publication date is given in the 1919 edition, and also the address of Editions de la Sirène, 12, rue la Boetie, very close to the galerie de l'Effort Moderne.

37.   Blaise Cendrars: *La Fin du monde filmée par l'Ange Notre-Dame*, Paris, 1919, no page number.

38.   Ibid., no page number.

39.   It is perhaps significant that Léger walked with Cendrars in the *cortège* of Apollinaire's funeral in November 1918; see Cendrars and Manoll: op. cit., p. 254.

40.   Entretiens de Fernand Léger avec Blaise Cendrars et Louis Carré sur *Le paysage dans l'oeuvre de Léger*, Paris, 1956.

41.   Blaise Cendrars: 'Modernités 8. De la Parturition des couleurs', *La Rose Rouge*, 17 July 1919, pp. 129–32.

42.   Cendrars, *Profond Aujourd'hui*, p. 13.

43.   No other oil versions are known to me.

44.   The circumstantial evidence is, first, the fact that the idea for the city setting of *Les Disques* with its wrought iron balconies seems to grow out of the little oil *L'Armistice*, recently in the Sidney Janis Gallery, New York, which must have been painted shortly after Armistice day (11 November 1918). Secondly its relationship with the small *Le Disque* recently in the Perls gallery, New York, which is dated on the back of the canvas, October 1918. That the *Etude* came first is indicated by the changes visible on *Les Disques* itself which are all *away* from conformations found in the *Etude*.

45.   See note 44, above.

46.   The relationship between the other disc theme *Le Disque rouge* (the most developed version of which, dated 1919, is in a New York private collection) and *L'Armistice* suggests that Léger used the disc as a pure replacement for the flags of the latter painting.

47.   Robert Delaunay: *Du Cubisme à l'art abstrait*, ed. Pierre Francastel, Paris, 1957, p. 126.

48.   Or it can take the place of flags hung out in celebration of peace, as in *Le Disque rouge* (see note 46, above).

49.   In Roger Garaudy: *Pour un réalisme du XXe siècle, dialogue posthume avec F. Léger*, Paris, 1968, p. 117.

50.   Unfortunately, no directly related study of this kind is available to prove the point, but that the process of translating modelled mechanical elements into flat discs was current is demonstrated by the Moscow *Composition (Etude pour la Partie de cartes)* (Plate 85).

51.   The inscription on the reverse reads: 'Les disques dans la ville, 1920', the date here conflicting with the date '21' on the front of the canvas. The fact that the painting was in the early 1920 Indépendants indicates that only touching up and minor changes must have occurred in 1921.

Chapter 7.

1.   For a more exact dating of Metzinger and Lipchitz's stays at Beaulieu-près-Loches, see *The Letters of Juan Gris*, trans. and ed. Douglas Cooper, London, 1956, pp. 52–8.

2.   Severini was soon to start on his book *Du Cubisme au classicisme*, which was published in Paris in 1921.

3.   Severini specifically mentions Plato and Pythagoras as having figured in the conversations, but he also made it clear that at this time he was deeply interested in the ideas of Alberti and Henry.

4.   Cf. Gino Severini: 'Tempo de "l'Effort Moderne"', *Tutta la vita di un pittore*, Nuovedizione Enrico Vallechi, 1968, p. 98.

5.   For an account of the application of proportional systems in the 'Section d'Or', see William A. Camfield: 'Juan Gris and the Golden Section', *Art Bulletin*, New York, 1965, pp. 128–34. Also worth referring to is Raynal's article on Severini in *Sic*, nos. 45–6, 15 and 31 May 1919.

6.   Raynal implores the artist to guard against 'un excès de méthode'. See Maurice Raynal: 'Quelques intentions du Cubisme', Paris, 1919; in *Bulletin de l'Effort Moderne*, no. 3, March 1924, p. 3.

7.   Ibid., p. 6.

8.   Léonce Rosenberg: 'Cubisme et Tradition' in *Bulletin de l'Effort Moderne*, nos. 25–7, dated 1920 in no. 26.

9.   Ibid., no. 25, p. 7.

10.   The contract is reproduced in full in *Fernand Léger, sa vie, son oeuvre, sa rêve*, Milan, 1972, no page number.

11.   The letter, which was apparently sent to all the artists of 'l'Effort Moderne', is quoted in Severini: op. cit., pp. 109–10.

12.   Other 1920 themes of this disintegrated kind are: *Les trois camarades*, an *état* of which is in the Stedelijk Museum, Amsterdam, and *Le Garcon au café*, an *état* of which is in the collection of Mr and Mrs Jacques Gelman, Mexico City.

13.   Picasso had at first sold to Léonce Rosenberg after the departure of Kahnweiler from Paris, and Léonce continued to deal in his work into the 1920s, including paintings by Picasso in his 1921 *exposition de groupe*.

14.   A small oil version exists in the Belgian collection of Victor Masurel.

15.   Cf. F. T. Marinetti: 'Le Futurisme', Paris, 1911; in *Opere di F. T. Marinetti*, Milan, 1968.

16.   Fernand Léger: 'L'Esthétique de la Machine, l'Objet fabriqué, l'artisan et l'artiste', first published in *Der Querschnitt*, Berlin, vol. 3, 1923, and in *Bulletin de l'Effort Moderne*, nos. 1 and 2, January and February 1924; in *Fonctions de la peinture*, Paris, 1965, p. 62.

17.   Most obviously of all, the mechanic's left arm has been broadened and there are signs of changes in the puffs of smoke from his cigarette.

18.   *L'Intransigeant* reported the Louvre open again on 14 January 1919. *L'Illustration*, 8 March 1919, reports the March opening of the Egyptian ivories and the fact that among the first rooms opened in January were one Assyrian and one Egyptian room. Also *Le Monde Illustré*, 22 March 1919, reports that new acquisitions, including Chaldean and Egyptian pieces, were exhibited in the Salle Lacaze that month.

19.   Amédée Ozenfant: 'Sur le Cubisme', *L'Elan*, no. 10, December 1916.

20. Ozenfant gives a clear picture of what his youthful enthusiasms were in his *Mémoires*, Paris, 1969, pp. 33–4, 39, 46–58.

21. Ozenfant mentions Poincaré's *Science et Méthode, Science at Hypothèse* and *La Valeur de la Science*; Ibid., p. 53.

22. See ibid., p. 72. The design was analysed in *Omnia*, December 1911, p. 157.

23. Ibid., p. 101, and Le Corbusier, *My Work*, London, 1960, p. 49.

24. Ibid., p. 102. Le Corbusier himself admitted that he had not painted earlier, see 'Souvenirs enregistrés de Le Corbusier', in *Hommes d'Aujourd'hui*, Paris, 1965.

25. Ibid., p. 102.

26. Amédée Ozenfant and Charles-Edouard Jeanneret: 'Le Purisme', *L'Esprit Nouveau*, no. 4, p. 369.

27. Amédée Ozenfant and Charles-Edouard Jeanneret: *Après le cubisme*, Paris, 1918, p. 32.

28. See ibid., p. 41.

29. Ibid., p. 41.

30. Ibid., pp. 16–17; cf. Amédée Ozenfant and Charles-Edouard Jeanneret: 'Le Purisme', *L'Esprit Nouveau*, no. 4.

31. Ozenfant and Jeanneret: *Après le cubisme*, pp. 42 and 43.

32. Ozenfant and Jeanneret: 'Le Purisme', *L'Esprit Nouveau*, no. 4, p. 370.

33. Ibid., pp. 370–1.

34. Ibid., p. 371.

35. Ibid., pp. 371–2.

36. Ibid., p. 373.

37. Cf. Ibid. Also see Le Corbusier, 'Les Tracés régulateurs', *L'Esprit Nouveau*, no. 5.

38. Cf. Ozenfant and Jeanneret: 'Le Purisme', *L'Esprit Nouveau*, no. 4, p. 381.

39. Charles Henry: 'Le Lumière, La Couleur, La Forme', *L'Esprit Nouveau*, nos. 8 and 9.

40. Ozenfant and Jeanneret: op. cit., p. 382.

41. See Ozenfant: *Mémoires*, p. 108.

42. Maurice Raynal contributed an appreciation of the work shown, in *L'Esprit Nouveau* no. 7.

43. Cf. Ozenfant and Jeanneret: op. cit., pp. 376–7.

44. See Ozenfant and Jeanneret: *Après le cubisme*, p. 45.

45. Cf. ibid., p. 46.

46. Ozenfant and Jeanneret: 'Le Purisme', *L'Esprit Nouveau*, no. 4, p. 374. Reyner-Banham has described the Purist law of Mechanical Selection as 'pseudo Darwinian'; see P. Reyner-Banham: *Theory and Design in the First Machine Age*, London, 1960, p. 212.

47. Ibid., p. 374.

48. Ibid., p. 374.

49. Cf. Ozenfant and Jeanneret: 'L'Angle droit', *L'Esprit Nouveau*, no. 18.

50. Ozenfant and Jeanneret: 'Les Idées d'Esprit Nouveau', *L'Esprit Nouveau*, no. 14, p. 1576.

51. Ozenfant and Jeanneret: *Après le cubisme*, p. 27.

52. The relationship between the articles and *Vers une architecture* is discussed fully in P. Reyner-Banham: op. cit., pp. 222–3.

53. Reyner-Banham demonstrates the degree to which technological reality was made to coincide with the Purists' geometrical and functional ideal by selection; see P. Reyner-Banham: 'Machine Aesthetic', *Architectural Review*, London, 1955, and op. cit., p. 242.

54. For photographs of the installation, see *Bulletin de l'Effort Moderne*, no. 1, January 1924.

55. *Fernand Léger*, Musée des Arts Décoratifs, Paris, 1956, p. 31.

56. See Ozenfant and Jeanneret: 'Le Purisme', *L'Esprit Nouveau*, no. 4, p. 283.

57. Waldemar George: 'Exposition de groupe', *L'Esprit Nouveau*, no. 9, p. 1040.

58. Although not mentioned in 'Curriculum Vitae de "l'Effort Moderne"', *Bulletin de l'Effort Moderne*, no. 1, January 1924, Mondrian was, as shown above, included in the Exposition de groupe of 1921, and his pamphlet, *Le néo-Plasticisme*, was published by the Editions de l'Effort Moderne in 1920.

59. Severini's important essay, 'La Peinture de l'avant-garde', was serialized between the second and sixth numbers of *De Stijl* (December 1917–18); and in the October 1919 number van Doesburg published the collection of 'l'Effort Moderne' texts also published that autumn in *Valori Plastici*.

60. *De Stijl*, Amsterdam, vol. 1, no. 3, January 1918, p. 52.

61. The publisher, significantly enough, was Editions de l'Effort Moderne.

62. Cf. Piet Mondrian: 'Le néo-Plasticisme', Paris, 1920; in *Bulletin de l'Effort Moderne*, no. 23, March 1926, p. 7.

63. Cf., for instance, the *Composition* of 1920 (Wilhelm Hack collection, Cologne).

64. Cf. Théo van Doesburg: 'Classique-Baroque-Moderne', Paris, 1920; in *Bulletin de l'Effort Moderne*, no. 23, March 1926, p. 1, and in *Bulletin de l'Effort Moderne*, no. 21, January 1926, p. 3.

65. Maurice Raynal: 'Quelques intentions du cubisme', Paris, 1919; in *Bulletin de l'Effort Moderne*, no. 3, March 1924, p. 4.

66. For Hieratic examples, see Ozenfant and Jeanneret: 'La peinture des cavernes à la peinture d'aujourd' hui', *L'Esprit Nouveau*, no. 15. Note the use of Pompeii as a model in Le Corbusier-Sanguier: 'Les Tracés régulateurs', *L'Esprit Nouveau*, no. 5.

67. Léonce Rosenberg: op, cit., in *Bulletin de l'Effort Moderne*, no. 25, May 1926, p. 5.

68. Ibid., p. 5.

69. Denys Sutton: *André Derain*, London, 1969, pp. 26–8.

70. See Gino Severini: *Tutta la vita di un pittore*, vol. 1, Rome–Paris, 1947, p. 246.

71. Cf. Sir Anthony Blunt: 'Picasso's Classical Period, 1917–25', *The Burlington Magazine*, London, April 1968, p. 187.

72. Cf. Phoebe Pool: 'Picasso's Neo-Classicism, 2nd Period, 1917–1925', *Apollo*, March 1967, p. 206.

73. Blunt, op. cit., p. 188.

74. Poole, op. cit., pp. 204–5

75. Blunt: op. cit., p. 188.

76. Jean Cocteau: *Le Rappel à l'ordrè*, Paris, 1926.

77. Sprigge and Kihm make this point, suggesting that certain verses are literally pastiche; see Elizabeth Sprigge and Jean-Jacques Kihm: *Jean Cocteau: The Man and the Mirror*, London, 1968, p. 82.

78. See Francis Poulenc: *Moi et mes amis*, Confidences recuellis par Stéphane Audel, Paris, 1963, pp. 89–90.

79. Jean Cocteau: *Le Coq et l'Arlequin*, Paris, 1918; in Cocteau: op. cit., p. 26.

80. The critic Henri Collet invented 'Les Six'; see Frederick Brown: *An Impersonation of Angels: A Biography of Jean Cocteau*, London, 1969. According to Poulenc, it was the accidental result of the frequent appearance of 'Les Six' on the same programme at the Théâtre de Vieux Colombier; see Poulenc: op. cit., p. 51.

81. The statement is published in Alfred H. Barr: *Picasso, 50 years of his art*, New York, 1946, pp. 270–1.

82. Jean Cocteau: 'D'un ordre considéré comme une anarchie', 3 May 1923, in Cocteau: op. cit., p. 248.

83. Jean Cocteau: 'Autour de La Fresnaye', *L'Esprit Nouveau*, no. 3, p. 322.

84. Jean Cocteau: 'Le Secret professionnel', in Cocteau: op. cit., p. 190.

85. Ibid., p. 179.

86.   Ibid., p. 194.
87.   Jean Cocteau: 'D'un ordre considéré comme une anarchie', in Cocteau: op. cit., p. 241.
88.   Jean Cocteau: 'Le Secret professionnel', in Cocteau: op. cit., p. 194.
89.   In Barr: op. cit., p. 270.
90.   Jean Cocteau: *Picasso*, Paris, 1921, in Cocteau: op. cit., p. 282.
91.   In Barr: op. cit., p. 271.
92.   Jean Cocteau: 'Le Secret professionnel', in Cocteau: op. cit., p. 210.
93.   Jean Cocteau: *Le Coq et l'Arlequin,* in Cocteau: op. cit., p. 21.
94.   Ibid., p. 30.
95.   Cf. Gino Severini: op. cit., pp. 266–7, and André Level: *Souvenirs d'un collectionneur*, Paris, 1959, p. 57.
96.   See Level: op. cit., p. 69.
97.   Ibid., p. 57; cf. Pierre Albert-Birot: 'Chroniques quelquefois rimée. Chez Paul Guillaume', *Sic.* no. 24, December 1917. Apollinaire was there and music by Debussy, Auric and Satie was played.
98.   See Blaise Cendrars and Michel Manoll: *Blaise Cendrars vous parle . . .,* Paris, 1952, p. 255.

Chapter 8.

1.   These are almost certainly related to Plates 147 and 149.
2.   The process of development behind this painting involves *Les deux femmes à la toilette* (private collection, Basle), and the small oil *Les trois femmes à la nature-morte* which has passed through the Perls gallery, New York.
3.   The *Femme couchée* (1921), recently in the Perls gallery, New York; the *Tasse de thé* (1921) (private collection, New York) and the two versions of *Fragment du Grand Déjeuner*, one now in a French private collection.
4.   A photograph of a highly finished and very well developed version, even closer to *Le Grand Déjeuner* than the Connecticut painting, exists in the Archives photographiques de Léonce Rosenberg.
5.   There are clear signs here, particularly where the paint is only patchily applied over the diamond floor-pattern area, both of a detailed guide-drawing and of squaring.
6.   Fernand Léger: 'Correspondance' (March 1922), in *Bulletin de l'Effort Moderne*, no. 4, April 1924, p. 11.
7.   A late 1920 date is indicated by the link with the Picasso gouaches, which Léger could not have seen until after Picasso's autumn return to Paris, and also by the stylistic link with a Léger dated '21 6' (June 1921), the *Mère et enfant* (Jewett Arts Centre, Wellesley College Museum, Mass.). This latter dated canvas indicates how late Léger continued with his synthetic style of the *Trois figures*.
8.   For a report of the reopening, see *L'Illustration*, 9 October 1920.
9.   See Léonce Rosenberg: 'Cubisme et Tradition', Paris, 1920; in *Bulletin de l'Effort Moderne*, no. 25, May 1926, p. 7; and Maurice Raynal: 'Quelques intentions du cubisme', Paris, 1919; in *Bulletin de l'Effort Moderne*, no. 3, March 1924, p. 5.
10.   'Jean Fouquet', *L'Esprit Nouveau,* no. 5, February 1921.
11.   Robert de Beauplan, 'Un Effort de Régénération du Cinéma française', *L'Illustration*, 17 December 1921. Gance conceived a scenario that would be part shot in the USA and part in Italy, among the archeological remains. *La Roue,* which was in fact shot mostly in Nice, was the outcome of the first part of the original concept.
12.   *L'Intransigeant*, 7 January 1919, p. 2.
13.   Albert Jeanneret: 'La rythmique', *L'Esprit Nouveau*, no. 2, November 1920, p. 183.
14.   D. Strohl: 'Danses gymnastiques', *La Danse*, September 1921. See also André Geiger: 'Jeanne Ronsay', *La Danse*, August 1921.

15. See *L'Illustration*, 27 December 1919. The quotation is from a letter sent by Gémier to the clubs and printed in *L'Illustration*.

16. See *L'Illustration*, 10 April 1920, pp. 186–7.

17. See Jacques-Charles: *Cent ans de Music-Hall*, Paris, 1956.

18. Fernand Léger, op. cit., p. 11.

19. Highly finished oil versions of the theme are known to me in the New York collections of Ralph Colin and Mr and Mrs Alan Emil, and the Soleure collection of Josef Müller. Clear signs of a detailed squaring-up and a very careful pencil guide-drawing show in the Basel version.

20. The catalogue records him as showing *La Femme et l'enfant* (no. 1531) and a *Dessin* (no. 1532). The description of the exhibited painting given by Marcel Hiver in 'Le Salon d'Automne', *Montparnasse*, 1 October 1922, p. 2, indicates that this was either the Basel *Mère et l'enfant* or a related painting, though there are anomalies in it.

21. It was part of the Pernolet legacy; see *L'Illustration*, 5 February 1919, for a report on the new acquisitions exhibition.

22. Maurice Raynal: 'Le Nain', *L'Intransigeant*, 4 February 1923, p. 1.

23. This view of the Le Nains is also echoed in an important 1922 article: Tristan Klingsor: 'Les Le Nain', *L'Amour de l'Art*, April 1922, pp. 97–100.

24. Cf. Robert Delevoy: *Léger*, Paris–Geneva, 1962, p. 12.

25. Marcel Hiver: 'Le Salon d'Automne', *Montparnasse*, 1 October 1922, p. 2.

26. Opened February 1922, at the Théâtre des Champs-Elysées.

27. Cf. Maurice Raynal on Léger's designs for *La Création du Monde*, *L'Intransigeant*, 5 November 1923.

28. The shooting of the film can be dated by reports in *L'Intransigeant*; see 5 and 11 October and 17 November 1923.

29. Report in *L'Intransigeant*, 13 June 1923.

30. It was first published in Paris in *Bulletin de l'Effort Moderne*, no. 1, January, and no. 2, February 1924.

31. The drawing is in the Ayala Zacks collection, Toronto.

32. See especially De Fayet (Le Corbusier): 'Mosaiques Romaines, début du IIIe Siècle Ap.J.-C', *L'Esprit Nouveau*, no. 19.

33. It is illustrated finished in *Bulletin de l'Effort Moderne*, no. 7, July 1924.

34. For illustrations of the other drawings, see Jean Cassou et Jean Leymarie: *Dessins et gouaches*, Paris, 1972, p. 76.

35. Fernand Léger: op. cit., p. 11.

36. The most revealing demonstration of Le Corbusier's interest in mass-production is his article on prefabricated housing: 'Les Maisons "Voisin"', *L'Esprit Nouveau*, no. 2. That there was popular interest too is demonstrated by an article on the subject in *Le Monde Illustré*, 16 August 1919, entitled 'Constructions rapides démontables "France"', p. 595.

37. For Gleizes's views on the subject, see A. Gleizes: *Du Cubisme*, Paris, 1921, p. 54. For the information on Léger's interest, see Laura Miner: *Abstract Art in Paris*, unpublished MA thesis, Courtauld Institute, University of London, 1971.

38. See *Lettre M. Frugès à Le Corbusier*, 3 November 1923, published in the invaluable *Le Corbusier et Pessac 1914–28*, by Brian Brace Taylor, Paris (Fondation Le Corbusier), 1972, p. 48.

39. For a fuller account, see Brian Brace Taylor: op. cit., pp. 27–31.

40. Ibid., pp. 29–30.

41. *Bytowa-Kultura*, Brno, March 1924. See Le Corbusier (ed.): *Almanach Architecture Moderne*, Paris, 1926, pp. 78–81.

42. Georges Charensol, 'Chez Fernand Léger', *Paris-Journal*, December 1924.

43. Cf. reports in *Le Monde Illustré*, 14 October 1922, and by M. Bouvry in *L'Intransigeant*, 6 October 1923. The latter, singling out the Renault models, concentrates entirely on the motor, carburettor, positioning of radiator, etc.

44. De Dion Bouton also made a point of mass-production in advertising their eight-cylinder model in *Le Monde Illustré* during 1919.

45. Hervé Lauwick: 'Taylorisations', *L'Intransigeant*, 26 April 1923.
46. A very careful preparatory drawing, squared up for enlargement, survives on the *Trois figures* theme, see Jean Cassou and Jean Leymarie: op. cit., p. 77.
47. A surviving photograph of Léger's Académie Moderne during its opening year (1924) shows the life class with a stiffly posed reclining nude holding just such a staff as appears in *Trois figures*.
48. Fernand Léger: op. cit., p. 11.
49. Elie Faure: 'Charlot', *L'Esprit Nouveau*, no. 6.
50. Fernand Léger, 'Le Ballet-Spectacle, l'objet-spectacle', in *Fonctions de la peinture*, Paris, 1965, p. 145.
51. See Darius Milhaud: 'Mon Ami Fernand Léger', *Europe*, August–September 1971, p. 27.
52. Armand Lunel: 'D'un lontain souvenir', *Europe*, August–September 1971, p. 48.
53. See 'La Vie fait l'oeuvre de Fernand Léger; propos de l'artiste recuellis par Dora Vallier', *Cahiers d'Art*, Paris, 1954, p. 152.

Chapter 9.

1. Fernand Léger: 'Correspondance' (March 1922), in *Bulletin de l'Effort Moderne*, no. 4, April 1924, p. 11.
2. There are two pencil studies, one in the St Louis collection of Richard Weil, which is squared up for enlargement.
3. Preparatory oil versions, and in the final versions careful pencil guide-drawings, with in some cases squaring-up, are typical of the *Paysages animés* as a whole.
4. Behind it lie at least one highly finished drawing, now in the Musée National de Fernand Léger at Biot, and a smaller oil illustrated as no. 60 in *Fernand Léger*, Grand Palais, Paris, 1971–2.
5. Piet Mondrian, *Le Néo-Plasticisme*, Paris, 1920; in *Bulletin de l'Effort Moderne*, no. 26, June 1926, pp. 5–6.
6. See especially 'Vie de Corot', *L'Esprit Nouveau*, no. 8, where they are called 'la partie la plus pure de sa production'.
7. Mondrian: op. cit., p. 6.
8. Amédée Ozenfant and Charles-Edouard Jeanneret: *Après le cubisme*, Paris, 1918.
9. See Le Corbusier-Sanguier: 'Des yeux qui ne voient pas', 1, *L'Esprit Nouveau*, no. 8.
10. Le Corbusier: 'Architecture III, Pure création de l'Esprit', *L'Esprit Nouveau*, no. 16.
11. This is a variant on the version in the Paris Musée National d'Art Moderne; its whereabouts are unknown to me, but a photograph of it is in the photographic archives of the galerie Louise Leiris, Paris, no. 7305/6529, with a note of its measurements: 92 × 65 cm.
12. This analogy was, of course, put into verbal form with the 'house-as-machine' idea in 1921 (*L'Esprit Nouveau*, no. 8), being repeated in *Vers une architecture* in 1923.
13. Le Corbusier: *Vers une architecture*, Paris, 1923, pp. 11–29.
14. Ozenfant and Jeanneret: op. cit.
15. Amédée Ozenfant and Le Corbusier: 'Formation de l'optique moderne', *L'Esprit Nouveau*, no. 21.
16. The opening of the Internationale Ausstelung Neuer Theater-technik in Vienna was on 19 September 1924, so he was probably back in Paris by the beginning of October. That this painting was not completed until then is suggested by the fact that it was not reproduced in the *Bulletin de l'Effort Moderne* until December, and by stylistic factors (the connection with de Chirico discussed below).
17. Letters in the Fondation Le Corbusier, Paris, make it clear that Le Corbusier

was at work on the Pavillon de L'Esprit Nouveau from April 1924, and therefore probably on the Voisin Plan too.

18. Georges Charensol: 'Chez Fernand Léger', *Paris-Journal*, December 1924.

19. The first attack came in *La Révolution Surréaliste*, 15 July 1925.

20. Soby rejects de Chirico's reported assertion that this is false, see James Thrall Soby: *Giorgio de Chirico*, New York, 1955, footnote, p. 11.

21. *12 Opere di Giorgio de Chirico*, Rome, 1919.

22. The probability of a late 1924 date is indicated by its illustration in the *Bulletin de l'Effort Moderne*, no. 10, December 1924.

23. Cf. especially the small *La Chaise verte*, 1922 (Kunstmuseum der Stadt, Düsseldorf), and the two oils on the theme of *La Choppe*, one in the Zurich collection of Gustave Zumsteg.

24. Amédée Ozenfant and Charles-Edouard Jeanneret: 'Les Idées de L'Esprit Nouveau', *L'Esprit Nouveau*, no. 14.

25. 'Autres Icones', *L'Esprit Nouveau*, no. 20.

26. See Amédée Ozenfant and Le Corbusier: 'L'Angle Droit', *L'Esprit Nouveau*, no. 18, on 'l'objet standard'; and especially Le Corbusier, '1925, Exposition des Arts Décoratifs, Besoins, types, meubles, types', *L'Esprit Nouveau*, no. 23.

27. Dating of the Paris *Eléments mécaniques* in the first six months of 1924 is established by its illustration in the *Bulletin de l'Effort Moderne*. no. 7, July 1924.

28. Report by Maurice Raynal: *L'Intransigeant*, 14 February 1924.

29. That Servranckx's view of the modern world was Purist is a point made by his 1925 lecture 'Les Voies nouvelles de l'Art Plastique', see *Bulletin de l'Effort Moderne*, no. 16, June 1925, no. 17, July 1925, no. 18, October 1925, and no. 19, November 1925.

30. Servranckx notes in 'Les Voies nouvelles de l'Art Plastique' that 'particularisme individualiste' is what strikes him whenever he makes personal contact with the French Cubists (including Léger); see *Bulletin de l'Effort Moderne*, no. 16.

31. An early 1924 date is indicated by the fact that the drawing is dated '23' and that the Basel version is illustrated in April 1924 in the *Bulletin de l'Effort Moderne*.

32. Georges Charensol talks about *Le Siphon* as a work under way in 'Chez Fernand Léger', *L'Intransigeant*, December 1924, and it was illustrated in the *Bulletin de l'Effort Moderne* in that month.

33. Le Corbusier, 1925: 'Exposition des Arts Décoratifs, Besoins, types, meubles, types', *L'Esprit Nouveau*, no. 23.

34. Georges Charensol: op. cit.

35. Fernand Léger: 'L'Esthétique de la Machine. L'Objet fabriqué, L'artisan et l'artiste', in *Fonctions de la peinture*, Paris, 1965, p. 54.

36. Ibid., p. 53.

37. Ibid., p. 56.

38. Ibid., p. 59.

39. Ibid., p. 61.

40. Cf.; the advertisement 'A la place Clichy', *L'Intransigeant*, 9 March 1924, p. 6; and 'Au Printemps', *L'Intransigeant*, 5 April 1924, back page.

41. See report in *L'Intransigeant*, 1 June 1923, p. 2.

42. This completion date is given by Robert de Beauplan in 'Un Effort de Régénération Française', *L'Illustration*, 17 December 1921.

43. See anon. review in *Montparnasse*, Paris, 1 November 1922.

44. Report in *Paris-Journal*, 1 February 1924, p. 3.

45. Pierre Descargues: *Fernand Léger*, Paris, 1955, p. 69.

46. Fernand Léger: 'Réponse à une enquête', *Le Théâtre et Comœdia illustré, Film*, March 1923. 'Il (Chaplin) est le seul a être devenu à l'écran *une image mobile* . . .'

47. Fernand Léger: 'Essai critique sur la valeur plastique du film d'Abel Gance La Roue', *Comoedia*, Paris, 16 December 1922; in *Fonctions de la peinture*, p. 162.

48. Abel Gance interviewed by Jean Mitry: *Le Théâtre et Comoedia illustré, Film*, 1 May 1924.

49. Fernand Léger: 'Réponse à une enquête'.

50. René Clair is particularly revealing on this, see 'Les Films du mois', *Le Théâtre et Comoedia illustré, Film*, March 1923.

51. See Pierre Leprohon: *Jean Epstein*, Paris, 1964.

52. Fernand Léger: op. cit.

53. See report on the making of *Paris qui dort* by André-L. Davan in *Le Théâtre et Comoedia illustré, Film,* October 1923.

54. For Clair's own account, see René Clair: *Cinéma d'hier, cinéma d'aujourd'hui*, Paris, 1970, pp. 25–9.

55. See report on first night in *L'Action*, Paris, 6 December 1924, p. 4.

56. René Clair: 'Exemples', *L'Intransigeant*, 13 January 1923, p. 4.

57. Marcel L'Herbier: 'Le Cinéma Leader de Gauche', *Paris-Journal*, Paris, 30 May 1924.

58. Jean Epstein: *Poésie d'aujourd'hui. Un nouvel état d'intelligence*, Paris, 1921, p. 170.

59. Jean Epstein: 'De quelques conditions de la photogénie', lecture given at the 1923 Salon d'Automne, published in *Paris-Journal*, 25 January 1924, p. 6.

60. René Clair: 'Les films du mois', *Le Théâtre et Comoedia illustré, Film*, 1 February 1924.

61. René Clair: op. cit., December 1923.

62. René Clair: op. cit., 1 February 1924.

63. Jacques Parsons: 'Une Grande Première cinématographique, *L'Inhumaine*', *L'Action*, 5 December 1924, p. 4.

64. René Bizet: 'Paris qui dort', *La Revue de France*, December 1924; quoted in Georges Charensol and Roger Regent: *Un Maître du Cinéma, René Clair*, Paris, 1952, p. 68.

65. Jean Epstein: op. cit.

66. 'Autour du *Ballet Mécanique*', undated statement in *Fonctions de la peinture*, p. 166.

67. Léger is quoted as saying that a reel was shown, in his interview of December 1924 with Georges Charensol published in *Paris-Journal*.

68. Fernand Léger: 'Ballet Mécanique', *L'Esprit Nouveau*, no. 28.

69. The film was divided into seven parts, each pulled together by links between images. Ibid.

70. Ibid. Pound's Vorticist connections are, of course, crucial here from the point of view of the take-over of the Vortographic technique from Coburn.

71. Fernand Léger: 'Réponse à une enquête'.

72. Epstein says that *La Roue* had '*Photogénie exterieure*: les machines, le mouvement formidable de leurs courses'; and '*Photogénie interieure*: La roue qui tourne derrière les roues—cinéma d'âme,' and he approves. Jean Epstein, interviewed by Jean Mitry: *Le Théâtre et Comoedia illustré, Film*, 15 June–15 September 1924.

73. Fernand Léger: 'Le Spectacle, Lumière, Couleur, Image Mobile, Objet-Spectacle', *Bulletin de l'Effort Moderne*, no. 7, July 1924 and no. 9, November 1924 (there dated May 1924); in *Fonctions de la peinture*, p. 132.

74. Ibid., p. 131.

Chapter 10.

1. Letter dated 23 April 1924 (copy) in the file E. N. Pavillon, E. Nouveau 1925, Arts Déco. 1925, 2A 13, Fondation Le Corbusier, Paris.

2. A letter from the commissaire générale, dated 2 February 1925, states that no trees were to be cut down or debranched. See E. N. Pavillon file, Fondation Le Corbusier, Paris.

3. A series of letters from the commissaire générale and M. Bonnier, the

Directeur des Services d'Architecture Parcs et Jardins, make this clear. See E. N. Pavillon file.

4. See letter from Bonnier, dated 11 May 1925, E. N. Pavillon file.

5. See *Almanach d'Architecture Moderne,* ed. Le Corbusier, Paris, 1926, p. 129. The names of some who attended are given here.

6. Le Corbusier himself reports Perret's hostility, ibid., p. 138.

7. A copy of Le Corbusier's request for aid from Michelin is in the E. N. Pavillon file; it is dated 3 April 1925.

8. The gun was also used at Pessac and on the Villa La Roche-Jeanneret.

9. *Almanach d'Architecture Moderne*, p. 140.

10. A bill for two tables with nickel-plated legs, dated 17 July 1925, is in the E. N. Pavillon file.

11. A letter to Freysinet (copy), dated 16 March 1925, is in the E. N. Pavillon file.

12. El Lissitzky did not like the article, and was himself commissioned to contribute one on 'Modern Architectural Problems in Russia', which unfortunately never appeared. See Sophie Lissitzky-Küppers, *El Lissitsky, Life and Letters,* Dresden, 1967. Letter from Lissitzky to Sophie Lissitzky-Küppers, 11 May 1924, mentioning the article.

13. Walter Gropius, 'Developpement de l'Esprit Architecturale Moderne en Allemagne', *L'Esprit Nouveau,* no. 27.

14. Lissitzky mentions such dealings with Rosenberg in a letter to Sophie Lissitzky-Küppers, 21 March 1924; in Lissitzky-Küppers: op. cit.

15. See Theo van Doesburg, 'Classique-Baroque-Moderne', Paris, 1920, in *Bulletin de l'Effort Moderne,* no. 22, February 1926.

16. See *L'Intransigeant,* 22 November 1923, and *Paris-Journal,* 30 November 1923, p. 5.

17. Keisler's installation is illustrated in *Bulletin de l'Effort Moderne,* no. 17, July 1925.

18. There is a short mention of the exhibition, naming exhibitors, in *L'Intransigeant,* 11 November 1924.

19. Note especially Waldemar George on the decision to exclude the Russians and Germans, in *Paris-Journal,* 25 April 1924; and Marcel Sauvage, 'Pourquoi les Allemands et les Russes ne sont-ils pas invités à l'Exposition Internationale de 1925?', *Paris-Journal,* 3 July 1924.

20. Tougendhold's visiting card, giving Exter's address, rue Broca, 154, Paris XIII, and letters asking for photographs and arranging a meeting are in the E. N. Pavillon file.

21. Waldemar George, 'L'Exposition des Arts Décoratifs et Industriels de 1925, Les Tendances Générales', *L'Amour de l'Art,* August 1925, p. 285.

22. Freidrich Keisler, *Manifesto, 1925,* quoted in *Architecture Forum,* February 1947.

23. Laura Miner, *Abstract Art in Paris,* unpublished MA thesis, Courtauld Institute, University of London, 1971. Miner uses an unpublished sketch book which she dates 1918–19 to prove her point, see Plates 17–20.

24. Herbin, letter to Léonce Rosenberg, September 1920, published in *Bulletin de l'Effort Moderne,* no. 13, March 1925.

25. See postscript to a letter from Rosenberg to Herbin, dated '11.6.19', in Miner, op. cit.

26. The fact that Waldemar George calls the project a project for a Hall in *L'Amour de l'Art,* February 1923, and that Maurice Hiver in *Montparnasse,* Paris, 1 March 1923, discusses the exterior factor in the design, indicates that the *Architecture Vivante* 'fresque' could well be directly linked with what was shown.

27. These possibly owe something to Vesnin's sets for Tairov's *Phèdre* seen at the Théâtre des Champs-Elysées in March 1923.

28. Marie Dormoy writes (incorrectly) that he had not built a single house by 1925, see 'L'Architecture Française moderne', *L'Amour de l'Art,* March 1925, p. 120. From the point of view of Viennese characteristics, it is perhaps significant that in 1923 *L'Amour de l'Art* carried a lavishly illustrated series of articles on

Austrian decorative art, including in the August number illustrations of the palais Stocklet.

29.   Le Corbusier, 'Le Salon d'Automne', *L'Esprit Nouveau*, no. 19.

30.   Material in the Fondation Le Corbusier shows that building did not actually begin on the Atelier Ozenfant until May 1923, and it has been shown that the final designs for the villa La Roche-Jeanneret were arrived at in September 1923; see Richard Francis, *Le Corbusier and Cubism*, unpublished MA thesis, Courtauld Institute, University of London, 1971.

31.   Ibid., footnote 56.

32.   Fernand Léger, 'L'Architecture polychromie', *L'Architecture Vivante*, autumn/winter 1924, translated by Charlotte Green in *Léger and Purist Paris*, the Tate Gallery, London, 1970–1, p. 96.

33.   Léon's opinion is reported in 'Faits divers' by Georges Charensol, *L'Art Vivant*, 15 June 1925, p. 38.

34.   See *Fernand Léger, 1881–1955*, Musée des Arts Décoratifs, Paris, 1956, p. 33; and Douglas Cooper, *Fernand Léger et le nouvel espace*, Geneva, 1949, p. 91.

35.   Fernand Léger, 'Peinture murale et peinture de chevalet', 1950, in *Fonctions de la peinture*, Paris, 1965, p. 31.

36.   Mlle I. Morillion of the Fondation Le Corbusier, very kindly on my behalf, has asked the daughter of Albert Jeanneret if she can recall the murals in the Pavillon, and received a very definite negative answer.

37.   A letter from Léger to Le Corbusier dated 7 November 1925 is in the E. N. Pavillon file at the Fondation Le Corbusier, Paris. Léger was apparently ill, and sent Otto Carlsund to pick up the paintings.

38.   *L'Architecture Vivante*, winter 1925, p. 50.

39.   The present whereabouts of this earlier painting is not known to me; it was sold as Lot 88 at Parke-Bernet, 14 October 1965.

40.   Jean Baldovici, in *L'Architecture Vivante*, autumn/winter 1924.

41.   Ibid.

42.   Theo van Doesburg, 'Towards a Plastic Architecture', 1924, in *Studio International*, March 1969.

43.   Theo van Doesburg and Cor van Eesteren, 'Vers un Construction collectif', Paris, 1923; in *Studio International*, March 1969.

44.   Fernand Léger, 'L'Architecture polychromie', p. 96.

45.   Entretien de Fernand Léger avec Blaise Cendrars et Louis Carré sur *Le Paysage dans l'oeuvre de Léger*, L. Carré, Paris, 1956.

46.   A lesser known, but equally impressive version, more recognizably related to an anglepoise lamp starting-point, is in the Soleure collection of Josef Müller; it measures 132×100 cm. That these paintings were conceived in the latter half of 1925 is indicated by the illustration of variants in the *Bulletin de l'Effort Moderne*, no. 19, November 1925, and no. 25, May 1926, none earlier. My statement that the Guggenheim *Composition* was painted 'only months' after the Vienna Theatre exhibition is misleading; cf. *Léger and Purist Paris*, p. 77.

Epilogue.

1.   The piece was first published under a Jeanneret alias de Fayet, as 'Le Vase Grec', *L'Esprit Nouveau*, no. 16.

2.   There are two smaller oil versions of the non-mirror image *Composition avec profil*. A *Nature-morte (profil)*, dated '26' ($25\frac{3}{4} \times 18\frac{1}{4}$ in.), and the *Nature-morte (profil)*, dated '26', sold at Sotheby's as Lot 102, 28 June 1961. A gouache for this idea is in a French private collection, see Jean Cassou and Jean Leymarie, *Léger, Dessins et gouaches*, Paris, 1972, p. 97. Another variant exists in a horizontal format, with three profiles, the *Trois profils*, dated '26', which was in the galerie Beyeler, Basle, in 1969. See *F. Léger*, galerie Beyeler, Basle, 1969, p. 26.

3.   See Fernand Léger, 'L'Architecture polychromie', *L'Architecture Vivante*, autumn/winter 1924, translated by Charlotte Green, in *Léger and Purist Paris*, the Tate Gallery, London, 1970–1, p. 96.

Index

344

345

347